BEGINNING

ReactJS Foundations

Building User Interfaces with ReactJS

BEGINNING

ReactJS Foundations

Building User Interfaces with ReactJS

AN APPROACHABLE GUIDE

Chris Minnick

A Wiley Brand

For Sam, who got such a kick out of being thanked in the last book. How about this?

ABOUT THE AUTHOR

Chris Minnick is a prolific author, blogger, trainer, speaker, and web developer. His company, WatzThis?, is dedicated to finding better ways to teach computer and programming skills to beginners.

Chris has been a full-stack developer for over 25 years and a trainer for over 10 years, and has taught web development, ReactJS, and advanced JavaScript at many of the world's largest companies as well as at public libraries, co-working spaces, and meetups.

Minnick has authored or co-authored over a dozen technical books for adults and kids, including *Beginning HTML5 and CSS3 for Dummies*, *Coding with JavaScript for Dummies*, *JavaScript for Kids*, *Adventures in Coding*, and *Writing Computer Code*.

ABOUT THE TECHNICAL EDITOR

Rick Carlino is a full-stack software developer from the greater Chicago area. He specializes in open source tools such as React. Rick has over a decade of experience both teaching and implementing modern web applications in React. During his time as a JavaScript instructor, he traveled the world to teach modern web application practices to countless students at large enterprises. He currently serves as the technical co-founder and lead software developer for FarmBot, an open source agricultural robotics platform (and React application!) that helps gardeners automate food production. Outside of work he volunteers his time as the co-founder of a makerspace that helps members of his community learn and access technology.

ACKNOWLEDGMENTS

THIS BOOK WOULD NOT HAVE been possible without the help, support, experience, and wisdom provided by my friends, family, colleagues, and team. I'd especially like to thank the following people:

- Carole Jelen and Maureen Maloney at Waterside Productions.

- Project editor Kelly Talbot. It's a real pleasure to work with as keen-eyed and experienced a professional as you.

- Technical editor Rick Carlino. Rick, you're a super-hero. Your suggestions and corrections are always spot-on, and you've spared me from innumerable embarrassments and mea culpas.

- Acquisitions editor Devon Lewis.

- Associate Publisher Jim Minatel.

- The rest of the team at Wiley (Saravanan Dakshinamurthy, Kim Cofer, Louise Watson). It takes more people to publish a book than I even know, but I know that you're all fantastic.

- Jill McVarish, Paul Brady, Mike Machado, and Richard Hain for being readers and testers or for helping me figure it out, even if you didn't know that's what you were doing.

- My mentors and teachers who taught me how to write, including Roger Smith, Ken Byers, Conrad Vachon, and Steven Konopacki.

- Everyone who has taken one of my classes or read my books.

- The incredible React community, whose blog posts, tweets, articles, books, and videos have enlightened and inspired me.

- My co-authors and co-conspirators over the years, especially Eva Holland and Ed Tittel.

- Sam, who taught me how to make wine and rescued me when I was being electrocuted (accidentally, I think) by Zach.

- You, the reader, for placing your trust in me as you begin or continue your journey toward mastery of React.

—CHRIS MINNICK

BEGINNING
REACTJS FOUNDATIONS BUILDING USER INTERFACES WITH REACTJS

INTRODUCTION . . . . *xxvii*

CHAPTER 1 Hello, World! 1
CHAPTER 2 The Foundation of React 11
CHAPTER 3 JSX 23
CHAPTER 4 All About Components 43
CHAPTER 5 React DevTools 105
CHAPTER 6 React Data Flow 123
CHAPTER 7 Events 199
CHAPTER 8 Forms 221
CHAPTER 9 Refs 233
CHAPTER 10 Styling React 243
CHAPTER 11 Introducing Hooks 257
CHAPTER 12 Routing 289
CHAPTER 13 Error Boundaries 319
CHAPTER 14 Deploying React 339
CHAPTER 15 Initialize a React Project from Scratch 351
CHAPTER 16 Fetching and Caching Data 369
CHAPTER 17 Context API 387
CHAPTER 18 React Portals 399
CHAPTER 19 Accessibility in React 413
CHAPTER 20 Going Further 425

INDEX **437**

CONTENTS

INTRODUCTION   *xxvii*

CHAPTER 1: HELLO, WORLD!   1

React without a Build Toolchain   1
Interactive "Hello, World" with Create React App and JSX   7
Summary   9

CHAPTER 2: THE FOUNDATION OF REACT   11

What's in a Name?   11
UI Layer   12
Virtual DOM   13
The Philosophy of React   14
  Thinking in Components   15
  Composition vs. Inheritance   15
  React Is Declarative   16
  React Is Idiomatic   17
  Why Learn React?   17
  React vs....   18
    React vs. Angular   18
    React vs. Vue   19
  What React Is *Not*   19
  React Is Not a Web Server   20
  React Is Not a Programming Language   20
  React Is Not a Database Server   21
  React Is Not a Development Environment   21
  React Is Not the Perfect Solution to Every Problem   21
Summary   21

CHAPTER 3: JSX   23

JSX Is Not HTML   23
What Is JSX?   30
  How JSX Works   30
  Transpiler . . . Huh?   31
    Compilation vs. Transpilation   31
    JSX Transform   31

Introducing Babel 31
Eliminating Browser Incompatibilities 33

Syntax Basics of JSX 33
JSX Is JavaScript XML 33
Beware of Reserved Words 33
JSX Uses camelCase 33
Preface Custom Attributes in DOM Elements with data- 34
JSX Boolean Attributes 34
Use Curly Braces to Include Literal JavaScript 35
Remember to Use Double Curly Braces with Objects 35
Put Comments in Curly Braces 35
When to Use JavaScript in JSX 36
Conditionals in JSX 36
Conditional Rendering with if/else and Element Variables 36
Conditional Rendering with the && Operator 37
Conditional Rendering with the Conditional Operator 38
Expressions in JSX 38
Using Children in JSX 40
React Fragments 40
Summary 41

CHAPTER 4: ALL ABOUT COMPONENTS 43

What Is a Component? 43
Components vs. Elements 44
Components Define Elements 44
Elements Invoke Components 45
Built-in Components 47
HTML Element Components 47
Attributes vs. Props 52
Passing Props 52
Accessing Props 52
Standard HTML Attributes 54
Non-Standard Attributes 56
Custom Attributes 56
User-Defined Components 56
Types of Components 56
Class Components 57
Stepping through a React Class Component 68
React.Component 68
Importing React.Component 68

The Class Header 69
The Constructor Function 69
Managing State in Class Components 71
The Render Function 73
Creating and Using Props 74
Function Components 76
What Are Function Components? 79
How to Write Function Components 79
Optimizations and Function Component Shortcuts 80
Managing State in Function Components 83
Differences between Function and Class Components 84

React Component Children **84**
this.props.children 85
Manipulating Children 86
React.Children 86
isValidElement 87
cloneElement 87

The Component Lifecycle **89**
Mounting 90
constructor() 90
static getDerivedStateFromProps 90
render 90
componentDidMount() 90
Updating 90
shouldComponentUpdate 91
getSnapshotBeforeUpdate 91
componentDidUpdate 92
Unmounting 92
componentWillUnmount 92
Error Handling 92
getDerivedStateFromError 92
componentDidCatch 92
Improving Performance and Avoiding Errors 92
Avoiding Memory Leaks 93
React.PureComponent 96
React.memo 97
React.StrictMode 98

Rendering Components **98**
Rendering with ReactDOM 98
Virtual DOM 100
Other Rendering Engines 101

React Native	101
ReactDOMServer	102
React Konsul	103
react-pdf	103
Component Terminology	103
Summary	104

CHAPTER 5: REACT DEVTOOLS — **105**

Installation and Getting Started	105
Inspecting Components	107
Working with the Component Tree	108
Searching for Components	110
Using the Search Input Box	110
Using Regular Expressions	110
Filtering Components	112
Selecting Components	114
Editing Component Data in DevTools	114
Working with Additional DevTools Functionality	118
Profiling	119
Summary	121

CHAPTER 6: REACT DATA FLOW — **123**

One-Way Data Flow	123
Understanding One-Way Data Flow	124
Why One-Way Data Flow?	125
Props	126
Components Receive Props	126
Props Can Be Any Data Type	126
Props Are Read-Only	127
Validating Incoming Props with PropTypes	129
What Is PropTypes?	130
Getting Started with PropTypes	131
What Can PropTypes Validate?	133
Default Props	141
React State	145
What Is state?	146
Initializing state	146
Initializing state in Class Components	146
Initializing State in Function Components	147

The Difference between state and props 149
Updating state 149
Updating a Class Component's state with setState 150
Updating state with Function Components 154
What to Put in State 161
Building the Reminders App 161
What Not to Put in State 168
Where to Put State 168
Lifting State Up 170
About the key Prop 177
Filtering the Reminders 183
Implementing the isComplete Changing Functionality 188
Converting to Class Components 190
Summary 198

CHAPTER 7: EVENTS   **199**

How Events Work in React 199
What Is SyntheticEvent? 201
Using Event Listener Attributes 202
The Event Object 203
Supported Events 204
Event Handler Functions 211
Writing Inline Event Handlers 211
Writing Event Handlers in Function Components 212
Writing Event Handlers in Class Components 213
Binding Event Handler Functions 214
Using bind 215
Using Arrow Functions 216
Passing Data to Event Handlers 218
Summary 219

CHAPTER 8: FORMS   **221**

Forms Have State 221
Controlled Inputs vs. Uncontrolled Inputs 222
Updating a Controlled Input 223
Controlling an Input in a Function Component 224
Controlling an Input in a Class Component 224
Lifting Up Input State 226
Using Uncontrolled Inputs 228
Using Different Form Elements 229

Controlling the Input Element   230
Controlling a textarea   230
Controlling a Select Element   231
Preventing Default Actions   231
Summary   232

CHAPTER 9: REFS   **233**

What Refs Are   233
How to Create a Ref in a Class Component   234
How to Create a Ref in a Function Component   234
Using Refs   234
Creating a Callback Ref   236
When to Use Refs   238
When Not to Use Refs   238
Examples   239
    Managing Focus   239
    Automatically Selecting Text   239
    Controlling Media Playback   241
    Setting Scroll Position   241
Summary   242

CHAPTER 10: STYLING REACT   **243**

The Importance of Styles   243
Importing CSS into the HTML File   244
Using Plain Old CSS in Components   245
Writing Inline Styles   247
    JavaScript Style Syntax   248
    Why to Use Inline Styles   249
    Why Not to Use Inline Styles   249
    Improving Inline Styles with Style Modules   249
CSS Modules   250
    Naming CSS Module Files   251
    Advanced CSS Modules Functionality   252
        Global Classes   252
        Class Composition   252
CSS-in-JS and Styled Components   253
Summary   255

CHAPTER 11: INTRODUCING HOOKS — 257

What Are Hooks? — 257
Why Were Hooks Introduced? — 257
Rules of Hooks — 259
The Built-in Hooks — 259
  Managing State with useState — 260
    Setting the Initial State — 262
    Using the Setter Function — 262
    Passing a Value to a Setter — 263
    Passing a Function to a Setter — 263
    Setter Function Value Comparison — 264
  Hooking into the Lifecycle with useEffect — 264
    Using the Default useEffect Behavior — 265
    Cleaning Up After Effects — 265
    Customizing useEffect — 266
    Running Asynchronous Code with useEffect — 270
  Subscribing to Global Data with useContext — 272
  Combining Logic and State with useReducer — 273
  Memoized Callbacks with useCallback — 275
  Caching Computed Values with useMemo — 278
    Solving Unnecessary Renders — 278
    Solving Performance Problems — 279
  Accessing Children Imperatively with useRef — 279
  Customizing Exposed Values with useImperativeHandle — 280
  Updating the DOM Synchronously with useLayoutEffect — 281
Writing Custom Hooks — 281
Labeling Custom Hooks with useDebugValue — 283
Finding and Using Custom Hooks — 285
  use-http — 285
  react-fetch-hook — 286
  axios-hooks — 286
  react-hook-form — 286
  @rehooks/local-storage — 287
  use-local-storage-state — 287
  Other Fun Hooks — 288
  Lists of Hooks — 288
Summary — 288

CHAPTER 12: ROUTING 289

What Is Routing? 289
How Routing Works in React 291
Using React Router 293
  Installing and Importing react-router-dom 293
  The Router Component 294
    Selecting a Router 294
    Using the Router Component 295
  Linking to Routes 296
    Internal Linking with Link 296
    Internal Navigation with NavLink 298
    Automatic Linking with Redirect 302
  Creating Routes 302
    Restricting Path Matching 304
    Using URL Parameters 304
    The component Prop 305
    Render Props 306
    Switching Routes 307
    Rendering a Default Route 308
    Routing with Redirect 308
  Behind the Scenes: location, history, and match 309
    The history Object 310
    The location Object 313
    The match Object 313
React Router Hooks 317
  useHistory 317
  useLocation 317
  useParams 317
  useRouteMatch 317
Summary 318

CHAPTER 13: ERROR BOUNDARIES 319

The Best Laid Plans 319
What Is an Error Boundary? 320
Implementing an Error Boundary 323
  Building Your Own ErrorBoundary Component 323
    getDerivedStateFromErrors Is a Static Method 324
    getDerivedStateFromErrors Runs During the Render Phase 325
    getDerivedStateFromErrors Receives the Error as a Parameter 325

getDerivedStateFromErrors Should Return an Object for
Updating State   325
Testing Your Boundary   326
Logging Errors with ComponentDidCatch()   327
Using a Logging Service   328
Resetting the State   333
Installing a Pre-Built ErrorBoundary Component   334
What Can't an Error Boundary Catch?   336
Catching Errors in Error Boundaries with try/catch   336
Catching Errors in Event Handlers with react-error-boundary 337
Summary   338

CHAPTER 14: DEPLOYING REACT   339

What Is Deployment?   339
Building an App   339
Running the build Script   340
Examining the build Directory   340
The Built index.html   341
The static Directory   342
asset-manifest.json   342
What's in a Name?   343
How Is a Deployed App Different?   343
Development Mode vs. Production   343
Putting It on the Web   344
Web Server Hosting   344
Node Hosting   345
Deploying with Netlify   345
Enabling Routing with Netlify   347
Enabling Custom Domains and HTTPS   348
Summary   349

CHAPTER 15: INITIALIZE A REACT PROJECT FROM SCRATCH   351

Building Your Own Toolchain   351
Initializing Your Project   352
The HTML Document   352
The Main JavaScript File   353
The Root Component   353
Running in the Browser   354
How Webpack Works   357
Loaders   358
Plugins   358

Automating Your Build Process   358
  Making an HTML Template   359
  Development Server and Hot Reloading   360
  Testing Tools   360
    Installing and Configuring ESLint   360
    ESLint Configuration   361
    How to Fix Errors   362
    Testing with Jest   363
  Creating NPM Scripts   364
Structuring Your Source Directory   365
  Grouping by File Type   366
  Grouping by Features   367
Summary   367

CHAPTER 16: FETCHING AND CACHING DATA   369

Asynchronous Code: It's All About Timing   369
JavaScript Never Sleeps   370
Where to Run Async Code in React   374
Ways to Fetch   376
Getting Data with Fetch   377
Getting Data with Axios   377
Using Web Storage   379
  Two Types of Web Storage   379
  When to Use Web Storage   380
  When Not to Use Web Storage   380
  Web Storage Is Synchronous   380
  Working with localStorage   381
  Storing Data with localStorage   381
  Reading Data from localStorage   382
  Removing Data from localStorage   384
Summary   385

CHAPTER 17: CONTEXT API   387

What Is Prop Drilling?   387
How Context API Solves the Problem   388
  Creating a Context   388
  Creating a Provider   389
  Consuming a Context   390
    Using Context in a Class Component   390
    Using Context in a Function Component   391

Common Use Cases for Context   391
When Not to Use Context   392
Composition as an Alternative to Context   392
Example App: User Preferences   396
Summary   398

CHAPTER 18: REACT PORTALS   **399**

What Is a Portal?   399
    How to Make a Portal   399
    Why Not Just Render Multiple Component Trees?   403
Common Use Cases   403
    Rendering and Interacting with a Modal Dialog   404
    Managing Keyboard Focus with Modals   409
Summary   411

CHAPTER 19: ACCESSIBILITY IN REACT   **413**

Why Is Accessibility Important?   413
Accessibility Basics   414
    Web Content Accessibility Guidelines (WCAG)   414
    Web Accessibility Initiative - Accessible Rich Internet
    Applications (WAI-ARIA)   415
Implementing Accessibility in React Components   415
    ARIA Attributes in React   416
    Semantic HTML   416
    Form Accessibility   417
    Focus Control in React   418
        Skip Links   418
        Managing Focus Programmatically   419
    Media Queries in React   420
        Media Queries in Included CSS   421
        Using useMediaQuery   422
Summary   422

CHAPTER 20: GOING FURTHER   **425**

Testing   425
    Mocha   426
    Enzyme   426
    Chai   427
        Assert   427
        Expect   428
        Should   428

Karma 428

Nightwatch.js 428

Server-Side Rendering **429**

Flux 430

Redux 430

GraphQL 432

Apollo 433

React Native 434

Next.js 434

Gatsby 434

People to Follow **435**

Useful Links and Resources **435**

Summary **436**

INDEX 437

INTRODUCTION

SINCE ITS CREATION BY FACEBOOK IN 2013, REACTJS has become one of the most popular and widely used front-end user interface libraries on the web. With the creation of React Native in 2015, ReactJS has become one of the most widely used libraries for mobile app development as well.

ReactJS has always been a bit of a moving target. It has gone through several major changes over the years, but through it all, the core principles of React have remained the same.

If you want to learn to develop next-generation cross-platform web and mobile apps using the latest syntax and the latest tools, you've come to the right place. My goal with this book is to save you from the countless hours of trial and error that were my experience with trying to piece together bits of old and new information from the web and books.

Whether you're coming to React as a mobile developer, a web developer, or as any other kind of software developer, this book is for you. If you have experience with ReactJS as it existed in the earlier days (before about version 16), this book is for you too!

In this book, I've attempted not only to give the most up-to-date syntax and patterns for developing ReactJS applications, but also to give enough background and timeless information for it to remain relevant for years to come.

So, welcome to ReactJS.

WHY THIS BOOK?

Thank you for choosing to begin, or continue, your React journey with me. My aim with this book is to provide an up-to-date and thorough explanation of React and the React ecosystem along with hands-on code that will prepare you to quickly start using React productively in the real world.

I'm thrilled to be writing this book at this time for a number of reasons:

1. I have the experience and knowledge to do it right.
2. React is one of the most popular JavaScript libraries today.
3. I believe React will be even more popular in the future.
4. Existing online resources and books too often give incomplete and/or outdated information about how to program with React.

Let's take a quick look at each of these points, starting with a little bit about who I am and how I came to React and this book.

About Me

I've been a web developer since 1997, and I've been programming in JavaScript since 1998. I've built or managed the building of web applications for some of the world's largest companies over the years. As a web developer, writer, and teacher, I've had to learn and use plenty of languages and JavaScript frameworks. There's a difference between learning something and applying it, and I've been working on projects with React and doing React consulting for several years now.

I've been teaching web development and JavaScript online and in person since 2000, and I've been teaching React since 2015. In the years that I've been teaching React, I've written three weeklong courses designed for in-person delivery, numerous short video courses, and two longer video courses. I've taught React on three continents, and my students have been web developers, Java and C programmers, COBOL programmers, database administrators, network administrators, project managers, graphic designers, and college students.

As I'm writing, the global COVID-19 pandemic has decimated the in-person training industry. While this situation has given me more time at home with the pets, it's also given me time to think deeply about React and about the React book that I wish existed today. This book is the result of my looking at all of the top React books, looking at the current state of how React is being used, and looking at what React is likely to look like in the future.

React Is Popular

React is a JavaScript library that was born out of Facebook's need to create scalable and fast user interfaces. Ever since Facebook released it to the world as an open source project, it has been one of the most widely used ways to build dynamic web and mobile applications.

One popular game among JavaScript developers is to think of a noun, add ".js", and search GitHub to find the JavaScript framework with that name. In a time when new JavaScript frameworks and libraries pop up and die off with shocking regularity, React is one of three libraries released since 2010 that have stuck around and gained the kind of developer usage that will guarantee that they will be supported and in widespread use for a long time to come.

React Is Both Progressive and Conservative

React has been able to stick around so long and gain so many users because it's always been a forward-looking framework that's not afraid to make big changes to adapt to new features in JavaScript, new ways of writing user interfaces, and feedback from developers. Over the years, React has gone through several major changes in how the basic unit of a React application, the component, is written. But, amidst all this change, React has stuck to a central paradigm and each major change to React has maintained compatibility with previous versions.

Don't Believe Everything on the Internet

While the end result of all this change is that React has gotten easier to write and more robust over the years, it's also caused a pileup of outdated and often wrong example code and tutorials on the internet and in books. If you've done any research on React prior to buying this book, you've surely noticed this, and you've likely been confused by it. Perhaps you bought this book after having a frustrating experience with learning React online only to learn that you learned about an old version of it.

This book aims to be a solid and complete guide to all of the most important (and some less important) features, concepts, and syntaxes used in React.

WHAT'S COVERED IN THIS BOOK?

This book covers everything you need to know to write high-quality React code. You'll learn about React components using the functional method of writing them as well as the class method. You'll learn about managing the state of your application using several different methods, including with React Hooks and with the setState method. You'll learn how to put components together to make complete and dynamic user interfaces. You'll learn how to fetch data from an external data source and use it in your application. And, you'll learn how to store data in the user's web browser to improve the performance and usability of your application. Speaking of usability, you'll learn about best practices for making your application work on mobile devices as well as on the desktop, and you'll also learn how to make sure that your application will be accessible.

Because React takes advantage of many of the latest and greatest improvements and enhancements to the underlying JavaScript language, I'll be giving you JavaScript lessons throughout the book. Some of the new JavaScript syntax can be a little confusing to those of us who first learned the language in its early days, but I'll provide plenty of simple and real-world examples to explain each new bit of syntax or shortcut.

WHAT'S NOT COVERED?

Although React is a JavaScript library, this is not a book for newcomers to JavaScript or to web programming. I expect that you've had at least some experience with JavaScript. If you're not familiar with the latest additions and revisions to JavaScript, that's not a problem. But, if you're new to JavaScript or to programming in general, I recommend that you learn the basics of programming with JavaScript before you tackle React.

Similarly, this is not a web design book. I assume that you're familiar with HTML and CSS and feel comfortable writing both. I also assume a basic knowledge of how web browsers work and how web pages are rendered in browsers.

Finally, this book is intended to teach the fundamentals of React to anyone who wants to gain the ability to write React applications. Although it does cover many of the most commonly used patterns and conventions in React development, and many of the more advanced topics in React are covered as well, there are many topics that will only be mentioned in passing or that had to be omitted for the sake of space. To cover everything having to do with more advanced React development would require several volumes, which would all need to be updated every couple of months.

Once you understand the fundamentals of React as taught in this book, you'll be more than qualified to explore the vast React online ecosystem and find tutorials, documentation, and example code to continue your React education.

Some of the more advanced topics that are beyond the scope of this book are: unit testing, building mobile applications with React Native, Redux, and isomorphic/universal React. If all that sounds like a bunch of nonsense jargon at this point, you came to the right place! You may not know everything about how to implement all these more advanced things by the end of the book, but you'll certainly know what they are and how to get started with them.

PREREQUISITES

Programming React can feel like assembling a complex piece of furniture from a Swedish furnishing store. There are a lot of parts that don't make much sense individually, but when you follow the instructions and put them together in the right way, the simplicity and beauty of the whole thing may surprise you.

Internet Connection and Computer

I assume that you have a connection to the internet and a reasonably modern desktop or laptop computer. Writing code on tablets or smartphones is possible, but it's not easy. My examples and screenshots will be from the perspective of a desktop and/or laptop computer, and I can't guarantee that my example code will all be usable on a smaller device. Furthermore, some of the tools that you'll be using to build React applications simply won't run on a smartphone or tablet.

Web Development Basics

As previously mentioned, an understanding of HTML, CSS, and JavaScript is essential before beginning your study of React. If your experience is mostly with copying and pasting code that others have written, but you feel comfortable with making changes and looking up things that you don't yet know, you'll do fine with this book.

Code Editor

You'll need a code editor. The one I currently use and recommend is Microsoft Visual Studio Code. It's available for free on MacOS, Linux, and Windows. If you're more comfortable using another code editor, that's fine too. I've used many different code editors over the years, and I believe that whichever code editor a developer chooses to use and can be most effective with is the right one.

Browser

You'll also need a modern web browser. Although Mozilla Firefox, Google Chrome, and Windows Edge will all work for our purposes, my screenshots throughout the book were taken in Google Chrome on MacOS. Feel free to use whichever of the three modern web browsers you prefer, but understand that your experience may differ slightly from the screenshots in the book and that some of the React developer tools are currently only available for Chrome and Firefox.

INSTALLING REQUIRED DEPENDENCIES

Although it is possible to write and run React applications with nothing more than a text editor and a web browser on a computer connected to the internet, if you want to build any applications that will be deployed to the public web you'll need to install some additional software packages on your computer. These packages, when combined, are what web developers refer to as a *toolchain*.

All of the tools in the React toolchain are free, open source, and easy to download and install. In the following pages, I'll take you step by step through installing and configuring your toolchain and I'll show you some of the things you'll be able to do with your new tools to help you efficiently build, compile, and deploy React applications in a modern, standard, and professional way.

Introducing Visual Studio Code

In my more than 25 years as a web developer, I've used many different code editors, and I still switch code editors from time to time depending on the project or the type of code I'm writing.

However, there always seems to be a "popular" code editor that the majority of web developers use. Which editor is the popular one has changed several times over the years, but as of this writing, the code editor that seems to be most widely used for writing front-end web code is Microsoft's Visual Studio Code (aka VS Code), shown in Figure I-1.

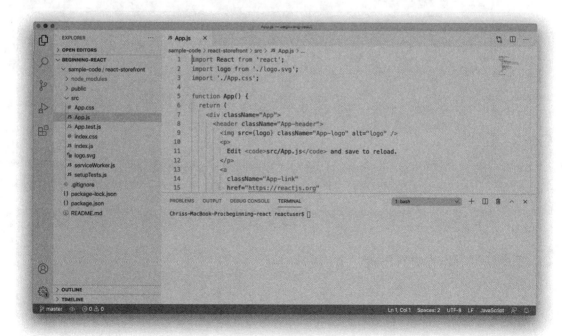

FIGURE I-1: VS Code

Visual Studio Code is free and open source, and it's available for Windows, Linux, and MacOS. It features built-in support for React development and many plugins have been developed for it that can be helpful for writing and debugging React projects.

For these reasons, I'll be using the latest version of Visual Studio Code in this book, and my screenshots and step-by-step instructions may be specific to Visual Studio Code in some places. If you choose to use a different code editor, be aware that you'll need to translate a few specific instructions to your environment.

If you don't already have Visual Studio Code installed, follow these steps to get it:

1. Open code.visualstudio.com in your web browser and click the download link for your operating system (Figure I-2).

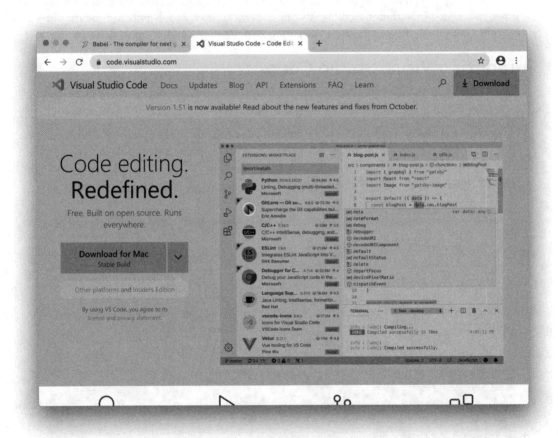

FIGURE I-2: Download VS Code

2. Double-click the downloaded file to start the installation process.

3. Accept the default options if you're presented with any options during installation.

Once you have Visual Studio Code, launch it. If this is the first time you've used it, you'll see the welcome screen, as shown in Figure I-3.

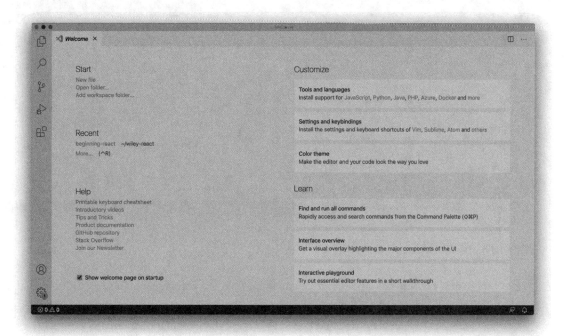

FIGURE I-3: The VS Code welcome screen

If you'd like to open the welcome screen at any point, you can do so by selecting Get Started from the Help menu.

The first and most important thing to learn about VS Code is how to use the Command Palette. The Command Palette gives you quick access to all of VS Code's commands. Follow these steps to become familiar with the Command Palette:

1. Open the Command Palette by selecting it from the View menu, or by pressing Command+Shift+P (on MacOS) or CTRL+Shift+P (on Windows). An input box will appear at the top of the VS Code interface, as shown in Figure I-4.

> **NOTE** *Since you're likely going to be using the Command Palette regularly, take a moment to memorize that keyboard shortcut.*

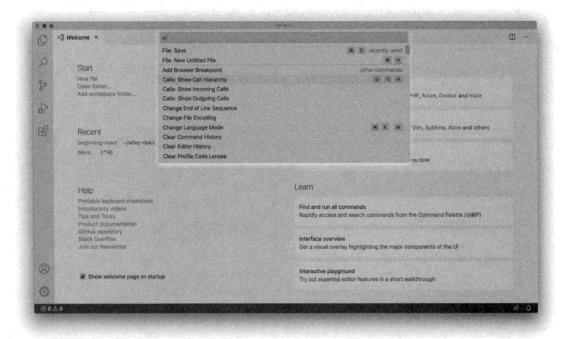

FIGURE I-4: The VS Code Command Palette

2. Type **new file** into the Command Palette input field. As you type, you'll see a list of available commands below your input.

3. When you see **File: New Untitled File** at the top of the Command Palette (as shown in Figure I-5), press Enter. A new untitled file will be created.

FIGURE I-5: Creating a new file using the Command Palette

4. Open the Command Palette again and start typing **save**. When File: Save is highlighted, press Enter to save your file. Give it a name ending with `.html` (such as `index.html`).

5. Type `!` on the first line of your new file and then press the Tab key. The scaffolding for a new HTML file will be written for you, which will look like Figure I-6. This magical code-generating feature is called Emmet. Emmet can be used to automate many routine tasks and speed the writing of code, and it would be a great idea to start getting familiar with it and practicing the use of it right away.

6. Use **CTRL+s** or the Command Palette to save your new file.

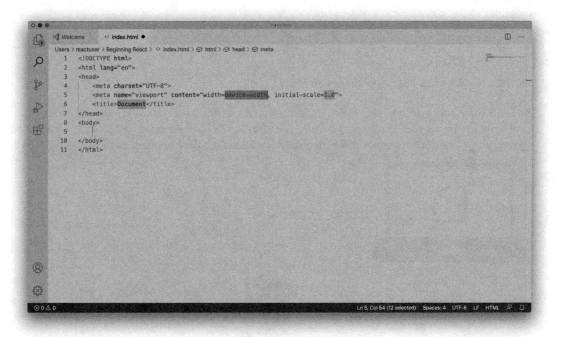

FIGURE I-6: Using Emmet to save typing

Node.js

Node.js started as a way to run JavaScript on web servers. The benefits of doing this are that, using Node.js (also known as just "Node"), programmers can use the same language on the client side (in the web browser) as they use on the web server (aka "server side"). Not only does this reduce the number of programming languages that a programmer or a team of programmers needs to be fluent in, but Node.js also makes communication between the server and web browsers easier because both are speaking the same language.

Figure I-7 shows a basic web application with Node.js running on the server and JavaScript running in a web browser.

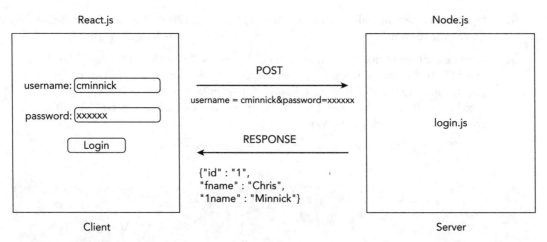

FIGURE I-7: Client-side React and server-side Node

As Node.js became popular, people also started to run it on their own computers as a way to run JavaScript programs outside of web browsers. Specifically, web developers used Node.js to run tools for automating many of the complex tasks involved in modern web development, as shown in Figure I-8.

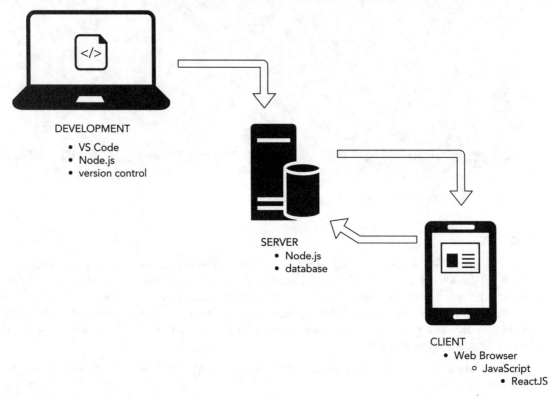

FIGURE I-8: Development, client-side, and server-side

Common tasks that take place in development and that can be aided by Node.js include:

➤ **Minification:** The process of removing spaces, line breaks, comments, and other code that's not required for the program to run, but that is helpful for people who work on the program. Minification makes scripts, web pages, and stylesheets more efficient and faster. Figure I-9 shows the difference between JavaScript code as it's written by a programmer and minified code.

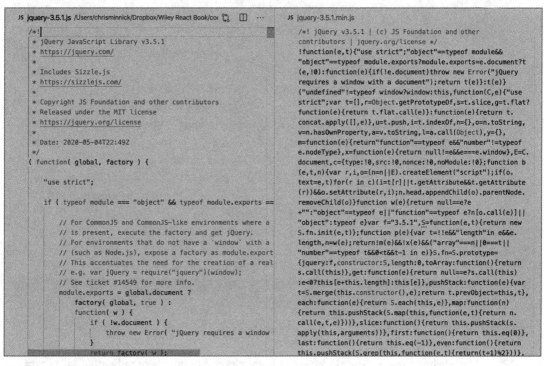

FIGURE I-9: Minification

➤ **Transpiling:** The process of converting programming code from one version of a programming language into another version. This is necessary in web development because not all web browsers support the same set of new JavaScript features, but they do all support some core subset of JavaScript features. By using a JavaScript transpiler, programmers can write code using the latest version of JavaScript and then the transpiled code can be run in any web browser. Figure I-10 shows an example use of JavaScript template strings, which were introduced in ES2015, along with their equivalent in an earlier version of JavaScript.

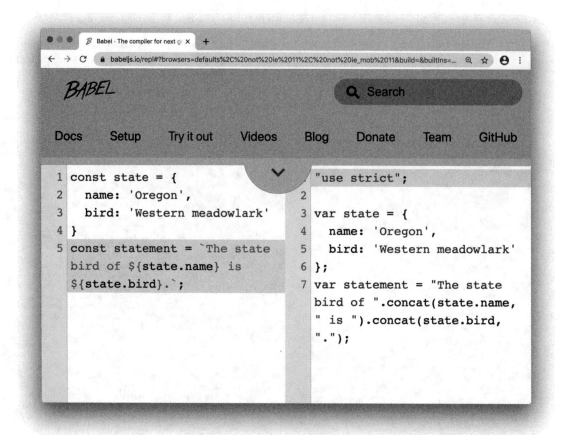

FIGURE I-10: Transpiling example

➤ **Module bundling:** A typical website can make use of hundreds of individual JavaScript programs. If a web browser had to download each of these different programs individually, it would significantly slow down web pages due to the overhead involved with requesting files from web servers. The main job of a module bundler is to combine (or "bundle") the JavaScript and other code involved in a web application to make serving the application faster. Because a bundler has to do work to all of the files in a program, it also is a good central place for tasks like minification and transpiling to take place, through the use of plugins. Figure I-11 illustrates the process of module bundling.

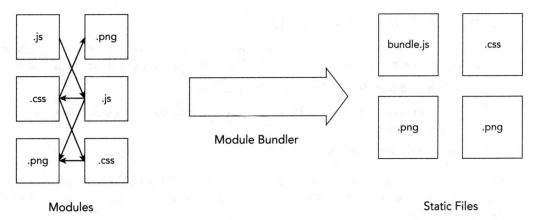

FIGURE I-11: Module bundling

➤ **Package management:** With so many different programs involved in JavaScript development, just installing, upgrading, and keeping track of them can be quite complex. A package manager is a program that helps you with tasks related to the management of all these programs (which are also known as "packages" in Node.js lingo).

➤ **CSS preprocessor:** A CSS preprocessor, such as SASS or LESS, allows you to write style sheets for your web application using a superset of CSS (such as SCSS) that supports the programmatic features that CSS lacks—things like variables, mathematic operations, functions, scope, and nesting. A CSS preprocessor produces standard CSS from code written using an alternative syntax.

➤ **Testing frameworks:** Testing is an essential part of any web project. Properly written tests can tell you whether each piece of your application is working as it was designed. The process of writing logic to test whether your application works as it should is also a powerful tool for helping you to write better code.

➤ **Build automation:** If you had to run each of the different tools involved in compiling a modern web app every time you wanted to test it out and deploy it to the web, you would have a very complex series of steps to follow and use to train anyone else who might work on the code. Build automation is the process of writing a program or script that runs all of the different tools for you in the right order to quickly and reliably optimize, compile, test, and deploy applications.

These are just a few of the different types of tools that are written in JavaScript and run in Node.js that front-end developers use on a regular basis. If you'd like to explore the vast universe of Node.js packages, visit the npm Package Repository at https://npmjs.com, or continue to the next section to learn about managing and installing Node.js packages.

Getting Started with Node.js

The most common way of interacting with Node.js is through commands typed into a UNIX-style terminal. You can access a terminal from within Visual Studio Code using three different methods:

1. By selecting **New Terminal** from the Terminal menu.

2. By right-clicking a folder in VS Code's file explorer and selecting **Open in Integrated Terminal**.

3. By using the keyboard shortcut **CTRL+~**.

Whichever way you choose (and I recommend getting comfortable with the keyboard shortcut to save yourself from having to switch to using your mouse), a window will open at the bottom of VS Code that looks like Figure I-12.

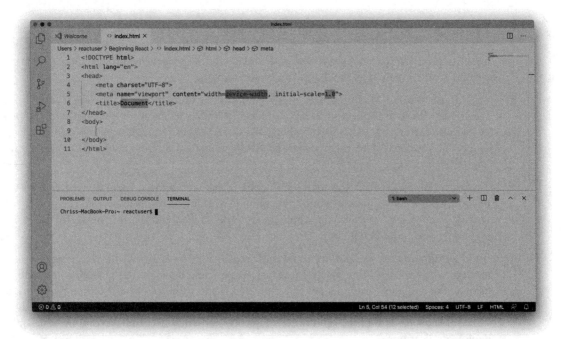

FIGURE I-12: The VS Code Terminal

The first step in learning to use Node.js is to make sure that it's installed on your computer. If you have a computer running MacOS or Linux, chances are good that it's already installed, but you may need to upgrade to a newer version. On Windows, it may not be installed, but that's easy to fix. Follow these steps to check whether you have Node.js installed, see what version is installed, and upgrade to the latest version:

1. Open the Terminal in Visual Studio Code.

2. In the Terminal, type **node -v**. If Node.js is installed, it will return a version number. If the version number is lower than 14.0, you'll need to upgrade. Proceed to step 4. If your version of Node.js is greater than 14.0, you may still want to proceed to step 4 and upgrade to the latest version of Node.js, but it's not required.

3. If Node.js is not installed, you'll get a message that node is an unknown command. Proceed to step 4.

4. Go to https://nodejs.org in your web browser and click the link to download the current LTS version of Node.js.

5. When the Node.js installer finishes downloading, double-click it and follow the instructions to install it.

6. If you have a Terminal window open in Visual Studio Code, close it and then re-open it.

7. Type **node -v** into your Terminal. You should now see that you have the latest version of Node.js installed.

Node.js Package Management with yarn or npm

Now that you have Node.js installed, the next step is to learn to use a package manager to install and upgrade Node.js packages. When you installed Node.js, you also installed a package manager called *npm*. This is the package manager that we'll be using in this book, because it's the most commonly used one, and because you already have it. There are other package managers, however. One of them, which has become quite widely used, for a number of reasons that we don't have the space to go into here, is called *yarn*. The commands that you use for npm and yarn are actually quite similar. If you'd like to find out more about yarn, and why you might want to use it, you can do so by visiting www.yarnpkg.com.

If you have Node.js installed, you already have npm installed. You can verify this by following these steps:

1. Open the Terminal in Visual Studio Code.

2. Type **npm -v** at the command line. You should get a response similar to the one shown in Figure I-13.

FIGURE I-13: Checking that npm is installed

If you have an older version of npm installed, it can cause some of the commands we'll run in this Introduction and the book's chapters to not work correctly. If you use MacOS, you can upgrade npm by entering the following command in the Terminal:

```
sudo npm install -g npm
```

After you type this command in the Terminal and press **Enter**, you'll be asked for a password. This is the password that you use to log in to your computer.

If you use Windows, you can upgrade npm by entering the following command:

```
npm install -g npm
```

Note that you must have administrative access to your computer to run this command.

The npm install command is how you can download and install Node.js packages to your computer so you can run them or so other programs can make use of them. When a computer program needs another computer program in order to run, we call the program it requires a *dependency*. Because Node.js programs are made up of small packages that often individually have reusable and limited functionality, it's not uncommon for a Node.js package to have hundreds of dependencies.

When you run npm install followed by the name of a Node.js package, npm looks for that package in the npm repository, downloads it (along with all of its dependencies), and installs it. Packages may be installed globally, which makes them available to any program on your computer, by specifying the **-g** flag after the npm install command. So, when we say npm install-g npm, what happens is that the npm package installs the latest version of itself. In other words, it upgrades.

In addition to being able to install packages globally, npm can also install packages locally, which makes them available only to the current project.

> **NOTE** Whenever possible, it's a good practice to only install packages locally in order to reduce the potential for version conflicts and to make your programs more reusable and more easily shared.

Follow these instructions to see the npm install command in action:

1. Open Visual Studio Code and click the File Explorer icon on the left toolbar.

2. Click **Open Folder** and use the file browser that it opens to create a new folder named **chapter-0** in your computer's Documents folder and open that folder.

3. Open the integrated Terminal application in Visual Studio Code. It will open a command-line interface and set the current directory to the folder that you have open.

4. Type npm init -y. Running npm init creates a new file called package.json, whose purpose is to track dependencies and other meta information about your node package.

5. Type `npm install learnyounode -g`, or `sudo npm install learnyounode -g` (on MacOS or Linux). This will install an npm package created by NodeSchool (`nodeschool. io`) that teaches you how to use Node.js. As the `learnyounode` package is downloaded and installed, you'll see some messages fly by on the screen (and possibly a few warnings or errors—these are normal and nothing to worry about).

6. When the package has finishing installing, type `learnyounode` in the Terminal to run it. Your command prompt will be replaced by a menu of lessons. I recommend going through at least the first one or two of these lessons at your convenience so that you can get a better idea of what Node.js is, although a deep understanding isn't necessary for learning React.

> **NOTE** *You may get an error message saying that running scripts is disabled when you try to run the* `npm install` *command on Windows. If you do, entering the following command into the Terminal should solve the problem:*
>
> ```
> Set-ExecutionPolicy -Scope Process -ExecutionPolicy Bypass
> ```

Chrome DevTools

Google's Chrome browser includes a powerful set of tools for inspecting and debugging websites and web applications. Follow these steps to get started with using Chrome DevTools:

1. Open your Chrome browser and go to `www.example.com`. You'll see a simple example web page. The simplicity of this page makes it a great place to start to learn about Chrome DevTools.

2. Open the Chrome DevTools panel by clicking the three dots in the upper-right corner of Chrome (this is known as the Chrome Menu) and selecting **More Tools ➤ Developer Tools** or by using the keyboard shortcut: **Command+Option+I** (on MacOS) **or CTRL+Shift+I** (on Windows). The keyboard shortcut is not only easier, it is also unlikely to ever change, whereas the location of the Developer Tools menu item has changed several times over the years. Either way you open it, a panel will open up in your browser, containing the DevTools, as shown in Figure I-14.

> **NOTE** *The default docking position for Chrome DevTools is on the right side of the browser window. You can change where the tools are docked by clicking the three dots (known as a "kebab" menu icon) in the upper-right corner of the DevTools pane.*

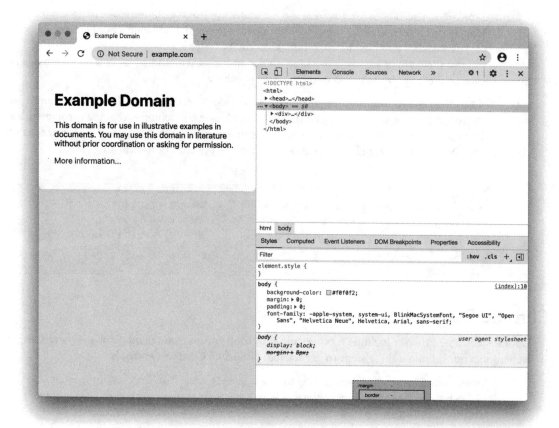

FIGURE I-14: Chrome DevTools

3. Look for the element selector tool in the upper-left corner of the DevTools panel and click it. You can use the element selector tool to inspect the different HTML elements in a web page.

4. Use the element selector tool to highlight different parts of the www.example.com web page. When you have the header of the page highlighted, click it. The HTML that creates the header will be highlighted in the source code view in DevTools, and the CSS styles that are applied to the header will be shown to the right of the source code.

5. Double-click the words Example Domain inside the `<h1>` element in the source code view. The words will become highlighted and editable.

6. With the words Example Domain highlighted in the source code view, type new words over them to replace them and then press Enter to exit the source editing mode. Your new text will appear in the browser window as the `<h1>` element.

7. Find the `<h1>` element style in the styles pane to the right of the source code window and double-click it.

8.   Try changing the styles that are applied to the `<h1>` element and notice that they modify what's showing in the browser window.

9.   Click the **Console** tab at the top of the DevTools pane. This will open the JavaScript console.

10.   Type the following JavaScript into the JavaScript console:

```
document.getElementsByTagName('h1')[0].innerText
```

When you press Enter, the text between the opening and closing `<h1>` tags will be logged to the console.

The important thing to know about everything we've done with the Chrome DevTools so far, and the first key to understanding how React works, is that you're not actually changing the HTML web page itself. That is safely stored on a web server. What you're changing is your web browser's in-memory representation of the web page. If you refresh the page, it will be re-downloaded and will appear as it did when you first loaded it.

The method that DevTools uses to manipulate the web page is through the *Document Object Model*, or DOM. The DOM is the JavaScript application programming interface (API) for web pages. By manipulating the DOM, you can dynamically alter anything in a web browser window. DOM manipulation is the way that JavaScript frameworks and libraries, including React, make web pages more interactive and more like native desktop applications.

React Developer Tools

To help developers debug React applications, Facebook created a browser extension called *React Developer Tools*. React Developer Tools is currently only available for Chrome and Firefox. Once installed, React Developer Tools gives you two new buttons in the browser developer tools: Components and Profiler.

Let's first look at how to install React Developer Tools and then we'll look at what it does.

Follow these steps to install React Developer Tools in Chrome:

1.   Go to the Chrome Web Store at `https://chrome.google.com/webstore` using your Chrome browser.

2.   Enter **React Developer Tools** into the search box. The first result will be the React Developer Tools extension by Facebook.

3.   Click the React Developer Tools extension and then click the **Add to Chrome** button. The extension will be installed in your browser.

Here's how to install the React Developer Tools AddOn in Firefox:

1.   Open your Firefox browser and go to `https://addons.mozilla.org/en-US/firefox/addon/react-devtools/`.

2.   Click the **Add to Firefox** button.

3. When Firefox asks you for permission to install the AddOn, click **Add**.

Once it's installed, follow these steps to get started with using the React Developer Tools:

1. Open the Chrome DevTools or the Firefox Developer Tools.

2. Notice that if you're not currently viewing a web page that uses React, you won't see any difference in the Developer Tools.

3. Go to `https://reactjs.org` in your browser. In the Developer Tools, you'll see new tabs for Components and Profiler appear.

4. Click the Components tab. You'll see a tree view of the React user interface, as shown in Figure I-15.

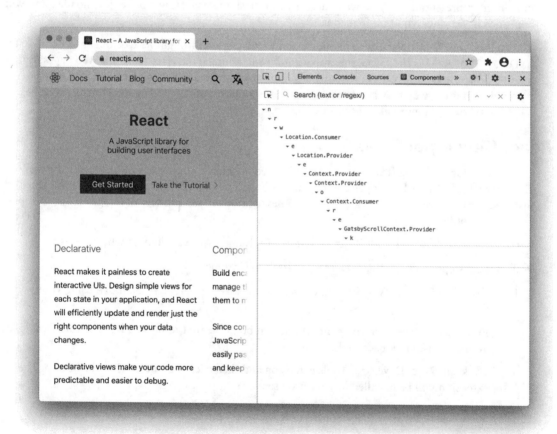

FIGURE I-15: React Developer Tools Components view

Each of the items in the React Components view is a different component in the React application. On most public websites that use React, the component names that display in the React Developer Tools won't make much sense, and the React Developer Tools are only of limited functionality. This is because there are actually separate versions of React for *development* (which is when you're building and debugging the application) and for *production* (which is when the application is deployed and available to end users).

The production version of React uses minified component names, and most of the debugging functionality is removed in order to increase performance and decrease the size of the download required for the browser to run React.

Spend a few minutes clicking around the Components tab and exploring the different components. Click the inspector icon in the React Developer Tools, which appears in the upper left of the window and resembles the icon for the Chrome DevTools element inspector you saw earlier.

The React Developer Tools' element inspector works similarly to the Chrome DevTools' element inspector (and to the Firefox element inspector too, for that matter). The difference between these two tools is an essential one to understand, however. Whereas the browser's element inspector can be used to highlight and view the HTML and styles that are in the browser's DOM, the React element inspector allows you to highlight and view the React components that were rendered on the page. You can think of the Components tab as a higher-level view.

The React components you can inspect through the React Developer Tools eventually produce the DOM nodes (which represent HTML and styles) that you can browse using the browser's element inspector.

The Profiler gives you information about the performance of your React application. Profiling is disabled in the production version of React, so this tab won't do much when you view a public web page that uses React. We'll explore and use the Profiler and show how it can be used to debug and tune your React applications in Chapter 5.

Intro to Create React App

The most common way to get started with React is to use a node package called *Create React App*. Create React App is an officially supported tool that installs a toolchain for React development and configures a boilerplate React application that you can use as a starting point for your applications.

To install and run Create React App, you can use a command that comes as part of the npm package manager called *npx*. npx is a package runner. Earlier in this Introduction, you used the npm install command to install a node package. Once a package is installed, you can run it by using the **npm start** command. npx is similar to a combination of npm install and npm start. If the package is already installed globally on your computer when you issue a command to run it with npx, the already-installed package will be run. If it's not installed, running it with npx will cause it to be downloaded, temporarily installed locally, and run.

To create a new React app using Create React App, use the npx command, followed by **create-react-app**, followed by a name that you want to give your new React app. For example:

```
npx create-react-app my-new-app
```

Naming Your React App

The name you choose for your new app is up to you, as long as it conforms to the rules of Node.js package names. These rules are:

➤ It must be less than 214 characters long.

➤ The name can't start with a dot or underscore.

➤ The name can't have uppercase letters.

➤ It can't contain any characters that aren't allowed in URLs (such as ampersands and dollar signs) and that are "unsafe" in URLs (such as the percent symbol and spaces).

In addition to these rules, there are several common conventions for how Node.js packages, and therefore apps created using Create React App, are named:

➤ Keep it simple and as short as possible.

➤ Use only lowercase letters.

➤ Use dashes in place of spaces.

➤ Don't use the same name as a common Node.js package.

Making Your First React App

Follow these steps to use Create React App to make your first React app:

1. Make or open a new folder in Visual Studio Code.

2. Open the Terminal and make your new folder the working directory. You can do this by right-clicking the folder name and choosing **Open in Integrated Terminal**, or by opening the Terminal and using the Unix cd (for change directory) command to change the working directory to the one where you want to make the new app. Note that if you're using Windows, your integrated terminal may be the Windows Command Prompt, in which case the command to change the working directory is dir.

3. Use npx to run create-react-app and give your new application a name. For example:

```
npx create-react-app my-test-app
```

4. Press **Enter** to start the installation of create-react-app and the configuration of your new app. You'll see a series of messages and progress bars in the Terminal. You may also see some errors and warnings, but often these aren't anything to be concerned about.

5. When the installation and configuration of your new React app finishes, change to the directory containing your new app by typing **cd** followed by the name you gave to your app:

```
cd my-test-app
```

6. Start up your app by using the npm start command. Note: npm start is actually shorthand for npm run start. What you're doing when you run npm start is that you're causing a script called start to run its commands.

7. Wait and watch as your generated React app starts up and then opens in a browser to reveal the React logo and a message, as shown in Figure I-16.

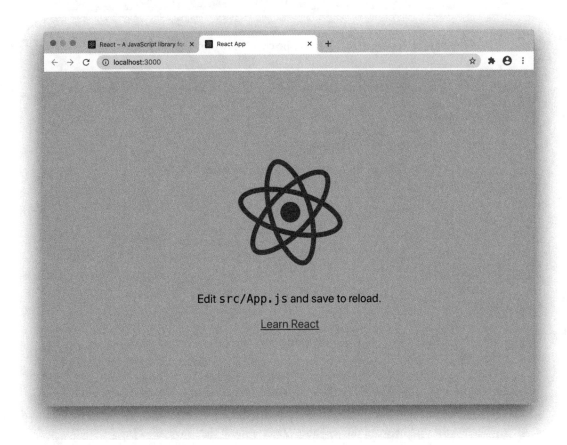

FIGURE I-16: The default Create React App boilerplate

8. Open the Chrome DevTools window and use the Components pane that you installed with the React Developer Tools to inspect your React app. Notice that this sample app is much smaller and less complex than the one that makes up the reactjs.org website, which you inspected earlier in this Introduction.

Now that you've created a React app, you can try making some changes to it by following these steps:

1. Leave the integrated Terminal in Visual Studio Code open and open src/App.js, which is located inside your application's folder.

> **NOTE** *React applications are made up of a hierarchy of components, and this one is the top-level component, and the only one in a default application generated by Create React App.*

2. Find the part of App.js that contains the code shown in Listing 0-1.

LISTING 0-1: The return statement in the default Create React App boilerplate

```
<div className="App">
  <header className="App-header">
    <img src={logo} className="App-logo" alt="logo" />
    <p>
      Edit <code>src/App.js</code> and save to reload.
    </p>
    <a
      className="App-link"
      href="https://reactjs.org"
      target="_blank"
      rel="noopener noreferrer"
    >
      Learn React
    </a>
  </header>
</div>
```

> **NOTE** *The HTML-like syntax you see here is JSX, which is a special feature of React projects that we will cover in detail in Chapter 3.*

3. Change the text between the <p> and </p> tags and then save App.js.

4. Switch back to your browser, and notice that the browser window has updated to reflect the change you made to App.js!

Congratulations, and Onward!

If you've made it this far, you're well on your way to learning React. You have your toolchain set up, you've learned the basics of using two in-browser testing tools (Chrome DevTools and React Developer Tools), you've installed Create React App, and you've used it to generate a boilerplate React application.

Feel free to play around with the tools and commands you learned in this Introduction, and to try making additional changes to the Create React App boilerplate code to see what happens.

When you're ready, move on to Chapter 1, where you'll get hands-on experience with building and modifying your first React components!

READER SUPPORT FOR THIS BOOK

You'll find hundreds of code listings in this book. I've designed these to be simple enough to be easily understandable, but practical enough to be helpful as you transition from learning React to practicing writing React code. To get the most out of this book, I recommend you try running and experimenting with each of the code listings.

To make running the examples easier, I've put them all online, including working examples where possible.

Companion Download Files

As you work through the examples in this book, you may choose either to type in all the code manually or to use the source code files that accompany the book. All the source code used in this book is available for download from `http://www.wiley.com/go/reactjsfoundations`.

Working examples of each code listing, supplemental information, and a link to the book's Github repository are available at `https://www.reactjsfoundations.com`.

If you prefer to download and run the example code on your own computer, you can clone the repository using Git and then follow the instructions in the README file to view working versions of every code listing.

If you don't have Git installed, you can go to `https://www.reactjsfoundations.com` in your browser and click the **Download** button to download all of the code to your computer.

In the event that a "but" may have made it into this book, or some unforeseen update to React has necessitated a change to any of the code in the book, you'll find corrections at `https://www.reactjsfoundations.com` as well.

How to Contact the Publisher

If you believe you've found a mistake in this book, please bring it to our attention. At John Wiley & Sons, we understand how important it is to provide our customers with accurate content, but even with our best efforts an error may occur.

In order to submit your possible errata, please email it to our Customer Service Team at wileysupport@wiley.com with the subject line "Possible Book Errata Submission."

Hello, World!

Since the beginning of time, the first program anyone learns to build in any new programming language is a program that displays the words "Hello, World." Of course, the words here aren't important, and I would encourage you to choose any words you like to replace this cliché phrase. The point of this chapter is to quickly build up your understanding of how React works by using a simple and inconsequential program. But, don't be deceived—the foundational tools and techniques that you learn about in this chapter are essential to learning React. If you only read one chapter of this book, this would be the one. In this chapter, you'll learn:

- ➤ How to use React without a toolchain.
- ➤ How to write your first React application.
- ➤ How to make and modify a React application built with Create React App.

REACT WITHOUT A BUILD TOOLCHAIN

Most React application development uses a build toolchain (such as the one created by Create React App) running in Node.js as its foundation. It is possible, however, to include React in an existing website or to build a website that makes use of React by just importing a couple of scripts into a web page. You can even use React code alongside JavaScript code written using another library or framework.

Follow these steps to make an HTML page and to add React to it:

1. Create a new folder in your Documents folder and open it in Visual Studio Code.

2. Open the Command Palette (**Command+Shift+P** on MacOS or **Control+Shift+P** on Windows) and run the **File: New File** command, or select **File** ⇨ **New File** from the top menu.

3. Save your new file as `index.html`.

4. Type **!** followed by the **Tab** key to generate an HTML template using emmet. If you prefer, you can also type the following code into your new blank file:

```
<!DOCTYPE html>
<html lang="en">
<head>
    <meta charset="UTF-8">
    <meta name="viewport" content="width=device-width, initial-scale=1.0">
    <title>Hello, React!</title>
</head>
<body>

</body>
</html>
```

5. Between the `<body>` and `</body>` tags, create an empty `div` element and give it an `id` attribute with the value of app. This is where you're going to tell React to render its output. In the React world, we call this the container element. The actual `id` value doesn't matter here, but app is a simple, easy to remember, and meaningful value that is very commonly used.

> **NOTE** You can put a React container element anywhere inside the body element of a web page.

6. Go to `https://reactjs.org/docs/cdn-links.html` in your browser and find the script tags for including React and ReactDOM from a content delivery network (CDN), as shown in Figure 1-1.

7. Copy both script tags and paste them right before the `</body>` tag in `index.html`.

> **NOTE** The reason these must go at the end of the body of your web page is that they can make changes to your web page. Because of the way JavaScript loads and then executes immediately after it loads, the browser will show an error message if your React code is loaded and executed before the container element is loaded.

The first script, `react.development.js`, is the actual React library that handles the rendering of React components, the flow of data between components, responding to events, and all of the functionality that you, as a React developer, have control over in React.

The second script, `react-dom.development.js`, handles the communication and translation between the React application that you write and the browser DOM. In other words, it controls how and when your component renders and updates in the browser.

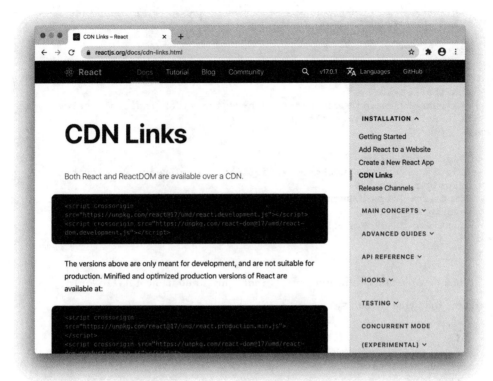

FIGURE 1-1: The React CDN Links

The CDN links that you copy from reactjs.org will explicitly specify the latest version of React at the time that you view the page. If you want to make sure that your page always uses the latest version of React, change the number following the @ to "latest" as shown here:

```
<script src="https://unpkg.com/react@latest/umd/react.development.js"
crossorigin></script>
<script src="https://unpkg.com/react-dom@latest/umd/react-dom.development.js"
crossorigin></script>
```

> **NOTE** Notice the "umd" in the URLs in step 7. UMD stands for Universal Module Definition. UMD is what allows the CDN version of React to work in browsers without requiring a compile step.

8. After the script tags that include the UMD versions of react and react-dom, write another script tag that includes a file (which we'll make shortly) named HelloWorld.js:

```
<script src="HelloWorld.js"></script>
```

Your index.html file should now match Listing 1-1.

LISTING 1-1: The HTML file for using React without a toolchain

```
<!DOCTYPE html>
<html lang="en">
<head>
    <meta charset="UTF-8">
    <meta name="viewport" content="width=device-width, initial-scale=1.0">
    <title>Hello, World!</title>
</head>
<body>
    <div id="app"></div>
    <script src="https://unpkg.com/react@latest/umd/react.development.js"
    crossorigin></script>
    <script src="https://unpkg.com/react-dom@latest/umd/react-dom.development.js"
    crossorigin></script>
    <script src="HelloWorld.js"></script>
</body>
</html>
```

9. Create a new file in the same directory as index.html and name it HelloWorld.js.

10. Add the following code to HelloWorld.js:

```
'use strict';

class HelloWorld extends React.Component {
  constructor(props) {
    super(props);
    this.state = { personName:'World' };
  }

  render() {
    return React.createElement('h1', null, 'Hello, ' + this.state.personName);
  }
}
```

11. Add the following to the end of HelloWorld.js, after the code you entered in step 10:

```
const domContainer = document.querySelector('#app');
ReactDOM.render(React.createElement(HelloWorld), domContainer);
```

12. Open index.html in a web browser. You should see the message "Hello, World" displayed as a first level heading, as shown in Figure 1-2.

13. Change the value of the personName property in the state object inside the constructor function in HelloWorld.js as shown in Listing 1-2.

LISTING 1-2: Changing the state data in a component

```
'use strict';

class HelloWorld extends React.Component {
  constructor(props) {
```

```
      super(props);
      this.state = { personName:'Murray' };
    }

  render() {
    return React.createElement('h1', null, 'Hello, ' + this.state.personName);
  }
}

const domContainer = document.querySelector('#app');
ReactDOM.render(React.createElement(HelloWorld), domContainer);
```

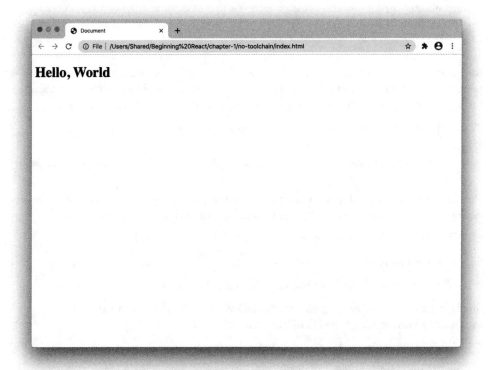

FIGURE 1-2: Hello, World running in a browser

14.   Save `HelloWorld.js` and refresh your browser window. You should see the update reflected.

Congratulations! You've now built your first custom React application.

Spend a few minutes examining the code for `HelloWorld.js`. If you're familiar with JavaScript objects and classes, you'll notice that there's nothing magic going on here. Everything is straightforward JavaScript.

Here's a quick line-by-line rundown of everything that's happening in this file:

1. We create a JavaScript class called `HelloWorld` that extends the `React.Component` class:

    ```
    class HelloWorld extends React.Component {
    ```

    > **NOTE** *You'll learn about using classes in JavaScript in Chapter 4.*

2. Next, we write the constructor:

    ```
    constructor(props) {
        super(props);
        this.state = { personName:'World' };
    }
    ```

    The constructor will run just once, before the component is mounted. In the constructor, we use the `super` method to import properties from the base class (which is `React.Component`). Finally, we create an object called `state` and give it a property called `personName`.

3. We create a new function in `HelloWorld` called `render()`:

    ```
    render() {
        return React.createElement('h1', null, 'Hello,' + this.state.personName);
    }
    ```

    The `render` function produces the output of every React component. This output is generated by using the `React.createElement` method, which takes three parameters:

    ➤ The HTML element to create

    ➤ Optional React element properties

    ➤ The content that should be put into the created element

4. Finally, we use the `render` method of ReactDOM to render the return value of the `HelloWorld` class inside of the HTML document:

    ```
    const domContainer = document.querySelector('#app');
    ReactDOM.render(React.createElement(HelloWorld), domContainer);
    ```

    > **NOTE** *Notice that we're using two different functions named* `render()`. *The first one,* `React.render()`, *creates the output of a component. The second one,* `ReactDOM.render()`, *causes that output to be displayed in the browser window.*

If this seems like a lot of work and code to just make a web page display text, you're right—it is.

Fortunately, there are much easier ways to write React code, thanks to the tools that you learned about in this book's Introduction—specifically, Node.js and Create React App.

Let's wrap up this chapter by combining everything you've learned so far into making an interactive version of the Hello, World application with Create React App.

INTERACTIVE "HELLO, WORLD" WITH CREATE REACT APP AND JSX

Although it's possible to use React without a toolchain by including the UMD build into an HTML file, this is far from an ideal way to do anything but a simple application.

By using a toolchain, you gain a set of testing and debugging tools that can help you write better code. You also gain the ability to compile your React components so that they'll run faster in the user's browser.

You've already seen how to use Create React App to build a boilerplate user interface. Now let's look at how to build something slightly more complex and interactive:

> **NOTE** *If you'd like to bypass the process of installing and configuring the Create React App boilerplate, you can skip the first three steps and use the same app you created in the book's Introduction.*

1. Using Visual Studio Code, create a new directory and open the integrated terminal.
2. Type `npx create-react-app react-js-foundations` into the terminal and press Enter.
3. Once Create React App finishes its work, type `cd react-js-foundations` followed by `npm start`. Create React App will start up your application and open it in a browser.
4. Open `src/App.js` in Visual Studio Code.
5. Update `App.js` to match Listing 1-3 and then save the file.

LISTING 1-3: An interactive Hello, World component

```
import React from 'react';
import './App.css';

function App() {
  const [personName,setPersonName] = React.useState('');

  return (
    <div className="App">
      <h1>Hello {personName}</h1>
      <input type="text" onChange={(e) => setPersonName(e.target.value)}/>
    </div>
  );
}

export default App;
```

6. Return to your browser, and notice that the default Create React App screen has been replaced with an input field and an h1 element above it.

> **NOTE** This ability of an app running in Create React App to detect when files have changed and update what's showing in the browser without you having to manually reload the page is called "hot reloading."

7. Type into the input field. Everything you type should appear inside the h1 element, as shown in Figure 1-3.

FIGURE 1-3: The finished interactive Hello, World component!

8. When you're done playing around with this component, return to the built-in terminal in VS Code and press **Ctrl+c** to stop the recompiling and hot reloading script.

SUMMARY

Congratulations! In the last few pages, you've experienced the most primitive way to write React code as well as the latest and most advanced way. The history of React has been one of gradually refining the methods and tools used to write React to make it easier for developers. In these two examples, you've seen the two extremes—a React application built without the aid of any tooling, and one built using Create React App and the latest enhancements and simplifications that have been added to React as of this writing.

In this chapter, you learned:

➤ How to write a React application with the UMD build of React.

➤ The difference between `React.render` and `ReactDOM.render`.

➤ How to write a component using `React.createElement`.

➤ How to write and run a basic interactive component using Create React App.

In the following chapters, you'll learn how all of this works. Continue on to the next chapter where you'll learn about the inner workings of React.js and how it fits into the big picture. After that, Chapter 3 takes you further into working with more code.

2

The Foundation of React

React is a JavaScript library for creating interactive user interfaces using components. It was created by Facebook in 2011 for use on Facebook's newsfeed and on Instagram. In 2013, the first version of React was released to the public as open source software. Today, it's used by many of the largest websites and mobile apps, including Facebook, Instagram, Netflix, Reddit, Dropbox, Airbnb, and thousands of others.

Writing user interfaces with React requires a bit of a shift in how you think about web applications. You need to understand what React is, how it works at a higher level, and the computer science ideas and patterns that it's based on. In this chapter, you'll learn:

➤ Why it's called React.

➤ What a Virtual DOM does.

➤ The difference between composition and inheritance.

➤ The difference between declarative and imperative programming.

➤ The meaning of "idiomatic" with regard to React.

WHAT'S IN A NAME?

Let's start with the name "React." Facebook designed React in response to its need to be able to efficiently update websites in response to events. Events that can trigger updates in websites include user input, new data coming into the application from other websites and data sources, and data coming into the application from sensors (such as location data from GPS chips).

Traditionally, the way that web applications have dealt with data that changes over time is to refresh themselves every so often, checking for new data in the process. Facebook wanted to create a way to more easily build applications that respond, or *react* to new data, rather than simply refreshing pages whether the underlying data has changed or not. You can think of the difference in approaches as *pull* (which is the traditional way of updating websites) vs. *push* (which is the reactive way to build websites).

This method of updating a user interface in response to data changes is called *reactive programming*.

UI LAYER

Web applications typically are built and described using the Model-View-Controller (MVC) pattern. The Model in MVC is the data layer, the Controller facilitates communication with the data layer, and the View is what the user sees and interacts with. In an MVC application, the View sends input to the Controller, which passes data between the data layer and the View. React is only concerned with the V in MVC. It takes data as input and presents it to the user in some form.

Figure 2-1 shows a diagram of the MVC pattern.

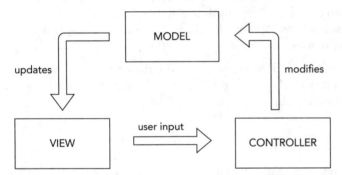

FIGURE 2-1: The MVC pattern

React itself doesn't care whether the user is using a mobile phone, a tablet, a desktop web browser, a screen reader, a command-line interface, or any other kind of device or interface that may be invented in the future. React just renders components. How those components get presented to the user is up to a separate library.

The library that handles rendering of React components in web browsers is called ReactDOM. If you want to render React elements to native mobile apps, you use React Native. If you want to render React components to static HTML, you can use ReactDOMServer.

ReactDOM has a number of functions for interfacing between React and web browsers, but the one that every React application makes use of is called ReactDOM.render. Figure 2-2 illustrates the relationship between React, ReactDOM, and a web browser.

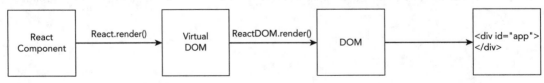

FIGURE 2-2: React and ReactDOM

ReactDOM is what makes it possible for user interfaces built in React to handle the quantity of screen changes required by modern web applications so efficiently. It does this through the use of a Virtual DOM.

VIRTUAL DOM

The Document Object Model, or DOM, is a web browser's internal representation of a web page. It converts HTML, styles, and content into nodes that can be operated on using JavaScript.

If you've ever used the `getElementById` function or set the `innerHTML` of an element, you've interacted with the DOM using JavaScript. Changes to the DOM cause changes to what you see in your web browser, and updates made in the web browser (such as when you enter data into a form) cause changes to the DOM.

Compared to other kinds of JavaScript code, DOM manipulation is slow and inefficient. This is because whenever the DOM changes, the browser has to check whether the change will require the page to be redrawn and then the redrawing has to happen.

Adding to the difficulty of DOM manipulation is that the DOM's functions aren't always easy to use and some of them have excessively long names like `Document.getElementsByClassName`. For both of these reasons, many different JavaScript DOM manipulation libraries have been created. The single most popular and widely used DOM manipulation library of all time was *jQuery*. It gave web developers an easy way to make updates to the DOM, and that changed the way we build user interfaces on the web.

Although jQuery made DOM manipulation easier, it left it up to programmers to program specifically when and how changes to the DOM would happen. The result was often inefficient user interfaces that were slower both to download and to respond to user interactions because of their use of jQuery. As a result, jQuery got a reputation for being slow.

When the engineers at Facebook designed React, they decided to take the details of how and when the DOM is modified out of the hands of programmers. To do this, they created a layer between the code that the programmer writes and the DOM. They called this intermediary layer the *Virtual DOM*.

Here's how it works:

1. A programmer writes React code to render a user interface, which results in a single React element being returned.

2. ReactDOM's `render` method creates a lightweight and simplified representation of the React element in memory (this is the Virtual DOM).

3. ReactDOM listens for events that require changes to the web page.

4. The `ReactDOM.render` method creates a new in-memory representation of the web page,

5. The ReactDOM library compares the new Virtual DOM representation of the web page to the previous Virtual DOM representation and calculates the difference between the two. This process is called *reconciliation*.

6. ReactDOM applies just the minimal set of changes to the browser DOM in the most efficient way that it can and using the most efficient batching and timing of changes.

By taking the programmer out of the process of actually making updates to the browser DOM, ReactDOM can decide on optimal timing and the optimal method for making required updates. This greatly improves the efficiency of making updates to a browser view.

Figure 2-3 is a diagram showing how the Virtual DOM works.

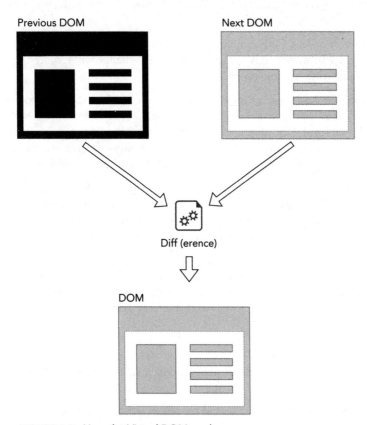

FIGURE 2-3: How the Virtual DOM works

THE PHILOSOPHY OF REACT

If you've used other JavaScript libraries, you may find React to be quite a bit different from your past experience with programming dynamic user interfaces. By understanding the thinking behind why React is like it is, you'll have a better understanding and appreciation of it.

Thinking in Components

React is a library for creating and putting together (or *composing*) components to build user interfaces. React components are independent pieces that can be reused and that can pass data to each other.

A component can be something as simple as a button or it can be more complex, such as a navigation bar that's made up of a collection of buttons and dropdowns.

As the programmer, it's your job to decide how big or how small each component in your application should be, but a good rule of thumb to think about is the idea of *single responsibility*.

The single responsibility principle, in programming, is the idea that a component should have responsibility for a single part of a program's functionality. Robert C. Martin, also known as "Uncle Bob," is one of the most important thinkers and writers on software design. He described the single responsibility principle this way:

> *Single Responsibility means that a class [or what we call a "component" in React] should have only one reason to change.*

Composition vs. Inheritance

In object-oriented programming (OOP), it's common to create variations of classes that inherit properties from a parent class. For example, a program might have a class called `Button`, which might have a child class called `SubmitButton`. `SubmitButton` would inherit all of the properties of `Button`, and then override or extend them to create its unique functionality and look.

Rather than using inheritance to create more specific components to deal with specific cases (such as a submit button), React encourages the creation of a single component that is more broadly reusable but that can be configured by passing data into it and then combining it with other components to handle more specific cases.

For example, in the case of a submit button, you might simply pass a parameter to a `Button` component called `label` and another parameter called `handleClick` that contains the action to be performed by the button. This generalized button can then serve multiple purposes, depending on the values of `label` and `handleClick` that are passed to it. Listing 2-1 shows what this component might look like.

LISTING 2-1: Creating configurable components

```
function Button(props){
  return(
    <button onClick={props.handleClick}>{props.label}</button>
  );
}
```

Once you've created a configurable component, you can create more specific components by combining more generalized ones. This technique is called *composition*. Listing 2-2 shows how you can create a specific `WelcomeDialog` component from a general `Dialog` one using composition.

LISTING 2-2: Using composition

```
function Dialog(props){
  return(
    <div className="dialogStyle">{props.message}</div>
  )
}

function WelcomeDialog(props){
  return(
    <Dialog message="Welcome to our app!" />
  )
}
```

React Is Declarative

One way to describe the difference in approach between programming with React and programming with many other JavaScript libraries is to say that React is *declarative* while many other libraries are *imperative*.

So, what is declarative programming? Traditionally, the job of a programmer has been to break down complex processes into steps so that a computer can perform them. For example, if you want to program a robot to make you a sandwich, you might start by figuring out the high-level steps involved in the process:

1. Get two slices of bread.
2. Find a knife.
3. Get the peanut butter.
4. Use the knife to spread the peanut butter.
5. Assemble the sandwich.

Of course, these steps are far too high-level for a robot to perform, so you need to break down each one into smaller steps:

1. Get two slices of bread.
    1a. Use visual sensors to locate bread.
        1aa. If bread is found, move toward it.
        1ab. If bread is not found, return to step 1.
    1b. Use grabber arm to attempt opening of bread package.

You get the idea. By breaking down a complex process into small steps, a task eventually becomes simple enough for a computer to perform. We call this step-by-step style of programming *imperative programming*. The imperative approach is the way that most DOM manipulation libraries worked prior to React.

To change a paragraph of text in the browser using jQuery, for example, you would do something like this:

```
$('#para1').html('<p>This is the new paragraph.</p>');
```

This code looks for a paragraph with the id attribute equal to para1 and changes its HTML content to the new content that's specified inside the parentheses.

React takes a different approach, which we call *declarative programming*. In declarative programming, the computer (or the computer language interpreter, rather) has some intelligence about the types of tasks that it can perform, and the programmer only needs to tell it what to do, rather than how to do it.

In declarative programming, our sandwich-making robot would know the steps for making sandwiches, and programming it would involve the programmer saying something like "make me a sandwich that looks like this."

Applied to DOM manipulation, the declarative approach that React takes is to allow the programmer to say, "Make the page look like this." React then compares the new way that the page should look with the way that it currently looks and figures out what's different and what needs to change and how to do it.

Building and updating a React user interface, from the programmer's perspective, is just a matter of specifying what the user interface should look like and telling React to render it.

React Is Idiomatic

React itself is a small library with limited functionality when compared to other JavaScript libraries. Except for a handful of concepts and methods that are unique to React, React components are just JavaScript. If the structure and code of a React component looks foreign to you, it's likely because it uses a style of JavaScript programming that you're not yet familiar with, or because it makes use of a new feature in JavaScript that you're not yet familiar with. The good news is that by getting better at JavaScript, you'll get better at programming with React.

You may hear the term "idiomatic JavaScript" used to describe React. What this means is that React code is easily understandable to people who program JavaScript. The reverse is also true: if you know JavaScript, understanding how to write React is not too much of a stretch.

Why Learn React?

If you've made it this far in the book, you probably already have your own reasons for learning React. You already know by now that you're in good company—React's popularity has been growing from day one of its release into the wild. Surveys of developers have consistently shown that it's at the top, or very near the top, of their preferred libraries, and the list of companies that have already migrated to React or that are in the process of migrating to React is impressive, to say the least.

React is going to be around for a long time to come, and there's never been a better time to learn it.

React vs....

The job of being a software developer today, especially one working with JavaScript and the web, requires some knowledge of a staggeringly large and growing number of libraries, frameworks, protocols, standards, best practices, and patterns. A great programmer not only knows how to apply whatever language and framework they are working in at any one time, but also how to quickly learn new languages and frameworks.

One good way to learn a new language is by comparing it to something that you already know, and the question "how does React compare to (x)" is one of the most common questions that my students ask me. In the following sections, I'll look at how React stacks up against its two closest rivals: Angular and Vue. While I don't like to take sides, I know enough about each to be able to give some facts and impressions.

React vs. Angular

Angular (`angular.io`) was created by Google, and it's been around longer than React in one form or another. Let's start with the similarities:

1. Purpose. Both Angular and React can create scalable and dynamic user interfaces.

2. Stability. Both Angular and React were created by one of the largest companies on the internet and they both have huge numbers of developers and enthusiasts.

3. Robustness. A major concern with any JavaScript library or framework is how safe, secure, and generally acceptable it is for enterprise development. Both Angular and React are popular and widely used in corporate software development.

4. License. Both frameworks use the MIT license, which allows for unlimited use and reuse for free as long as the original copyright and license notices are included in any copy of the source code.

Angular has gone through some major changes in the years since React came onto the scene. Prior to what we now call "Angular" there was AngularJS, which was replaced in 2016 with Angular 2.0. Angular 2.0 was a major change and was not compatible with AngularJS. Its introduction led to many developers deciding to learn React instead of the rewritten Angular.

Angular is considered to be a "framework," while React calls itself a "library." The difference between a library and a framework is that a framework is usually an all-encompassing way of doing something, while a library is generally seen as a tool for a more specific purpose.

The React library itself is a tool for making user interfaces out of components. Angular, on the other hand, is a complete system for building front-end web applications. By assembling components and libraries, React can do everything that Angular can do. But, if you need something smaller, such as to generate some HTML, React can do that as well.

Angular has a steeper learning curve than React. In addition to the learning curve required to use the framework itself, Angular requires the use of Microsoft's TypeScript, which is a superset of JavaScript that's designed for the development of large applications. It's possible to use TypeScript to write React as well, but with Angular it's a requirement.

Unlike React, Angular operates on the real DOM, rather than on a Virtual DOM, and it optimizes changes to the DOM by using an approach it calls Change Detection. When an event causes data changes in Angular, the framework checks each component and updates it as needed. You may recognize this approach as a more imperative approach (as compared to React's declarative approach) to DOM manipulation.

React and Angular also differ in how data flows within an application. React, as you'll see, uses one-way data flow. What this means is that every change that happens in the browser starts out as a change in the data model. This differs from both Angular and Vue, which both feature two-way data binding, in which changes in the browser can affect the data model directly and changes to the data model can affect the view.

React vs. Vue

Vue.js (`vuejs.org`) is a relative newcomer to the universe of JavaScript frameworks, but it has been growing in popularity and is now considered one of the top three, along with React and Angular.

Like React and Angular, Vue is open source. Unlike React and Angular, however, Vue isn't backed or controlled by a large corporation. Instead, it's the work of many programmers and companies donating their skills to maintain and support it. This can be seen as either a plus or a minus, depending on your view of giant internet companies.

Vue takes a middle ground between the bare-bones approach of React and the smorgasbord approach of Angular. Like Angular, it has built-in functionality for state management, routing, and managing CSS. But, like React, it's a small library (even smaller than React in terms of total kilobytes that must be downloaded to the browser) and how you use it is highly customizable.

Of the three libraries, Vue is probably the easiest to learn.

What React Is *Not*

It's important to keep in mind not only what React is, but what it isn't. Beyond the often repeated (and largely semantic) argument about whether React is a library or a framework are the more important distinctions between front-end libraries, back-end libraries, and the development environment.

React, as it's used most often, is a front-end library. This means that everything React does happens in the web browser. It can't directly control or access remote databases (except through the web), and it doesn't serve web pages.

When I'm asked about the differences between front-end, back-end, and development environments in my classes, I like to draw something like the diagram in Figure 2-4.

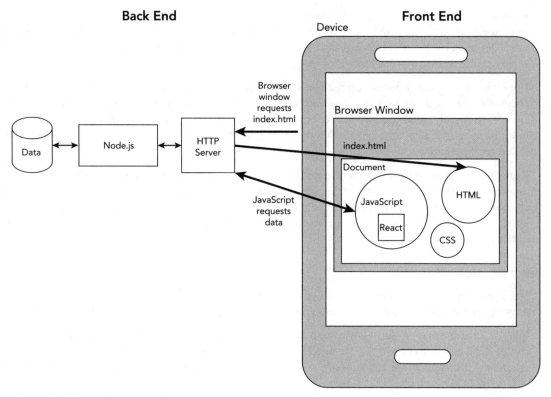

FIGURE 2-4: How the web works

You know already that React is a front-end JavaScript library. As you can see from the preceding diagram, there are many other pieces of the web ecosystem. Here are a few of the things that React is *not*.

React Is Not a Web Server

A web server, also known as an HTTP server, has as its primary job to accept requests for web pages from web browsers and then return those web pages to the browser along with all of their linked images, CSS files, and JavaScript files.

The React library and the user interfaces you create using React are among the linked JavaScript files that a web server sends to a web browser, and React itself has no ability to handle requests from web browsers, although it can interact with the browser, just as any JavaScript code can, through the browser's application programming interfaces (APIs).

React Is Not a Programming Language

React is a JavaScript library, which means that it is just a collection of JavaScript functions that programmers can make use of. The idea of a library is to simplify common tasks that programmers need to do frequently so that they can just focus on writing the code that makes a program unique.

If you had enough time and knowledge, you could rewrite every bit of the React library yourself using JavaScript—but, of course, there's no reason to do that, because the React developers have done it for you.

React Is Not a Database Server

React doesn't have any abilities to store data in a secure way or in a permanent way. Instead, React user interfaces (like every web and mobile web user interface) communicate with server-side databases over the internet to store and receive data such as login information, ecommerce transaction data, news feeds, and so forth.

The data that React uses to make user interfaces dynamic, and the data that you're viewing at any one time in a React user interface (what we call "session" data), is not persistent. Unless your React user interface saves session data in the web browser (using cookies or the browser's local storage), it all gets erased when you navigate to a different URL or refresh your browser window.

React Is Not a Development Environment

As you saw in the book's Introduction, you'll use plenty of different tools to program with React. Collectively, these are known as your development environment. I present the most commonly used tools (and, in some cases, just my own personal preferences), but there's nothing about React that requires you to use these specific tools. In many cases, there are alternatives available, and you may discover that you prefer different ones than I do (or, you may discover a better tool that I'm not currently aware of). It's possible to write perfect React code using any tools you want, or using no tools at all (other than a text editor).

React Is Not the Perfect Solution to Every Problem

React works well for many types of applications, but it's not always the best solution. This is true of any JavaScript library, and it's probably true of every single tool ever invented. It's important to know about a wide variety of different languages and libraries so that you can make good choices and know when the tools you prefer to use or that you know the best are the best and when they might not be the best.

SUMMARY

Because React is a different way of writing user interfaces for the web, it does have some concepts and foundational ideas behind it that are important to understand before you can work with it effectively. In the end, however, writing React user interfaces is straightforward:

1. You write components to describe how the user interface should look and act.

2. React renders your components to create a tree of nodes.

3. A React renderer figures out the differences between the latest rendered component tree and the previous one and updates the user interface accordingly.

In this chapter, you learned:

➤ Why React is called React, and what is meant by the term "reactive programming."

➤ The purposes of the React library and of the ReactDOM library.

➤ What composition is.

➤ About declarative programming and how it's different from imperative programming.

➤ Why you should learn React.

➤ How React compares to Angular and Vue.js.

➤ The role of React in a web application and what roles React does not fill within the web application ecosystem.

In the next chapter, you'll learn about one of the most fundamental tools used to write React components: JSX.

3

JSX

Newcomers to React often remark on how it appears that React breaks one of the cardinal rules of web development, which is to not mix your programming logic with your HTML. This chapter explains where this misperception about React comes from and introduces JSX, which gives us an easy, HTML-like syntax for composing React components. In this chapter, you'll learn:

➤ How to write JSX.

➤ How modules work in JavaScript.

➤ What a transpiler does.

➤ How to include literal JavaScript in JSX code.

➤ How to do conditional rendering in React.

➤ How to render children in JSX.

JSX IS NOT HTML

Take a look first at Listing 3-1. If you know some HTML, you can probably guess what the result of this function will be—a form containing two input fields and a button will be returned.

LISTING 3-1: A React component

```
import React from "react";

function Login(){

    const handleSubmit = (e)=>{
        e.preventDefault();
        console.log(`logging in ${e.target[0].value}`);
```

continues

LISTING 3-1 *(continued)*

```
        // do something else here
    }

    return (
        <form id="login-form" onSubmit={handleSubmit}>
            <input  type="email"
                id="email"
                placeholder="E-Mail Address"/>
            <input type="password"
                id="password"/>
            <button>Login</button>
        </form>
    );
}

export default Login;
```

But, if you know some JavaScript, you might think the result of running this JavaScript function should be an error—HTML is not valid JavaScript, and so the value of the `return` statement will cause this function to fail.

However, this is a perfectly well-formed React component and that markup inside of the `return` statement actually isn't HTML. Instead, it's written in JSX, which is an extension of JavaScript that's used as a visual aid to help you describe what a component should look like.

JAVASCRIPT LESSON: MAKING SENSE OF MODULES WITH AMD, CJS, AND ESM

Modularization is a fundamental concept in software development in which a program is organized into reusable units of code. Modularization makes software easier to build, debug, test, and manage and it also enables team development of software. Just as functions create units of functionality that can be reused in a JavaScript file, modules create JavaScript files that can be reused within a program.

A computer program made up of modules might look something like this:

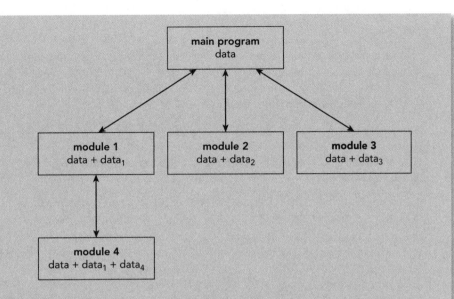

THE HISTORY OF JAVASCRIPT MODULES

JavaScript started its life as a scripting language for web browsers. In its early days, scripts written in JavaScript were small. Because it was seen as less than a "real" programming language, no thought was given to including a way to create modules in JavaScript. Instead, programmers would just write their JavaScript in a single file and import it into HTML files using the script element, or write all of their JavaScript directly into the script element.

As JavaScript became a more powerful language, and as the number of things that people were doing with JavaScript began to grow, so too did the complexity and size of JavaScript files.

The Rise of the JavaScript Module

Because JavaScript couldn't do modules natively, when the need for and benefits of breaking up large JavaScript programs into smaller pieces became apparent, Java-Script developers did what they always do and created new libraries that could be used to add modularization into JavaScript.

RequireJS

The library that became the most popular way to modularize JavaScript in the web browser was RequireJS. The method used by RequireJS to load modules is called Asynchronous Module Definition (AMD).

As the name implies, AMD modules are loaded asynchronously, meaning that all of the imports in a module run prior to any of the code in those modules being executed.

continues

(continued)

With RequireJS, you can create modules by using the `define` function, and then those modules can be included into other JavaScript code using the `require()` function. All you have to do to use RequireJS is to include the RequireJS script into your HTML file using a `script` tag, like this:

```
<script data-main="scripts/main" src="scripts/require.js">
</script>
```

The preceding script tag specifies that the single entry point into the app is `scripts/main.js`.

Once you've included the script tag in your HTML file, you can create individual modules in other files by using RequireJS's `define` function, like this:

```
// messages.js
define(function () {
    return {
        getHello: function () {
            return 'Hello World';
        }
    };
});
```

Modules you define can then be loaded into `main.js` using the `requirejs` function, where individual functions from the module can be assigned to variables and used, like this:

```
requirejs(["messages"], function(messages) {
 // module usage here
});
```

This function is called when `scripts/messages.js` is loaded. If `messages.js` calls `define`, then this function is not fired until `messages`'s dependencies have loaded, and the `messages` argument will hold the module value.

CommonJS

While RequireJS created a way to have modules in the web browser, web browsers aren't the only place where JavaScript code runs. Prior to 2009, there was no agreed-upon standard way to modularize JavaScript code running outside the browser.

This changed when *CommonJS* (also known as CJS) was created. CommonJS was built into Node.js and quickly became the most widely used modularization library for server-side JavaScript.

With CommonJS, you can export variables, functions, or objects from a file by using the `exports` function, like this:

```
// mathhelpers.js
exports.getSum = function(num1,num2) { return num1 + num2; }
```

Once you've defined a module, you can import it into any other JavaScript files by using the `require` function:

```
const mathHelpersModule = require('mathHelpers.js');
var theSum = mathHelpersModule.getSum(1,1);
```

Unlike RequireJS, CommonJS loads and parses modules synchronously, parsing and executing each module as it's loaded.

The following image illustrates the difference between how CommonJS and AMD systems like RequireJS load modules.

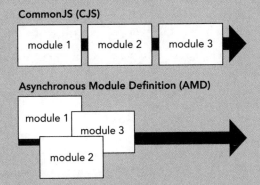

ES Modules

Having more than one way to create and use modules made modules less reusable, however, and the ultimate dream of JavaScript programmers was always that JavaScript would someday have a built-in way to modularize code. This dream became a reality with the standardization of ECMAScript Modules (ESM).

ESM features asynchronous module loading, like RequireJS, but has a simple syntax, like CommonJS. The statements that you use to create and use ES Modules are `import` and `export`.

USING IMPORT AND EXPORT

React components are JavaScript modules, and so you'll see `import` and `export` statements everywhere in React. The most basic thing to know about `import` and `export` is that the `export` statement creates modules, and the `import` statement imports modules into other JavaScript code. Since `import` and `export` are built into JavaScript now, there's no need to include a separate library to make use of them.

continues

(continued)

export Creates Modules

Let's say that you have a function that calculates shipping charges for your ecommerce store. The basic skeleton of this function might look something like this:

```
function calculateShippingCharge(weight,shippingMethod){
  // do something here
  return shippingCharge;
}
```

Turning this function into a module would make it more reusable, since you'd then be able to simply include it into any file that needs to calculate shipping charges, and you could even make use of it in different programs as well.

The basic syntax for using export is to put the export keyword before the definition of the function, like this:

```
export function calculateShippingCharge(weight,shippingMethod){
  // do something here
  return shippingcharge;
}
```

Now, you can put this module into a file with other modules (maybe the file would be named ecommerce-utilities.js) and you can import individual functions, or every function, from this file into any other file in your program.

import Imports Modules

To import a function, variable, or object from a JavaScript module, you use the import statement. To use import, name at least one module, followed by the from keyword, followed by the path to the file that contains the module or modules you want to import.

You can import individual items from a file by surrounding them with curly braces, like this:

```
import { shippingMethods, calculateShippingCharges } from
'./modules/ecommerce-utilities.js';
```

Using Default Exports

Another way to use export is to create a *default export*. A default export can be used to specify a default function provided by a module:

```
function calculateShippingCharge(weight,shippingMethod){
  // do something here
}
export default calculateShippingCharge;
```

You can only have one default export per file. When you have a default export, you can import the module specified with the default export by using the import statement without the curly braces, like this:

```
import calculateShippingCharge from
'./modules/calculateShippingCharge.js';
```

React components are usually created using default exports, unless you're creating a library of components.

Note: you'll often see the path to a module specified without the .js at the end. For example:

```
import calculateShippingCharge from
'./modules/calculateShippingCharge';
```

When you omit .js at the end of a filename in an import, the import will work exactly the same as if you had specifically written it. Also notice that the path to the module file starts with './'. This is the UNIX way of saying to start with the current directory and to create a relative path from it. ES Modules require that the path to the module is a relative path, so it will always start with ./ (the current directory) or ../ (indicating the parent directory). Oftentimes, you may need to have more than one ../, if the module you want to load is higher up in the file hierarchy.

So, in the previous case, the modules folder is a subdirectory of the directory containing the file that's importing the module.

If you've installed Node.js packages using npm, such as the React library itself, you don't need to use ./ or to specify the path to the Node.js package when you import it. For example, components that use the React library's functions have an import statement that imports React. This usually looks like this:

```
import React from 'react';
```

Although you may also see individual objects from the React library imported separately, like this:

```
import React, {Component} from 'react';
```

Some Important ES2015 Module Rules

There are just a few more important rules for how to use import and export:

➤ Both import and export statements need to be at the top level of your JavaScript file—that is, not inside of a function or any other statement.

➤ Imports must be done before any other statements in a module.

➤ import and export can only be used inside modules (not inside of ordinary JavaScript files).

WHAT IS JSX?

JSX is an XML-based syntax extension to JavaScript. In plain English, it's a way to write JavaScript code using XML. Although it's not specific to React, and it's not even required in order to write React components, JSX is an integral part of how every React developer writes components because it makes writing components so much easier and has no negative impact in terms of performance or functionality.

How JSX Works

React uses JSX elements to represent custom components (which are also known as *user-defined components*). If you create a component named SearchInput, you can make use of that component in other components by using a JSX element named SearchInput, as shown in Listing 3-2.

LISTING 3-2: Using a user-defined React component in JSX

```
import {useState} from 'react';
import SearchInput from './SearchInput';
import SearchResults from './SearchResults';

function SearchBox() {
  const [searchTerm,setSearchTerm] = useState(");

  return (
    <div id="search-box">
      <SearchInput term={searchTerm} onChange={setSearchTerm}/>
      <SearchResults term={searchTerm}/>
    </div>
  )
}

export default SearchBox;
```

In the same way, React has components built into it for each of the elements in HTML5, and you can use any HTML5 element name when you write your React components and the result will be that React will output that HTML5 element. For example, say you want your React component to result in the rendering of the following piece of HTML markup:

```
<label class="inputLabel">Search:
  <input type="text" id="searchInput">
</label>
```

The JSX code for telling your React component to output that HTML would look like this:

```
<label className="inputLabel">Search:
  <input type="text" id="searchInput"/>
</label>
```

If you study both of the preceding snippets closely, you'll find a couple of differences. The difference between them, and the fact that JSX is not HTML, are of vital importance to understanding what JSX is really doing.

It's fully possible to create React components without using JSX by using the `React.createElement` method. Here's what the code to output the previous HTML markup looks like when you write it using `React.createElement`:

```
React.createElement("label", {className: "inputLabel"}, "Search:",
    React.createElement("input", {type: "text", id: "searchInput"}));
```

If you examine this JavaScript code closely, you should be able to figure out basically how it works. The `React.createElement` method accepts an element name, any attributes of the HTML element, the element's content (`"Search:"` in this example) and its child element or elements. In this case, the `label` element has one child, `input`.

That's pretty much all there is to `React.createElement`. If you're interested in learning the exact syntax of `React.createElement`, you can read more about it here:

`https://reactjs.org/docs/react-without-jsx.html`

In reality, however, very few React developers ever have to think about `React.createElement`, because we use a tool called a *transpiler* as part of our development environment.

Transpiler . . . Huh?

Before you can run a React application that uses JSX and modules, it must first be compiled. During the compile (also known as "build") process, all of the modules are joined together and the JSX code is converted into pure JavaScript.

Compilation vs. Transpilation

Compilation of React applications is somewhat different from how programmers of truly "compiled" languages (like C++ or Java) understand compilation. In compiled languages, the code that you write is converted into low-level code that can be understood by the computer's software interpreter. This low-level code is called *bytecode*.

When React applications are compiled, on the other hand, they're converted from one version of JavaScript to another version of JavaScript. Because the React compilation process doesn't actually create bytecode, a more technically correct word for what happens is *transpilation*.

JSX Transform

One of the steps in the transpilation of React code is the JSX Transform. The JSX Transform is a process in which the transpiler takes JSX code (which isn't natively understood by web browsers) and converts it into plain JavaScript (which is natively understood by web browsers).

Introducing Babel

The tool we use for transpilation in JavaScript is called *Babel*. Babel is integrated into Create React App and is an automatic part of compiling a React app built with Create React App.

> **NOTE** *Prior to version 17 of React, the JSX Transform converted JSX into* `React.createElement()` *statements. With React 17, the JSX Transform was rewritten so that it transforms JSX into browser-readable code without using* `React.createElement()`. *The result is that developers no longer need to import React into every component in order to use JSX.*

It can be interesting sometimes to see how Babel converts JSX into JavaScript, and you can do this by either viewing the source code for a running React application or by pasting your JSX code into the web-based version of Babel at `https://babeljs.io/repl`, as shown in Figure 3-1.

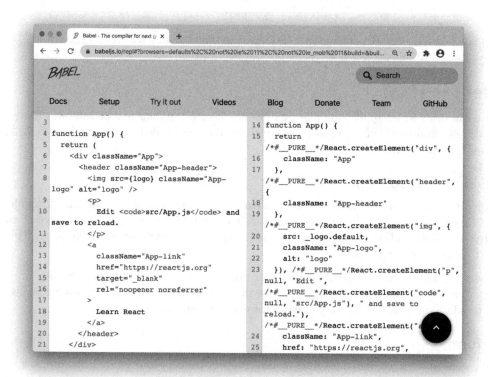

FIGURE 3-1: Trying out Babel on the web

Babel does much more than just convert JSX into JavaScript. It also takes JavaScript in your components that's written using new and experimental syntax that might not be supported by all of your target web browsers and converts it into JavaScript that can be understood and run in any web browser that you expect to access your React user interface.

Eliminating Browser Incompatibilities

Using transpilation does away with the age-old problem of browser incompatibilities and having to wait until every browser supports a new JavaScript language feature before using it. Rather than developers having to write special code and multiple `if/then` branches to accommodate older browsers, Babel makes it possible for developers to just write JavaScript using the latest syntax and then transpile that new JavaScript into a common denominator that will run in any web browser that's likely to access the app.

SYNTAX BASICS OF JSX

As I may have mentioned (and I'll mention again, because it's a really important point), JSX is not HTML. Because it's not HTML, you can't write JSX in the same loosey-goosey way that you may be used to writing HTML.

JSX Is JavaScript XML

The first thing to know about JSX is that it's XML. So, if you know a little bit about XML (or if you've used XHTML), the rules of writing JSX should sound familiar. Namely:

- ➤ All elements must be closed.
- ➤ Elements that cannot have child nodes (so-called "empty" elements) must be closed with a slash. The most commonly used empty elements in HTML are `br`, `img`, `input`, and `link`.
- ➤ Attributes that are strings must have quotes around them.
- ➤ HTML elements in JSX must be written in all lowercase letters.

Beware of Reserved Words

Because JSX compiles to JavaScript, there is the potential that an element name or attribute name that you use in your JSX code can cause errors in your compiled program. To guard against this, certain HTML attribute names that are also reserved words used in JavaScript have to be renamed, as follows:

- ➤ The `class` attribute becomes `className`.
- ➤ The `for` attribute becomes `htmlFor`.

JSX Uses camelCase

Attribute names in HTML that contain more than one word are camel-cased in JSX. For example:

- ➤ The `onclick` attribute becomes `onClick`.
- ➤ The `tabindex` attribute becomes `tabIndex`.

Preface Custom Attributes in DOM Elements with data-

Prior to version 16 of React, if you needed to add an attribute to a DOM element that doesn't exist in the HTML or SVG specification for the element, you had to preface it with `data-`, or else React would ignore it. Listing 3-3 shows a JSX HTML equivalent element with a custom attribute.

LISTING 3-3: Custom attributes in HTML must start with data-

```
<div data-size="XL"
     data-color="black"
     data-description="awesome">
     My Favorite T-Shirt
</div>
```

Starting with React 16, however, you can use any custom attribute name with built-in DOM elements. Custom attributes in DOM elements can be useful for including arbitrary data with your markup that doesn't have any special meaning or affect the presentation of the HTML in the browser. Although it is possible to use custom attributes for DOM elements, this is not generally considered a good practice.

User-defined elements, on the other hand, can have custom attributes with any name, as shown in Listing 3-4.

LISTING 3-4: User-defined elements can have any attributes

```
import MyFancyWidget from './MyFancyWidget';

function MyFancyComponent(props){
  return(
    <MyFancyWidget
      widgetSize="huge"
      numberOfColumns="3"
      title="Welcome to My Widget" />
  )
}
export default MyFancyComponent;
```

Using custom attributes with user-defined elements is the primary way that React passes data between components, as you'll see in Chapter 4.

JSX Boolean Attributes

In HTML and in JSX, certain attributes don't require values, because their presence is interpreted as setting their value to a Boolean `true`. For example, in HTML, the `disabled` attribute of `input` elements causes an input to not be changeable by the user:

```
<input type="text" name="username" disabled>
```

In JSX, the value of an attribute can be omitted when it is explicitly true. So, to set the `disabled` attribute of a JSX `input` element to `true`, you can do either of the following:

```
<input type="text" name="username" disabled = {true}/>
<input type="text" name="username" disabled/>
```

Use Curly Braces to Include Literal JavaScript

When you need to include a variable or a piece of JavaScript in your JSX that shouldn't be interpreted by the transpiler, use curly braces around it. Listing 3-5 shows a component whose `return` statement includes literal JavaScript in JSX attributes.

LISTING 3-5: Using literal JavaScript inside of JSX

```
function SearchInput(props) {

    return (
      <div id="search-box">
        <input   type="text"
                 name="search"
                 value={props.term}
                 onChange={ (e)=>{props.onChange(e.target.value)}}/>
      </div>
    )
}

export default SearchInput;
```

Remember to Use Double Curly Braces with Objects

One common mistake is to forget that if you're including a JavaScript object literal inside of JSX, the JSX code will have double curly braces, as shown in Listing 3-6.

LISTING 3-6: Object literals in JSX result in double curly braces

```
function Header(props){
return (
  <h1 style={{fontSize:"24px",color:"blue"}}>
    Welcome to My Website
  </h1>
  )
}
export default Header;
```

Put Comments in Curly Braces

Because JSX is actually a way of writing JavaScript, HTML comments don't work in JSX. Instead, you can use JavaScript block comment syntax (`/*` and `*/`).

However, because you don't want to transpile your comments, they must be enclosed in curly braces, as shown in Listing 3-7.

LISTING 3-7: Enclose comments in curly braces

```
function Header(props){
return (
  <h1 style={{fontSize:"24px",color:"blue"}}>
    {/* Todo: Make this header dynamic */}

    Welcome to My Website
  </h1>
  )
}
export default Header;
```

When to Use JavaScript in JSX

The concept of separation of concerns in programming says that layout code should be separated from logic. What this means in practice is that code that does calculations, retrieves data, combines data, and controls the flow of an application should be written as functions outside of the `return` statement in a component, rather than inside of curly braces in JSX.

Limited amounts of logic are necessary and perfectly normal inside of the `return` statement, however. There's no hard-and-fast rule for how much is too much, but, generally, any JavaScript that you write in your JSX should only have to do with presentation, and it should be single JavaScript expressions, rather than functions or complex logic.

An example of purely presentational JavaScript would be the case of conditional rendering.

Conditionals in JSX

Oftentimes, a component needs to output different subcomponents, or hide certain components, based on the results of expressions or the values of variables. We call this *conditional rendering*.

There are three ways to write conditional statements in JavaScript, and you may use any of these to do conditional rendering.

Conditional Rendering with if/else and Element Variables

JSX elements can be assigned to variables, and these variables can be substituted for the elements inside a component's `return` statement, as shown in Listing 3-8.

LISTING 3-8: Using element variables

```
import Header from './Header';

function Welcome(){
```

```
    let header = <Header/>;
    return(
      <div>
        {header}
      </div>
    );
}
export default Welcome;
```

By using a conditional statement, you can assign a different element to a variable and thus change what gets rendered, as shown in Listing 3-9.

LISTING 3-9: Conditional rendering with element variables

```
import Header from './Header';
import Login from './Login';

function Welcome({loggedIn}) {
    let header;

    if (loggedIn) {
      header = <Header/>;
    } else {
      header = <Login/>;
    }
    return (
      <div>
        {header}
      </div>
    );
}

export default Welcome;
```

Conditional Rendering with the && Operator

Rather than having your conditional logic outside of the `return` statement, you can write it inline by using the logical AND operator, `&&`. The `&&` operator evaluates the expressions on its left and right. If both expressions evaluate to a Boolean `true`, the `&&` will return the one on the right. If either side of the `&&` operator is false, then a value of `false` will be returned.

By applying this fact, you can conditionally return an expression from the right side of `&&` if the left side of `&&` is `true`.

This can be a little confusing at first. Take a look at Listing 3-10. This code will render the `Header` component if `loggedIn` evaluates to `true`.

LISTING 3-10: Conditional rendering with &&

```
import Header from './Header';

function Welcome({loggedIn}){
    return (
      <div>
        {loggedIn&&<Header />}
        Note: if you don't see the header messsage,
        you're not logged in.
      </div>
    )
  }

export default Welcome;
```

Conditional Rendering with the Conditional Operator

The conditional operator is a way to combine the simplicity and conciseness of inline conditional rendering with the ability to have an `else` case that element variables combined with `if` and `else` gives us.

Listing 3-11 shows an example of using the conditional operator.

LISTING 3-11: Using the conditional operator

```
import Header from './Header';
import Login from './Login';

function Welcome({loggedIn}){
    return(
      <div>
        {loggedIn ? <Header /> : <Login />}
      </div>
    )
  }

export default Welcome;
```

In this example, the expression to the left of the question mark is evaluated. If it's true, the `WelcomeMessage` component is returned. If it's false, the `Login` component is returned.

Expressions in JSX

You can use any JavaScript expression inside of your JSX or inside of React element attribute values by surrounding it with curly braces. JSX elements themselves are JavaScript expressions as well, because they get converted into function calls during compilation.

To understand what JavaScript you can and can't include in JSX, let's take a brief look at what a JavaScript expression is.

An expression is any valid unit of code that resolves to a value. Here are some examples of valid JavaScript expressions:

➤ Arithmetic: `1+1`

➤ String: `"Hello, " + "World!"`

➤ Logical: `this !== that`

➤ Basic keywords and general expressions: This includes certain keywords (such as `this`, `null`, `true`, and `false`) as well as variable references and function calls.

Examples of structures in JavaScript that do not return a value (and are thus not expressions) include `for` loops and `if` statements, as well as function declarations (using the `function` keyword). You can still use these in your React components, of course, but you'll need to use them outside of the `return` statement, as we did in Listing 3-9.

Functions can be included in JSX, provided that they're invoked immediately and that they return a value that can be parsed by JSX, or that they're passed as values for an attribute. The component in Listing 3-12 has a `return` statement that includes a function as an event handler.

LISTING 3-12: Using an arrow function as an event handler

```
import {useState} from 'react';

function CountUp(){
  const [count,setCount] = useState(0);
  return (
    <div>
      <button onClick={()=>setCount(count+1)}>Add One</button>
      {count}
    </div>
  );
}

export default CountUp;
```

Listing 3-13 shows an example of using a function that's immediately invoked and that's valid in JSX.

LISTING 3-13: Immediately invoking a function in JSX

```
function ImmediateInvoke(){
    return(
        <div>
          {(()=><h1>The Header</h1>)()}
        </div>
    );
}
export default ImmediateInvoke;
```

Using Children in JSX

The `return` statement in a React component can only return one thing. This one thing can be a string, a number, an array, a Boolean, or a single JSX element. Keep in mind, however, that a single JSX element can have as many children as you like. As long as you start and end your `return` statement with a matching opening tag and closing tag, everything in between (provided that it's valid JSX or a JavaScript expression) is fine.

Here's an example of an invalid JSX return value:

```
return(
  <MyComponent />
  <MyOtherComponent />
);
```

One way to make this a valid JSX return value is to wrap two elements with another element, like this:

```
return(
  <div>
    <MyComponent />
    <MyOtherComponent />
  </div>
);
```

With the `div` element wrapping the two user-defined elements, we now have a single element being returned.

React Fragments

Although it's quite common to see multiple elements wrapped with a `div` element or another element for the purpose of returning a single JSX element, adding `div` elements just for the sake of eliminating errors in your code, rather than to add necessary meaning or structure to your code, creates code bloat and decreases the accessibility of your code.

To prevent the introduction of unnecessary elements, you can use the built-in `React.Fragment` component. `React.Fragment` wraps your JSX into a single JSX element, but doesn't return any HTML.

You can use the `React.Fragment` component in one of three ways:

1. By using dot notation: `<React.Fragment></React.Fragment>`
2. By importing `Fragment` from the react library using curly braces
3. By using its short syntax, which is just a nameless element: `< > < / >`

Listing 3-14 shows how to use `React.Fragment` in a component.

LISTING 3-14: Using React.Fragment

```
import {Fragment} from 'react';

function MyComponent() {
```

```
    return(
      <Fragment>
        <h1>The heading</h1>
        <h2>The subheading</h2>
      </Fragment>
    );
  }

  export default MyComponent;
```

Listing 3-15 shows how to use the short syntax for React.Fragment.

LISTING 3-15: Using React.Fragment's short syntax

```
function MyComponent(){
  return(
    <>
      <h1>The heading</h1>
      <h2>The subheading</h2>
    </>
  );
}

export default MyComponent;
```

> **NOTE** Notice that when you use React.Fragment's short syntax, you don't need to import Fragment from React.

The result of running either Listing 3-14 or Listing 3-15 is that just the h1 and h2 HTML elements will be returned.

SUMMARY

JSX is an important tool that is used in the development of nearly every React component. In this chapter, you learned:

➤ Why we use JSX, the XML language that React uses to make it easier to visualize and write the output of components.

➤ That JSX is not HTML, but that React uses JSX to generate HTML.

➤ The history of JavaScript modules, which make distributed development and reusable components possible, and how to use import and export to create and use modules.

➤ What transpiling is.

➤ How to write JSX code.

➤ What conditional rendering is and how to do it in JSX.

➤ How to use JavaScript expressions inside JSX.

➤ How to use comments in JSX.

➤ How to use `React.Fragment` to group elements together without returning extra HTML elements.

In the next chapter, you'll learn about the React library itself, and about the basic unit of every React user interface: the component.

All About Components

Up until now, we've mostly been talking about the tools that make React development possible, including your development environment, Node.js, ReactDOM, JavaScript modules, and JSX. Now it's time to dig deeply into the heart of what makes React tick: the component. In this chapter, you'll learn:

- ➤ The relationship between components and elements.
- ➤ How to use React's HTML elements.
- ➤ How to pass data between components with props.
- ➤ How to write class components.
- ➤ How to write function components.
- ➤ How to bind functions in JavaScript.
- ➤ How to manage React state.

WHAT IS A COMPONENT?

Components are the building blocks of React applications. A React component is a function or a JavaScript class that optionally accepts data and returns a React element that describes some piece of the user interface. A React user interface is made up of a hierarchy of components that build up to a single component (called the *root component*) that is rendered in the web browser.

Figure 4-1 shows an example of a React component tree.

It's possible to create a React application with only a single component, but for all but the smallest apps, breaking your app up into multiple components makes development and management of the code easier.

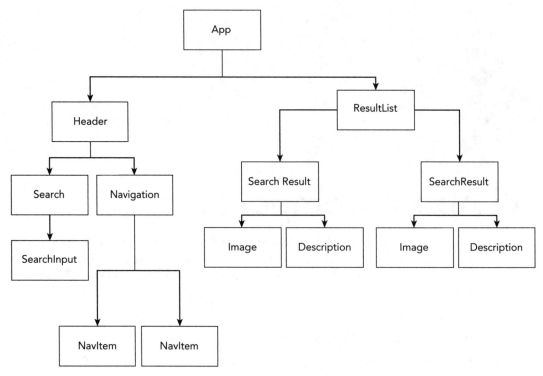

FIGURE 4-1: A tree of react components

COMPONENTS VS. ELEMENTS

Before we talk about components, it's important to understand the relationship between components and elements in React.

Components Define Elements

The job of a component is to return an element.

Each component within an application has a unique name, which is how you use it. The component name becomes the name of the React element when you include a component in another component, as shown in Listing 4-1.

LISTING 4-1: Components define elements

```
function WelcomeMessage(){
  return "Welcome!";
}
export default WelcomeMessage;
```

In this very simple example, `WelcomeMessage` is a React component that was created using a function and exported as a JavaScript module. Once it's exported, `WelcomeMessage` can be imported into any other React component where you need to make use of its functionality, as shown in Listing 4-2.

LISTING 4-2: Components can be imported into other components

```
import WelcomeMessage from './WelcomeMessage';

function WelcomeTitle(){
    return <h1><WelcomeMessage /></h1>;
}

export default WelcomeTitle;
```

It's not a requirement that each component have its own module, but that's the most common way components are defined. In components created using a default export, the file containing the module usually takes the name of the component defined in the file.

Once you import a component into another component, this is where React elements come in.

Elements Invoke Components

Once you've imported a component into another component, the imported component's functionality can be included in your new component's JSX using an element. You can include as many components inside another component as you need to, and there's no limit to how many levels of components a tree of components can have. Once you import a component, you can use the element it defines as many times as you need to and each usage will create a new instance of the component with its own data and memory.

In general, the point of using components is to provide a higher level of abstraction that reduces the complexity of an application and enables reuse. Listing 4-3 shows an example of a top-level React component that uses the functionality of other components to display a shopping cart user interface.

LISTING 4-3: Using components to reduce complexity

```
import React from 'react';
import CartItems from './CartItems';
import DisplayTotal from './DisplayTotal';
import CheckoutButton from './CheckoutButton';
import styles from './Cart.css.js';

function Cart(props){
  return(
    <div style={styles.cart}>
      <h2>Cart</h2>

        <CartItems items = {props.inCart} />
```

continues

LISTING 4-3 *(continued)*

```
        <DisplayTotal items = {props.inCart} />

        <CheckoutButton />

    </div>
  );
}


export default Cart;
```

Notice that the component in Listing 4-3 uses a combination of ordinary JavaScript and imported modules to return a combination of custom elements and HTML elements. It's fairly trivial to figure out the gist of what will be rendered by this component just by looking at the return statement.

The entire component could have been written with everything in a single file, as shown (partially) in Listing 4-4, but the result would be a file that would be much larger, more difficult to work with, and more difficult to maintain.

Don't worry if much of the code in Listing 4-4 looks strange or unfamiliar to you. Remember that React is just JavaScript, and this example uses several relatively new JavaScript tools and functions that I'll explain later in this chapter.

LISTING 4-4: Putting everything in one component

```
import React,{useState} from 'react';
import styles from './Cart.css.js';

function Cart(props){

  const [inCart,setInCart] = useState(props.inCart);

  const removeFromCart = (item)=>{
    const index = inCart.indexOf(item);
    const newCart = [...inCart.slice(0, index), ...inCart.slice(index + 1)];
    setInCart(newCart);
  };

  const calculatedTotal = inCart.reduce((accumulator, item) => accumulator +
(item.price || 0), 0);

  let ItemList = inCart.map((item)=>{
    return (<div key={item.id}>{item.title} – {item.price}
      <button onClick={()=>{removeFromCart(item)}}>remove</button></div>)
  });

  return(
    <div style={styles.cart}>
      <h2>Cart</h2>
```

```
                {ItemList}

                <p>total: ${calculatedTotal}</p>

                <button>Checkout</button>

            </div>
        );
    }

    export default Cart;
```

BUILT-IN COMPONENTS

React has built-in components for the most commonly used HTML elements and their attributes. There are also built-in components for Scalable Vector Graphics (SVG) elements and attributes. These built-in components produce output in the DOM and are the base for your custom components.

HTML Element Components

React's built-in HTML element components have the same names as elements from HTML5. Using them in your React app causes the equivalent HTML element to be rendered.

Many React developers (and web application developers in general) tend to use the div element for every type of container in their user interfaces. While this is convenient, it's not always recommended. HTML is a rich and descriptive language when used correctly, and using meaningful (aka semantic) HTML elements to mark up your content makes it more accessible for search engines and people as well.

Table 4-1 shows all the HTML elements that React supports, along with a brief explanation of each element. If an element that you want to use in your user interface isn't on this list, try using it to see if it's been added since this list was compiled. If it isn't, you can submit a request to Facebook that the element be added to React by filing an issue in the React github.com repository at https://github.com/facebook/react/issues/new.

TABLE 4-1: HTML Elements Supported by React

HTML ELEMENT	DESCRIPTION
a	Creates a hyperlink.
abbr	Represents an abbreviation or acronym.
address	Indicates that the containing HTML includes contact information.
area	Defines a clickable area in an imagemap.
article	Represents a self-contained composition (such as a story or an article) in a page.
aside	Represents content that is indirectly related to the main content.

continues

TABLE 4-1 (*continued*)

HTML ELEMENT	DESCRIPTION
audio	Embeds sound content.
b	Used to draw the reader's attention to the contents. Previously, this was the "bold" element, but it's now called the "Bring to Attention" element to separate its purpose from how it's styled.
base	Specifies the base URL for all relative URLs in the document.
bdi	Bidirectional Isolate. Isolates text that may flow in a different direction from text around it.
bdo	Bidirectional Text Override. Changes the direction of text.
big	Renders text at a font size one level larger (obsolete).
blockquote	Indicates an extended quotation.
body	Represents the content of an HTML document.
br	Produces a line break.
button	Represents a clickable button.
canvas	Creates an area for drawing with the canvas API or WebGL.
caption	Specifies a caption for a table.
cite	Describes a reference to a cited work.
code	Indicates that its content should be styled as computer code.
col	Defines a column within a table.
colgroup	Defines a group of columns in a table.
data	Links content to a machine-readable translation.
datalist	Contains `option` elements indicating the permissible options available for a form control.
dd	Provides the definition for a preceding term (specified using `dt`).
del	Represents text that has been deleted from a document.
details	Creates a widget in which information is visible when the widget is toggled to its "open" state.
dfn	Indicates the term being defined within a sentence.
dialog	Represents a dialog box, subwindow, alert box, or other such interactive element.
div	A generic container with no effect on content or layout.

HTML ELEMENT	DESCRIPTION
dl	Represents a description list.
dt	Specifies a term in a definition list. Used inside `dl`.
em	Marks text that has emphasis.
embed	Embeds external content in the document.
fieldset	Groups controls and labels within a form.
figcaption	Describes the contents of a parent `figure` element.
figure	Represents self-contained content, optionally with a caption.
footer	Represents a footer for its nearest sectioning content.
form	Represents a document section containing interactive controls.
h1	First-level section heading.
h2	Second-level section heading.
h3	Third-level section heading.
h4	Fourth-level section heading.
h5	Fifth-level section heading.
h6	Sixth-level section heading.
head	Contains machine-readable information about the document.
header	Represents introductory content.
hr	Represents a thematic break between sections.
html	Represents the root of an HTML document.
i	Represents idiomatic text that is set off from the normal text.
iframe	Represents a nested browser context.
img	Embeds an image into the document.
input	Creates interactive controls for web-based forms.
ins	Represents a range of text that has been added to the document.
kbd	Represents a span of text denoting textual user input.
keygen	Facilitates generation of key material and submission of the public key in an HTML form.
label	Represents a caption for an item in a user interface.
legend	Represents a caption for an element in a `fieldset`.

continues

TABLE 4-1 (*continued*)

HTML ELEMENT	DESCRIPTION
li	Represents an item in a list.
link	Specifies a relationship between the document and an external resource. Commonly used to link stylesheets.
main	Represents the dominant content of the body of a document.
map	Used with area elements to define an imagemap.
mark	Represents marked, or highlighted, text.
menu	Represents a group of commands.
menuitem	Represents a command in a menu.
meta	Represents metadata that can't be represented with other metadata elements (such as title, link, script, or style).
meter	Represents a fractional value or a scalar value within a known range.
nav	Represents a section containing navigation links.
noscript	Represents a section to be inserted if a script type is unsupported or if scripting is disabled in the browser.
object	Represents an external resource.
ol	Represents an ordered list.
optgroup	Creates a grouping of options within a select element.
option	Defines an item in a select or optgroup.
output	Creates a container for the results of a calculation or for user input.
p	Represents a paragraph.
param	Defines parameters for an object.
picture	Contains source elements and an img element to provide alternative versions of an image.
pre	Represents preformatted text which should be presented exactly as written.
progress	Displays an indicator showing progress towards the completion of a task, such as a progress bar.
q	Indicates that its content is a quotation.
rp	Used to provide fallback content for browsers that don't support ruby annotations using the ruby element.
rt	Specifies the ruby text component of a ruby annotation.
ruby	Represents annotations for showing the pronunciation of East Asian characters.

HTML ELEMENT	DESCRIPTION
s	Represents a strikethrough.
samp	Encloses text that represents sample output from a computer program.
script	Embeds executable code or data.
section	Represents a standalone section in a document.
select	Represents a control that shows a menu of options.
small	Represents small print, such as copyright or legal text.
source	Specifies multiple media resources for `picture` and `audio` elements.
span	A generic inline container.
strong	Indicates that its contents have strong importance.
style	Contains style information for a document.
sub	Specifies inline text that should be displayed as subscript.
summary	Specifies a summary, legend, or caption for `details` content.
sup	Specifies inline text that should be displayed as superscript.
table	Represents tabular data.
tbody	Encapsulates table rows in a `table`.
td	Defines a cell in a `table`.
textarea	Represents a multi-line text editing control.
tfoot	Defines a set of rows summarizing the columns in a table.
th	Defines a cell as a header of a group of table cells.
thead	Defines a set of rows defining the head of the columns in a table.
time	Represents a period of time.
title	Defines the title that is shown in the browser's title bar and browser tab.
tr	Defines a row of cells in a table.
track	Contains timed text tracks (such as subtitles) for audio and video content.
u	Originally the underline element, specifies that text should be rendered in a way that indicates that it has non-textual annotation (whatever that means).
ul	Represents an unordered list (usually rendered as a bulleted list).
var	Represents the name of a variable in mathematic or programming context.
video	Embeds a media player that supports video playback.
wbr	Represents a word break opportunity, where the browser may optionally break a line.

Attributes vs. Props

In markup languages (such as XML and HTML), attributes define properties or characteristics of the element, and are specified using the `name=value` format.

Because JSX is an XML markup language, JSX elements can have attributes, and there's no limit to the number of attributes that a single JSX element can have.

Passing Props

Attributes that you write in JSX elements are passed to the component represented by the element as properties, or *props* for short. You can access props inside the component using the component's `props` object.

To illustrate how props are used for passing data between components, I'll use the example of a component called `Farms`, which includes multiple instances of the `Farm` component, as shown in Listing 4-5. Props that you pass into the `Farm` component are what make it possible for the generic `Farm` component to represent any farm.

Note that a string can be passed into a component by surrounding it with quotes, and that any other type of data can be passed to a component by using curly braces to indicate that the value should be treated as JavaScript.

LISTING 4-5: Passing props

```
import Farm from './Farm';

export default function Farms(){
  return(
    <>
      <Farm
        farmer="Old McDonald"
        animals={['pigs','cows','chickens']} />
      <Farm
        farmer="Mr. Jones"
        animals={['pigs','horses','donkey','goat']} />
    </>
  )
}
```

Accessing Props

Once values have been passed as props, you can access that data inside the component. Listing 4-6 shows the `Farm` component and how it makes use of the data passed into it.

LISTING 4-6: Using props inside a component

```
export default function Farm(props){

  return (
```

```
    <div>
      <p>{props.farmer} had a farm.</p>
      <p>On his farm, he had some {props.animals[0]}.</p>
      <p>On his farm, he had some {props.animals[1]}.</p>
      <p>On his farm, he had some {props.animals[2]}.</p>
    </div>
    )

  }
```

As in all JavaScript functions, if data is passed into a function component, you can give that data a name inside the function arguments. This name, technically, could be anything. However, since React's class-based components accept passed data using `this.props`, it's standard practice and smart to use the name `props` in function components as well.

Notice that when you use props inside the `return` statement, you have to enclose them in curly braces. You can use props elsewhere inside a component as well, as shown in the slightly improved version of the `Farm` component shown in Listing 4-7.

LISTING 4-7: An improved version of the Farm component

```
export default function Farm(props){
    let onHisFarm = [];
    if(props.animals){
        onHisFarm = props.animals.map((animal,index)=>
            <p key={index}>On his farm he had some {animal}.</p>);
    }
    return (
      <>
      <p>{props.farmer} had a farm.</p>
      {onHisFarm}
      </>
      )
    }
```

JAVASCRIPT LESSON: USING ARRAY.MAP()

JavaScript's `Array.map` function creates a new array using the result of applying a function to every element in an existing array. The `map` function is commonly used in React to build lists of React elements or strings from arrays.

The syntax of `Array.map` is as follows:

```
array.map(function(currentValue, index, arr),thisValue)
```

Take a closer look at the details:

➤   The `array` is any JavaScript array. The function passed into the `map` function will run once for every element in the array.

continues

(continued)

➤ The `currentValue` is the value passed into the function and will change with every iteration through the array.

➤ The `index` parameter is a number representing the current value's position in the array.

➤ The `arr` parameter is the array object that the `currentValue` belongs to.

➤ The `thisValue` parameter is a value to be used as the "this" value inside the function.

The only required parameter is `currentValue`. It is also what you will most commonly see in real-world React applications. Here's how you can use `Array.map()` to make a series of list items from an array:

```
const bulletedList = listItems.map(function(currentItem){
    return <li>{currentItem}</li>
}
```

For performance reasons, React requires each item in a list of JSX elements (such as one built from an array) to have a unique `key` attribute. One way to give each element a unique `key` is to use the `index` parameter, like this:

```
const bulletedList = listItems.map(function(currentItem,index){
    return <li key={index}>{currentItem}</li>
}
```

Standard HTML Attributes

As you saw in Chapter 3, React's HTML components support most of the standard HTML attributes, but with a couple of important differences, which I'll reiterate and expand upon here.

Attributes Use camelCase

Whereas HTML5 attributes use all lowercase letters, and a few of them use dashes between multiple words (such as the `accept-charset` attribute), all attributes in React's HTML components use capital letters for words in the attribute after the first one. This type of capitalization is commonly called *camelCase*.

For example, the HTML `tabindex` attribute is represented by `tabIndex` in React and `onclick` is represented by `onClick`.

Two Attributes Are Renamed

In a couple of cases, React attributes for built-in elements have different names than HTML attributes. The reason for this is to avoid potential clashes with reserved words in JavaScript. The attributes that are different in React are:

➤ `class` in HTML is `className` in React.

➤ `for` in HTML is `htmlFor` in React.

React Adds Several Attributes

Several attributes that are available for React's built-in HTML components don't exist in HTML. Chances are good that you'll never need to use any of these special attributes, but I'm including them here for completeness. These are:

➤ `dangerouslySetInnerHTML`, which allows you to set the `innerHTML` property of an element directly from React. As you can tell by the name of the attribute, this is not a recommended practice.

➤ `suppressContentEditableWarning`, which suppresses a warning that React will give you if you use the `contentEditable` attribute on an element that has children.

➤ `suppressHydrationWarning`. No, it's not a way to tell React to stop nagging you to drink more water. This attribute will suppress a warning that React gives you when content generated by server-side React and client-side React produce different content.

Some React Attributes Behave Differently

Several attributes behave differently in React than they do in standard HTML:

➤ `checked` and `defaultChecked`. The `checked` attribute is used to dynamically set and unset the checked status of a radio button or checkbox. The `defaultChecked` attribute sets whether a radio button or checkbox is checked when the component is first mounted in the browser.

➤ `selected`. In HTML, when you want to make an option in a dropdown be the currently selected option, you use the `selected` attribute. In React, you set the `value` attribute of the containing `select` element instead.

➤ `style`. React's `style` attribute accepts a JavaScript object containing style properties and values, rather than CSS, which is how the `style` attribute in HTML works.

React Supports Many HTML Attributes

The following list contains the standard HTML attributes supported by React's built-in HTML components:

```
accept acceptCharset accessKey action allowFullScreen allowTransparency alt async
autoComplete autoFocus autoPlay capture cellPadding cellSpacing charset challenge
checked classID className cols colSpan content contentEditable contextMenu
controls coords crossOrigin data dateTime defer dir disabled download draggable
encType form formAction formEncType formMethod formNoValidate formTarget frame-
border headers height hidden high href hrefLang htmlFor httpEquiv icon id
inputMode keyParams keyType label lang list loop low manifest marginHeight
marginWidth max maxLength media mediaGroup method min minLength multiple muted
name noValidate open optimum pattern placeholder poster preload radioGroup rea-
dOnly rel required role rows rowSpan sandbox scope scoped scrolling seamless
selected shape size sizes span spellCheck src srcDoc srcSet start step style
summary tabIndex target title type useMap value width wmode wrap
```

Non-Standard Attributes

In addition to the standard HTML attributes, React also supports several non-standard attributes that have specific purposes in some browsers and meta-data languages, including:

➤   `autoCapitalize` and `autoCorrect`, which are supported by Mobile Safari.

➤   `property` is used for Open Graph meta tags.

➤   `itemProp`, `itemScope`, `itemType`, `itemRef`, and `itemID` for HTML5 microdata.

➤   `unselectable` for Internet Explorer.

➤   `results` and `autoSave` are attributes supported by browsers built using the WebKit or Blink browser engines (including Chrome, Safari, Opera, and Edge).

Custom Attributes

As of version 16, React will pass any custom attributes that you use with HTML components through to the generated HTML, provided that the custom attributes are written using only lower-case letters.

USER-DEFINED COMPONENTS

Have you ever thought that it would be awesome if you weren't just limited to the standard set of HTML elements? What if you could, for example, make an element called `PrintPageButton` that you could use anywhere that you need to display a functional print button in your app? Or what if you had an element called `Tax` that would calculate and display the taxes in your online store's shopping cart?

Essentially, this is what React components enable through custom components. Custom components, also known as user-defined components, are the components that you make by putting together built-in components and other custom components.

The possibilities for custom components are infinite. Even better, if you design your components to be reusable, you can reuse components not only inside of a single React application, but across any number of React applications. There are even hundreds of open source libraries of custom components created by other developers that you can repurpose inside your own apps.

Writing useful and reusable React components can sometimes require considerable work up front, but the benefits of writing them the right way are that you can reduce work for yourself overall and make apps that are sturdier and more dependable.

In the rest of this chapter, you'll learn about writing custom components and putting them together to build robust user interfaces.

TYPES OF COMPONENTS

React components can be written in two different ways: by using JavaScript classes or by using JavaScript functions.

In most cases, making a component with a function is much simpler and requires less code and less detailed knowledge of the inner workings of JavaScript than the class method. However, both methods are widely used, and it's important to have a good understanding of how to write components using classes as well as using functions.

> **NOTE** *Having a knowledge of JavaScript classes and class components is necessary in order for you to get a complete picture of how React works, but it is possible to write complete React applications without using classes. An explanation of classes can get pretty dense and theoretical, but don't let it bog you down. If this chapter's "Class Components" section confuses you, feel free to skip ahead or skim it for now and go straight to the "Function Components" section, which is what we'll be working with for most of the rest of the book. You can come back and learn all about class components and JavaScript classes when you need to.*

Class Components

Classes were new to JavaScript when React was first released. The early versions of the React library had a function called `React.createClass`, which was the only way to create components. To use `React.createClass`, you could pass an object containing the component's properties as a parameter to the function and the result would be a React component.

In one of the bigger changes made to React in its lifetime so far, `React.createClass` was deprecated as of React 15.5.

You can still use `createClass` if you need to by installing the `create-react-class` package. Listing 4-8 shows the code for a component created using `createClass`.

LISTING 4-8: Creating a component with React.createClass

```
import React from 'react';
import createClass from 'create-react-class';

const UserProfile = createClass({
  render() {
    return (
      <h1>User Profile</h1>
    );
  }
});

export default UserProfile;
```

Beginning with React 15.5, the preferred way of writing classes was by extending the `React.Component` base class directly.

Listing 4-9 shows how to write the component from Listing 4-8 using a class that extends `React.Component`.

LISTING 4-9: Creating a component using a class

```
import React from 'react';

class UserProfile extends React.Component {

  constructor(props) {
    super(props);
  }

  render() {
    return (
      <h1>User Profile</h1>
    );
  }
};

export default UserProfile;
```

JAVASCRIPT LESSON: CLASSES

Classes in JavaScript resemble classes in traditional object-oriented languages, such as Java or C, but with some fundamental differences.

Traditional classes are blueprints for creating objects. In JavaScript, classes are objects themselves that serve as a template for objects. In other words, JavaScript has *prototypes*, not true classes.

You may see the term "syntactic sugar" used to describe classes and some other new features of JavaScript that were introduced in ES2015 and more recent versions of JavaScript. Syntactic sugar refers to a simplified or abstracted way of writing something that makes it easier to write or to understand, but doesn't actually do anything that you couldn't previously do. It helps the medicine go down, you might say.

The introduction of the class syntax in JavaScript didn't create any new functionality. Classes merely expose existing functionality in JavaScript using a different syntax that's more familiar to developers who have worked with class-based languages (such as Java or C).

More specifically, the class syntax in JavaScript is just a new way to use *function constructors* and *prototypal inheritance*. So, to understand classes, you first need to understand the basics of function constructors and prototypal inheritance.

Prototypal Inheritance

JavaScript objects are collections of properties. JavaScript has several ways to create objects:

➤ By using Object Literal notation.

➤ By using the `Object.create` method.

➤ By using the `new` operator.

Using the new Operator

One way to use the `new` operator is to write a constructor function and then invoke the function with the `new` keyword.

To see how it works, open your browser's JavaScript console (by pressing Cmd+Shift+j (on Windows) or Cmd+Option-j (on Mac) and enter the following code:

```
let a = function () {
  this.x = 10;
  this.y = 8;
};
let b = new a();
```

The result of creating the b object will be an object with two properties, x and y. Type the following two statements to confirm this:

```
b.x; // 10
b.y // 8
```

These properties are called the object's "own" properties, and a is the prototype for b.

Modifying and Using the Prototype

You can add new properties to an object's prototype, like this:

```
a.prototype.z = 100;
```

In the preceding statement, we added a new property, z, to the prototype of b. In prototypal inheritance, every object inherits properties and methods from its prototype object.

Here's where things get interesting. When you try to access the property z on the b object, JavaScript will look first for an "own" property of b named z. If it doesn't find one, it will look at the object's prototype. If it doesn't find it there, it will look at the prototype's prototype. This will happen all the way up to the built-in `Object` object, which is the prototype for every JavaScript object.

Try it out!

```
b.z; // 100
```

continues

(continued)

Methods Are Properties Too

A property of an object can have a function as its value. A property with a function value is what we refer to as a "method" in JavaScript.

You can use the `this` keyword in methods, and it refers to the inheriting object, not the prototype.

For example, add a method called `sum()` to the prototype object:

```
a.prototype.sum = function() { return this.x + this.y };
```

Now, change the values of x and y on the b object:

```
b.x = 1000
b.y = 2000
```

And then invoke the `sum` function on the b object:

```
b.sum() // 3000
```

Even though b doesn't have its own function called `sum`, JavaScript runs the `sum` function on the prototype but uses the `this` values from b.

Summary

To sum it all up, every object that you create in JavaScript is a copy of another object, which is called its prototype. Objects inherit properties and values from their prototype and have a link back to their prototype. If a property is referenced on an object and that object doesn't contain that property, JavaScript will look at the object's prototype and so on up the chain of prototypes until it gets to the built-in `Object`.

Now that we've covered prototypal inheritance, let's get back to talking about classes and the most commonly used features of classes used in React.js.

Understanding JavaScript Classes

To define a class, you can use either a class declaration or a class expression.

Class Declarations

A class declaration starts with the `class` keyword followed by the name of the class. The following is an example of a class declaration:

```
class Pizza {
  constructor(toppings,size) {
    this.toppings = toppings;
    this.size = size;
  }
}
```

Class declarations are similar in structure to function declarations. Here's an example of a function declaration:

```
function Pizza(toppings,size) {
  this.toppings = toppings;
  this.size = size;
}
```

An important difference between class declarations and function declarations, however, is that function declarations are *hoisted*. Function hoisting means that you can reference a function created using a function declaration anywhere in a script, even before the function declaration actually appears in the file. For example, the following code will function just fine even though we invoke the `Pizza()` function before it appears in the order of the code:

```
let MyPizza = new Pizza(['sausage','cheese'],'large');
function Pizza(toppings,size) {
  this.toppings = toppings;
  this.size = size;
}
```

However, the class version of this code will produce an error, because the class named `Pizza` doesn't exist when this code tries to use it:

```
let MyPizza = new Pizza(['sausage','cheese'],'large');
class Pizza {
  constructor(toppings,size) {
    this.toppings = toppings;
    this.size = size;
  }
}
```

Class Expression

To create a class using a class expression, you use either a named or unnamed class and assign it to a variable. Here's an example of a class expression that uses an unnamed class:

```
let Pizza = class {
  constructor(toppings, size) {
    this.toppings = toppings;
    this.size = size;
  }
};
```

Here's an example of a class expression that uses a named class:

```
let Pizza = class MyPizza {
  constructor(toppings,size) {
```

continues

(continued)

```
        this.toppings = toppings;
        this.size = size;
    }
};
```

Note that when you use a class expression with a named class, the name you specify after the `class` keyword becomes the value of the `name` property of the class:

```
console.log(Pizza.name); // Output: "MyPizza"
```

Using a named class expression is not a way of extending an existing class. It's just a convenient way to give a class instance a `name` property.

Class Body and the Constructor Method

The body of a class, like the body of a function, is the part between the curly braces. Inside the class body, you can define class members, such as its methods, fields, and constructor.

The `constructor` method of a class can be used to initialize objects created using the class. It isn't required that you include a constructor in classes you create. If you don't include it, your class will have a default constructor, which is just an empty function.

When you instantiate a class, you can optionally pass in arguments and these arguments become the arguments to the constructor method. Inside the constructor, you can create a property in the new instance by assigning these values to `this`, which represents the new object.

For example, the following `Pizza` class's constructor takes three parameters:

```
class Pizza {
    constructor(sauce,cheese,toppings){
        this.sauce = sauce;
        this.cheese = cheese;
        this.toppings = toppings;
    }
}
```

To create an instance of `Pizza`, you use the `new` keyword and pass in arguments, like this:

```
let myPizza = new Pizza('tomato','mozzarella',['basil','tomato',
'garlic']);
```

Inside the `myPizza` object, `sauce` is equal to `tomato`, `cheese` is equal to `mozzarella`, and `toppings` is equal to the array of toppings that was passed in.

When you assign each value to a new property of `this`, you create an instance property that can be accessed inside of the instance using `this.[property]` and outside the instance by using the instance name followed by a period and the property name.

Inside myPizza:

```
this.cheese;
```

Outside myPizza:

```
myPizza.cheese;
```

Creating Subclasses with extends

You can use the extends keyword in a class declaration or a class expression to create a child of any existing class. If the new class doesn't have a constructor, the properties it inherits from the parent will be automatically accessible in the new instance. For example, here's a class that we'll use as the parent for our new child class:

```
class Animal {
  constructor(numberOfLegs,weight){
    this.numberOfLegs = numberOfLegs;
    this.weight = weight;
  }
}
```

You can use extends to create a subclass, like this:

```
class Insect extends Animal {
}
```

Once you extend a class, you can define methods in the new subclass that reference inherited properties:

```
class Insect extends Animal {
  countLegs() {
    console.log(`This insect has ${this.numberOfLegs} legs.`);
  }
}
```

If you do include a constructor method in the subclass, you must specifically call the super method from within the constructor before you can use the this keyword, as in this example:

```
class Insect extends Animal {
  constructor(numberOfLegs,weight,name) {
    super(numberOfLegs,weight);
    this.name = name;
  }
  countLegs() {
    console.log(`The ${this.name} has ${this.numberOfLegs}
legs.`);
  }
}
```

In the preceding example, the constructor of Insect calls the constructor of Animal and passes in the arguments that were used to instantiate the Insect class, making the properties defined in Animal's constructor available in Insect even though they're not specifically defined inside of Insect's constructor.

continues

(continued)

For example, let's take the `numberOfLegs` out of the `Animal` class and make it specific to the `Insect` subclass. We'll leave `weight` as a property of `Animal`, since all animals have a weight:

```
class Animal {
  constructor(weight){
    this.weight = weight;
  }
}

class Insect extends Animal {
  constructor(numberOfLegs,weight) {
    super(weight);
    this.numberOfLegs = numberOfLegs;
  }
}
```

With these two classes defined, we can now create an instance of the `Insect` class `Fly`:

```
let Fly = new Insect(6,.045);
```

Now, the `Fly` instance can reference its own `weight` and `numberOfLegs` properties internally using the `this` keyword, and these properties can be referenced externally using the name of the instance:

```
console.log(Fly.weight); // .045
```

Understanding this

One of the really interesting (some would say confusing) things about JavaScript is that it sometimes looks like an object-oriented programming language, but it's actually a functional programming language.

In functional programming, programs are created by applying and composing functions, and functions are "first-class citizens." What this means is that JavaScript functions are treated like any other variable. They can be passed as values into other functions, they can return other functions, and they can be assigned as a value to a variable.

Because functions are so versatile, you can define functions as part of a class, or you can pass functions as arguments into a class to be used by that class.

The `this` keyword plays a vital role in the ability of functions to be used inside of and shared between objects.

Having a good understanding of what the `this` keyword does and how to use it to bind functions to objects is important to being able to write React code with classes.

this Doesn't Have a Value until Invocation

Function (or method) invocation in JavaScript happens when an expression that evaluates to a function is followed by open and close parentheses, optionally with a comma-separated list of arguments between them. For example, here's a function, followed by an invocation of the function:

```
// function definition
function sum(a,b){
  return a+b;
}
// function invocation
let mySum = sum(2,5);
console.log(mySum); // 7
```

What Is this in a Function?

By default, when you use the this keyword inside a function and then invoke that function, this gets set to the global object, which in a web browser is the window object:

```
function sum(a,b){
  this.secretNumber = 100;
  return a+b;
}

let mySum = sum(2,5);
console.log(window.secretNumber); // 100
```

What Is this in "strict" Mode?

If your JavaScript code is running in strict mode, however, this will be set to undefined instead of the global object:

```
function getSecretNumber(){
'use strict';
  this.secretNumber = 100;
  return this.secretNumber;
}

console.log(getSecretNumber()); // error: cannot set property
'secretNumber' of undefined.
```

The reason for the different behavior of this in strict mode is that use of global variables should be discouraged because when every function has access to a variable, it makes it difficult to know which functions make use of or modify the variable, and chaos ensues.

More often than not, when you add properties to the global object, it's a mistake. Strict mode makes this mistake have immediate consequences, rather than letting your code appear to work correctly while containing potentially dangerous global variables.

continues

(continued)

What Is this in Methods?

Remember that a method is a function that's stored in a property of an object. Method invocation is when you access a method followed by parentheses (with optional arguments between the parentheses).

In the following code, the `author` object has a method named `write`, and we can invoke it using `author.write`:

```
const author = {
  write: function(){
    return 'Writing!';
  }
}
let status = author.write();
```

JavaScript also allows you to write methods using "method" syntax. In method syntax, you can eliminate the colon and the `function` keyword. So, the preceding object declaration can also be written like this:

```
const author = {
  write() {
    return 'Writing!';
  }
}
```

More often than not, this shorter syntax is what you'll see used in React components.

In method invocation, `this` is the object that owns the method:

```
const author = {
  totalWords: 0,
  write: function(words) {
    this.totalWords += words;
    return this.totalWords;
  }
}
let totalWords = author.write(500);
```

This is all well and good, but remember it's often the case that you'll want to use a function with different objects, as in this case:

```
const author1 = {
  totalWords: 0
}
const author2 = {
  totalWords: 0
}
```

```
const write = function(words) {
  this.totalWords += words;
  return this.totalWords;
}
```

If you invoke the `write` function now, `this.totalWords` will be `undefined` (in strict mode) or will try to access `window.totalWords` (if not in strict mode). To associate the `totalWords` function with an object, you need to *bind* it to the object by using `call`, `apply`, or `bind`.

Function Binding with call

The JavaScript `call` function binds a function with an object and invokes the function. It accepts the name of the object you want to bind the function to, followed by a list of individual arguments to pass into the function. To invoke the `write` function within the context of the `author1` object and pass in the number `500`, you can use this statement:

```
write.call(author1,500);
```

Function Binding with apply

The `apply` function also binds a function with an object and invokes the function. It accepts the name of the object you want to bind the function to, followed by an array that will be passed into the function. To invoke the `write` function within the context of the `author1` object and pass in an array you can use this statement:

```
write.apply(author1,[500]);
```

Function Binding with bind

The `bind` function works the same as `call`, but instead of invoking a function, it returns a new function that's bound to the specified object. To create a new function that will invoke the `write` function within the context of the `author1` object and pass in `500` each time it's invoked, you can use this statement:

```
let write500Words = write.bind(author1,500);
write500Words();
```

The second argument to `bind` is optional. In React, it's most common to see `bind` used with only the first argument.

Function binding is important in React components, because it allows you to define a function in one component and then pass it as a variable into other components, while still operating on the component where the function was initially defined.

This method of passing a bound function to a child component looks like this:

continues

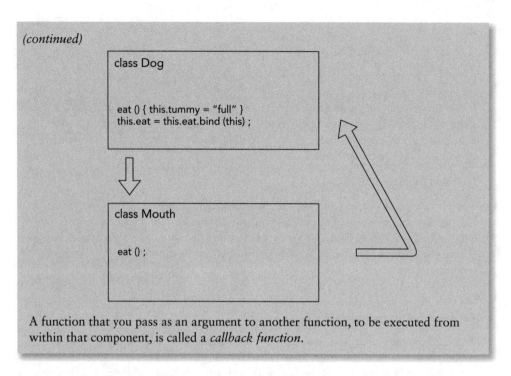

(continued)

class Dog

eat () { this.tummy = "full" }
this.eat = this.eat.bind (this) ;

class Mouth

eat () ;

A function that you pass as an argument to another function, to be executed from within that component, is called a *callback function*.

Stepping through a React Class Component

Once you have an understanding of how prototypal inheritance works in JavaScript, and you know that classes are just another way to use function constructors, creating React components using the class method is actually quite easy and it becomes a powerful tool in your React toolbox.

Let's take a look, piece by piece, at a basic class component.

React.Component

`React.Component` is the base class for every class component that you'll make. It defines a number of methods, lifecycle methods, class properties, and instance properties that you can make use of and extend in your components.

Importing React.Component

Because a custom component is a subclass of `React.Component`, any file that defines a class component (or more than one class component, in the case of a library) must start by importing React. You'll see two ways that this is typically done: by importing the entire React library, or by importing individual objects from the React library.

Here's the `import` statement for importing the entire React library:

```
import React from 'react';
```

This import is called a "default import."

You potentially save a few keystrokes inside your component by using a named import to import the Component class specifically, as shown here:

```
import {Component} from 'react';
```

The Class Header

If you import the entire library into your new component module, the first line of your new component will be as follows (assuming that your component is named MyComponent):

```
class MyComponent extends React.Component{
```

If you import Component using a named import, the header of your new component will look like this:

```
class MyComponent extends Component{
```

The Constructor Function

Next up is the constructor. If you include a constructor in your class, it will run one time when an instance of the class is created. The constructor is where you will bind event handler functions to the instance of the class and set up the local state for the instance.

A typical constructor in a component looks like this:

```
constructor(props) {
  super(props);
  this.state = {
    score: 0;
    userInput: ''
  }
  this.saveUserInput = this.saveUserInput.bind(this);
  this.updateScore = this.updateScore.bind(this);
}
```

After the constructor header and the call to the super function, this constructor has two purposes—it initializes the component instance's state, and it binds event handler methods to the component instance.

Initializing Local State

Each instance of a React component maintains its own state, and the constructor is where you initialize this state. The state of a component determines whether and when a component should re-render.

State and state management is at the heart of how React works, so I'll introduce the topic here and I'll go into much more detail about it in Chapter 6. For now, just know that the state of a component is stored in an object called state, and every time state changes, React attempts to re-render the UI.

The other object in a component instance that stores data is called props (which is short for properties). This is data that is passed to a component by its parent component in a React component hierarchy. If you're going to use the props object in the constructor, you need to pass it to the superclass's constructor when you call super.

In a component that makes use of the `state` object, the basic constructor should now look like this:

```
import {Component} from 'react';

class MyComponent extends Component {

  constructor(props){
    super(props);
    this.state = {};
  }
  ...
}

export default MyComponent;
```

Binding Event Handlers

Event handlers are the functions that run in response to events. Binding makes the `this` keyword work. By binding an event handler to the component instance, you also make it possible to share the function with other components while maintaining its link to the state of the instance with which it's bound. The result is that no matter where the event handler is, it always uses and affects the data from its bound object.

Listing 4-10 shows what happens when you don't properly bind your event handler.

LISTING 4-10: Not binding your functions results in errors

```
import React from 'react';

class Foo extends React.Component{
  constructor( props ){
    super( props );
    this.message = "hello";
  }

  handleClick(event){
    console.log(this.message); // 'this' is undefined
  }

  render(){
    return (
      <button type="button" onClick={this.handleClick}>
        Click Me
      </button>
    );
  }
}

export default Foo;
```

What's happening here is that we're passing `this.handleClick` into the button component as a prop. When we do that, it's passed as a variable and becomes an ordinary function without an owner object. When the click event happens inside the button component, this falls back to refer-ring to the global object, and we get an error because this.message doesn't exist.

To solve this problem, you can use the bind function to create a new function that's bound to the Foo class, as shown in Listing 4-11. Once you do that, you can pass handleClick as a prop to other components and it will always run within the context of Foo.

LISTING 4-11: Binding a function and using it in another class

```
import React from 'react';

class Foo extends React.Component{
  constructor( props ){
    super( props );
    this.message = "hello";
    this.handleClick = this.handleClick.bind(this);
  }

  handleClick(event){
    console.log(this.message); // 'hello'
  }

  render(){
    return (
      <button type="button" onClick={this.handleClick}>
        Click Me
      </button>
    );
  }
}

export default Foo;
```

You'll learn much more about the importance of binding event handlers in React, as well as how to avoid having to think about it at all, in Chapters 6 and 7.

Managing State in Class Components

The constructor function is the only place where you should ever directly update the state object of a component. For updating the state after the constructor function has run (during the life of the component, in other words), React provides a function called setState.

The setState function tells React to update the state of the component using an object or function that you pass into it.

Listing 4-12 shows a class component that displays a counter and has a button for incrementing that counter.

LISTING 4-12: Using state and setState in a class component

```
import {Component} from 'react';

class Counter extends Component {
  constructor(props) {
    super(props);
    this.state = {count: 0};
    this.incrementCount = this.incrementCount.bind(this);
  }
  incrementCount() {
    this.setState({count: this.state.count + 1});
  }
  render() {
    return (
      <div>
        <p>The current count is: {this.state.count}.</p>
        <button onClick = {()=>{this.incrementCount(this.state.count+1)}}>
          Add 1
        </button>
      </div>
    );
  }
}

export default Counter;
```

A very important point to remember about the setState function (and one that I'll repeat frequently because it's so important and can be the cause of many bugs in React apps) is that setState is asynchronous, and changes to state that you make using setState may be batched for performance reasons.

The reason that the asynchronous nature of setState is important is that if you try to access state immediately after setting it, you may get the old value rather than the new value that you expect. In Listing 4-13, I've added a console.log statement immediately after the setState function in the incrementCount method. Even though the console.log statement appears after setState, it will log the value of this.state.count prior to the incrementing happening, as shown in Figure 4-2.

We'll talk about how to work with state to avoid this problem in Chapter 6.

LISTING 4-13: setState() is asynchronous

```
import {Component} from 'react';

class Counter extends Component {
  constructor(props) {
    super(props);
    this.state = {count: 0};
    this.incrementCount = this.incrementCount.bind(this);
  }
  incrementCount() {
    this.setState({count: this.state.count + 1});
```

```
      console.log(this.state.count);
    }
    render(){
      return (
        <div>
          <p>The current count is: {this.state.count}.</p>
          <button onClick = {()=>{this.incrementCount(this.state.count+1)}}>
            Add 1
          </button>
        </div>
      );
    }
  }

export default Counter;
```

FIGURE 4-2: Using state immediately after calling setState() may produce unexpected results

The Render Function

The render function is the only function that's required in a class-based React component. It runs when the component mounts and then again each time the component updates. It contains a return statement that outputs the piece of the user interface that the component is responsible for.

Like any JavaScript function, the `render` function may contain JavaScript functions and variables. The `return` statement inside the `render` function contains JSX or variables with JSX values.

Listing 4-14 shows a component that outputs a simple static figure and caption.

LISTING 4-14: Rendering a figure and caption

```
import {Component} from 'react';

class BasicFigure extends Component {

  render() {
    return(
      <figure>
        <img src="images/cat.jpeg" alt="a cat" />
        <figcaption>This is a picture of a cat.</figcaption>
      </figure>
    );
  }
}
```

Remember that the `return` statement can only return one thing, such as one element, or one array, or one string. In the preceding example, it returns a single `<figure>` element.

The beauty of React is that once you've built a simple component such as the one in Listing 4-14, you can reuse it as many times as you need to. However, there's a major piece missing from this `BasicFigure` component. It will currently output the same image and caption every time you use it. To fix that, we need to use props.

Creating and Using Props

Props are the arguments that you pass into a component from a parent component. With JSX, the attributes that you write (which take the form of `name=value` in JSX elements) become properties inside the props object of the resulting component instance.

To illustrate how props work, let's create a component that will make use of the `BasicFigure` component. I'll call this component `FigureList`. The code for `FigureList` is shown in Listing 4-15.

LISTING 4-15: The FigureList component

```
import {Component} from 'react';
import BasicFigure from './BasicFigure';

class FigureList extends Component {
  render() {
    return (
      <>
        <BasicFigure />
        <BasicFigure />
        <BasicFigure />
      </>
```

```
      )
    }
  }
}
export default FigureList;
```

You can probably figure out from looking at the code for this component and the `BasicFigure` component that the result of rendering `FigureList` will be that three identical figures and captions will be outputted. To make our figures different, we need to pass data from `FigureList` to `BasicFigure`. This is where props come in, as shown in Listing 4-16.

LISTING 4-16: Using props to pass data to a child component

```
import {Component} from 'react';
import BasicFigure from './BasicFigure';

class FigureList extends Component {
  render() {
    return (
      <div style={{display:"flex"}}>
        <BasicFigure filename="dog.jpg" caption="Chauncey" />
        <BasicFigure filename="cat.jpg" caption="Murray" />
        <BasicFigure filename="chickens.jpg" caption="Lefty and Ginger" />
      </div>
    )
  }
}
export default FigureList;
```

With these attributes in place, the first part of rendering different output from a single component is in place. The `BasicFigure` component instances are all receiving different props.

The next step is to modify the `BasicFigure` component so that it makes use of the received props. We can do this by inserting variables in place of static values in the `return` statement, as shown in Listing 4-17.

LISTING 4-17: Using props in a class component

```
import {Component} from 'react';

class BasicFigure extends Component {

  render() {
    return(
      <figure>
        <img src={this.props.filename} alt={this.props.caption}/>
        <figcaption>{this.props.caption}</figcaption>
      </figure>
    );
  }
}

export default BasicFigure;
```

With that done, the `FigureList` component will now render three `BasicFigure` components, each of which will output a `figure` element with different images and captions. I've changed the value of the `display` style property to `flex` so that they'll display in a row, rather than vertically, as shown in Figure 4-3.

Chauncey

Murray

Lefty and Ginger

FIGURE 4-3: The result of rendering FigureList

Function Components

Now that you understand JavaScript classes, how the `this` keyword works in JavaScript, what the constructor is, and the basics of writing React components using the class method, we can get to the good stuff.

Although a knowledge of classes is important for understanding how React works, the React world is moving very quickly away from using classes whenever possible. The reason: using classes is complicated, and many people don't understand how `this` works. If you do have an understanding of classes and how the `this` keyword works in JavaScript, you'll have a better appreciation and understanding of how function components work, so I do recommend learning about classes still.

The function component was created to simplify the creation of React components. To illustrate how much easier writing a function component can be than a class component, consider the simple To Do List example class in Listing 4-18.

LISTING 4-18: A typical class component

```
import React from 'react';

class ToDoClass extends React.Component{
  constructor(props){
    super(props);
    this.state = {
        item: '',
        todolist: []
    }
    this.handleSubmit = this.handleSubmit.bind(this);
    this.handleChange = this.handleChange.bind(this);
  }
```

```
handleSubmit(e){
  e.preventDefault();
  const list = [...this.state.todolist, this.state.item];
  this.setState({
      todolist:list
  })
}

handleChange(e){
  this.setState({item:e.target.value});
}

render(){
  const currentTodos = this.state.todolist.map(
    (todo,index)=><p key={index}>{todo}</p>);
  return (
    <form onSubmit={this.handleSubmit}>
    <input type="text"
            id="todoitem"
            value={this.state.item}
            onChange={this.handleChange}
            placeholder="what to do?" />
    <button type="submit">
      Add
    </button>
    {currentTodos}
    </form>
  );
  }
}

export default ToDoClass;
```

Listing 4-19 shows how you can write a component that does the same thing as the class in Listing 4-18 using a function component.

LISTING 4-19: A typical function component

```
import React,{useState} from 'react';

function ToDoFunction(props){
  const [item,setItem] = useState('');
  const [todolist,setTodoList] = useState([]);

  const handleSubmit = (e)=>{
    e.preventDefault();
    const list = [...todolist, item];
    setTodoList(list)
  }
  const currentTodos = todolist.map((todo,index)=><p key={index}>{todo}</p>);
  return (
    <form onSubmit={handleSubmit}>
    <input type="text"
```

continues

LISTING 4-19 *(continued)*

```
                id="todoitem"
                value={item}
                onChange={ (e)=>{setItem(e.target.value)}}
                placeholder="what to do?" />
        <button type="submit">
        Add
        </button>
        {currentTodos}
        </form>
    );
}

export default ToDoFunction;
```

Notice how much simpler the function component version is. There's no `render` method, no constructor, and no binding of `this`. It's even possible to further simplify this function component by removing the import of React, since we're not directly using it, using an arrow function for the component, and moving the `export` statement up to the function expression, as shown in Listing 4-20.

LISTING 4-20: Further simplifying a function component

```
import {useState} from 'react';

export const ToDoFunction = (props)=>{
  const [item,setItem] = useState('');
  const [todolist,setTodoList] = useState();

  const handleSubmit = (e)=>{
    e.preventDefault();
    const list = [...todolist, item];
    setTodoList(list)
  }
  const currentTodos = todolist.map((todo,index)=><p key={index}>{todo}</p>);
  return (
    <form onSubmit={handleSubmit}>
    <input type="text"
            id="todoitem"
            value={item}
            onChange={ (e)=>{setItem(e.target.value)}}
            placeholder="what to do?" />
    <button type="submit">
    Add
    </button>
    {currentTodos}
    </form>
  );
}
```

Note that in this example, we've changed the export from a default export to a named export. To import this component into another component, you'll need to surround the name of the component with curly braces, like this:

```
import {ToDoFunction} from './ToDoFunction';
```

Now that you've seen how much more simple function components can be than class components, let's look at how to write them and what their limitations are.

What Are Function Components?

Function components are JavaScript functions that return React elements.

When they were first introduced into React, function components were a simplified way to write certain kinds of components called "stateless functional components." Stateless functional components are also known as "dumb components" or "presentational components."

Stateless functional components simply accept props from their parent and return a piece of the user interface. They don't perform additional operations, such as fetching and posting data, and they don't have their own internal state data.

In version 16.8 of React, however, a new feature was added to React called *hooks*. Hooks allow function components to do most of the things that class components can do, such as interacting with data stores and using state. The result is that function components have now become the primary way that most React components are written.

React's official documentation states that class components will continue to be supported for the foreseeable future. At this point, however, no one can foresee how much longer they'll be necessary. If you're currently writing class components, there's no need to convert them to function components. If you're coming to React from a background working with object-oriented languages, you may feel more comfortable working with class components than with function components and that's fine too.

With function components being so much simpler to work with, you may very well want to use them exclusively, and that's great! Be aware, however, that fully functional function components weren't introduced into React until years after it became one of the most popular UI libraries, so you're going to come into contact with a lot of class components. As long as you understand them and how to convert them to function components (which we'll cover in detail in Chapter 11), you may never need to write another class component.

How to Write Function Components

Since a function component is simply a JavaScript function, it starts the same way as any other function—as either a function expression or a function declaration. The choice of whether to use an expression or a declaration is mostly a matter of style and personal choice.

Here's an example of a function component created using a function declaration:

```
function Foo(props){
   return <h1>Welcome</h1>;
}

export default Foo;
```

Here's an example of a function component created using a function expression:

```
const Foo = function(props){
  return <h1>Welcome</h1>;
}

export default Foo;
```

Components created using function expressions can also be written using JavaScript's arrow function syntax, which saves several characters. For example:

```
const Foo = (props) => {
  return <h1>Welcome</h1>;
}

export default Foo;
```

The difference in terms of performance or actual bytes of data between using the function keyword and using an arrow function is negligible. Many React developers opt for the arrow syntax because it allows additional shortcuts (as described in the following section), and because arrow functions are generally more convenient to use internally inside of components, why not use them everywhere and be consistent? Also, arrow functions look kind of cool.

Whether you choose to use function expressions or function declarations for your function components, it's a good practice (and looks cleaner) if you stick to one or the other for every function component you write.

Optimizations and Function Component Shortcuts

One of the challenges in writing any type of computer code is to balance readability with conciseness. JavaScript offers many ways to minimize the number of characters and lines of code required to perform tasks, and React developers, in particular, are fond of using the shorthand syntax whenever possible.

For example, the following is a perfectly valid function component:

```
export const Foo = props => <h1>Hello, World!</h1>;
```

That's the whole thing! The preceding code snippet takes advantage of the following rules of arrow functions:

1. The parentheses around the parameter list are optional when a function only takes one parameter.

2. The `return` keyword is optional when an arrow function doesn't do anything except return data.

3. The curly braces around the function body are optional if you skip the `return` keyword.

JAVASCRIPT LESSON: VARIABLES

With the ES2015 version of JavaScript, we gained two new keywords for declaring variables: `const` and `let`. We also gained some new ways to work with variables, including the *destructuring assignment* syntax.

If it's been a while since you've written any JavaScript, the new keywords and ways to work with variables will be new to you. They are widely used and relied upon by most React apps, however, so it's important that you understand when, why, and how to use these new tools.

Goodbye to var

In the original JavaScript syntax, and up until 2015, the way to create a variable was with the `var` keyword. The `var` keyword is still present in JavaScript, and it always will be. The simplest form of using `var` looks like this:

```
var x;
```

When you want to assign a value to x or change the value of x, you can simply use the assignment operator:

```
x=10;
```

You can also initialize a variable created using `var` at the same time as you declare it:

```
var x=10;
```

JavaScript evaluates declarations first within their scope through a process called *hoisting*. When you use the `var` keyword to declare a variable, JavaScript also initializes the variable with a value of `undefined` during the hoisting. What this means in practice is that it's possible to use a variable created with `var` before it's declared, as in the following example:

```
x = 10;
console.log(x);
var x;
```

The previous example, when compiled by a JavaScript interpreter, is exactly the same as:

```
var x;
x = 10;
console.log(x);
```

and

```
var x=10;
console.log(x);
```

Variables created using `var` have *function scope*. What this means is that if you declare a variable inside a function, you can use that variable anywhere in the function.

continues

continued

If you declare a variable outside of a function, it will have *global scope*, meaning that you can use it anywhere in your program.

In reality, if a global is what you want (and if you're not using "strict" mode) you didn't even need to use the var keyword, because if you just assigned a value to a name, the result will be a global variable, no matter where in your program you do the assignment. Another way to think about what happens when you create a variable without declaring it is that a new property is created on the global object (window in the case of a browser). This "feature" of loose-mode JavaScript is called *implicit globals*, and it can be very dangerous, which is why strict mode disallows it.

In modern JavaScript, even variables created using the var keyword are considered to be dangerous, and their use is discouraged. The reason is that function scope is almost always unnecessarily broad and it makes it too easy to accidentally overwrite or redeclare a variable.

Most developers and experts now recommend using the new const and let keywords exclusively.

Using const

The const keyword creates a variable that can only have one value during its lifetime, which we call a *constant*. To create a constant, just use the const keyword followed by a valid name:

```
const x;
```

However, because you can't change a constant, and because declaring a variable automatically assigns it a value of undefined, if you want your constant to have a value other than undefined, you must initialize it at the same time as the declaration:

```
const x = 10;
```

Attempting to change the value of a const will result in an error in JavaScript. Note, however, that if you assign an object or an array to a constant, you can still change the properties of that object or the items in the array. You would not be able to reassign the variable with a completely new object or array, however.

Block Scoped Variables with let

The other new way to declare variables is with the let keyword, which creates a block-scoped variable. This is also known as *lexical variable scoping*. In JavaScript, a block is created by a pair of curly braces. Since loops and conditional statements as well as functions create blocks, let makes it possible to have variables that are function-scoped in practice (by declaring them at the top level of a function), but it also enables you to create variables that have more limited scope, such as inside of a loop.

Variables created using const also have block scope.

> **Destructuring Assignment**
>
> Destructuring assignment syntax lets you create variables by unpacking the elements in an array or the properties of an object. For example, say you have the following object:
>
> ```
> const User = {
>     firstName: 'Lesley',
>     lastName: 'Altenwerth',
>     userName: 'roosevelt86',
>     address: '81592 Daniel Underpass',
>     city: 'Haileeshire',
>     birthday: '1963-10-12'
> }
> ```
>
> If you want to create individual variables from the properties in this object, one way to do it is to declare and assign individual variables, like this:
>
> ```
> const firstName = User.firstName;
> const lastName = User.lastName;
> const userName = User.userName;
> ...
> ```
>
> Using destructuring syntax, you can do it all in one statement:
>
> ```
> const {firstName,lastName,userName,address,city,birthday} = User;
> ```
>
> To use destructuring with arrays, use square brackets:
>
> ```
> const [firstName,lastName] = ['Lesley','Altenwerth'];
> ```

Managing State in Function Components

Each time a JavaScript function runs, the variables inside it are initialized. Because functional components are merely JavaScript functions, it's not possible for them to have persistent local variables.

React provides *hooks* to allow functional components to create and access data that persists from one invocation of a functional component to the next (aka "state").

Hooks are functions that let you "hook" into functionality of class components without writing a class. React has many built-in hooks and even lets you write your own hooks. The hook that lets you persist data with functional components is useState.

The first step in using useState is to import it from the React library, like this:

```
import {useState} from 'react';
```

Once imported, you can invoke useState inside your functional component as many times as you need to. The useState function accepts an initial value as an argument and each time you invoke useState it returns an array containing a stateful variable and a function for updating that variable. Using destructuring syntax, you can extract this array and function into two variables:

```
const [todos, setTodos] = useState([{item: 'Learn About Hooks'}]);
```

Listing 4-21 shows a functional component that uses `useState` to create and update a counter.

LISTING 4-21: Using state in functional components

```
import {useState} from 'react';

function Counter() {
  const [count, setCount] = useState(0);

  return (
    <div>
      <p>The current count is: {count}.</p>
      <button onClick = {()=>{setCount(count+1)}}>
        Add 1
      </button>
    </div>
  );
}

export default Counter;
```

I'll cover hooks in detail in Chapter 11.

Differences between Function and Class Components

Table 4-2 summarizes the main differences between function components and class components.

TABLE 4-2: Functions vs. Classes

FUNCTION COMPONENTS	CLASS COMPONENTS
Accepts props as arguments and returns a React element	Extends React.Component
No render method	Requires a render method
No internal state (can be simulated using hooks)	Has internal state
Can use hooks	Cannot use hooks
Cannot use lifecycle methods (can be simulated using hooks)	Can use lifecycle methods

REACT COMPONENT CHILDREN

Components that are rendered inside other components are called *children*, and the component they're rendered inside of is called their *parent*. As in the physical world, being a child doesn't prevent a component from being a parent to some other child, and all parents except for the root component are also children.

A React UI of any complexity will have many components nested within other components and the parent/child terminology is how their relationships are described.

In the React component shown in Listing 4-22, the `UsernameInput`, `PasswordInput`, and `LoginSubmit` components are all children of `LoginForm`. Technically, the built-in `form` component is the child of `LoginForm`, and the three custom components are its grandchildren.

LISTING 4-22: A component made up of three child components

```
export default function LoginForm() {
  return (
    <form>
      <UsernameInput />
      <PasswordInput />
      <LoginSubmit />
    </form>
  )
}
```

this.props.children

Every component in a React UI has a property called `children` that stores the children of that component. By using `this.props.children` (or `props.children` in the case of function components) in the `return` statement of a component, you can create components where the child components aren't known until the component is invoked.

For example, Listing 4-23 shows a component named `ThingsThatAreFunny`, which you can wrap around any other components and it will render them with a title of "Here are some funny things."

LISTING 4-23: Presenting ThingsThatAreFunny

```
export default function ThingsThatAreFunny(props) {
  return (
    <>
      <h1>Here are some funny things.</h1>
      {props.children}
    </>
  )
}
```

To use the `ThingsThatAreFunny` component, split it into starting and ending tags instead of using the self-closing slash at the end of the component element name. Between the starting and ending tags, include child elements that you want to be rendered inside of it, as shown in Listing 4-24.

LISTING 4-24: Passing children into a component

```
import ThingsThatAreFunny from './ThingsThatAreFunny';
import Joke from './Joke';
```

continues

LISTING 4-24 (continued)

```
export default function ThingsILike(props){
  return (
    <ThingsThatAreFunny>
      <ul>
        <li><Joke id="0" /></li>
        <li><Joke id="1" /></li>
      </ul>
    </ThingsThatAreFunny>
  )
}
```

Assuming that the Joke component outputs one joke, the result of rendering the ThingsILike component is shown in Figure 4-4.

The following things are funny.

- Did you hear about the mathematician who's afraid of negative numbers? He'll stop at nothing to avoid them.
- What sound does a limping turkey make? Wobble Wobble.

FIGURE 4-4: Rendering the ThingsILike component

Manipulating Children

React provides several built-in ways to access information about and manipulate elements. These are:

➤ isValidElement

➤ cloneElement

➤ React.Children

React.Children

React.Children provides several utility functions that operate on the children of a component. For each of these, you can pass in props.children as an argument. These utilities are:

➤ React.Children.map. Invokes a function for each immediate child element and returns a new array of elements.

➤ React.Children.forEach. Invokes a function for each immediate child but doesn't return anything.

➤ React.Children.count. Returns the number of components in children.

➤ React.Children.only. Verifies that children only has one child.

➤ React.Children.toArray. Converts children to an array.

isValidElement

The `isValidElement` function takes an object as an argument and returns either `true` or `false` depending on whether the object is a React element.

cloneElement

The `cloneElement` function creates a copy of an element passed into it. Here's the basic syntax for `cloneElement`:

```
const NewElement = React.cloneElement(element,[props],[children]);
```

With `cloneElement`, you can create new elements from a component's child elements, and modify them in the process. For example, say you have a `NavBar` component that has `NavItem` children. You can render these in your `App` component, as shown in Listing 4-25.

LISTING 4-25: Rendering a NavBar inside of App

```
import NavBar from './NavBar';
import NavItem from './NavItem';

function App(props){
  return (
    <NavBar>
      <NavItem />
      <NavItem />
      <NavItem />
    </NavBar>);
}

export default App;
```

The `NavBar` component in this example could use `props.children` to render all of the `NavItems` that are children of it, as shown in Listing 4-26.

LISTING 4-26: Rendering the children using props.children

```
function NavBar(props){
  return (
    <div>
      {props.children}
    </div>
  )
}
export default NavBar;
```

However, what if you want to add an `onClick` attribute to each `NavItem` from within the `NavBar` component? Because `props.children` isn't actually the children (it's a *descriptor* of the children), you can't modify the children by using `props.children`.

Instead, what you need to do is to clone the children from within the `NavBar` component and then add or change properties in them, as shown in Listing 4-27.

LISTING 4-27: Cloning the children in NavBar.js

```
import React from 'react';

function NavBar(props){
  return (
    <div>
      {React.Children.map(props.children, child => {
        return React.cloneElement(child, {
          onClick: props.onClick })
    })}
    </div>
    )
}

export default NavBar;
```

With that done, you can then pass a function into `NavBar`, as shown in Listing 4-28, and it will be added to each of its child components.

LISTING 4-28: Passing onClick into the parent component

```
import NavBar from './NavBar';
import NavItem from './NavItem';

function App(props){
  return (
    <NavBar onClick={()=>{console.log('clicked');}}>
      <NavItem />
      <NavItem />
      <NavItem />
    </NavBar>);
}

export default App;
```

The child components can then make use of this new prop, as shown in Listing 4-29.

LISTING 4-29: Making use of props in a child component

```
function NavItem(props){
  return (
    <button onClick={props.onClick}>Click Me</button>
  )
}

export default NavItem;
```

THE COMPONENT LIFECYCLE

During the time when a React application is running, components become active, do their thing, and are destroyed. At each stage in the life of a component, certain events are fired and methods are invoked. These events and methods make up the *component lifecycle*.

The stages of a component's life are:

➤ **Mounting:** Mounting is where a component is constructed using the props passed into it and the default state, and the JSX returned by the component is rendered.

➤ **Updating:** Updating happens when the state of the component changes and the component is re-rendered.

➤ **Unmounting:** Unmounting is the end of the component lifecycle, when the component is removed from the active application.

➤ **Error handling:** The error handling methods run when an error happens during a component's lifecycle.

In class components, you can override the lifecycle methods to run your own code in response to lifecycle events. Function components can simulate lifecycle methods using a hook called `useEffect`, which I'll cover in detail in Chapter 11.

Understanding the main events in the lifecycle of a component is key to understanding how React works. Figure 4-5 shows the component lifecycle as a flowchart.

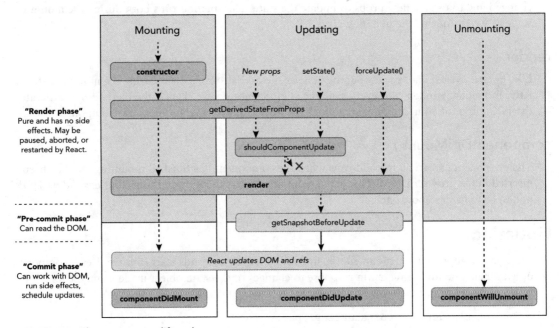

FIGURE 4-5: The component lifecycle

The following sections will examine the four stages of the component lifecycle and then will explore how you can avoid errors and improve performance with the lifecycle as well.

Mounting

The mounting stage includes everything from when a component is first constructed until it is inserted into the DOM. During the mounting lifecycle stage, the following methods run, in this order:

➤ `constructor`

➤ `static getDerivedStateFromProps`

➤ `render`

➤ `componentDidMount`

constructor()

You've already learned about the `constructor`. This is the method that automatically runs in an instance of a class when it's created. In a React component, it may include a call to the `super` method, initialization of the component's state object, and binding of event handlers.

static getDerivedStateFromProps

This method is a static method, meaning that it doesn't have access to the `this` keyword. The purpose of `getDerivedStateFromProps` is to check whether the props that the component uses have changed and to use the new props to update the state. This method runs both during the mounting stage as well as during the updating stage.

render

Like `getDerivedStateFromProps`, the `render` method also runs once during the mounting stage. After mounting, `render` runs every time the component updates. This is the method that generates the JSX output of your component, and it's the only required method in a class component.

componentDidMount()

The `componentDidMount` method runs when the component has finished mounting and has been inserted in the browser DOM. This is the point at which it's safe to do things that depend on DOM nodes, or to fetch remote data.

Updating

After your component has mounted, the updating lifecycle methods start running. React components update their data and re-render in response to changes to the state object made using the `setState` function. Every time a component updates, the following methods run, in this order:

➤ `static getDerivedStateFromProps`

➤ `shouldComponentUpdate`

➤ `render`

➤ `getSnapshotBeforeUpdate`

➤ `componentDidUpdate`

The `getDerivedStateFromProps` and `render` methods serve the same purposes in the updating stage as they do during the mounting stage. So, let's take a look at the three lifecycle methods that are unique to the updating stage.

shouldComponentUpdate

The default behavior of a React component is to update every time the state changes. There are times, however, when you might want to tell React that a change to the state doesn't affect a component and so it's not necessary to go through the updating process.

This method, when it's present, must return either `true` or `false`. If you have a component that you know will never need to be updated once it's mounted, you can prevent it from updating by using this code:

```
shouldComponentUpdate(){
   return false;
}
```

More often, the way `shouldComponentUpdate` is used is to compare the previous props and state with the new props and state and to decide whether to update the component. This is possible because React passes the props and state that will be used for the upcoming rendering into `shouldComponentUpdate`. In Listing 4-30, the value of a prop is compared with the value of that prop in the `nextProp` object to determine whether to re-render.

LISTING 4-30: Comparing previous and next props in shouldComponentUpdate

```
class ToDoItem extends Component {
    shouldComponentUpdate(nextProps, nextState) {
        return nextProps.isChecked != this.props.isChecked;
    }
    ...
}
```

getSnapshotBeforeUpdate

This lifecycle method happens right before the rendered output from the component is made active in the DOM. The purpose of this method is to allow you to capture information about the state of the browser (or other output device) prior to it changing.

Although it's rare that you'll have a need to use this lifecycle method, one example use for it is to maintain the scroll position of an element (such as a text box) between renders. If an update to the browser DOM would affect what the user is currently viewing in the browser, `getSnapshotBeforeUpdate` can be used to find out the relevant information about the browser DOM so that it can be restored after the update happens.

componentDidUpdate

This method runs immediately after a component updates. It's useful for performing network requests based on new props passed to the component, or for performing operations that depend on the snapshot of the DOM created during the `getSnapShotBeforeUpdate` method.

If your component has a `shouldComponentUpdate` method that returns `false`, the component won't update and this method won't run.

Unmounting

The process of removing a component from the DOM is called *unmounting*. Only one lifecycle method, `componentWillUnmount`, happens during this process.

componentWillUnmount

As its name implies, `componentWillUnmount` is invoked right before a component is removed from the DOM. If you need to do any cleanup in your application related to the component that will be unmounted, this is the place to do it. Examples of tasks that are commonly done in the `componentWillUnmount` method include:

➤ Stopping any network requests that are in progress.

➤ Stopping timers.

➤ Removing event listeners created in `componentDidMount`.

Error Handling

The fourth type of lifecycle methods are the ones that only run when something goes wrong with your component. These lifecycle methods are `getDerivedStateFromError` and `componentDidCatch`. I'll talk about both of these methods further in Chapter 13, but I want to introduce them to you here.

getDerivedStateFromError

If an error occurs in a component's descendant components, the component will run the `getDerivedStateFromError` method. This lifecycle method receives the error that occurred and should return an object that will be used to update the state.

componentDidCatch

The `componentDidCatch` lifecycle method runs after a descendant component throws an error. Because `componentDidCatch` doesn't run during the render phase of the lifecycle, it's useful for performing tasks such as error logging.

Improving Performance and Avoiding Errors

Lifecycle methods can be used to improve the performance of your React application and to prevent errors. In the following sections I'll talk about a few tools and techniques you can use to make your components the best they can be.

Avoiding Memory Leaks

To demonstrate the use of several lifecycle methods, we can look at a common problem in React applications—a memory leak—and how to fix it.

A memory leak is a fault in a computer program where memory is allocated unnecessarily. This can happen when a component is unmounted without removing timers or network requests involving the component continue to happen after the unmounting.

Because a memory leak is a wasted use of resources, having a memory leak in your program can lead to reduced performance and unexpected behaviors. Memory leaks have a tendency to build up the longer a program is running, and so you may not notice them at first but things can start to get weird as they accumulate. So, it's best to take action to avoid them.

To avoid memory leaks, you should always make sure to properly clean up after your components using the `componentWillUnmount()` method.

Listing 4-31 shows a component that uses the JavaScript `setInterval` function to increment a counter.

LISTING 4-31: A React component with a potential memory leak

```
import {Component} from 'react';

class Counter extends Component{
    constructor(){
      super();
      this.state = {count: 0};
      this.incrementCount = this.incrementCount.bind(this);
    }

    incrementCount(){
      this.setState({count: this.state.count + 1});
      console.log(this.state.count);
    }

    componentDidMount(){
      this.interval = setInterval(()=>{
        this.incrementCount();
      },1000)
    }

    render(){
      return (<p>The current count is: {this.state.count}.</p>);
    }
}
export default Counter;
```

The component's parent has a method, invoked using a button, that toggles whether the `Counter` component is rendered or not, as shown in Listing 4-32.

LISTING 4-32: Toggling the rendering of the Counter

```
import {useState} from 'react';
import {Counter} from './Counter';
function CounterController() {
  const [displayCounter,setDisplayCounter] = useState(true);

  function toggleCounter(){
    setDisplayCounter(!displayCounter);
  };

  return (
    <div className="App">
      {displayCounter ? <Counter /> : null}
      <button onClick={toggleCounter}>Toggle Count</button>
    </div>
  );
}
export default CounterController;
```

When the App component mounts, the Counter component will also mount and the timer will start running and incrementing the counter in the browser and in the console, as shown in Figure 4-6.

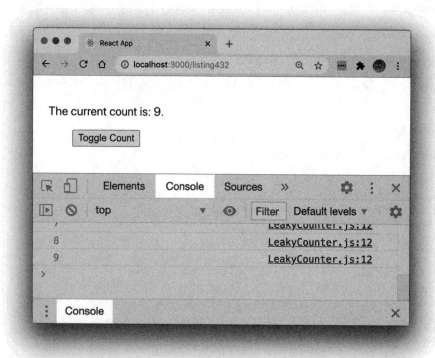

FIGURE 4-6: Incrementing a counter

When you click the Toggle Count button, the `Counter` component will disappear. However, the timer created by the `setInterval` function in the `Counter` component is never cleared, and so it continues to run after the component is removed.

After the component is unmounted, React will log a message to the browser console to tell you that you're attempting to call `setState` on an unmounted component, as shown in Figure 4-7.

FIGURE 4-7: The result of attempting to call setState on an unmounted component

Trying to call `setState` on an unmounted component won't do anything, since an unmounted component doesn't have state. But, as React's error message points out, it's indicative of a memory leak.

To fix this problem, you can use the `componentWillUnmount` method in the `Counter` component to call `clearInterval`, which will stop the timer before the `Counter` component is unmounted, as shown in Listing 4-33.

LISTING 4-33: Fixing a memory leak

```
import {Component} from 'react';

class Counter extends Component{
    constructor(){
      super();
      this.state = {count: 0};
      this.incrementCount = this.incrementCount.bind(this);
    }

    incrementCount(){
      this.setState({count: this.state.count + 1});
      console.log(this.state.count);
    }

    componentDidMount(){
      this.interval = setInterval(()=>{
        this.incrementCount();
      },1000)
    }

    componentWillUnmount(){
      clearInterval(this.interval);
    }

    render(){
      return (<p>The current count is: {this.state.count}.</p>);
    }
}
    export default Counter;
```

Now Counter will be properly unmounted and the timer will be cleared when it's removed from the browser. If you click the Toggle Counter button again, the counter will start over as you would expect it to, because a new timer will be created.

React.PureComponent

If you have a component that only accepts props and returns JSX, without modifying state or affecting anything outside of itself, that component is known as a "pure component." It gets this name from the concept of a pure function.

A key characteristic of a pure function is that it always returns the same result when given the same input.

Pure components are opportunities to improve the performance of your React user interface. Because their output only depends on props passed to them, a simple comparison of the previous props and the new props will tell you whether the component will change when re-rendered.

One way to do this comparison is by using the shouldComponentUpdate lifecycle method along with React's shallowCompare function, as shown in Listing 4-34.

LISTING 4-34: Using shouldComponentUpdate and shallowCompare

```
import React from 'react';
import shallowCompare from 'react-addons-shallow-compare';

class ShallowCompare extends React.Component {

  shouldComponentUpdate(nextProps, nextState) {
    return shallowCompare(this, nextProps, nextState);
  }

  render() {
    return <div>foo</div>;
  }
}

export default ShallowCompare;
```

Another way to accomplish the same thing as the code in Listing 4-34 is to write your class component by extending `React.PureComponent` instead of `React.Component`, as shown in Listing 4-35.

LISTING 4-35: Extending React.PureComponent

```
import React from 'react';

class PureComponentExample extends React.PureComponent {
    render() {
      return <div>foo</div>;
    }
}

export default PureComponentExample;
```

React.memo

Function components can also be pure components, but because they can't use lifecycle methods or extend `React.PureComponent`, a different method is required to optimize them.

`React.memo()` is a higher-order function, meaning that it wraps around another function and adds its functionality to that function. When you wrap your function component in `React.memo()`, it performs a comparison of the previous and next props and skip rendering if they're the same.

The name of `React.memo()` refers to memoization, which is the caching of the results of a function and using the cached result if the function has the same input as when the cache was created.

Listing 4-36 shows how to use `React.memo()`.

> **LISTING 4-36:** Using React.memo

```
import React from 'react';

function ExampleComponent(props){
  return (<p>Hi, {props.firstName}. This component returns the same thing when
given the same props.</p>);
}

export default React.memo(ExampleComponent);
```

React.StrictMode

`React.StrictMode` is a component that you can wrap around your components to activate additional checks of your code and produce warning messages that can be helpful during development.

The default Create React App application wraps the root component with a `<StrictMode>` element to turn on strict mode for the entire component tree. But, you can also just use `<StrictMode>` on parts of your application by applying it more selectively.

RENDERING COMPONENTS

The end result of the mounting and updating stages of the lifecycle in React is a single rendered component, called the root component. Remember that by "rendered" we mean that all of the JSX for the root component and its subcomponents has been parsed and the resulting tree of components has been created.

Once React's work has been done and the tree of components has been created, it's the job of a separate node package to render the component in a way that it can be seen and used by people.

Rendering with ReactDOM

The most common place for a tree of React elements to end up being used is in a web browser. The library responsible for converting a React component into HTML and inserting it into the DOM and then managing updates to the DOM is ReactDOM.

ReactDOM includes several methods that you can use to interact with the DOM, but the one that's absolutely necessary for every React application designed for the browser to use is `ReactDOM.render`.

If you look at the `index.js` file at the root of the `src` folder in a React project created using Create React App, you'll see where `ReactDOM.render` is invoked and where a single React element (which may be optionally wrapped with a `React.StrictMode` component) is passed in, as shown in Listing 4-37.

LISTING 4-37: ReactDOM.render renders a single element in the DOM

```
ReactDOM.render(
  <React.StrictMode>
    <App/>
  </React.StrictMode>,
  document.getElementById('root')
);
```

The beauty of `ReactDOM.render` is that it performs an incredible number of calculations and DOM manipulations, controls the timing of DOM updates, manages the virtual DOM, and more—but as far as you, the programmer, are concerned, it's a black box. All you need to do is feed it a valid React component and a DOM node where you want that component to be rendered and `ReactDOM.render` takes it from there.

If you examine the code in Listing 4-37, you'll see that, in this case, we're telling `ReactDOM.render` to render the `App` component (you can ignore the `StrictMode` wrapper) inside the HTML element node that has an `id` attribute with a value of `root`.

Every React application designed for rendering to web browsers will have a single HTML file that imports the React and ReactDOM libraries, plus all the rest of the JavaScript that the application needs. In the case of a Create React App application, this file is `public/index.html`. Listing 4-38 shows a version of Create React App's `index.html` file (with the HTML comments and unimportant meta tags removed to save space). When a JavaScript application lives within a single HTML file like this, we call it a *single page app*.

LISTING 4-38: Create React App's index.html file

```
<!DOCTYPE html>
<html lang="en">
  <head>
    <meta charset="utf-8" />
    <link rel="icon" href="%PUBLIC_URL%/favicon.ico" />
    <meta name="viewport" content="width=device-width, initial-scale=1" />
    ...
    <title>React App</title>
  </head>
  <body>
    <noscript>You need to enable JavaScript to run this app.</noscript>
    <div id="root"></div>
    ...
  </body>
</html>
```

Virtual DOM

After the root component has been mounted, the job of `ReactDOM.render` is to monitor changes to the rendered element coming in from React and figure out the most efficient way to update the browser DOM to match the newly rendered application through a process called *reconciliation*.

As a programmer, you can think of rendering a React UI as a continual process of replacing a previous tree of elements with a new one: and this is in fact what React is doing. But, once a new tree of elements gets to `ReactDOM.render`'s reconciliation process, it looks for the minimal set of changes and just makes those.

For example, compare the element shown in Listing 4-39 with the element in Listing 4-40. The second listing could be the `<nav>` element that results from the user clicking the "About Us" link.

LISTING 4-39: The initial element tree

```
<nav>
  <ul>
    <li><a href="/" className="active navlink">Home</a></li>
    <li><a href="/aboutus" className="navlink">About Us</a></li>
  </ul>
</nav>
```

LISTING 4-40: The element tree after the user clicks a link

```
<nav>
  <ul>
    <li><a href="/" className="navlink">Home</a></li>
    <li><a href="/aboutus" className="active navlink">About Us</a></li>
  </ul>
</nav>
```

The only difference between these two element trees is which one has the `active` class. `ReactDOM.render` will find this difference during reconciliation and will simply remove `active` from the first link's class element and add it to the second link's class element without modifying anything else.

This process of rendering the new UI in memory and then comparing it with the previous UI and figuring out the minimal set of changes that can be applied to the browser DOM to make the previous state match the new one is what we call the *Virtual DOM*.

One important thing to know about how reconciliation works is that updates to the browser DOM won't always happen in the same order as when they were rendered in the Virtual DOM. This is because `ReactDOM.render` may batch changes if it creates more efficiency.

Once again, the Virtual DOM's inner workings happen without your intervention, and you won't need to know exactly what's happening in the reconciliation process (except perhaps in very rare cases). Knowing that it exists is important, however.

If you'd like to learn more about how reconciliation works, you can read about it in more detail at https://reactjs.org/docs/reconciliation.html.

Other Rendering Engines

React doesn't care whether you render the elements that it outputs in a web browser, on a billboard, as a mobile app, as text in a terminal application, or in any other user interface device.

Although ReactDOM is the most commonly used rendering engine, and thus the one that most books and tutorials on React focus on, other rendering engines can and do exist. The following sections explore a few of the most common ones.

React Native

React Native converts React elements into native mobile applications. React Native has a set of built-in elements that, when rendered, result in the creation of commonly used native app components such as View, Text, ScrollView, and Image.

After React renders a tree of React Native elements, the React Native rendering engine compiles these elements into platform-specific code for different mobile operating systems (such as Android or iOS).

Listing 4-41 shows a "Hello, World" component written with React Native.

LISTING 4-41: Your first React Native component

```
import React from 'react';
import { Text, View } from 'react-native';

const YourApp = () => {
  return (
    <View style={{ flex: 1, justifyContent: "center", alignItems: "center" }}>
      <Text>
        Hello, World!
      </Text>
    </View>
  );
}

export default YourApp;
```

Everything here is standard React and JavaScript, and everything you're learning about React also applies to React Native. The only difference is that React Native adds a library of components that are relevant to native mobile apps, and React Native components are compiled into native mobile apps rather than for web browsers.

After you write your React Native code, it needs to be compiled to generate platform-specific code that you can deploy on mobile devices or to app stores. You can compile React Native components using a Node.js program called Expo CLI (CLI stands for "command-line interface"), or by using the React Native CLI.

React Native CLI requires you to have the appropriate native app development tools installed (either XCode for iOS apps, or Android Studio for Android apps). Expo CLI compiles your apps and deploys them inside a wrapper Expo mobile app on mobile phones.

While React Native CLI is more familiar to developers who already have experience with mobile app development, Expo is great because it's so easy to use and will have you writing functioning mobile apps very quickly.

Figure 4-8 shows the "Hello, World!" app from Listing 4-41 running on an iPhone.

FIGURE 4-8: Hello, React Native

ReactDOMServer

ReactDOMServer renders React components and returns an HTML string. It can be used on a web server to generate the initial HTML for a React application, which can then be served to web browsers to speed up the initial loading of the user interface.

Once the initial HTML for the application is rendered on the server and served to a web browser, the regular ReactDOM renderer takes over and handles updates. This technique is referred to as "Isomorphic React" or "Universal React."

React Konsul

React Konsul renders React components to the browser console. It includes a handful of built-in components, including `container`, `text`, `image`, `button`, and `group`, that allow developers to create interactive views inside the JavaScript console of a browser.

The use cases for React Konsul are rather limited, but it can render images, interactive buttons, and styled text instead of the simple plain text console log messages that JavaScript outputs by default.

react-pdf

With react-pdf, you can use React components to render PDF files. The built-in components for assembling PDFs include `Document`, `Page`, `View`, and `Text`. Once you've composed your PDF document using these components, you can render them in the browser using `ReactDOM.render`, or you can save them as PDF documents using `ReactPDF.render`.

COMPONENT TERMINOLOGY

Components and elements are the building blocks of React. If you understand components and JavaScript, you're more than halfway to being a React developer. React components come with a lot of terminology, however. To help you keep everything straight, here's a handy overview of some of the most commonly used lingo in React component development:

➤ **Class component:** A class component is a React component created by extending `React.Component` or `React.PureComponent`.

➤ **Function component:** A function component is a JavaScript function that returns JSX code.

➤ **State:** State is the data in a React user interface that determines when updates will happen.

➤ **Props:** Props are the data that's passed from a parent component to a child component. In JSX, props are created using attributes (in the `name=value` format).

➤ **Stateful component:** A stateful component is a component that has internal state, stored in either the state object (in the case of class components) or created using hooks (in the case of function components).

➤ **Stateless component:** A stateless component is one that doesn't have its own internal state. Stateless components are also known as "dumb" components or "presentational" components.

➤ **Pure component:** A pure component is one that always returns the same output when given the same input.

➤ **Root component:** The root component is the single component that contains all the other components in your React application. Rendering the root component (using ReactDOM) causes the entire component tree to be rendered.

➤ **Parent component/child component:** As in the HTML DOM, the relationship between components in a React component tree is described using the terms parent and child.

➤ **Component lifecycle:** The component lifecycle is the progression of events and methods that happen during the life of a React component. It starts with mounting and ends with unmounting. In between mounting and unmounting, the update lifecycle methods happen.

SUMMARY

React components are the building blocks of React. In this chapter, you learned:

➤ The two methods for creating React components: class and function.

➤ How React components return React elements.

➤ How to use React's built-in components.

➤ How to pass data between components by using JSX attributes.

➤ How data passed using attributes in React elements becomes props in child components.

➤ How to manage state in a class component.

➤ How to manage state in a function component.

➤ What lifecycle methods are and how to use them in a class component.

➤ How to prevent memory leaks in React components.

➤ How to use `PureComponent` and `React.memo`.

➤ How to render React components using ReactDOM.

In the next chapter, you'll learn how to use in-browser tools to inspect and test React components. Onward!

5

React DevTools

React applications can get rather large and complex. With a large tree of components and sub-components and all of their props and state and events, having a way to easily see what's going on inside each component, as well as to be able to filter out the noise and focus on just the components that you're interested in, becomes essential to debugging problems. React DevTools can also show you where performance issues exist in your code. In this chapter, you'll learn:

- ➤ How to install React DevTools.
- ➤ How to inspect components with React DevTools.
- ➤ How to search for components in React DevTools.
- ➤ Filtering and selecting components in React DevTools.

INSTALLATION AND GETTING STARTED

In this book's Introduction, you installed React Developer Tools (also known as React Dev-Tools) and I briefly covered how it works. If you haven't yet installed React DevTools, follow the instructions in the Introduction to install it in Google Chrome or Mozilla Firefox, then return to this chapter.

Before we can experiment with any of the React DevTools features, we first need an app to work with. I've created the beginnings of a bookstore app, as shown in Figure 5-1, which you can download and use for working with the React DevTools.

React Bookstore is a simple store and shopping cart application that displays a randomized grid of books, using data from an external file. Each book in React Bookstore has an Add To Cart button underneath it that will add the book to the cart, and that toggles to a button for removing the book from the cart.

React Bookstore's shopping cart simply displays a list of the books that have been added to the shopping cart and calculates a total price. The React Bookstore is part of my GitHub repository for this book.

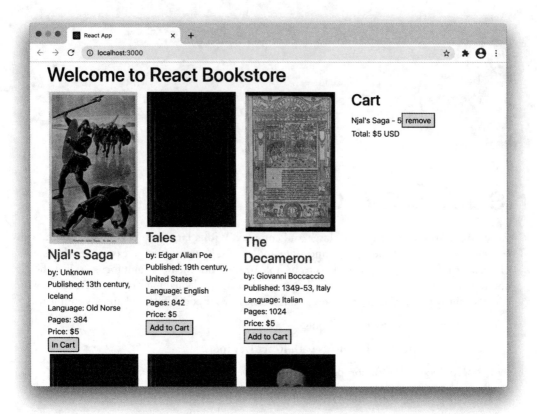

FIGURE 5-1: The React Bookstore sample app

If you haven't already downloaded and installed the repository, use the following steps to do so:

1. Open the integrated terminal in Visual Studio Code.

2. Type the following command to check whether you have the Git version control system installed on your computer:

   ```
   git --version
   ```

   If Git is installed, the terminal will respond with a version number, and you can skip to step 3. If it's not installed, you can download the latest version for your operating system from https://git-scm.com/downloads.

3. You may need to close and re-open the VS Code terminal before you'll be able to do this step. Make sure that the current working directory in VS Code's terminal is where you want to place the example files. If it's not, you can either right-click a directory in the VS Code Explorer pane and select **Open in Integrated Terminal** or you can use the UNIX cd command to change the directory from within the terminal.

4. Clone my repository by entering this command into the terminal:

```
git clone https://github.com/chrisminnick/react-js-foundations
```

After a moment, all of the files will be downloaded.

> **NOTE** *If you have any issues using Git to clone the example code repository, you can simply use a browser to go to the repository URL and download it as a* `.zip` *file by clicking the Code link.*

5. Install and start up the React Bookstore example:

```
cd react-js-foundations/react-book-store
npm install
npm start
```

The React Bookstore example is a work in progress that you can use throughout this book to try out new things you learn about React. The application shows a randomized list of 100 great books, and you can add and remove the books from a shopping cart.

It's obviously a simple app which is as yet unfinished, but it's a good starting point for learning about React and React DevTools.

> **NOTE** *The React Bookstore is open source, and you can do whatever you want with it. I make no claims as to its suitability for anything more than learning React.*

INSPECTING COMPONENTS

The most common reason to use React DevTools is to inspect your React component tree. Follow these steps to get started with the DevTools Components window:

1. Start up the `react-book-store` app if it isn't already running.

2. Open the Developer Tools in your browser. If the current browser window contains a React app, you'll see the React DevTools Components and Profiler tabs, as shown in Figure 5-2.

3. Click the Components tab and you'll see the list of components that make up the React Bookstore, as shown in Figure 5-3.

4. Click the components on the left to inspect each one.

Inspecting the components in a React app will show you the relationship between the components, any hooks or state being using in the component, the data and functions that were passed to the component, and the file that contains the source code for each component.

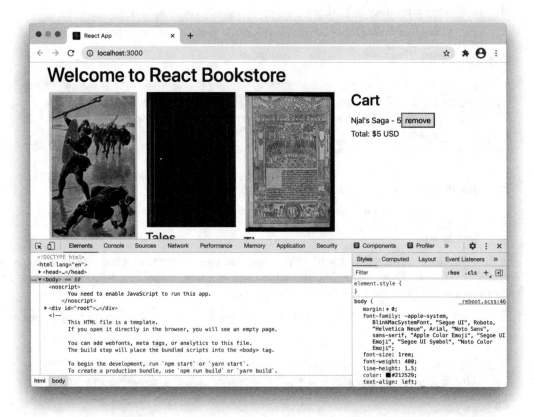

FIGURE 5-2: The Chrome Developer Tools with React DevTools installed

Working with the Component Tree

The left side of the Components window shows a nested list containing each of the components that make up the current view in the browser. In the React Bookstore app, this includes the root component, App, the ProductList component, a long list of Product components, and the Cart component.

Each parent component has an arrow next to it, which you can click to expand or collapse the children within that component. For example, if you collapse the ProductList, the outline will look like Figure 5-4.

With ProductList collapsed, you can see that the React Bookstore is made up of two main sections: the list of products, and the cart. The list of products includes all of the products being viewed (which is currently all of them) and the cart contains any items that are currently in your shopping cart.

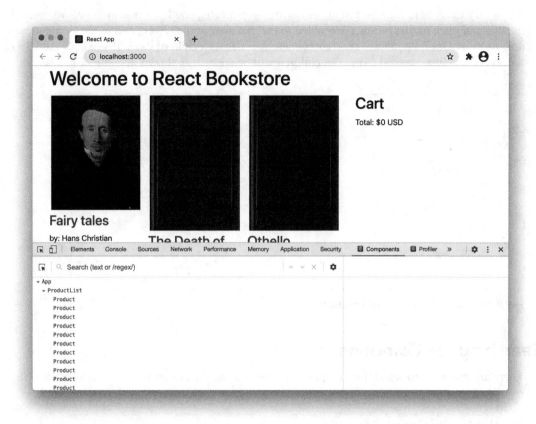

FIGURE 5-3: The React DevTools Components tab

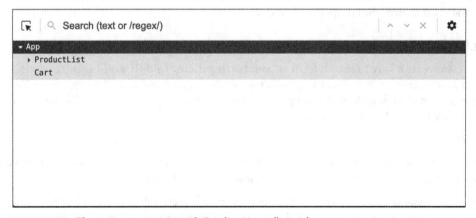

FIGURE 5-4: The component tree with ProductList collapsed

If you click the **Add to Cart** button under one of the products, you'll see that in the browser window, the title and price of that product are added to the cart area of the screen, and in the Component window of React DevTools, a CartItem component is added as a child of Cart. If you click **Add To Cart** for several products, several CartItem children will be created, as shown in Figure 5-5.

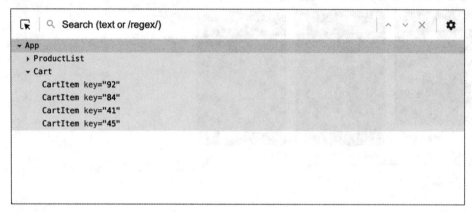

FIGURE 5-5: Creating new CartItem children

Searching for Components

There are two ways to search for components. One is using the Search input box. The other is using regular expressions.

Using the Search Input Box

In a large tree of components, the Search input box above the component tree view can be very helpful for locating specific components. The search box can accept either a string or a *regular expression* that will be matched against the component names.

Using Regular Expressions

Regular expressions are a way to search for text based on a pattern. To distinguish regular expressions from ordinary text searches, React DevTools uses slashes before and after the expression. For example, if you wanted to find all of the components that contain the word "Product," you could do so using the following regular expression:

```
/Product/
```

Right now, however, this regular expression will highlight the exact same list of components as if you just searched for the word "product" without the slashes before and after it.

Where regular expressions come in handy is for more complex searches than can be done with ordinary text searches. For example, if you wanted to select all of the Product components, but not the ProductList component, you could use a regular expression such as this one:

```
/Product$/
```

The dollar sign at the end indicates that you're only looking for component names that end with the word "Product."

If you want to find components that match the name `Cart` or the name `ProductList`, you can use the *OR operator*, which is a vertical bar in regular expressions, like this:

```
/(Cart$|ProductList)/
```

In addition to the "ends with" operator ($), regular expressions also have a "begins with" operator, which is the caret (^). For example, the following regular expression search will find any component with a "c" in its name:

```
/c/
```

The result of running the preceding regular expression search is shown in Figure 5-6.

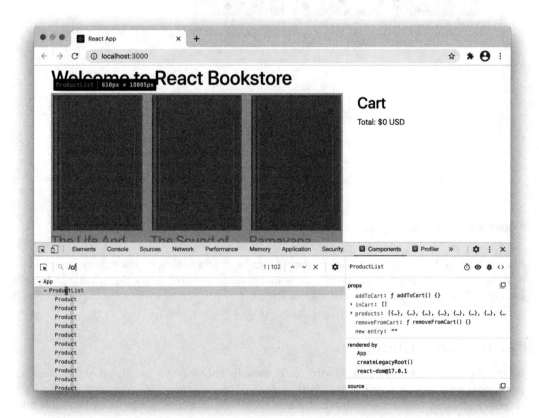

FIGURE 5-6: Searching for components containing "c"

If you add a ^ to the beginning of the search term, it will only show the `Cart` and `CartItem` components, as shown in Figure 5-7.

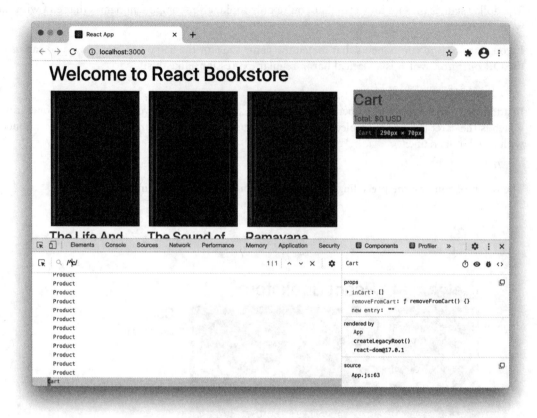

FIGURE 5-7: Searching for components starting with "c"

I've only touched on a few of the capabilities of regular expressions here. For a more complete list of the capabilities of regular expressions and more examples of how to use them, visit the Mozilla Developer Network Regular Expressions Cheatsheet at `https://developer.mozilla.org/en-US/docs/Web/JavaScript/Guide/Regular_Expressions/Cheatsheet`.

Filtering Components

When you first open the React DevTools, you're actually only seeing a partial list of the React components that make up your user interface. Although all of the custom components that make up what's currently on the screen are showing, the built-in HTML components (which React DevTools refers to as "host components") are hidden.

To reveal all of the host components as well as the custom components, you can adjust the filtering in the View Settings.

Click the gear icon in the upper right of the Component window's tree view, and the settings dialog box will open, as shown in Figure 5-8.

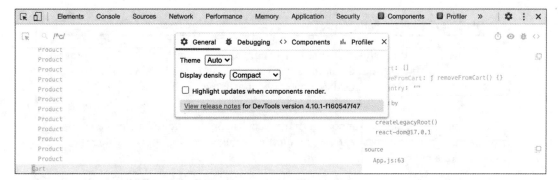

FIGURE 5-8: React DevTools' View Settings

The Components tab in the settings dialog will be open, and you'll see a checkbox for expanding the tree of components by default. Underneath that is an area where you can define filters that will be applied to the component tree.

The default component tree filter hides all host components. If you disable this filter, you'll see why you may also want to uncheck the "Expand component tree by default" checkbox and why it's so important for React DevTools to have a Search feature—when you include the host components, the list of components becomes very long (as shown in Figure 5-9).

```
🔍 Search (text or /regex/)                    ∧  ∨  ×    ⚙

▼ App
  ▼ div
    ▼ header
      ▼ div
          h1
    ▼ div
      ▼ div
        ▼ ProductList
          ▼ ul
            ▼ li key="87"
              ▼ Product
                ▼ div
                  ▼ a
                      img
                  ▼ div
                    ▼ h3
                        a
                      div
                      div
                      div
                      div
                      div
                      button
            ▼ li key="52"
              ▼ Product
```

FIGURE 5-9: The component tree view with the default filter disabled

HIGHER-ORDER COMPONENTS

In functional programming, a higher-order function is a function that takes another function as an argument and whose return value is a function. In React, a higher-order component is one that takes a component as input and returns another component.

The reason for writing a component that accepts a component and returns a component is that it's a convenient way to add functionality to components using the concept of composition.

Often in React, we refer to the component that is passed to a higher-order component as the "wrapped" component. If you think of a higher-order component as like wrapping paper, you'll understand the idea. When you wrap a box with gift wrapping paper, the result is a new thing that we might call a "present," which includes both the box and the wrapping. We can express the wrapping of a box like this in JavaScript code:

```
const Present = wrappingPaper(Box);
```

Higher-order components are not a feature of React, but rather a pattern for using React.

You'll see more examples of higher-order components in future chapters, including in Chapter 12, where we'll talk about how to give a component the ability to have React applications respond to the browser URL with React Router.

The filter feature in the settings dialog allows you to create filters based on the location, name, type, and whether components are higher-order components.

Selecting Components

In addition to finding components using the Search input box, you can also select components just by clicking on them in the tree view, or by using the Select tool, which is shown in Figure 5-10.

No matter how you select a component, once you do, the inner workings of that component will show up in the pane on the right side of the Components window. If multiple components are selected, the details for the first selected component will be shown.

EDITING COMPONENT DATA IN DEVTOOLS

The right side of the Components window in React DevTools displays information about the currently selected component, including its state and props data, hooks used by the component, the ancestors of the component, and the location of the component's source code, as shown in Figure 5-11.

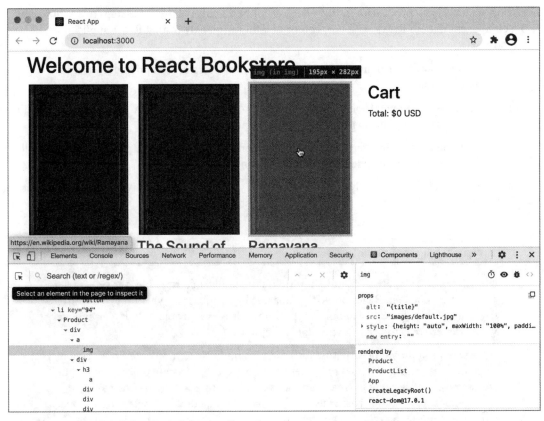

FIGURE 5-10: The React DevTools Select tool

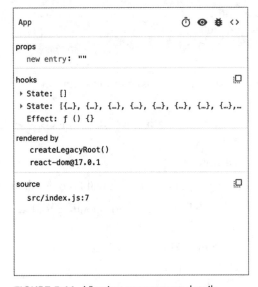

FIGURE 5-11: Viewing component details

The hooks, state, and props data in this pane can all be edited. Follow these steps to see how editing component data in React DevTools can be helpful for quickly testing React applications in the browser:

1. If it's not already running, start up the React Bookstore demo app and open it in your browser.

2. Open the Developer Tools window in your browser and click the Components tab. You'll see a list of the components that make up the React Bookstore.

3. Click the root component (App) in the component tree view. App's props and hooks will show up on the right side of the DevTools window.

4. Notice that App currently has two state hooks. The first one displayed is the state of the cart. The second one is the state of the products list.

HOOKS AND STATE

Because of the way React handles multiple state hooks in a function, the only way to tell the two hooks in React Bookstore apart is by the order in which they appear and the data within them. In a simple application, this isn't a problem. In larger applications, better ways to organize the state are required.

One way to improve the structure of the state data in React Bookstore is by emulating how state works in class components and using a single state object. For example, the App component currently contains two calls to `useState`—one to create the `products` state, and one to create the `inCart` state. To combine these into a single tree, you can use the following statement:

```
const [state,setState] = useState({products:[],inCart:[]});
```

With this done, you can access `state.products` and `state.inCart`, and you can modify your state data by calling the `setState` function.

---

5. Expand the first state hook. When the React Bookstore first loads, it just contains an empty array.

6. In the browser window, click the **Add to Cart** button underneath one of the products to add the product to the cart.

7. Notice that a new item is added to the first state array.

8. Double-click the value of the item you just added to the `inCart` state. It will become editable.

9. Change the number to any number between 0 and 99. The product corresponding to that number will appear in the cart.

10. Try using a number that's higher than 99 or lower than 0. The result will be an error, as shown in Figure 5-12.

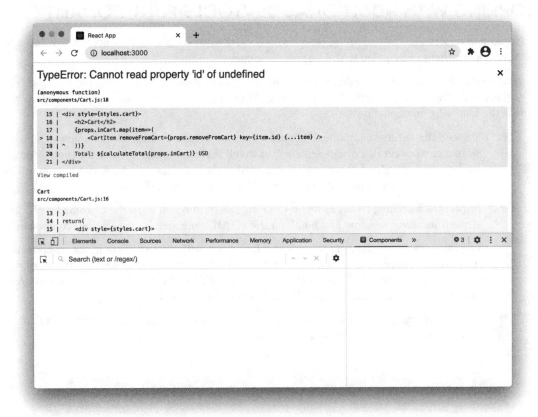

FIGURE 5-12: Attempting to add an out-of-range ID to the cart

11. Click your browser's refresh button to restore the default state.

12. Try adding a non-numeric character to the inCart array. This will also result in an error.

13. Change a value inside the first object in the product state array and see how it changes in the browser window.

14. Click the ProductList component in the component tree view. Notice how the state hook inside App becomes props inside ProductList.

15. Click the first Product component in the component tree view, and notice that it receives a single object (one product) from the ProductList component.

16. See how many different ways you can break the application by changing the data contained within or passed to a component, and think about how you might modify the application to prevent the possibility of this error happening.

WORKING WITH ADDITIONAL DEVTOOLS FUNCTIONALITY

In addition to viewing and inspecting component data, the DevTools Components window has a few other options that can help you with an app's components.

Look at the icons in the upper-right corner of the component data window. Hovering over each one of these will give you a description of its purpose. As of this writing, there are four icons, which provide the following functionality:

➤   Suspend the selected component. Suspense is a new feature in React which allows you to wrap a component in a `Suspense` element to tell that component to wait for some code to be loaded. If a highlighted component is wrapped in the `Suspense` element, this button in Dev-Tools will cause a component to go into this waiting (suspended) state.

➤   Inspect the matching DOM element. Clicking this button will open the Chrome DevTools element inspector window and highlight the HTML generated by the selected component.

➤   Log this component data to the console. This option will cause the data in the component data inspection window to be output to the JavaScript console. After clicking this button, switch to the Console in Chrome DevTools and you'll see the data for the selected component under a link titled [**Click to expand**], as shown in Figure 5-13.

➤   View source for this element. This option will take you to the JavaScript source file that creates the element, such as the function or class that defines the component.

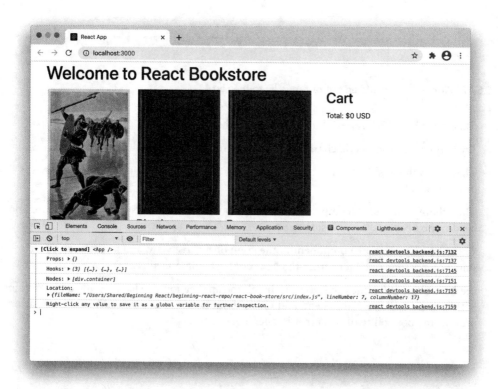

FIGURE 5-13: Logging component data to the console

React DevTools is a powerful tool for quickly viewing a list of the React components in your application and drilling down into them to see their state and props. Being able to access the inner data of components as they run in the browser is the first step in being able to fix bugs and improve your components.

PROFILING

The React DevTools Profiler tab gives you information about the performance of a React application. To use it, start by recording or importing a usage session that you wish to analyze.

1. Click the **Start Profiling** icon in the upper-left corner of the Profiler, which will turn into a red **Stop Profiling** icon to indicate that recording is in progress.

2. Interact with the application in the browser window. Click buttons, fill out and submit any forms, and so forth.

3. Click the red **Stop Profiling** icon.

Once you've recorded some Profiler data, you can switch to the Flamegraph tab to see how your components render. The Flamegraph chart is shown in Figure 5-14.

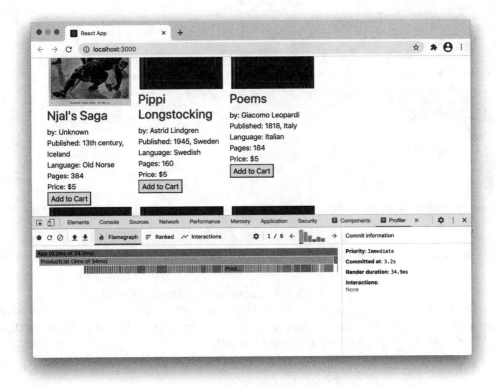

FIGURE 5-14: The Flamegraph chart

For each time you did something while profiling the app that caused a state change (and therefore a re-rendering of the UI), there will be a separate Flamegraph chart.

You can navigate through each rendering by clicking items in the bar graph in the upper right of the Flamegraph window or by clicking the arrows to the left and right of the bar graph.

The Ranked chart shows each of the components that rendered during your profiling, in order of how long they took to render. In our React Bookstore app, the component that takes the longest to render, by far, is `ProductList`, as shown in Figure 5-15.

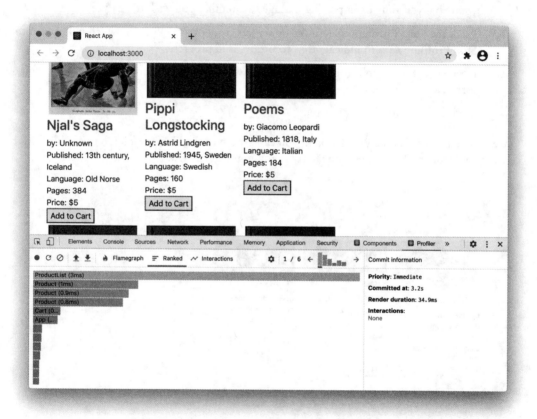

FIGURE 5-15: Viewing the Ranked chart

It's pretty easy to see `ProductList` is the slowest component—each rendering of `ProductList` requires 100 `Product` components to be rendered. There are several ways to optimize this. The most effective ways involve rendering fewer components. For example, you could require the user to click a "View More" button after the first batch of books is displayed.

Another way is to use a technique called *list virtualization* or *windowing*. List virtualization optimizes long lists by only rendering a small subset of the list at a time.

The simplest technique for optimizing the `ProductList` component is to use memoization. Since the `ProductList` component always renders the same data when given the same props, this data can all be cached by React and re-rendering can be minimized.

Figure 5-16 shows the Ranked chart after wrapping the `ProductList` and `Product` components in the `React.memo` function.

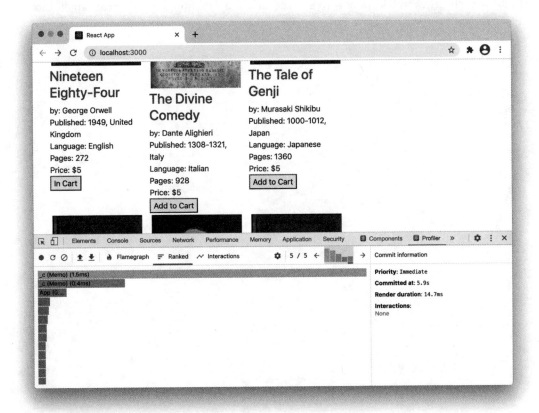

FIGURE 5-16: Ranked chart after optimizing

SUMMARY

Inspecting and optimizing your code are critical and ongoing processes in any software development project. React DevTools is a powerful tool for looking inside your React user interfaces while they're running and for testing the performance of individual components as well as an entire React app.

In this chapter, you learned:

➤ How to access React DevTools.

➤ How to navigate and search the DevTools component tree.

➤ How to filter components in the DevTools tree.

➤ How to modify component data in DevTools.

➤ How to inspect components in DevTools.

➤ How to use the DevTools Profiler to analyze component performance.

In the next chapter, you'll learn how to manage data and data flow within a React application.

React Data Flow

Data, and moving data between the different parts of an application, is a critical piece of any interactive user interface. In this chapter, you'll learn:

- ➤ What one-way data flow means.
- ➤ The benefits of one-way data flow.
- ➤ How to initialize state in a React user interface.
- ➤ How to decide where the state should "live."
- ➤ How to decide what data should be in state.
- ➤ Methods for updating state.
- ➤ How and why to treat state as immutable.
- ➤ How to pass data between components.
- ➤ The value of "shallow" copying and merging.
- ➤ How to validate incoming props with `PropTypes`.
- ➤ How and why to provide default props.
- ➤ New JavaScript syntax for working with props and state.
- ➤ How to convert between function and class components.

ONE-WAY DATA FLOW

One of the defining characteristics of React that distinguishes it from most other front-end UI libraries is its use of *one-way data flow*, also known as *unidirectional data flow*. One-way data flow means that all of the data in a React application flows from parent components to child components. Another common way to describe the flow of data in React is "Data flows down (or downstream), and events flow up (or upstream)."

While one-way data flow eliminates a common cause of complexity and errors in user interfaces, it can also create confusion and frustration unless you fully understand the ins and outs of using it to your advantage. In this chapter, I'll take a step-by-step and thorough approach, with plenty of example code, to covering everything you need to know about data flow within React, using both class components and function components.

Understanding One-Way Data Flow

Figure 6-1 illustrates how unidirectional data flow works.

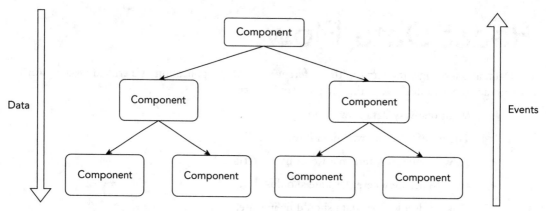

FIGURE 6-1: Unidirectional data flow

Unidirectional data flow doesn't mean that child components can't send data to parent components. Sending data from child components (for example, an input form) to parent components (for example, the form containing the input) is a critical part of interactivity. However, one-way data flow does mean that the way you send data from a child component to a parent component or between sibling components is different from how you pass data from a parent to a child.

To understand one-way data flow, it's helpful to look at an example of two-way data flow. To use two-way binding in Angular, you can use a combination of brackets, like this:

```
<search-form [(term)]="searchTerm"></search-form>
```

Assuming that the preceding code causes a search form to be rendered, the combination of square brackets and parentheses indicate that the searchTerm variable should be passed into the component represented by the search-form element (downstream data flow) and that when the value of the search term changes within the component represented by the search-form element, the value of the searchTerm variable should be updated (upstream data flow).

In React, passing data downstream is done using props, like this:

```
<SearchForm term={searchTerm} />
```

However, because of unidirectional data flow, updating the value of the searchTerm variable from within the SearchForm component requires an event to be triggered. In function components, the event that allows you to pass data upstream is created when you use the useState hook.

Before we get to how that works, let's look briefly at why React uses one-way data flow and the benefits of it.

Why One-Way Data Flow?

Two-way data flow, also known as bidirectional data flow, where a component's data can be modified by its parent and changes within the component can directly affect data in the parent, is convenient. However, it also increases the complexity of a user interface, and this, in turn, increases the potential for errors.

Figure 6-2 shows an example of a user interface that makes use of two-way data flow. Notice that there are multiple ways for data in the model to be changed, and the controller is required in order to manage changes.

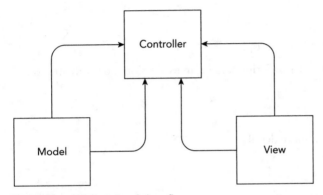

FIGURE 6-2: Bidirectional data flow

In bidirectional data flow, it's not possible to tell whether the view was updated by the user interacting with the view or by the data in the model changing.

Figure 6-3 shows a diagram of one-way data flow in a user interface. The only way that a view (what's displayed in the browser) can be changed is by changing the data in the model (which is the `state` object in React).

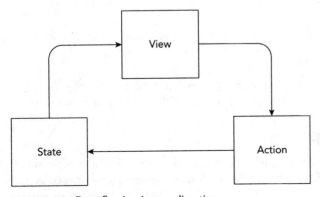

FIGURE 6-3: Data flowing in one direction

A view in unidirectional data flow can be expressed as a simple function:

```
V = function(data)
```

If you want to test whether a piece of data in unidirectional data flow is being properly updated, or test that the change to a variable in unidirectional data flow has the intended consequences, there's only one thing to test: whether changing the state of the application modifies the view as expected.

PROPS

Props in React are the primary way that data is shared between parent components and child components. To create a prop, simply give a React custom element an attribute, using the `name=value` format. Inside the component instance created by that element, the attribute will become a property of the `props` object.

Here are some key points about props:

➤ A component can receive any number of props.

➤ A prop's value can be of any type of JavaScript data or an expression that evaluates to a value or function.

➤ Props are read-only.

Let's take a look at each of these points in more detail.

Components Receive Props

When you write a JSX element in React, the attributes that you give an element are passed to the component as properties in an object. For example, consider this JSX element:

```
<Taco meat="chicken" produce={[cabbage,radish,cilantro]} sauce="hot" />
```

If `Taco` is a function component, this element is the same as the following JavaScript function call:

```
Taco({meat:"chicken",produce:[cabbage,radish,cilantro],sauce:"hot"});
```

Inside the `Taco` function's header, the object passed to the function is given the name `props`, which is how you can access it inside of the function:

```
function Taco(props){
  return (<p>Your {props.sauce} {props.meat} taco will be ready shortly.</p>
}
export default Taco;
```

Because `props` is a JavaScript object, you can have as many or as few properties in the prop object as you need, and there's no requirement that each prop be passed each time you use a component.

Props Can Be Any Data Type

The props you pass to a component can be any type of JavaScript data, including any of the six primitive data types (undefined, Boolean, Number, String, BigInt, and Symbol) as well as objects, functions, arrays, and even `null`.

Because of JSX's ability to include JavaScript expressions through the use of curly braces, the data passed to a component through the `props` object can be determined through the use of a variable or any JavaScript expression or function call.

Props Are Read-Only

Once data has been passed to a component using props, that data is treated as immutable. This means that although a component receives props, once those props are values inside the component, your component can't change them.

This is the strictest rule in React: a component must act like a pure function with regard to its props.

The reason for this rule is that React only re-renders components in response to state changes. Props are the mechanism for updating components according to state changes. If you were to change the value of a prop inside a component, it would cause the internal data of your component to be out of sync with what's displayed in your browser and the value of the prop would be reset by the parent component with the next render. In other words: changing props inside a component won't have the effect that you want.

If you attempt to change the value of a prop, you'll get an error. However, the problem with mutating props can be illustrated by looking at what happens when you change any variable inside a component without triggering a re-render.

In Listing 6-1, a stateful variable is passed as a prop from a parent component (`App`) to a child component (`PropsMutator`). Inside `PropsMutator`, a local variable is created to hold the value of the prop. This local variable is also used inside the `return` statement.

A function called `changeProp` increments the value of the local copy of the prop and then logs it to the console.

LISTING 6-1: Changing local variables doesn't update the view

```
import {useState} from 'react';

function App(){
    const [theNumber,setTheNumber] = useState(0);
    return (
        <PropsMutator theNumber = {theNumber} setTheNumber = {setTheNumber} />
    )
}

function PropsMutator(props){
  let myNumber = props.theNumber;

  const changeProp = ()=>{
    myNumber = myNumber + 1;
      console.log("my number is: " + myNumber);
    }

  return (
      <>
```

continues

LISTING 6-1 *(continued)*

```
            <h1>My number is: {myNumber}</h1>
            <h1>props.theNumber is: {props.theNumber}</h1>
            <button onClick = {changeProp}>change myNumber</button><br />
            <button onClick={()=>{props.setTheNumber(props.theNumber + 1)}}>
              use setTheNumber
            </button>
        </>
    )
}

export default App;
```

Figure 6-4 shows what happens when you run this component and click the **change myNumber** button several times.

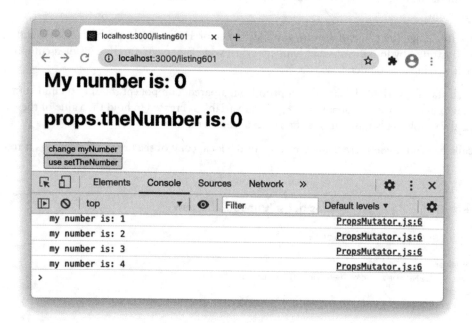

FIGURE 6-4: Changing local variables doesn't update the view

The second button in Listing 6-1 shows the correct way to modify a value that will be used in the `return` method. In this button, we call a state change function, `setTheNumber` (which is passed to the component from its parent) and pass in a new value. The state change function modifies the state variable and then re-renders, which causes the new value to be passed into the child component.

Figure 6-5 shows the result of clicking the **change myNumber** button several times, followed by clicking the **use setTheNumber** button, followed by clicking **change myNumber** again.

Make sure that you understand this example before moving on to the next section, because if you see what's happening in Figure 6-5, the distinction between props and state will make perfect sense and you'll have a much better idea of when to use each.

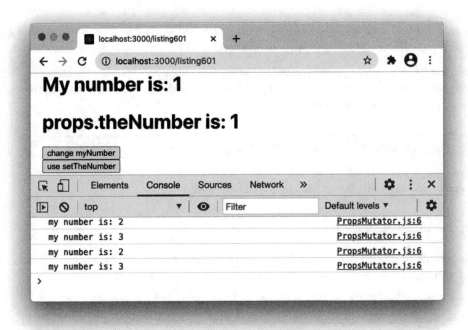

FIGURE 6-5: Local variable and props confusion

Validating Incoming Props with PropTypes

When you invoke a JavaScript function and pass in arguments, the function doesn't care what type of data the arguments are, whether they're passed in at all, or whether more or fewer arguments are passed in than the function defines. The same things are true with props that you pass from a parent component to a child component.

For programs to operate correctly, however, it often is important that the props that are passed to a component are the same type of data that the component is expecting. For example, if your component expects a prop called itemPrice to be a number, an error may occur if a parent component passes itemPrice as an object.

React programmers (and programmers in general) must account for the possibility of incorrect data types being passed to any function that receives arguments. But, it's not always easy to figure out and detect possible data type problems with a dynamically typed language such as JavaScript.

To help with keeping track of a component's expected input and finding possible problems, we can use a tool called *PropTypes*.

What Is PropTypes?

PropTypes is a tool for type checking and documenting props in React components. For each prop in your component, you can specify rules that the value coming into the prop will be tested against. If the prop value doesn't pass those rules, a message will be displayed in the JavaScript console in your browser.

PropTypes only displays these warning messages when you're using the development version of React. Once your app is deployed and using the production version of React, PropTypes is silent.

For example, the `WelcomeMessage` component in Listing 6-2 uses a prop called `firstName` to display a customized header message. You can tell from looking at the code in this component that the value of the `firstName` prop should be a string.

LISTING 6-2: A component that uses a string prop

```
function WelcomeMessage(props){
  return (<p>Welcome back, {props.firstName}!</p>);
}

export default WelcomeMessage;
```

By now, you should be able to guess what the output of this component will be when you pass a first name into it through an element like the following:

```
<WelcomeMessage firstName = "Grover" />
```

But, what happens if you pass something that's not a string into the `firstName` prop? The following element passes an array into the `firstName` prop:

```
<WelcomeMessage firstName = {['Jimmy','Joe']} />
```

The result may not be what you'd expect, as shown in Figure 6-6.

React doesn't consider this case to be an error, so it may not be obvious at first what the cause of the unexpected output is. This is especially true in components that make use of many different props.

Listing 6-3 shows how you can use PropTypes to validate this prop.

LISTING 6-3: Validating that a prop is a string

```
import PropTypes from 'prop-types';

function WelcomeMessage(props){
  return (<p>Welcome back, {props.firstName}!</p>);
}

WelcomeMessage.propTypes = {
  firstName:PropTypes.string
}

export default WelcomeMessage;
```

FIGURE 6-6: Passing the wrong prop type

With the PropType specified for `firstName`, when `WelcomeMessage` receives a value of `firstName` that isn't a string, a warning message will be displayed in the console, as shown in Figure 6-7.

Use of PropTypes in React is optional, and whether you use it or not, it won't fix errors by itself. It also won't cause your application to not compile if a prop fails its checks. It's purely a development tool. However, it's a great way to catch bugs in your components and to document your components. Getting into the habit of using PropTypes will improve your React components and make it easier for other programmers who may use your component in the future to know what data it requires.

Getting Started with PropTypes

PropTypes is not part of the core React library. To use it, you first have to install it. If you boot-strapped your app with Create React App, it's already been installed for you. Otherwise, you can install it by running the following command from the root of your project:

```
npm install prop-types --save
```

Once PropTypes is installed, you'll need to include the PropTypes library into each component where you use it. At the beginning of the file containing your component, use the following import:

```
import PropTypes from 'prop-types;
```

Once imported, PropTypes works the same with both function and class components, but where you place the PropTypes may differ.

FIGURE 6-7: PropTypes displaying a warning

To use PropTypes, you just need to add a property called `propTypes` to the component. Note that the PropTypes library, which contains different ways of validating props, starts with a capital P. The property that you add to your component to cause it to do type checking starts with a lowercase p.

The `propTypes` property is a static property, meaning it operates at the component level, not the component instance. In class components, this means that you can use the static keyword to put your `propTypes` property in the body of your class, as shown in Listing 6-4.

LISTING 6-4: PropTypes inside a component's body

```
import PropTypes from 'prop-types';
import {Component} from 'react';

class WelcomeMessage extends Component {

  static propTypes = {
    firstName: PropTypes.string
  }

  render(){
    return(<h1>Welcome, {this.props.firstName}!</h1>);
  }
}

export default WelcomeMessage;
```

You can also add the `propTypes` object into your class component by putting it outside of the class body, as shown in Listing 6-5.

LISTING 6-5: Putting propTypes outside the class body

```
import PropTypes from 'prop-types';
import {Component} from 'react';

class WelcomeMessage extends Component {

  render(){
    return(<h1>Welcome, {this.props.firstName}!</h1>);
  }
}

WelcomeMessage.propTypes = {
  firstName: PropTypes.string
}

export default WelcomeMessage;
```

In function components, the `propTypes` object always goes outside of the function body, as shown in Listing 6-6.

LISTING 6-6: Using propTypes with a function component

```
import PropTypes from 'prop-types';

function MyComponent(props){
  return (<p>The value is {props.itemValue}</p>);
}

MyComponent.propTypes = {
  itemValue: PropTypes.number
}

export default MyComponent;
```

What Can PropTypes Validate?

PropTypes can perform a wide variety of checks on a component's props, including the data type (as you've seen), whether required props are passed, the shape of properties passed as objects, and more. In this section, I'll explain and demonstrate all of the different validation rules contained in PropTypes.

Validating Data Type

You've already seen how to check whether a prop is one of JavaScript's data types. The validators for JavaScript types are:

➤   `PropTypes.array`

➤ PropTypes.bool

➤ PropTypes.func

➤ PropTypes.number

➤ PropTypes.object

➤ PropTypes.string

➤ PropTypes.symbol

The purpose of each of these should be self-evident, but note that a couple of the validators, bool and func, have names that are different from the names of the JavaScript data types.

When you use one of these data type validators by itself, PropTypes will treat the prop as optional. In other words, a missing prop won't trigger a PropType warning message by default.

Validating Required Props

If a component requires a prop to be passed to it, you can indicate to PropTypes that a prop is required by appending the isRequired validator to the data type validator, as shown in Listing 6-7.

LISTING 6-7: Appending the isRequired validator

```
MyComponent.propTypes = {
  firstName: PropTypes.string.isRequired,
  middleName: PropTypes.string,
  lastName: PropTypes.string.isRequired
}
```

Beyond whether a prop exists and is of a particular data type, you can also do checks that are specific to how the prop data functions within React.

Validating Nodes

The node validator checks whether the prop's value is something that can be rendered. React calls anything that can be rendered in a component a *node*. The things that can be rendered in a component are numbers, strings, elements, and arrays containing numbers, strings, or elements:

```
userMessage: PropTypes.node
```

The node validator is useful in cases where you may not care whether the value of the prop is a string or number or element, but you do care that it can be rendered.

If one of your components does try to render a prop that isn't a node, it will cause your program to crash and display an error in the browser as well as in the console even if you're not using PropTypes. You can view this default error message by trying to render a prop value that isn't a number, string, element, or an array of renderable data. For example, the component in Listing 6-8 renders the values passed into the url and linkName props.

LISTING 6-:8 Trying to render a non-node value

```
function SiteLink(props) {
  return (
    <a href={props.url}>{props.linkName}</a>
  );
}

export default SiteLink;
```

The following element invokes the `SiteLink` function component, passing in an object as
the `linkName`:

```
<SiteLink url="http://example.com" linkName={{name:'Example'}} />
```

Figure 6-8 shows the error message that displays when you try to render an object. Notice that the
error message doesn't specify which prop caused the error, just that there was one and the element in
which it occurred.

FIGURE 6-8: The not-renderable error message

You can use `PropTypes.node` to find out which prop caused the error.

Listing 6-9 shows how to use `PropTypes.node` to validate that `props.linkName` can be rendered, and Figure 6-9 shows that attempting to render an object still causes the same error messages to be displayed, but PropTypes displays which prop caused the error.

LISTING 6-9: Using PropTypes.node

```
import PropTypes from 'prop-types';

function SiteLink(props) {
  return (
    <a href="{props.url}">{props.linkName}</a>
  );
}

SiteLink.propTypes = {
  linkName: PropTypes.node
}

export default SiteLink;
```

FIGURE 6-9: PropTypes tell which attribute caused the error

In order to properly handle a case where an object value may be passed into a prop that will be rendered, you can use error boundaries, which you'll learn about in Chapter 13.

Validating React Elements

If you want to make sure that a prop is a React element, you can use `PropTypes.element`. You might use the element validator to test whether the `children` prop contains an element, as shown in Listing 6-10.

LISTING 6-10: Validating React elements

```
import PropTypes from 'prop-types';

function BorderBox(props){
  return(
    <div style={{border:"1px solid black"}}>{props.children}</div>
  )
}

BorderBox.propTypes = {
  children: PropTypes.element.isRequired
}

export default BorderBox;
```

Here's an example of a use of the `BorderBox` element defined in Listing 6-10 that will cause the `PropType.element` validation to fail:

```
<BorderBox>
  <p>The first paragraph</p>
  <p>The second paragraph</p>
</BorderBox>
```

Figure 6-10 shows the warning message that will be displayed in the preceding case.

Element Type Validation

If you want to test whether the prop value is a React element type, you can use `elementType`, as shown in Listing 6-11.

LISTING 6-11: Using the elementType validator

```
FamilyTree.propTypes = {
  pet: PropTypes.elementType
}
```

The difference between the `element` validator and the `elementType` validator is that the `element` validator checks for a rendered element (for example, `<MyComponent />`), while the `elementType` validator checks for an unrendered element (for example, `MyComponent`).

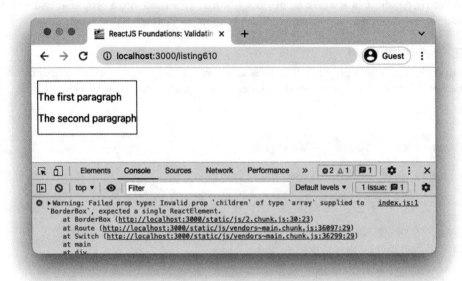

FIGURE 6-10: Failing PropTypes.element validation

JavaScript Class Validation

`PropTypes.instanceOf` tests that the supplied prop is an instance of a particular JavaScript class (meaning that it has this class in its prototype chain). To use it, you can use the `instanceOf` validator, as shown in Listing 6-12. The `instanceOf` validator uses the JavaScript `instanceOf` operator.

LISTING 6-12: Validating that a prop is an instance of a class

```
import {Component} from 'react';
import {PropTypes} from 'prop-types';
import Person from './Person';

class FamilyTree extends Component {
    render(){
        return(
            <p>{this.props.father.firstName}</p>
        )
    }
}

FamilyTree.propTypes = {
    father: PropTypes.instanceOf(Person)
}

export default FamilyTree;
```

Limiting Props to Certain Values or Types

`PropTypes.oneOf` is a function that tests whether the value of a prop is one of the specific items in a list. To use it, pass an array of possible values into the `oneOf` function, as shown in Listing 6-13.

LISTING 6-13: Using PropTypes.oneOf

```
import PropTypes from 'prop-types';

function DisplayPrimaryColor(props){
  return(
    <p>You picked: {props.primaryColor}</p>
  )
}

DisplayPrimaryColor.propTypes = {
  primaryColor:PropTypes.oneOf(['red','yellow','blue'])
}

export default DisplayPrimaryColor;
```

With the `oneOfType` validator, you can check whether the value of a prop is one of a list of data types. To use it, pass an array containing the allowed data types, using names of PropTypes's data type validators:

```
Component.propTypes = {
  myProp:PropTypes.oneOfType([
    PropTypes.bool,
    PropTypes.string,
    PropTypes.number
  ])
}
```

Additional Validators

`PropTypes.arrayOf` tests that the prop is an array in which each of the elements matches a provided type:

```
MyComponent.propTypes = {
  students: PropType.arrayOf(
    PropTypes.instanceOf(Person)
  )
}
```

`PropTypes.objectOf` tests that the prop is an object in which each of the properties of the object match a provided type:

```
MyComponent.propTypes = {
  scores: PropTypes.objectOf(
    PropTypes.number
  )
}
```

`PropTypes.shape` tests whether a prop value is an object containing specific properties:

```
MyComponent.propTypes = {
  userData: PropTypes.shape({
    id: PropTypes.number,
    fullname: PropTypes.string,
    birthdate: PropTypes.instanceOf(Date),
    isAdmin: PropTypes.bool
  })
}
```

`PropTypes.exact` performs a strict object match on the prop, meaning that it must include only the specified properties, each of which must pass its validation:

```
MyComponent.propTypes = {
  toDoItem: PropTypes.exact({
    description: PropTypes.string,
    isFinished: PropTypes.bool
  })
}
```

Creating Custom PropTypes

If what you want to validate isn't covered by any of the built-in validators, you can create your own. A custom validator is a function that will automatically receive three arguments when it's used:

➤ An object containing all of the props received by the component.

➤ The prop being tested.

➤ The name of the component.

In a custom prop, you can write the `Error` object that is returned when the validation fails.

For example, you might write a custom validator to check whether a prop is a 10-digit phone number, as shown in Listing 6-14.

LISTING 6-14: Using a custom validator to test for a phone number

```
import PropTypes from 'prop-types';

function Contact(props){
    return(
        <li>{props.fullName}: {props.phone}</li>
    )
}

const isPhoneNumber = function(props, propName, componentName) {
const regex = /^(\+\d{1,2}\s)?\(?\d{3}\)?[\s.-]\d{3}[\s.-]\d{4}$/;

if (!regex.test(props[propName])) {
    return new Error(`Invalid prop ${propName} passed to ${componentName}.
Expected a phone number.`);
}
```

```
}

Contact.propTypes = {
  fullName: PropTypes.string,
  phone: isPhoneNumber,
}

export default Contact;
```

Figure 6-11 shows the browser console returning the custom error message when this PropType fails.

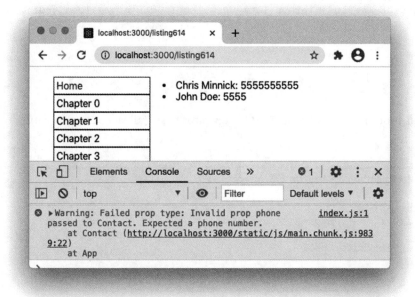

FIGURE 6-11: A custom PropType validator failing

Default Props

PropTypes can tell you when a component doesn't receive a prop or when it receives the wrong data type, but using PropTypes by itself won't fix any of the problems it reveals. To solve problems revealed by PropTypes, you often need to look at the parent component that's passing incorrect data to the component. But, ideally, each component in a React app should be able to function in some capacity without crashing your entire user interface, even if something unexpected happens in a parent component. This is where setting default values for props comes in.

For example, the StoresNearYou component in Listing 6-15 renders a Map component and a StoreList component based on location data passed into it as props.latitude and props.longitude. Many things can go wrong with geolocation, however, and it's possible that the parent component won't be able to pass this required data. The result is that the values passed to the Map and StoreList components would be invalid and could even result in the app crashing.

LISTING 6-15: A component without default props

```
import Map from './Map';
import StoreList from './StoreList';

function StoresNearYou(props){
  return(
    <>
      <div id="map-container">
        <Map latitude={props.latitude} longitude={props.longitude} />
      </div>
      <div id="store-list">
        <StoreList latitude={props.latitude} longitude={props.longitude} />
      </div>
    </>
  )
}

export default StoresNearYou;
```

One way to solve this problem is by using the || (OR) operator to set fallback values for latitude and longitude, as shown in Listing 6-16.

LISTING 6-16: Setting defaults with the OR operator

```
import Map from './Map';
import StoreList from './StoreList';

function StoresNearYou(props){
  return(
    <>
      <div id="map-container">
        <Map
          latitude={props.latitude || "37.3230"}
          longitude={props.longitude || "122.0322"}
        />
      </div>
      <div id="store-list">
        <StoreList
          latitude={props.latitude || "37.3230"}
          longitude={props.longitude || "122.0322"}
        />
      </div>
    </>
  )
}

export default StoresNearYou;
```

However, this can quickly get messy and confusing in larger components involving many different props, and using inline default values like this creates duplication of effort.

The next improvement to this code might be to separate the properties in the props object into variables outside of the return statement and set the default values just once, as shown in Listing 6-17.

LISTING 6-17: Destructuring props and setting defaults

```
import Map from './Map';
import StoreList from './StoreList';

function StoresNearYou(props){
  const latitude = props.latitude || "37.3230";
  const longitude = props.longitude || "122.0322";

  return(
    <>
      <div id="map-container">
        <Map
          latitude={latitude}
          longitude={longitude}
        />
      </div>
      <div id="store-list">
        <StoreList
          latitude={latitude}
          longitude={longitude}
        />
      </div>
    </>
  )
}

export default StoresNearYou;
```

This is a great improvement in terms of the cleanliness of the code, but it does introduce additional variables, perhaps unnecessarily. We can do better.

React components have a defaultProps object that can be used to set values for props that aren't passed into a component. Like propTypes, defaultProps is a property of the component, rather than of an instance of the component. Therefore, to set defaultProps in a class component, you can either define it inside the component by using the static keyword, or set it outside of the component.

Listing 6-18 shows how to set defaultProps as a static property, and Listing 6-19 shows how to set it outside of the class definition.

LISTING 6 18: Setting defaultProps as a static property

```
import {Component} from 'react';

class StoresNearYou extends Component{
```

continues

LISTING 6-18 *(continued)*

```
static defaultProps = {
  latitude: "37.3230",
  longitude: "122.0322"
}

render(){
  return(
    <>
      <div id="map-container">
        <Map
          latitude={this.props.latitude}
          longitude={this.props.longitude}
        />
      </div>
      <div id="store-list">
        <StoreList
          latitude={this.props.latitude}
          longitude={this.props.longitude}
        />
      </div>
    </>
  )
}
}

export default StoresNearYou;
```

LISTING 6-19: Setting defaultProps outside of the component body

```
import {Component} from 'react';

class StoresNearYou extends Component{

  render(){
    return(
      <>
        <div id="map-container">
          <Map
            latitude={this.props.latitude}
            longitude={this.props.longitude}
          />
        </div>
        <div id="store-list">
          <StoreList
            latitude={this.props.latitude}
            longitude={this.props.longitude}
          />
        </div>
      </>
    )
```

```
    }
  }

StoresNearYou.defaultProps = {
  latitude: "37.3230",
  longitude: "122.0322"
}

export default StoresNearYou;
```

You can set `defaultProps` in function components outside of the function body, as shown in Listing 6-20.

LISTING 6-20: Setting defaultProps for a function component

```
function StoresNearYou(props) {
  return (
    <>
      <div id="map-container">
        <Map latitude={props.latitude} longitude={props.longitude} />
      </div>
      <div id="store-list">
        <StoreList latitude={props.latitude} longitude={props.longitude} />
      </div>
    </>
  )
}

StoresNearYou.defaultProps = {
  latitude: "37.3230",
  longitude: "122.0322"
}

export default StoresNearYou;
```

With the `defaultProps` property set, `StoresNearYou` will use the default values for `props.latitude` and `props.longitude` if it's invoked without passing props, or if it's rendered before it receives props (which can often happen in cases where a component depends on the result of an asynchronous function).

REACT STATE

If all you want to do is render a static component that never changes, all you need is props. However, the real value of React is in how it enables interactive web applications and manages updates to components in response to input.

The key to React's ability to be reactive is the concept and object called *state*.

What Is `state`?

In a React component, `state` is an object containing a set of properties that may change over the lifetime of the component. Changes to the properties in the `state` object control the behavior and updating of the component.

Initializing `state`

Initializing state is the process of defining the properties of the `state` object and setting their initial values. The initial values are the values that will be used for the first rendering of a component.

Initializing `state` in Class Components

Prior to the introduction of React Hooks, class components were the only place where you could use state. Hooks made it possible to use state in function components, but if you want to take advantage of the full power of React, including all of the lifecycle methods, classes are still the best (and in some cases the only) way to go.

There are a few important rules about initializing the state of a class component:

1.   The `state` object of a class component can have as many or as few properties as you need.

2.   Not all class components need to have state.

3.   If your component does make use of state, you must initialize it.

4.   The `constructor` function is the only place where you can change state directly.

In a class component, the most common way to initialize the `state` object is in the `constructor` function, as shown in Listing 6-21.

LISTING 6-21: Initializing state in a class component

```
import {Component} from 'react'

class NewsFeed extends Component {

  constructor(props) {
    super(props);
    this.state = {
      date: new Date(),
      headlines: []
    }
  }
  render() {
    return(
      <>
        <h1>Headlines for {this.state.date.toLocaleString()}</h1>
        ...
```

```
        </>
      )
    }
  }
}

export default NewsFeed;
```

The reason for initializing the `state` object in the `constructor` function is that it's the first method to be called when you create an instance of a component.

It is possible to initialize the `state` object without a `constructor` function by using a class property, which is also known as a *public instance field*, or a *public field*. A public field works the same as defining a property of the class in the `constructor`, and the resulting property will exist in every instance of the class that's created. Listing 6-22 shows how to set the initial state with a class property.

LISTING 6-22: Initializing state using the class property

```
import {Component} from 'react'

class NewsFeed extends Component {

  state = {
    date: new Date(),
    headlines: []
  }

  render(){
    return(
      <>
        <h1>Headlines for {this.state.date.toLocaleString()}</h1>
        ...
      </>
    )
  }
}

export default NewsFeed;
```

Initializing State in Function Components

In JavaScript functions, data doesn't persist between invocations of the function. Prior to React Hooks, React function components also had no way to preserve data between calls. For this reason, function components were previously known as *stateless components*.

With React Hooks, function components can *hook into* functionality of React, including the `state` object. The hook that makes this possible is `useState`.

The first time a function component containing the `useState` function is rendered, `useState` creates a stateful variable and a function for setting that variable. For all subsequent renders of the component, `useState` makes use of the variable created on that first render.

The first time a function component renders, useState serves the same purpose as initializing the state object in the constructor or using a public field in a class component.

Listing 6-23 shows how to initialize a stateful variable in a function component.

LISTING 6-23: Initializing state in a function component

```
import {useState} from 'react'

function NewsFeed(props) {

const [date,setDate] = useState(new Date());
const [headlines,setHeadlines] = useState([]);

  return(
    <>
      <h1>Headlines for {date.toLocaleString()}</h1>
      ...
    </>
  )
}

export default NewsFeed;
```

Notice that Listing 6-23 includes two calls to useState. This is the recommended way to manage state with React Hooks—for each stateful variable, you can make a call to useState and return the new stateful variable and the function for updating that variable.

Another way to initialize state in a function component is shown in Listing 6-24.

LISTING 6-24: Another approach to initializing state in a function component

```
import {useState} from 'react'

function NewsFeed(props) {

const [state,setState] = useState({date:new Date(),headlines:[]});

  return(
    <>
      <h1>Headlines for {state.date.toLocaleString()}</h1>
      ...
    </>
  )
}

export default NewsFeed;
```

While the method of managing state shown in Listing 6-24 does have the advantage of more closely simulating how class components have just a single state object, having multiple variables gives you more flexibility with regard to splitting your component into smaller components and for memoization.

> ### setSTATE IS NOT setSTATE
>
> Another important point to keep in mind (which we'll discuss in more detail shortly) is that the function returned by useState (which I named setState in Listing 6-24) doesn't work the same as a class component's setState function. In short: setState in a class component merges objects, while the setState function returned by useState replaces the value of the stateful variable.

The Difference between state and props

Props and state look similar at first glance:

➤   They're both JavaScript objects.

➤   Changes to each of them cause components to update.

➤   Both are data that are used by a component to generate the HTML output of the component.

The differences between props and state are in their roles.

The basic difference is that the props object is passed to a component by its parent, while state is managed within a component.

To put it another way, props is similar to a function parameter, while state is similar to a local (private) variable defined inside the function. You can pass values from the state of a parent component to a child component (where they become part of the props object), but a component cannot modify the state of its children.

Table 6-1 summarizes the similarities and differences between props and state.

TABLE 6-1: Comparing props and state

	PROPS	STATE
Is it passed from the parent?	Yes	No
Can it change inside a component?	No	Yes
Can it be changed by the parent?	Yes	No
Can it be passed to child components?	Yes	Yes

Updating state

Once the initial state of a component has been set and the component has been rendered, updates to the component (and to its children, if it has any) happen when the state changes.

You might be wondering how React knows that the `state` object has changed. It actually doesn't. The reason that changes to state update components is that all changes to state must be done using a function provided for that purpose. This function updates the state and then triggers a re-render of the component.

The method that you use for updating a component's state depends on whether you're using a class component or a function component.

Updating a Class Component's state with setState

In class components, the `setState` method is the only way to modify the state once it's been initialized. You can use the `setState` method inside any method in a class component except the constructor.

The `setState` method takes an object or a function as its argument and uses this argument to schedule an update of the component's `state` object.

Passing an Object to setState

Listing 6-25 shows a simple example of a class component that initializes a `state` object and then updates it using `setState` each time a button is clicked.

LISTING 6-25: Using setState

```
import {Component} from 'react';

class CounterClass extends Component {
  constructor(props) {
    super(props);
    this.state = {count:0};
    this.increment = this.increment.bind(this);
  }

  increment() {
    this.setState({count: this.state.count + 1});
  }

  render() {
    return (
      <button onClick={this.increment}>{this.state.count}</button>
    )
  }

}
export default CounterClass;
```

This simple counter example demonstrates a basic usage of `setState`. In the `increment` function, I passed a new object containing a new value for the `count` property. If you run this component, you'll see that it works as follows:

➤ Clicking the button triggers the `increment` method in the component.

➤ The increment method calls the `setState` function, passing in a new value for `this` `.state.count`.

➤ Calling `setState` updates the value of `state.count` and then causes the component to re-render.

➤ The new value of `state.count` is displayed on the button.

While this simple example can be fairly easily understood, it doesn't do much to illuminate how `setState` actually functions. For that, we'll need a slightly more complex example with multiple properties in the `state` object.

Merging an Object into state with setState

Listing 6-26 simply adds another `count` property to the component, along with another button and another increment function.

LISTING 6-26: Using setState with multiple state properties

```
import {Component} from 'react';

class CounterClass extends Component {
  constructor(props) {
    super(props);
    this.state = {count1:0, count2:0};
    this.incrementCount1 = this.incrementCount1.bind(this);
    this.incrementCount2 = this.incrementCount2.bind(this);

  }

  incrementCount1() {
    this.setState({count1: this.state.count1 + 1});
  }
  incrementCount2() {
    this.setState({count2: this.state.count2 + 1});
  }

  render() {
    return (
      <>
        <button onClick={this.incrementCount1}>Count 1: {this.state.count1}</button>
        <button onClick={this.incrementCount2}>Count 2: {this.state.count2}</button>
      </>
    )
  }

}
export default CounterClass;
```

If you run the example in Listing 6-26, you'll see that clicking each of the buttons increments the respective property in the `state` object. Notice, though, that each count's increment function only passes the single property that's being modified to `setState` and `setState` only updates the property passed to it.

While the previous example is not particularly thrilling, and the code could be simplified and made considerably more flexible, it demonstrates how the first way to use setState works: when you pass an object into setState, it merges that object with the existing state object.

Calls to setState are Asynchronous

When you call setState, it may not immediately update the state object. Instead, it actually just schedules, or enqueues, an update to the component's state. The reason for this behavior is that it reduces the number of unnecessary component re-renders, which improves performance of the React app.

It's helpful to think of a call to setState as a request, rather than an immediate operation.

For example, if a parent and child component both call setState in response to the same click event, this would cause two re-renders of the component if setState were to update state immediately. Because calls to setState are asynchronous, however, React will wait until both components have called setState before re-rendering.

Why Should You Care that setState Is Asynchronous?

The asynchronous nature of setState is a frequent cause of bugs or unexpected behavior in React. The problem is that if you try to use the state object immediately after calling setState, you may not get the most current state.

In Listing 6-27, I've written a method called incrementTwice that calls setState twice each time the button is clicked. To show the difference between what the expected value of this.state .count is and the new value, the component also increments and logs the value of a property named testCount.

LISTING 6-27: Demonstrating setState's asychronous nature

```
import {Component} from 'react';

class CounterClass extends Component {
  constructor(props){
    super(props);
    this.state = {count:0};
    this.testCount = 0;
    this.incrementTwice = this.incrementTwice.bind(this);
  }

  incrementTwice(){
    this.setState({count: this.state.count + 1});
    this.testCount ++;
    this.setState({count: this.state.count + 1});
    this.testCount ++;
    console.log("Count should be: " + this.testCount);
  }

  render(){
    return(
```

```
        <button onClick={this.incrementTwice}>{this.state.count}</button>
    )
  }

}
export default CounterClass;
```

If you didn't know that setState is asynchronous, you would think that each click of the button would increase the value of state.count by two. But, if you try out the component, you'll discover that it only increments by one. The reason is that the second call to setState happens before state.count has been updated by the first call. It therefore uses the same value of state.count that the first call used and the result is that both calls to setState change the value of state.count to the same number.

Figure 6-12 shows the result of clicking the button in the CounterClass component in Listing 6-27.

FIGURE 6-12: The result of clicking the CounterClass button

To solve this problem, you can pass a function into the setState function, rather than an object, to ensure that setState uses the most up-to-date value for the state object.

Passing a Function into setState

When you pass a function that returns an object into setState, the inner function receives the current state and props of the component and returns an updated state object. This function is called an *updater function*. The updater function variant of setState takes this form:

```
setState((state,props)=>{ return {};}
```

The updater function is guaranteed to receive the latest state and props. For this reason, you should always use an updater function when the new state depends on the current state.

To make it clear that the state received by the updater function is the most current state, it's a common practice to name this parameter `current`. In our increment function, we can use an updater function to update the value of `state.count` like this:

```
setState((current)=>{
  return {count: current.count + 1};
});
```

Listing 6-28 shows how the updater function solves the problem in the `incrementTwice` function from Listing 6-27.

LISTING 6-28: Using the updater function with setState

```
import {Component} from 'react';

class CounterClass extends Component {
  constructor(props){
    super(props);
    this.state = {count:0};
    this.testCount = 0;
    this.incrementTwice = this.incrementTwice.bind(this);
  }

  incrementTwice(){
    this.setState((current)=>{return {count: current.count + 1};});
    this.testCount++;
    this.setState((current)=>{return {count: current.count + 1};});
    this.testCount++;
    console.log("Count should be: " + this.testCount);
  }

  render(){
    return(
      <button onClick={this.incrementTwice}>{this.state.count}</button>
    )
  }

}

export default CounterClass;
```

Figure 6-13 shows the result of clicking the button in Listing 6-28. Notice that the `testCount` property is now in sync with `state.count`.

Updating state with Function Components

When you call the `useState` hook, it returns an array. The first element of the array is a stateful variable. The second element is a setter function.

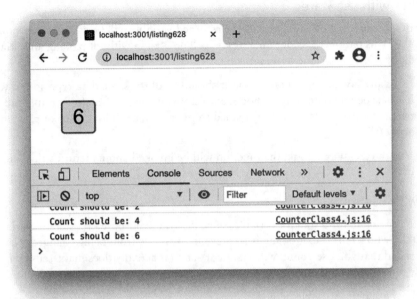

FIGURE 6-13: The fixed counter class

To assign the state variable and the function to separate variables, use array deconstruction. For example, to create a state variable called `counter` and a setter function for changing the value of `counter`, use the following statement:

```
const [counter,setCounter] = useState(0);
```

The variable name can be any valid JavaScript variable name. The function should be the name of the state variable prefixed with "set," although this is just a convention and not enforced by React.

Initializing and updating state in function components is considerably simpler than doing so with class components. Here are a few important things to know about using state in function components and the `useState` hook:

1. The value you pass into `useState` will be the initial value for the stateful variable.

2. Use `const` rather than `let` when creating stateful variables and setter functions.

3. Unlike `setState` in class components, the setter function returned by `useState` replaces the value of the stateful variable with the new value you pass into it, rather than merging it with the current state.

4. After updating the stateful variable, the setter function causes a re-render of the component.

Each of these four points deserves a bit more explanation, so let's take a look at them one by one.

Setting Initial State with useState

The first time a function component calls useState, the returned variable will be assigned the value you pass into useState. This parameter is optional. If you call useState without passing an initial value, the variable will be assigned a value of undefined.

The initial state can be of any JavaScript data type, but it should be of the same data type as you will be setting the variable to inside your component. For example, if you create a stateful variable called products to hold an array of products that will be loaded from an API, the initial value of products should be an empty array ([]).

If you pass a function to the useState hook, the function will be invoked and its return value will be used as the initial state.

Why Use const with useState?

It may seem wrong to use const for a stateful variable, since the whole purpose of a stateful variable is to be changed and the whole purpose of const is to prevent a variable from being changed. Nevertheless, it is recommended that you use const with useState, and it actually does make sense when you think about how functions (and therefore function components) work.

Consider the example of a stateful variable named counter and a setter function called setCounter. Calling setCounter and passing it a new value sets the value of a property in React's state object and then re-renders the component. Unlike class components, where the render method can be called and use the same properties of the class each time, a function starts its life over each time it's invoked.

When React re-renders a function component, the function calls useState again, and useState returns a new variable with the latest state value. So, the setter function doesn't actually modify the variable in the function at all—the function gets a new const each time it's invoked.

Because the whole point of a stateful variable is to trigger a re-render, the only way a stateful variable should be updated is with the setter function returned by useState.

The Setter Function Replaces the State

The function returned by the useState hook replaces the current value of the stateful variable with the value you pass into it. This makes working with stateful variables in functions simpler, but it also introduces some additional complexity, especially when working with more complex state.

State in function components is *immutable*. That is, you can't change it; you can only replace it with a new state. If the new state of a function component depends on the previous state, this creates some interesting problems and coding patterns—especially when the stateful variable's value is an object or array.

To set a stateful variable that's a primitive data type, simply pass the new value to the function:

```
setCounter(4);
```

If the new value depends on the previous value, you should use a function to access the previous state and return the new value:

```
setCounter((prevState)=>{return prevState+1});
```

If your stateful variable contains an object or array, you can replace the value by passing in a new object or array. But, if your new state depends on the old state, you'll need to make a copy of the existing array or object, modify it, and then pass the copy of the array into the setter function.

The copy you make of an object or array can't be just any copy. It needs to be a *shallow copy*. One of the easiest ways to make a shallow copy, which is widely used in React, is by using the spread operator (. . .).

JAVASCRIPT LESSON: SHALLOW COPIES AND THE SPREAD OPERATOR

One of the most useful new tools in JavaScript is the *spread operator*. The spread operator is made up of three periods (. . .) and its job is to expand (or spread) the value of a string, array, or object into separate parts.

To see how the spread operator works, we'll start with a very simple example. The following function accepts three numbers and returns the sum of the numbers:

```
function sum(x,y,z){
   return x+y+z;
}
```

If you have an array of three numbers that you want to find out the sum of, you could invoke the sum function and pass in each element of the array separately, like this:

```
sum(myNumbers[0],myNumbers[1],myNumbers[2]);
```

Or you could just spread the array into its component parts, which accomplishes the same thing:

```
sum(...myNumbers)
```

The spread operator is useful in cases where you want to include all of the elements of an array or object in a new object or array, such as when you're creating a new array or object that's partially made up of an existing one.

In React, the spread operator is commonly used to work with immutable state variables, especially in function components.

When you're working with mutable data in JavaScript and you have an array and you want to add an element to it, you can use the Array.push function, like this:

```
let temperatures = [31,29,35];
temperatures.push[32];
```

The result of these statements is that the temperatures array will look like this:

```
[31,29,35,32]
```

Because React state is immutable and can only be changed using the setState function or the function returned by useState, if you want to change the value of an array or object inside the state, you need to make a new array or object rather than mutating the existing one.

continues

continued

Copying an Array with Spread

JavaScript arrays are *reference values*. When you use the = operator to make a copy of an array, the new array still has a reference to the old one. Follow these steps to see the consequences of this:

1. Open the JavaScript console in Chrome.

2. Create a new array, such as the following one:

   ```
   let arr = ['red','green','blue'];
   ```

3. Use the = operator to make a new array from the original one:

   ```
   let newArr = arr;
   ```

4. Add an element to the new array:

   ```
   newArr.push('orange');
   ```

5. Write out the value of the original array to the console:

   ```
   arr
   ```

The following image shows the result, which is that adding a new element to the copy created using the = operator also changes the original array.

```
> let arr = ['red','green','blue'];
<· undefined
> let newArr = arr;
<· undefined
> newArr.push('orange');
<· 4
> arr
<· ▶ (4) ["red", "green", "blue", "orange"]
>
```

To make a copy of an array that doesn't reference the original one, you need to copy each element in the original array into a new array. The new array created in this way is called a *shallow copy*. As with everything in JavaScript, there are several ways to make a shallow copy of an array. One way is by using a loop, like this:

```
let numbers = [1, 2, 3];
let numbersCopy = [];

for (i = 0; i < numbers.length; i++) {
  numbersCopy[i] = numbers[i];
}
```

Another method is to use the slice function. slice returns a shallow copy of an array based on the start and end element indexes you provide. If you call slice on an array without passing in any arguments, it returns a shallow copy of the whole array:

```
numbersCopy = numbers.slice();
```

Using the spread operator makes this same operation even easier. You simply use square brackets to create a new array, and then populate it with each element in the old array by prefacing the name of the old array with the spread operator:

```
numbersCopy = [...numbers];
```

Changing an Array with Spread

JavaScript has several different methods for modifying, adding, and removing elements from arrays. For example, if you want to add an element to the end of an array, you can use the `Array.push` method:

```
numbersCopy.push(4);
setNumbers(numbersCopy);
```

Other array methods include:

➤ `Array.pop`: Removes an element from the end of an array.

➤ `Array.shift`: Adds an element to the beginning of an array.

➤ `Array.unshift`: Removes an element from the beginning of an array.

Each of these array methods actually modifies, or *mutates*, the array, however. To work with immutable data, such as React state, the spread operator can be used to accomplish each of these tasks. For example, if you want to copy an array and add an element to the end of it, you can do that like this:

```
numbersCopy = [...numbers,14];
```

If you want to change the value of a certain element in an array, you need to know the index of that element, then you can use what I refer to as the "sandwich" method—two slices and spread:

```
const newArray = [ ...oldArray.slice(0, indexToChange),
                   updatedValue,
                   ...oldArray.slice(indexToChange+1) ];
```

Although it may look strange and confusing at first, this method of modifying an element in an array is actually quite simple, and it's widely used in React programming. If you know the index of the element in the array you want to modify, you make a shallow copy of the original array from the first element in the array (0) up to the element you want to change. Then, you insert the new value into the array. Finally, you insert the rest of the elements in the array into the new array by passing just the number of the next element in the original array into `slice`.

Copying an Object with Spread

The spread operator can also be used to create a shallow copy of an object. A shallow copy of an object is a copy that only includes the properties, and not the prototype:

```
let obj1 = { foo: 'bar', x: 0 };
let clonedObj = { ...obj1 };
```

continues

continued

Combining two objects with spread is as simple as combining two arrays:

```
let obj1 = { foo: 'bar', x: 0 };
let obj2 = { food: 'taco', y: 1 };

let mergedObj = { ...obj1, ...obj2 };
```

The new object will look like this:

```
{foo: 'bar', x: 0, food: 'taco', y: 1}
```

Changing a property while cloning or merging objects is also simple with objects. Just use the spread operator to expand the object, and then overwrite one or more existing properties:

```
let newObj = {...obj1, x: 42 };
```

The resulting object will now look like this:

```
{foo: 'bar', x:42}
```

Bonus JavaScript Lesson: Rest Parameters

Once you're comfortable with how the spread operator works, understanding its twin, *rest parameters*, is easy. Rest parameters use the same three-period operator as spread syntax. What's different about it is where rest parameters are used. As the name implies, rest parameters are parameters that you can define in function definitions. Here's an example:

```
function(a,b,...c){
  // do something here
}
```

When you use a rest parameter, the function will aggregate the arguments passed into the function where the rest parameter is and any following arguments into an array inside the function.

For example, in the following function the first two arguments will become function-scoped variables, and an array named `toppings` will be created with however many arguments are passed into the function after the first two:

```
function pizza(size,crust,...toppings){
  // do something here
}
```

In the following example, the `add` function will take any number of arguments and return the sum of them, using the `Array.reduce` function:

```
function add(..numbers) {
  return numbers.reduce((sum, next) => sum + next)
}
```

Now that you know about the rest and spread operators, you'll recognize and be able to understand their role in JavaScript code, as well as their special powers when used in React and JSX.

What to Put in State

Whether you use class components or function components, changes to state data are what initiate changes to your user interface. If you think of the data in your React user interface as a river, state is the melting snow in the mountains that sets everything off.

One of the first steps in designing any React user interface is to figure out what the state of your application is. While it may not always be immediately obvious at first, as you become more comfortable with React, you'll get better at identifying the state.

As a rule, if a piece of data changes over time in response to data coming in from an external source or user input, it is likely state.

Building the Reminders App

Let's take a look at a demo application and determine what its state is, and then implement it. Before we can implement state, however, we need to take a brief detour to build the structure of the application.

Figure 6-14 shows a mockup of a user interface for a simple reminders app. The user can enter a task into the form and set a due date. The app will show a list of tasks and the user can filter tasks using a dropdown menu and mark tasks as completed.

Typically, once you've created a mockup of an app, the next step in the development of a React user interface is to figure out what components will make up the app and then make a "static" version of the app. A static version simply passes props from parents to children and doesn't have any interactivity.

Before I get started with building the app, I'll set up the development environment using Create React App. If you plan to follow along, open your terminal in VS Code and create a new project by entering the following command:

```
npx create-react-app reminders-app
```

After Create React App finishes its work, you'll see the new project in the file explorer in VS Code.

Open the `src` directory inside the `reminders-app` directory, and delete everything from there except for the following files:

➤   `index.js`

➤   `index.css`

➤   `reportWebVitals.js`

Now we're ready to get started.

From my initial evaluation of the mockup in Figure 6-14, I've determined that the Reminders app should have the following components:

➤   An entry form and submit button component.

➤   A filter select dropdown component.

➤ A list of reminders.

➤ An individual reminder component (which will be reused for each reminder in the list).

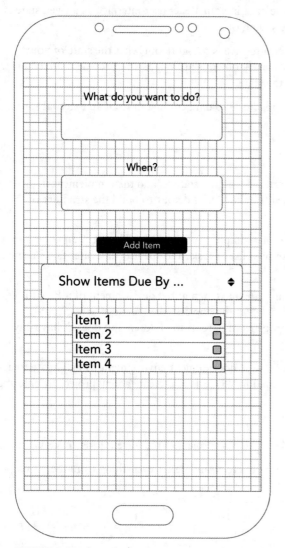

FIGURE 6-14: A reminders app

In addition to these components, there's one more component that we need to make this app complete: a container. The container component will enclose all of the other components in the app and will provide an overall structure and style to the app. The container component is frequently named App, although, as with most things in React, you're free to call it whatever you like.

Now that I've figured out what components I'll need to make, the next step is to think up names for the components and then write static versions of them.

The first component I'll make is App, and I'll include import statements and JSX elements for its sub-components (which I have yet to make). Listing 6-29 shows a static version of the App component.

LISTING 6-29: The static version of the App component

```
import InputForm from './InputForm';
import FilterSelect from './FilterSelect';
import RemindersList from './RemindersList';

function App(){
  return(
      <div>
          <InputForm />
          <FilterSelect />
          <RemindersList />
      </div>
  );
}

export default App;
```

Notice that I didn't pass props into App. Since App is the top-level component, we won't be passing any props to it, so there's currently no need to specify props in the parameter list.

Once you've created the container component, the next step is to create empty files for each of the components that App imports, and to make shell components for each one. Listing 6-30 shows an example of the start of the InputForm component.

LISTING 6-30: A shell component for InputForm

```
function InputForm(props){
  return(
    <div>Input form here</div>
  );
}
export default InputForm;
```

You can copy and modify this basic shell component for each of the rest of the components. Listing 6-31 shows a shell component for FilterSelect, Listing 6-32 shows one for RemindersList, and Listing 6-33 shows the one for the Reminder component.

LISTING 6-31: A shell component for FilterSelect

```
function FilterSelect(props){
  return(
      <div>Filter the List</div>
  );
}
export default FilterSelect;
```

LISTING 6-32: A shell component for RemindersList

```
function RemindersList(props){
  return(
      <div>Reminders List</div>
  );
}
export default RemindersList;
```

LISTING 6-33: A shell component for Reminder

```
function Reminder(props){
  return(
      <div>Reminder</div>
  );
}
export default Reminder;
```

On a simple app such as this, you can now just go through the components and start to make each one's `return` statement look a little bit more like what you think the final component will need to be. Don't worry about getting everything perfect. Writing React code is usually an iterative process—write some code, see what it looks like, improve it, and then write some more.

The first thing you might want to do to improve on what we have so far is to link in the `Reminder` component. The `RemindersList` component will contain all of the instances of the `Reminder` component, so we can import `Reminder` into it and also put in a couple instances of the `Reminder` element, as shown in Listing 6-34.

LISTING 6-34: RemindersList with Reminder imported

```
import Reminder from './Reminder';

function RemindersList(props){
  return(
    <div>
      <Reminder />
      <Reminder />
      <Reminder />
    </div>
  );
}
export default RemindersList;
```

If you compile and build this app as it is so far (using a Create React App boilerplate application to provide the toolchain and basic structure), you'll see something like what's shown in Figure 6-15.

Clearly, this is far from being a full static version of the app, but it's a great start. Let's go through another round of changes and get this static app to look a bit more like the mockup. We'll also define some props and pass some fake data down to child components.

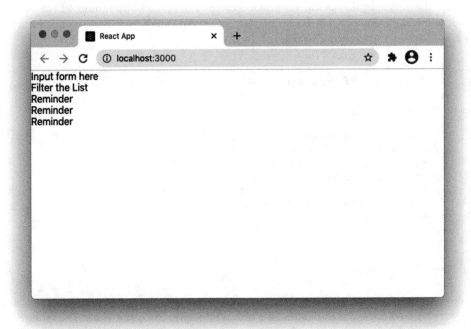

FIGURE 6-15: The first round static version

The App component can stay how it is for now. We'll add functionality and style to it eventually, but that can come later.

The InputForm component should have a text input, a date input, and a button. I'll also add in a couple of attributes for the input element and change the container element for these elements to a form element. Listing 6-35 shows the InputForm component with these improvements made.

LISTING 6-35: Round two of InputForm

```
function InputForm(props) {
  return(
    <form>
      <input id="reminderText" type="text" placeholder="What do you want to do?" />
      <input id="dueDate" type="date" />
      <button>Add Item</button>
    </form>
  );
}
export default InputForm;
```

The FilterSelect component should contain a select input with several options. I'll define these options in my second round of changes, as shown in Listing 6-36. We'll assume that the filter will be applied when the selected value changes, so there's no need to add a button to the `FilterSelect` component. If you recall from Chapter 3, `select` elements in React JSX have a `value` attribute that determines which option is currently selected.

LISTING 6-36: Round two of FilterSelect

```
function FilterSelect(props){
  return(
    <label htmlFor="filterReminders">Show tasks due:
      <select id="filterReminders" value="2day">
        <option value="2day">within 2 Days</option>
        <option value="1week">within 1 Week</option>
        <option value="30days">within 30 Days</option>
        <option value="all">any time</option>
      </select>
    </label>
  );
}
export default FilterSelect;
```

The `RemindersList` component's purpose is to contain one `Reminder` element for each reminder in the list. For our static version, we can pass sample text, a due date, and a status from `RemindersList` to each `Reminder`, as shown in Listing 6-37.

LISTING 6-37: Round two of RemindersList

```
import Reminder from './Reminder';

function RemindersList(props){
  return(
    <div>
      <Reminder reminderText="Pick up Wesley" dueDate="2364-01-15"
isComplete={false} />
      <Reminder reminderText="Meet with Jean-Luc" dueDate="2364-01-29"
isComplete={false} />
      <Reminder reminderText="Holodeck time!" dueDate="2364-06-01"
isComplete={false} />
    </div>
  );
}
export default RemindersList;
```

The `Reminder` component can now accept the props data from `RemindersList` and display it, as shown in Listing 6-38. Because the Boolean value from `props.isComplete` won't display in the browser, we can convert it to a string in the JSX.

LISTING 6-38: Round two of Reminder

```
function Reminder(props){
  return(
    <div>item: {props.reminderText}
         due date: {props.dueDate}
         Completed?: {String(props.isComplete)}
    </div>
  );
}
export default Reminder;
```

Our Reminders app still isn't pretty, as you can see in Figure 6-16, but more of the pieces are in place now and we have a foundation upon which we can start to implement the dynamic data, or state.

FIGURE 6-16: A static version of the Reminders app

After you've made your static version, you can figure out what data in the app causes the app to change—what should be in the state of the app, in other words.

In the case of the Reminders app, it has the following pieces of data:

➤ The user's current textual input.

➤ The currently selected due date.

➤ The list of reminders.

➤ Individual reminders.

➤ The reminder status (completed or not completed).

➤ The selected filter.

➤ The filtered list of tasks.

Think for a moment about which pieces of data should or should not be state. Here's what I've come up with:

➤ The user's current input is certainly state, since it changes as the user types.

➤ The selected due date, likewise, is state.

➤ The list of reminders changes as new tasks are added, so it is state.

➤ The individual tasks within the list are unchanging, and are not state.

➤ The completed status of each task is state, since the user can change it.

➤ The selected filter is state.

➤ The filtered list is not state.

In the next section, I'll explain why some of these items should not be state. Oftentimes, your initial judgment about what needs to be state changes as you code your app. It's important to stay flexible and look for opportunities to reduce the size of your state object. The more data in your app can be moved out of state and into props, the simpler (and perhaps faster and more efficient) your app will be.

What Not to Put in State

Another way to think about what should be state is to follow a few rules for determining what *isn't* state:

➤ If it's passed from a parent component to a child component, it's not state.

➤ If it remains unchanged throughout its life, it's not state.

➤ If it can be computed based on other values, it's not state.

Generally speaking, individual task items should not be kept in state. My reasoning for this is that these tasks, once created, are unchanging. Also, as you'll learn, the tasks are going to be stored in the parent component and passed down to the individual task components using props.

The filtered list of tasks that displays when you select a time period from the dropdown list also should not be stored in state. This is because this list will be computed based on the due dates. Because it can be computed and displayed based on other props and state, it's not state itself.

Where to Put State

Once you've determined what is and what isn't state, the next step in the development of a React user interface is to figure out where each piece of state should be located. In other words, which component should we initialize the state inside of by either using the class-based component method of setting this.state, or by using the useState hook.

So, let's take another look at each piece of state that we identified and decide what component it should be declared in. Here's an outline of our current user interface, taken from the components created during the building of the static version:

```
App
- InputForm
- Filter
- RemindersList
- Reminder
```

And here, once again, is the list of state items that we've identified in the app so far:

➤ User input.

➤ Selected due date.

➤ Reminder list.

➤ Reminder status.

➤ Selected filter.

Now, I'll go through each of these candidates for state and figure out where to put them in the component hierarchy:

➤ The current user input seems like it should be stored in the component that contains the form, so we'll put that in the InputForm component.

➤ The currently selected due date seems like it should be stored with the user input. So, we'll put that in the InputForm component as well.

➤ The list of reminders, logically, would seem to go into the RemindersList component.

➤ The isComplete status of each reminder item probably belongs inside of each Reminder component.

➤ The filter that is currently selected can go with the Filter component.

Now that we've put each piece of state into a component, let's look at the outline of components again, with the state values that each one contains:

```
<App>
- <InputForm>
    - currentInput
    - selectedDate
- <Filter>
    - selectedFilter
- <RemindersList>
```

```
        - reminders

    - <Reminder>

        - isComplete
```

Although it seems logical, the organization of the state in our app has some serious problems that become apparent as you think about how it will actually function. Here are a few of the bigger issues:

1. In the preceding outline, each reminder keeps track of its own completed status. If we wanted the `RemindersList` component to only list the completed tasks, or only list the uncompleted ones, `RemindersList` would first need to query each `Reminder` and find out its status.

2. The `Filter` and `RemindersList` components are siblings. If you recall that data always flows down in a React app, you'll see a problem here. If `Filter` maintains its own state about which filter is currently selected, there's no way to get that information to the `RemindersList` component so that the correct `Reminder` components can be displayed.

3. `InputForm` is also a sibling of `RemindersList`. Since the goal of the user input form is to add a new item to the list of reminders, we need the current user input to be able to be passed to the `RemindersList` component. With these components being siblings, there's no easy way to do this.

It seems that our little Reminders app is getting pretty complicated. We'll need to figure out how the `RemindersList` component will query all of the `Reminders` for their status, we'll need to figure out how to get around this problem with passing data between sibling components, and we have all this state data spread throughout our app that we're going to need to remember and keep track of. There must be a simpler way, you say.

There is, and it's called *lifting state up*.

Lifting State Up

Having a lot of components that each independently maintain their own state can very quickly increase the complexity of your app, and therefore the chances of something breaking. A good rule of thumb, therefore, is that the majority of your components should be stateless pure functions.

A pure function, as you'll recall from Chapter 4, is one in which the output of the function is solely a result of the input to it. In other words, a pure function will always produce the same output when given the same input.

To turn stateful components into stateless components, React developers use a technique called "lifting state up." This means that, instead of a component controlling its own state, you can have a component at a higher level in the hierarchy of your user interface control the state. This state can then be passed down as props to the components that need it.

Lifting state up gives you the benefit of having fewer components that can possibly cause your user interface to change, it makes your components more easily reusable, and it makes your app easier to test.

To determine where to lift your state up to, think about where each piece of state in your application is needed, and then find a parent common to all of the components that use each piece of state.

For example, in our Reminders app, the list of reminders is used by the `InputForm`, `Filter`, `RemindersList`, and `Reminder` components. The only component in our application that's a common parent to all of these is the `App` component. So, that's where that piece of stateful data should live.

In fact, if you look through the list of stateful variables we identified for the Reminders app, you'll discover that each one of them actually should belong to the `App` component, and also that some of them can be combined.

The `reminders` and `isComplete` values, for example, can be combined into a single array of objects, with each object having a `reminderText` property, an `isComplete` property, and a `dueDate` property:

```
[
    {reminderText:"do laundry",dueDate:"2022-01-01",isComplete:false},
    {reminderText:"finish chapter",dueDate: "2022-02-01",isComplete:false},
    {reminderText:"make Pizza",dueDate: "2022-03-01",isComplete:false}
]
```

Likewise, the `currentInput` and `selectedDate` can also be combined into an object. This has the benefit of creating exactly the right data structure for insertion into the reminder list.

Since the `useState` hook not only creates the stateful variable, but also creates the function for setting that variable, you can pass both of these down to the proper components as props.

With those changes done, our `App` component with the lifted-up state is shown in Listing 6-39.

LISTING 6-39: App with lifted state

```
import {useState} from 'react';
import InputForm from './InputForm';
import FilterSelect from './FilterSelect';
import RemindersList from './RemindersList';

function App(){
  const [reminders,setReminders] = useState();
  const [userInput,setUserInput] = useState();
  const [selectedFilter,setSelectedFilter] = useState("all");

  return(
    <div>
      <InputForm userInput={userInput}
                 setUserInput={setUserInput} />
      <FilterSelect selectedFilter={selectedFilter}
                    setSelectedFilter={setSelectedFilter} />
      <RemindersList reminders={reminders} />
    </div>
  );
}

export default App;
```

Next, I'll receive and make use of the stateful data, which I've passed down to the subcomponents as props, and write all of the subcomponents of `App` as pure functions. Listing 6-40 shows the

InputForm component, Listing 6-41 shows the FilterSelect component, and Listing 6-42 shows the RemindersList component.

LISTING 6-40: Pure InputForm

```
function InputForm(props){
  return(
    <form>
      <input value={props.userInput.reminderText}
             id="reminderText"
             type="text"
             placeholder="What do you want to do?" />
      <input value={props.userInput.dueDate}
             id="dueDate"
             type="date" />
      <button>Add Item</button>
    </form>
  );
}
export default InputForm;
```

LISTING 6-41: Pure FilterSelect

```
function FilterSelect(props){
  return(
    <label htmlFor="filterReminders">Show tasks due:
      <select id="filterReminders" value={props.selectedFilter}>
        <option value="2day">within 2 Days</option>
        <option value="1week">within 1 Week</option>
        <option value="30days">within 30 Days</option>
        <option value="all">any time</option>
      </select>
    </label>
  );
}
export default FilterSelect;
```

LISTING 6-42: Pure RemindersList

```
import Reminder from './Reminder';

function RemindersList(props){

  const reminders = props.reminders.map((reminder,index)=>{
    return (<Reminder reminderText={reminder.reminderText}
                      dueDate={reminder.dueDate}
                      isComplete={reminder.isComplete}
                      id={index}
                      key={index} />);
  });
```

```
    return(
        <div>
            {reminders}
        </div>
    );
}
export default RemindersList;
```

Figure 6-17 shows what happens when you try to run the app at this point.

FIGURE 6-17: Cannot read property

The reason we get this error is that we're trying to read a property of an object (userInput) that doesn't yet exist.

The solution to this problem, and to many other problems in React, is to make use of PropTypes for validating props, and defaultProps to set initial values for the props. I'll start again with the child components and work through each one and make some necessary improvements.

The InputForm component receives two props: userInput and setUserInput. The userInput prop is an object with two properties. We can use propTypes.shape to validate that the object the component receives has the correct properties and that those properties are the correct type of data. I'll also set default values that will be used for each property of userInput in case the prop is not received, as shown in Listing 6-43.

LISTING 6-43: Adding PropTypes and default values to InputForm

```
import PropTypes from 'prop-types';

function InputForm(props){
  return(
      <form>
        <input value={props.userInput.reminderText}
               id="reminderText"
               type="text"
               placeholder="What do you want to do?" />
        <input value={props.userInput.dueDate}
               id="dueDate"
               type="date" />
        <button>Add Item</button>
      </form>
  );
}

InputForm.propTypes = {
  userInput: PropTypes.shape({
    reminderText: PropTypes.string,
    dueDate: PropTypes.string
  }),
  setUserInput: PropTypes.func
}

const date = new Date();
const formattedDate = date.toISOString().substr(0,10);

InputForm.defaultProps = {
  userInput: {
    reminderText:"",
    dueDate:formattedDate
  }
}

export default InputForm;
```

You may have a question about how the default value for the date picker is being set. The HTML date picker control accepts a string in the format 'YYYY-MM-DD'. To set its default value, I'll get the current date (by creating a new Date object) and then I'll use the JavaScript toISOString function to convert the current date to a string containing the date and time, in the format 'YYYY-MM-DDTHH:mm:ss.sssZ'. Since I only care about the date portion of this string, I'll use the substr function to get the first 10 characters of the result of the toISOString function.

Because the actual value used by the date input is a string, the correct PropType to validate it against is string rather than date.

If you run the app now (or just refresh the browser window if the development server is still running), you'll see that the reminderText error is gone, but we have a new one, as shown in Figure 6-18.

This isn't the last time you'll see this error in your dealings with React. In plain English, it's telling us that we're trying to run the Array.map function on something that's not an array.

FIGURE 6-18: Cannot read property 'map' of undefined

RemindersList receives the reminders variable as a prop and uses Array.map to create an array of Reminder elements from it. Any time you use Array.map in a component, you have to be certain that the component won't try to render before the array that Array.map is used on is populated. If it does try to render before the array is received, the render will fail with an error, as you saw in Figure 6-18. Using a default prop value is one way to eliminate the possibility of this type of failure. Listing 6-44 shows the RemindersList component with default props and propTypes defined.

LISTING 6-44: RemindersList with default props and PropTypes

```
import PropTypes from 'prop-types';
import Reminder from './Reminder';

function RemindersList(props){

  const reminders = props.reminders.map((reminder,index)=>{
    return (<Reminder reminderText={reminder.reminderText}
                      dueDate={reminder.dueDate}
                      isComplete={reminder.isComplete}
                      id={index}
                      key={index} />);
  });

  return(
    <div>
      {reminders}
    </div>
  );
```

continues

LISTING 6-44 *(continued)*

```
}

RemindersList.propTypes = {
  reminders: PropTypes.array
}

const date = new Date();
const formattedDate = date.toISOString().substr(0,10);

RemindersList.defaultProps = {
  reminders: [{
    reminderText:"No Reminders Yet",
    dueDate:formattedDate,
    isComplete: false
  }]
}

export default RemindersList;
```

Another way to prevent map from trying to run on a prop that's not yet an array is to set the initial value of the stateful variable in App to an empty array, like this:

```
const [reminders,setReminders] = useState([]);
```

However, if you set the initial value of reminders to an empty array, the default "No Reminders Yet" reminder doesn't show up. If you remove the empty square brackets passed into the useState function that creates the reminders variable, the default props defined in RemindersList will render, as shown in Figure 6-19.

FIGURE 6-19: Displaying the default prop

About the key Prop

Any time you make a list of components, as we do in the `RemindersList` component, each element in the list must have a prop named `key`. The value of `key` must be unique to each item in the list. Since the index position of an element in an array is a unique value, this makes a convenient value for the `key` prop.

The `key` prop is used by React to help facilitate updating of items in the list. The value of `key` is not available as part of the `props` object inside the component. You'll notice that `RemindersList` passes the same value (the index position of the reminder in the array) to both the `key` prop and to a prop called `id`. This is necessary so we can make use of this value to update the reminders list, as you'll see when we start coding the functionality of the app.

> **NOTE** In this example, I used the index of the `reminders` array as the key. In a real-world application, it would be a better practice to have a separate, unique ID property for each reminder and to use that as the key. The reason is that the key is used by React to identify elements in the array. If your application changes the order of elements in the array or adds or removes elements from inside the array (none of which ours currently does), React will assume that the same keys represent the same DOM elements. The result can be that wrong data will be displayed or your app will break. For a more detailed explanation of the problems with using the index as the key, see Robin Pokorny's blog post at https://robinpokorny.medium.com/index-as-a-key-is-an-anti-pattern-e0349aece318.

Now let's look at the `FilterSelect` component. `FilterSelect` also receives two props: `selectedFilter` and `setSelectedFilter`. I'll set `selectedFilter` to `all` by default and validate the types for both, as shown in Listing 6-45.

LISTING 6-45: Validating and setting defaults for FilterSelect

```
import PropTypes from 'prop-types';

function FilterSelect(props) {
  return(
    <label htmlFor="filterReminders">Show tasks due:
      <select id="filterReminders" value={props.selectedFilter}>
        <option value="2day">within 2 Days</option>
        <option value="1week">within 1 Week</option>
        <option value="30days">within 30 days</option>
        <option value="all">any time</option>
      </select>
    </label>
  );
}
```

continues

LISTING 6-45 *(continued)*

```
FilterSelect.propTypes = {
  selectedFilter: PropTypes.string,
  setSelectedFilter: PropTypes.func
}

FilterSelect.defaultProps = {
  selectedFilter:'all'
}

export default FilterSelect;
```

The Reminder component receives three props: reminderText, dueDate, and isComplete. There shouldn't be a possibility of Reminder not receiving props, because its parent component, RemindersList, has default props set. But, it's always a good idea to set defaults and validate your props using PropTypes, because it makes your component more reusable and independent. Listing 6-46 shows the Reminder component with propTypes and default props set.

LISTING 6-46: Reminder with PropTypes and defaultProps

```
import PropTypes from 'prop-types';

function Reminder(props){
    return(
        <div>item: {props.reminderText}
            due date: {props.dueDate}
            Completed?: {String(props.isComplete)}</div>
    );
  }

Reminder.propTypes = {
    reminderText: PropTypes.string,
    dueDate: PropTypes.string,
    isComplete: PropTypes.bool
}

const date = new Date();
const formattedDate = date.toISOString().substr(0,10);

Reminder.defaultProps = {
    reminderText:"No Reminder Set",
    dueDate:formattedDate,
    isComplete: false
}

export default Reminder;
```

Now that we have state and props being passed down through the components and default values set for the props, the initial render of the app is starting to take shape and there shouldn't be any PropType warnings in the JavaScript console (although you will see a couple of other warnings), as you can see in Figure 6-20.

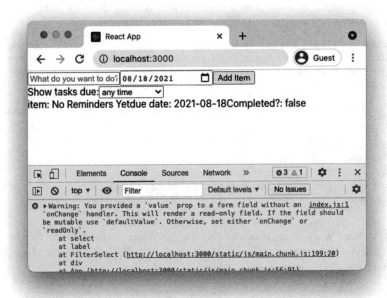

FIGURE 6-20: The initial render of the Reminders app

The warnings that you see in the console now are expected, and they point to the one big thing left to do before this is a somewhat functional app: we need to implement event listeners that will trigger state changes.

Since we're building this app entirely with function components, we already created the functions that will set the state variables. All we need to do now is pass those functions down to the correct component and then set up event listeners to call the functions.

I'll start with the `userInput` object and its setter function, `setUserInput`. The `setUserInput` function is already passed to the `InputForm` component. What we want to happen is for it to be called and to store the reminder text and date when the text field and date field change.

It's common to define an intermediary function between the event handler and the setter function. Often, this function will take the name of the event that triggers it, prefaced by `handle`. In the `InputForm` component, we'll define a function called `handleTextChange`, one called `handleDateChange`, and one called `handleClick`. The purpose of `handleTextChange` and `handleDateChange` is to get the data from the field's change event into the correct form to be stored in state and then to call the `setUserInput` function. The purpose of `handleClick` will be to use the current values from the `userInput` object to add a new element to the `reminders` array each time the button is clicked.

Recall that the setter functions created by the `useState` hook replace the value of the stateful variable, rather than updating it like `setState` does. As a result, each time we call `setUserInput`, we need to re-create the `userInput` object, but with the new value. This is easily done by using the spread operator. The `handleTextChange` function in `InputForm` looks like this:

```
const handleTextChange = (e)=>{
  const newUserInput = {...props.userInput,reminderText:e.target.value}
  props.setUserInput(newUserInput);
}
```

The `handleDateChange` function is very similar, but it requires the date to be massaged into the correct format:

```
const handleDateChange = (e)=>{
  const date = new Date(e.target.value);
  const formattedDate = date.toISOString().substr(0,10);
  const newUserInput = {...props.userInput,dueDate:formattedDate};
  props.setUserInput(newUserInput);
}
```

Because we've done all of the hard work of creating the `userInput` object as the user was typing it, adding a new reminder to the `reminders` array when the button is clicked is just a matter of adding the new object along with an `isComplete` property.

We'll write a function to update the reminders list. To avoid having to pass the `reminders` array down to the `InputForm` component unnecessarily, we'll instead define a function in `App` and then pass that down to `InputForm`.

Here's the `addNewReminder` function to add to `App`:

```
const addNewReminder = (itemToAdd) => {
  setReminders([...reminders,itemToAdd]);
}
```

Add a new attribute to the `InputForm` element to pass `addNewReminder` down to the `InputForm` component:

```
<InputForm userInput={userInput}
           setUserInput={setUserInput}
           addNewReminder={addNewReminder} />
```

And, of course, don't forget to validate the `PropType` for `setUserInput` inside `InputForm`:

```
InputForm.propTypes = {
  userInput: PropTypes.shape({
    reminderText: PropTypes.string,
    dueDate: PropTypes.string
  }),
  setUserInput: PropTypes.func,
  addNewReminder: PropTypes.func
}
```

Now, inside of `InputForm`, we can define a `handleClick` function that will call the `addNewReminder` function when the button is clicked. HTML buttons have a default action, which is to submit a form and reload the page. We need to prevent this default action so that we don't reload the page (and React) every time the button is clicked (thus losing the state):

```
const handleClick = (e)=>{
  e.preventDefault();
```

```
      const itemToAdd = {...props.userInput,isComplete:false};
      props.addNewReminder(itemToAdd);
    };
```

To invoke these new functions, add event listener attributes to the form elements. Event listener attributes in React work like HTML event listener attributes. When the specified event happens on the element containing the attribute, the function specified will be run.

> **NOTE** *I'll cover events and event handling in React in more detail in Chapter 7.*

The value of an event listener attribute can be the name of a function (or a prop with a function value), or an arrow function definition. Here's the `reminderText` input element with the event listener function specified:

```
<input value={props.userInput.reminderText}
       id="reminderText"
       type="text"
       placeholder="What do you want to do?"
       onChange={handleTextChange} />
```

Here's the `dueDate` input with its event listener attribute:

```
<input value={props.userInput.dueDate}
       id="dueDate"
       type="date"
       onChange={handleDateChange} />
```

And here's the `button` with its event listener attribute:

```
<button onClick={handleClick}>Add Item</button>
```

At this point, the code for the `InputForm` component should look like Listing 6-47.

LISTING 6-47: The InputForm component with event handlers and event listeners

```
import PropTypes from 'prop-types';

function InputForm(props) {
  const handleTextChange = (e) =>{
    const newUserInput = {...props.userInput,reminderText:e.target.value}
    props.setUserInput(newUserInput);
  }

  const handleDateChange = (e) =>{
    const date = new Date(e.target.value);
    const formattedDate = date.toISOString().substr(0,10);
    const newUserInput = {...props.userInput,dueDate:formattedDate};
    props.setUserInput(newUserInput);
  }
```

continues

LISTING 6-47 *(continued)*

```
const handleClick = (e) =>{
  e.preventDefault();
  const itemToAdd = {...props.userInput,status:false};
  props.addNewReminder(itemToAdd);
};


return(
  <form>
    <input value={props.userInput.reminderText}
           id="reminderText"
           type="text"
           placeholder="What do you want to do?"
           onChange={handleTextChange} />

    <input value={props.userInput.dueDate}
           id="dueDate"
           type="date"
           onChange={handleDateChange} />

    <button onClick={handleClick}>Add Item</button>
  </form>
);
}

InputForm.propTypes = {
  userInput: PropTypes.shape({
    reminderText: PropTypes.string,
    dueDate: PropTypes.string
  }),
  setUserInput: PropTypes.func,
  addNewReminder: PropTypes.func
}

const date = new Date();
const formattedDate = date.toISOString().substr(0,10);

InputForm.defaultProps = {
  userInput: {
    reminderText:"",
    dueDate:formattedDate
  }
}

export default InputForm;
```

With these three event listeners set to trigger our event handler functions, you should be able to start up Create React App's development server (using **npm start**). When you try to add a new reminder, however, you'll get a new error: `TypeError: reminders is not iterable`. This indicates that we're trying to use the spread operator on `reminders` before it's an array. And, in fact, that's what's happening in the `addNewReminder` function.

As with the solution to the error we got when we tried to use the `Array.map` function on `reminders` before it was populated, the solution here is to add a default value. You could set the initial value of `reminders` to an empty array, or you could use a third method and test the value of `reminders` inside of `addNewReminders` and take the appropriate action. Here's what that looks like:

```
const addNewReminder = (itemToAdd) => {
  if (reminders===undefined){
    setReminders([itemToAdd]);
  } else {
    setReminders([...reminders,itemToAdd]);
  }
}
```

With that done, now you'll be able to add new reminders to the list, as shown in Figure 6-21.

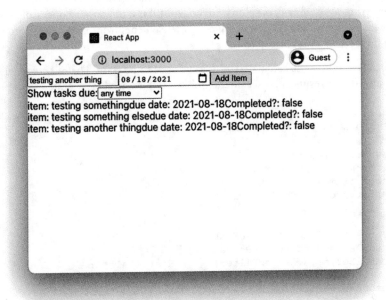

FIGURE 6-21: Adding Reminders to the list

Filtering the Reminders

The `FilterSelect` component uses a dropdown menu containing various time frames to calculate a filtered list of the reminders. To figure out how to code the functionality of this component, let's step through the basic process of filtering the list:

1. The user changes the selected item in the `select` input.

2. The change to the `select` input causes a function to be called.

3. The called function receives the full list of reminders and the selected filter.

4. A subset of the full reminders list is created.

5. The subset of the list is displayed.

The default filter in our app is `"all"`, which displays all of the reminders. Since there's no way to shut off the filter selector, what is displayed in the app should always be a filtered list (even if the filtered list contains all of the reminders). So, the first step in programming the filter functionality is to create a new variable for the filtered list and pass that down to the `RemindersList` component instead of the full list of reminders.

For now, I'll do this by just copying the reminders list into a new array called `filteredReminders` in App (using the spread operator) and then passing down this new `filteredReminders` array as the value of the `reminders` attribute in `RemindersList`, as shown in Listing 6-48.

Once again, the spread operator will produce an error unless you give `reminders` a default value or do a test before trying to use `Array.map` on `reminders`. I'll use the ternary operator this time to check whether `reminders` is defined. If it is, I'll copy the elements from `reminders` into `filteredList`. If it isn't, I'll set `filteredList` to `undefined`.

Remember, because the `filteredList` is calculated, it doesn't need to be state. The `selectedFilter`, on the other hand, is changed as a result of a user interaction, so it does need to be state.

LISTING 6-48: Creating a new filteredReminders array

```
import {useState} from 'react';
import InputForm from './InputForm';
import FilterSelect from './FilterSelect';
import RemindersList from './RemindersList';

function App(){
  const [reminders,setReminders] = useState();
  const [userInput,setUserInput] = useState();
  const [selectedFilter,setSelectedFilter] = useState("all");

  const addNewReminder = (itemToAdd) => {
    if (reminders===undefined){
      setReminders([itemToAdd]);
    } else {
      setReminders([...reminders,itemToAdd]);
    }
  }

  const filteredList = reminders?[...reminders]:undefined;

  return(
    <div>
      <InputForm userInput={userInput}
                 setUserInput={setUserInput}
                 addNewReminder={addNewReminder} />
      <FilterSelect selectedFilter={selectedFilter}
                    setSelectedFilter={setSelectedFilter} />
      <RemindersList reminders={filteredList} />
```

```
        </div>
    );
}

export default App;
```

At this point, the app will function exactly the same as before, but the groundwork is properly laid to be able to filter the list. The next step is to write a function that will filter the reminders list based on the date. For that, we can use Array.filter. Array.filter takes a function as its argument, and creates a new array containing all of the elements that pass a test in the function.

Listing 6-49 shows the function that I came up with for filtering the list.

LISTING 6-49: Filtering the reminders list

```
function filterList(reminders,selectedFilter){
        if (selectedFilter === "all"){
            return reminders;
        } else {

        let numberOfDays;

        switch(selectedFilter){
                case "2day":
                  numberOfDays = 2;
                  break;
                case "1week":
                  numberOfDays = 7;
                  break;
                case "30days":
                  numberOfDays = 30;
                  break;
                default:
                  numberOfDays = 0;
                  break;
        }

        const result = reminders.filter(reminder=>{
            const todaysDate = new Date().toISOString().substr(0,10);
            const todayTime = new Date(todaysDate).getTime();
            const dueTime = new Date(reminder.dueDate).getTime();
            return dueTime < (todayTime + (numberOfDays * 86400000));
        });
        return result;
    }
}
```

If you examine this function, you'll see that it first checks whether the selected filter is "all", and just exits out of the rest of the function if so. If the selected filter isn't "all", it converts the selected filter into a number of days. Then it uses Array.filter to go through each element in the reminders array and make a list of the reminders that have a due date earlier than the current time (which is in the number of milliseconds since the beginning of UNIX time) plus the number of milliseconds in the selected filter.

To implement this function, place it outside of the `return` statement in the `App` component, and then call it, passing in `reminders` and `selectedFilter`, as shown in Listing 6-50.

LISTING 6-50: Implementing the filterList function

```
import {useState} from 'react';
import InputForm from './InputForm';
import FilterSelect from './FilterSelect';
import RemindersList from './RemindersList';

function App(){
  const [reminders,setReminders] = useState();
  const [userInput,setUserInput] = useState();
  const [selectedFilter,setSelectedFilter] = useState("all");

  const addNewReminder = (itemToAdd) => {
    if (reminders===undefined){
      setReminders([itemToAdd]);
    } else {
      setReminders([...reminders,itemToAdd]);
    }
  }

  const filteredList = filterList(reminders,selectedFilter);

  function filterList(reminders,selectedFilter){
    if (selectedFilter === "all"){
        return reminders;
    } else {

    let numberOfDays;

    switch(selectedFilter){
        case "2day":
          numberOfDays = 2;
          break;
        case "1week":
          numberOfDays = 7;
          break;
        case "30days":
          numberOfDays = 30;
          break;
        default:
          numberOfDays = 0;
          break;
    }

    const result = reminders.filter(reminder=>{
        const todaysDate = new Date().toISOString().substr(0,10);
        const todayTime = new Date(todaysDate).getTime();
```

```
         const dueTime = new Date(reminder.dueDate).getTime();
         return dueTime < (todayTime + (numberOfDays * 86400000));
      });
      return result;
      }
   }
   return(
     <div>
       <InputForm userInput={userInput}
                  setUserInput={setUserInput}
                  addNewReminder={addNewReminder} />
       <FilterSelect selectedFilter={selectedFilter}
                     setSelectedFilter={setSelectedFilter} />
       <RemindersList reminders={filteredList} />
     </div>
   );
}

export default App;
```

The next thing we need to do is to add the event listener and handler to the `FilterSelect` component so that selecting a filter from the dropdown will update the `selectedFilter` state variable.

In the `FilterSelect` component, I'll define a new function called `handleChange`, which will pass the value of the `select` input to the `setSelectedFilter` component. Then, I'll set an `onChange` event handler on the `select` input to call `handleChange`. The `FilterSelect` component, with this event listener and event handler specified, is shown in Listing 6-51.

LISTING 6-51: FilterSelect with an event handler and event listener

```
import PropTypes from 'prop-types';

function FilterSelect(props){

function handleChange(e){
  props.setSelectedFilter(e.target.value);
}

return(
   <label htmlFor="filterReminders">Show tasks due:
     <select id="filterReminders" value={props.selectedFilter}
onChange={handleChange}>
       <option value="2day">within 2 Days</option>
       <option value="1week">within 1 Week</option>
       <option value="30days">within 30 days</option>
       <option value="all">any time</option>
     </select>
   </label>
   );
}

FilterSelect.propTypes = {
```

continues

LISTING 6-51 *(continued)*

```
    selectedFilter: PropTypes.string,
    setSelectedFilter: PropTypes.func
}

FilterSelect.defaultProps = {
    selectedFilter:'all'
}

export default FilterSelect;
```

Implementing the isComplete Changing Functionality

The last thing left to do for now is to implement the `isComplete` status changing functionality. This should just be a checkbox to the right of each reminder that, when clicked, will indicate that the item is complete.

The first thing to do is to implement the checkbox in the `Reminder` component. Checkboxes don't have a `value` property. Instead, they have a property called `checked` which is either `true` or `false`. Our checkbox in the `Reminder` component should look like this:

```
<input type="checkbox" checked={props.isComplete} onChange={handleChange} />
```

The full `Reminder` component should now look like Listing 6-52.

LISTING 6-52: Reminder with the checkbox

```
import PropTypes from 'prop-types';

function Reminder(props){
  function handleChange(){
    props.setIsComplete(!props.isComplete,props.id);
  }

  return(
    <div className="item">item: {props.reminderText}
      <span className="due-date">due date: {props.dueDate}</span>
      <span className="is-complete">
         Completed?: <input type="checkbox"
                       checked={props.isComplete}
                       onChange={handleChange} /></span>
    </div>
    );
  }

Reminder.propTypes = {
  reminderText: PropTypes.string,
  dueDate: PropTypes.string,
  isComplete: PropTypes.bool
}
```

```
const date = new Date();
const formattedDate = date.toISOString().substr(0,10);

Reminder.defaultProps = {
  reminderText:"No Reminder Set",
  dueDate:formattedDate,
  isComplete: false
}

export default Reminder;
```

Next, we can define the `handleChange` function, which will call a function called `setIsComplete` that we'll pass down via props. The `handleChange` function will pass the index of the current reminder in the array (which we're passing down as the `id` prop) and the opposite of the current `isComplete` (so, if `isComplete` is true, false will be passed to the `setIsComplete` function):

```
function handleChange(){
  props.setIsComplete(!props.isComplete,props.id);
}
```

Next, we have to define the `setIsComplete` function. Remember that `isComplete` is a property inside the `reminders` array. Since the `reminders` array lives in the `App` component, we'll define the `setIsComplete` function there as well. This function will simply change the `isComplete` property of the element in the array matching the index passed to it. Here's how that's done, using the "sandwich" method (two slices and spread):

```
function setIsComplete(isComplete,index){
  const newReminders = [ ...reminders.slice(0, index),
                         {...reminders[index],isComplete},
                         ...reminders.slice(index+1) ];
  setReminders(newReminders);
}
```

To get the `setStatus` function down to the `Reminders` component, you'll need to pass it first to the `RemindersList` component, like this:

```
<RemindersList reminders={filteredList} setIsComplete={setIsComplete}/>
```

And then you'll need to pass it from the `RemindersList` component down to the `Reminder` component, like this:

```
<Reminder reminderText={reminder.reminderText}
          dueDate={reminder.dueDate}
          isComplete={reminder.isComplete}
          setIsComplete={props.setIsComplete}
          id={index}
          key={index} />
```

When you run the app and add a couple of reminders, you can now check and uncheck each one's status checkbox independently of the others, as shown in Figure 6-22.

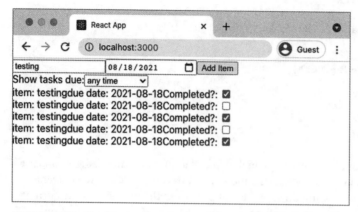

FIGURE 6-22: Checking and unchecking isComplete checkboxes

CONVERTING TO CLASS COMPONENTS

Now that we've gone through how to write this app the easy way, let's look at how to write this application using class components. The functionality of the app will remain the same, but the class method of writing components is commonly used, even since the introduction of React Hooks, and so understanding how to switch between the two methods is important:

1. Start with the root component, App. All of our state variables will still be defined in this component, but in a class component, this is done inside the constructor. Import Component instead of useState from the react library, then create the render method and initialize the properties of this.state as shown in Listing 6-53.

LISTING 6-53: Initializing state in App

```
import {Component} from 'react';
class App extends Component{
  constructor(props){
    super(props);
    this.state = {
      reminders:undefined,
      userInput:undefined,
      selectedFilter:"all"
    }
  }
  render(){
    return();
  }
}

export default App;
```

2. Copy the JSX from the function version of App to the class version, import the child components, and update the names of the state properties to reference this.state and update the names of functions to methods of the class, as shown in Listing 6-54.

LISTING 6-54: Copying and modifying JSX in App

```
import {Component} from 'react';
import InputForm from './InputForm';
import FilterSelect from './FilterSelect';
import RemindersList from './RemindersList';

class App extends Component{
  constructor(props){
    super(props);
    this.state = {
      reminders:undefined,
      userInput:undefined,
      selectedFilter:"all"
    }
  }
  render(){
    return(
      <div>
        <InputForm userInput={this.state.userInput}
                   setUserInput={this.setUserInput}
                   addNewReminder={this.addNewReminder} />
        <FilterSelect selectedFilter={this.state.selectedFilter}
                      setSelectedFilter={this.setSelectedFilter} />
        <RemindersList reminders={filteredList} setIsComplete={this.setIsComplete} />
      </div>
    );
  }
}

export default App;
```

3. Create methods for `setUserInput`, `setSelectedFilter`, `addNewReminder`, and `setIsComplete`. Change references to state properties and methods to refer to properties of the class, and bind these methods to the component, as shown in Listing 6-55.

LISTING 6-55: Adding methods and binding them to App

```
import {Component} from 'react';
import InputForm from './InputForm';
import FilterSelect from './FilterSelect';
import RemindersList from './RemindersList';

class App extends Component{
  constructor(props){
    super(props);
    this.state = {
      reminders:undefined,
      userInput:undefined,
      selectedFilter:"all"
    }
```

continues

LISTING 6-55 *(continued)*

```
    this.setUserInput = this.setUserInput.bind(this);
    this.setSelectedFilter = this.setSelectedFilter.bind(this);
    this.addNewReminder = this.addNewReminder.bind(this);
    this.setIsComplete = this.setIsComplete.bind(this);
  }

  setUserInput(newInput){
    this.setState({userInput:newInput});
  }

  setSelectedFilter(newFilter){
    this.setState({selectedFilter:newFilter});
  }

  addNewReminder(itemToAdd) {
    if (this.state.reminders===undefined){
      this.setState({reminders:[itemToAdd]});
    } else {
      this.setState((current)=>{
        return (
          {
            reminders:[...current.reminders,itemToAdd]
          }
          )
      });
    }
  }

  setIsComplete(isComplete,index){
    const newReminders = [ ... this.state.reminders.slice(0, index),
                    { ... this.state.reminders[index],isComplete},
                        ... this.state.reminders.slice(index+1) ];
    this.setState({reminders:newReminders});
  }

  render(){
    return(
      <div>
        <InputForm userInput={this.state.userInput}
                   setUserInput={this.setUserInput}
                   addNewReminder={this.addNewReminder} />
        <FilterSelect selectedFilter={this.state.selectedFilter}
                      setSelectedFilter={this.setSelectedFilter} />
        <RemindersList reminders={filteredList} setIsComplete={this.setIsComplete} />
      </div>
    );
  }
}

export default App;
```

4. Copy over the `filterList` function and update its reference to `this.state.reminders`.

5. Use a call to `filterList` inside the `render` method to create the `filteredList`, since we want it to be recalculated when the component re-renders.

With these steps done, the App component should be fully converted to a class, and the Reminders app will function the same as it did before. The final code for the converted App component is shown in Listing 6-56.

LISTING 6-56: The converted App component

```
import {Component} from 'react';
import InputForm from './InputForm';
import FilterSelect from './FilterSelect';
import RemindersList from './RemindersList';

class App extends Component{
  constructor(props){
    super(props);
    this.state = {
      reminders:undefined,
      userInput:undefined,
      selectedFilter:"all"
    }
    this.setUserInput = this.setUserInput.bind(this);
    this.setSelectedFilter = this.setSelectedFilter.bind(this);
    this.addNewReminder = this.addNewReminder.bind(this);
    this.setIsComplete = this.setIsComplete.bind(this);
  }

  setUserInput(newInput){
    this.setState({userInput:newInput});
  }

  setSelectedFilter(newFilter){
    this.setState({selectedFilter:newFilter});
  }

  addNewReminder(itemToAdd) {
    if (this.state.reminders===undefined){
      this.setState({reminders:[itemToAdd]});
    } else {
      this.setState((current)=>{
        return (
          {
            reminders:[...current.reminders,itemToAdd]
          }
        )
      });
    }
  }
}
```

continues

LISTING 6-56 *(continued)*

```
    setIsComplete(isComplete,index){
      const newReminders = [ ...this.state.reminders.slice(0, index),
                        {...this.state.reminders[index],isComplete},
                        ...this.state.reminders.slice(index+1) ];
      this.setState({reminders:newReminders});
    }

    filterList(reminders,selectedFilter){
      if (selectedFilter === "all"){
          return reminders;
      } else {

      let numberOfDays;

      switch(selectedFilter){
          case "2day":
            numberOfDays = 2;
            break;
          case "1week":
            numberOfDays = 7;
            break;
          case "30days":
            numberOfDays = 30;
            break;
          default:
            numberOfDays = 0;
            break;
      }

      const result = this.state.reminders.filter(reminder=>{
          const todaysDate = new Date().toISOString().substr(0,10);
          const todayTime = new Date(todaysDate).getTime();
          const dueTime = new Date(reminder.dueDate).getTime();
          return dueTime < (todayTime + (numberOfDays * 86400000));
      });

      return result;
      }
    }
  render(){
    const filteredList =
this.filterList(this.state.reminders,this.state.selectedFilter);

    return(
      <div>
        <InputForm userInput={this.state.userInput}
                   setUserInput={this.setUserInput}
                   addNewReminder={this.addNewReminder} />
        <FilterSelect selectedFilter={this.state.selectedFilter}
                      setSelectedFilter={this.setSelectedFilter} />
```

```
            <RemindersList reminders={filteredList} setIsComplete={this.setIsComplete} />
          </div>
        );
      }
    }

    export default App;
```

Since all of the state of our application lives in the App component, converting the other components is straightforward and simple. I'll show how to convert the first InputForm to a class, and then the same steps can be followed to convert the others:

1. Import Component from react at the very beginning of the file:

```
import {Component} from 'react';
```

2. Replace the function header with a class header:

```
class InputForm extends Component {
```

3. Wrap the event handler functions and the return statement with the render method and change references to props to references to this.props:

```
render(){
  const handleTextChange=(e)=>{
    const newUserInput = {...this.props.userInput,reminderText:e.target.value}
      this.props.setUserInput(newUserInput);
  }

  const handleDateChange=(e)=>{
    const date = new Date(e.target.value);
    const formattedDate = date.toISOString().substr(0,10);
    const newUserInput = {...this.props.userInput,dueDate:formattedDate};
    this.props.setUserInput(newUserInput);
  }

  const handleClick=(e)=>{
    e.preventDefault();
    const itemToAdd = {...this.props.userInput,isComplete:false};
    this.props.addNewReminder(itemToAdd);
  }

  return(
    <form>
      <input value={this.props.userInput.reminderText}
             id="reminderText"
             type="text"
             placeholder="What do you want to do?"
             onChange={handleTextChange} />

      <input value={this.props.userInput.dueDate}
             id="dueDate"
             type="date"
             onChange={handleDateChange} />
```

```
          <button onClick={handleClick}>Add Item</button>
        </form>
      );
    }
```

Once you've made these changes, start up the app and test it. If you did everything correctly, it should function the same as before. The converted InputForm component is shown in Listing 6-57.

LISTING 6-57: The converted InputForm component

```
import {Component} from 'react';
import PropTypes from 'prop-types';

class InputForm extends Component {

  render(){

    const handleTextChange=(e)=>{
      const newUserInput = {...this.props.userInput,reminderText:e.target.value}
      this.props.setUserInput(newUserInput);
    }

    const handleDateChange=(e)=>{
      const date = new Date(e.target.value);
      const formattedDate = date.toISOString().substr(0,10);
      const newUserInput = {...this.props.userInput,dueDate:formattedDate};
      this.props.setUserInput(newUserInput);
    }

    const handleClick=(e)=>{
      e.preventDefault();
      const itemToAdd = {...this.props.userInput,isComplete:false};
      this.props.addNewReminder(itemToAdd);
    }
    return(
        <form>
            <input value={this.props.userInput.reminderText}
                id="reminderText"
                type="text"
                placeholder="What do you want to do?"
                onChange={handleTextChange} />

            <input value={this.props.userInput.dueDate}
                id="dueDate"
                type="date"
                onChange={handleDateChange} />

            <button onClick={handleClick}>Add Item</button>
        </form>
      );
```

```
    }
  }

InputForm.propTypes = {
  userInput: PropTypes.shape({
    reminderText: PropTypes.string,
    dueDate: PropTypes.string
  }),
  setUserInput: PropTypes.func,
  addNewReminder: PropTypes.func
}

const date = new Date();
const formattedDate = date.toISOString().substr(0,10);

InputForm.defaultProps = {
  userInput: {
    reminderText:"",
    dueDate:formattedDate
  }
}

export default InputForm;
```

This same basic method can be applied to the other components to convert them to class components. However, there is one important gotcha to be aware of. In the `InputForm` and `RemindersList` functions, we defined the internal event handler functions using the `function` keyword. When you define functions using the `function` keyword and then reference `this` inside of them, `this` refers to the function, not to the object the function is a part of. The result is that the following function will result in an error:

```
function handleChange(e){
  this.props.setSelectedFilter(e.target.value);
}
```

The easiest solution (but not the only solution) is to simply redefine the function as an arrow function. The `this` keyword inside an arrow function references the object that the function is a part of:

```
const handleChange = (e)=> {
  this.props.setSelectedFilter(e.target.value);
}
```

If you're really set on using the `function` keyword, another solution is to use the `bind` function to specify that the function should run in the context of the current object. You can bind the function in the constructor (as you've previously seen) or in the `onChange` event listener attribute, like this:

```
        <select id="filterReminders"
                value={this.props.selectedFilter}
                onChange={this.handleChange.bind(this)}>
```

SUMMARY

One-way data flow is a large part of what makes React user interfaces able to handle updates efficiently and reliably. Although some of the patterns and techniques used to implement one-way data flow may be unfamiliar to many JavaScript programmers, they are just JavaScript, and they become second nature as you work with React more. Especially since the introduction of React Hooks, and the useState hook in particular, basic state management in React has become simpler while also remaining compatible with previous methods of writing React components.

In this chapter, you learned:

- ➤ How one-way data flow works.
- ➤ How to pass data to child components with props.
- ➤ How to initialize state.
- ➤ How to change state variables in class components and in function components.
- ➤ How to work with the asynchronous nature of setState.
- ➤ What immutability is.
- ➤ The importance of shallow copies.
- ➤ How to validate props using PropTypes.
- ➤ How to set default prop values using defaultProps.
- ➤ How to use the rest and spread operators.
- ➤ The steps to build an app from mockup to reactivity.
- ➤ How to "lift state up."
- ➤ How to convert between function components and class components.

In the next chapter, we'll go into more depth about how events, event listening, and event handling work in React.

Events

Events, and the functions that run in response to events, are what make React reactive. In this chapter, you'll learn:

➤ How and where to use event listeners.

➤ The difference between native events and SyntheticEvents.

➤ How to write event handlers in class and function components.

➤ How to use the Event object.

➤ How to bind functions to class components.

➤ How to pass data to event handlers.

➤ How to use arrow functions for inline event handlers.

➤ How passing functions to child components works.

HOW EVENTS WORK IN REACT

To put it simply, listening for events in a React component and handling events is done similarly to how HTML event attributes trigger actions in a browser.

In HTML, it's possible to use event attributes to call JavaScript functions. These event attributes have names starting with "on" and they take a function call as their value. For example, the HTML onsubmit event attribute can be used with the <form> element to invoke a function when the form is submitted. Listing 7-1 shows an example of using the HTML onsubmit attribute. This example assumes that a JavaScript function named validate() has been defined or imported elsewhere in the HTML file.

LISTING 7-1: Using an event attribute in HTML

```
<form id="signup-form" onsubmit="validate()">
  <input type="text" id="email">
  <input type="text" id="fullname">
  <input type="submit">
</form>
```

Because HTML event attributes violate the "separation of concerns" rule that says markup and scripts should be kept separate, it's generally not a good practice to rely on them too heavily in web apps. Instead, most JavaScript programmers use the `addEventListener` DOM method to attach event listeners to HTML elements, as shown in Listing 7-2.

LISTING 7-2: Using addEventListener

```
<html>
  <head>
    <script>
      function validate(e){
        //do something here
      }
    </script>
  </head>
  <body>
    <form id="signup-form">
      <input type="text" id="email">
      <input type="text" id="fullname">
      <input type="submit">
    </form>
    <script>
      document.getElementById("signup-form").addEventListener("submit",validate);
    </script>
  </body>
</html>
```

> **NOTE** In Listing 7-2, the event listener is registered at the end of the body of the document, so the `form` element will be loaded beforehand. Another way to accomplish the same thing is to add another event listener to the document that waits until the entire page (the HTML document) is loaded before registering event listeners.

In React, setting event listeners is a hybrid between the two approaches for doing so in HTML. The syntax in the JSX code looks very similar to an HTML event attribute, but because it's JSX, it actually compiles to something that more closely resembles using `addEventListener`.

Listing 7-3 shows how to set an event listener in a React component to listen for a form's submit event.

LISTING 7-3: Setting an event listener in a React component

```
function MyForm(props){
  return (
    <form onSubmit={props.handleSubmit}>
      <input type="text" id="fullName" />
      <input type="text" id="phoneNumber" />
      <button>Submit</button>
    </form>
  );
}
export default MyForm;
```

As you'll frequently see in React, it would seem that the use of an event listener attribute would violate the same separation of concerns rule that dictates that the use of event attributes in HTML should be avoided. However, keep in mind that JSX is, essentially, JavaScript. So, in reality, it's not that you're using HTML to trigger JavaScript, but that you're using JavaScript to write HTML and to add an event listener to the `form` element created using JavaScript.

The two biggest clues as to what's really going on when you write event attributes in JSX are:

1. As with the DOM `addEventListener` method, React event attributes take a function, rather than a string containing a function call, as their value. The value of a React event attribute must be in curly braces and it should not have the pair of parentheses after the function name.

2. React event attributes use JavaScript-style camelCase names, rather than the HTML-style lowercase attribute names used by HTML event attributes.

React events are actually a wrapper around native HTML DOM events, which take the same names as the native events (albeit with different capitalization). These wrapped events are instances of a React class called *SyntheticEvent*.

WHAT IS SYNTHETICEVENT?

`SyntheticEvent` is a cross-browser wrapper around the browser's native events. Historically, web browsers have always had slightly different ways of handling events. Most famously, in Microsoft's now defunct Internet Explorer browser, the `event` object was a global property of the browser's `window` object, whereas in Chrome and Firefox, it was a property passed to event handlers (as is the case with SyntheticEvent). Another important difference between how browsers handle events is at what point in the propagation of events do the event listeners handle them. Today, every modern browser handles events during the event "bubbling" phase, but in the earlier days of web browsers, Internet Explorer handled events during the "capture" phase.

> **NOTE** *Event bubbling refers to the upward propagation of an event from a lower level in the element hierarchy to a higher one. Event capture is the opposite. In event bubbling, an event that happens on a button (such as a click) is dispatched by the button before the* form *element that contains the button dispatches it.*

These historic and major differences between how web browsers handle events have largely been ironed out, and today the real value of having a cross-browser wrapper for events is that it can provide additional and consistent properties across every browser.

SyntheticEvent also shields developers from the implementation details of exactly how events in React are translated to DOM events in the browser. The React documentation is intentionally vague about exactly how SyntheticEvents map to native events (although it is possible to find this out, as you'll see). Except in rare cases, these details won't matter to a React developer, and because these details are not part of the official React documentation, they are subject to change at any time.

USING EVENT LISTENER ATTRIBUTES

To create an event listener in React, use one of the supported event listener attributes on a built-in HTML DOM element. If the HTML event that will be created by a React component supports a certain event, it should also be supported by the React component, except in a few cases where things work differently in React.

Using an event listener attribute in an element created by a custom component won't have any effect on the custom component except to create a prop inside of it with same name as the event listener attribute. For example, inside the following element, a prop named onClick will be created:

```
<MyButton onClick={handleEvent} />
```

The preceding onClick attribute is not an event listener attribute. It's common to use the names of event listener attributes to pass event handlers between custom components, but doing so doesn't actually add the event listener to the resulting browser DOM.

In order for the MyButton component to actually be able to handle events, you must have an HTML DOM element inside the MyButton component that has an event listener attribute. For example, here's what the return statement of the MyButton component might look like:

```
return (
  <button onClick={props.onClick}>Click Me</button>
);
```

THE EVENT OBJECT

When an event happens in React, it triggers an event in the DOM. This, in turn, creates an instance of the `Event` object, which triggers the creation of a SyntheticEvent object in React. This is what we mean by SyntheticEvent being a wrapper around native DOM events.

The `Event` object contains the properties and methods that are common to all events. The most important of these base `Event` properties and methods are the following:

➤ `Event.cancelable` indicates whether an event can be canceled. Canceling an event prevents the event from happening. Canceling events is useful when you want to prevent a user from clicking something or to prevent a `form` element from submitting a form, for example.

➤ `Event.target` references the object onto which the event was originally dispatched (such as an element that was clicked or a form input that was typed into).

➤ `Event.type` contains the name of the event, such as `click`, `change`, `load`, `mouseover`, and so forth.

➤ `Event.preventDefault` cancels an event if it's cancelable.

The wrapper that React creates around the JavaScript `Event` object is named `SyntheticBaseEvent`.

To access the properties and methods of the `SyntheticBaseEvent` object, specify a parameter in the function definition for your event handler. The `SyntheticBaseEvent` object will take the name of this parameter inside the function. It's a standard practice for this parameter to be named either `event` or simply `e`, but there's no restriction in React or JavaScript on what valid JavaScript variable name you give it.

Listing 7-4 is a React component that listens for a `click` event on a button and then prints out the properties of the dispatched `SyntheticBaseEvent` object to the console.

LISTING 7-4: Viewing the properties of the Event object

```
function EventProps(){
    const logClick=(e)=>{
        console.dir(e);
    }
    return(
        <button onClick={logClick}>Click Me</button>
    )
}

export default EventProps;
```

With modifications, this basic function can be used to view the properties of the `SyntheticBaseEvent` object for any event. Figure 7-1 shows the object that's output to the console when you click the button in this component.

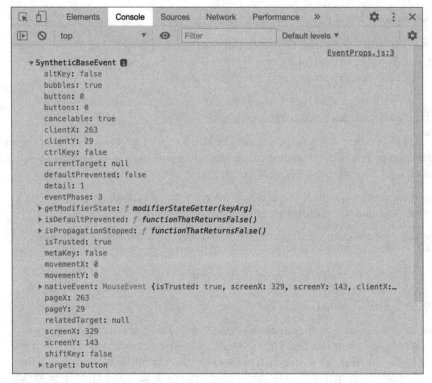

FIGURE 7-1: Viewing the properties of a SyntheticEvent

The `SyntheticBaseEvent` object has a property called `NativeEvent`, which is an object that contains all the properties from the native `Event` object that `SyntheticBaseEvent` wraps around. Compare the properties in this `NativeEvent` object, shown in Figure 7-2, with the properties in the `SyntheticEvent` shown in Figure 7-1.

SUPPORTED EVENTS

All interactivity in a web browser happens as a result of events. Events are what is emitted (or "fired") by software in reaction to interactions or significant things (including automated processes) happening in the browser. For example, when a user clicks a mouse button while the pointer is hovered over a button, that causes the button element to emit a `click` event. The movement of the mouse pointer within the browser window and the mouse pointer hovering over an element trigger additional events.

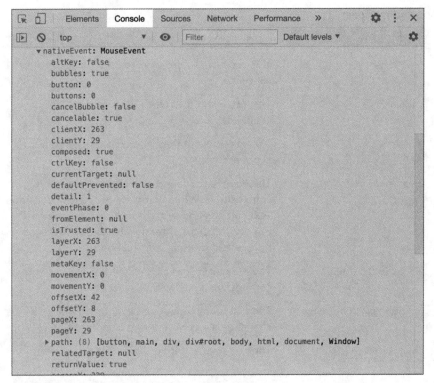

FIGURE 7-2: The NativeEvent properties

Many DOM events are defined in official specifications, and others are defined and used by specific browsers. These events can be detected using the HTML DOM and responded to using JavaScript running in the browser.

React supports listening for and handling many of the standard DOM events. Many of these events add properties to the `Event` object, which you can use to find out more about the event. For example, the keyboard events include properties that tell which key was pressed.

Table 7-1 lists the events that are currently supported within React, along with a brief description of each one. To view the properties added to the `Event` object, you can log the `Event` object to the console, as shown in Listing 7-4, or visit the excellent Event API documentation available at `https://developer.mozilla.org/en-US/docs/Web/API/Event`.

TABLE 7-1: Events Supported by React

CATEGORY	EVENT LISTENER	DESCRIPTION
Clipboard Events	onCopy	The `copy` event fires when data is copied to the clipboard.
	onCut	The `cut` event fires when data is cut to the clipboard.
	onPaste	The `paste` event fires when data is pasted from the clipboard.
Composition Events	onCompositionEnd	The `compositionend` event fires when a text composition system completes or cancels a session. Text composition systems include input method editors (IMEs) for entering Chinese, Japanese, or Korean text using a Latin keyboard.
	onCompositionStart	The `compositionstart` event fires when a text composition system starts a session.
	onCompositionUpdate	The `compositionupdate` event fires when a new character is received during a composition session.
Keyboard Events	onKeyDown	The `keydown` event fires when a key is pressed.
	onKeyPress	The `keypress` event fires when a key that produces a character is pressed.
	onKeyUp	The `keyup` event fires when a key is released.
Focus Events	onFocus	The `focus` event fires when an element receives focus, for example when an `input` element is selected.
	onBlur	The `blur` event fires when an element loses focus, for example when an `input` element becomes unselected (by tabbing out of it or clicking another input element).
Form Events	onChange	The `change` event is fired for `input`, `select`, and `textarea` elements when the value of the input is changed by the user.
	onInput	The `input` event fires when the value of an element changes.
	onInvalid	The `invalid` event fires when a submittable element's content is checked and doesn't meet its constraints. For example, when a number input receives a number outside of the range specified by `min` and `max` attributes.

CATEGORY	EVENT LISTENER	DESCRIPTION
	`onReset`	The `reset` event fires when a form is reset.
	`onSubmit`	The `submit` event fires when a form is submitted.
Generic Events	`onError`	The `error` event fires when a resource fails to load.
	`onLoad`	The `load` event fires when a resource finishes loading.
Mouse Events	`onClick`	The `click` event fires when a pointing device (such as a mouse) has been pressed and released.
	`onContextMenu`	The `contextmenu` event fires when the right mouse button is clicked.
	`onDoubleClick`	The `doubleclick` event fires when the mouse button is double-clicked.
	`onDrag`	The `drag` event fires while an element or text selection is being dragged.
	`onDragEnd`	The `dragend` event fires when a drag event ends (such as when the mouse button is released).
	`onDragEnter`	The `dragenter` event fires when a draggable element enters a drop target.
	`onDragExit`	The `dragexit` event fires when a draggable element exits a drop target. Note: `onDragExit` may not work in all browsers. Use `onDragLeave` instead.
	`onDragLeave`	The `dragleave` event fires when a draggable element exits a drop target.
	`onDragOver`	The `dragover` event fires while a draggable element is being dragged over a drop target.
	`onDragStart`	The `dragstart` event fires when the user begins dragging an element.
	`onDrop`	The `drop` event fires when an element is dropped on a drop target.
	`onMouseDown`	The `mousedown` event fires when a pointing device button (such as a mouse button) is pressed on an element.
	`onMouseEnter`	The `mouseenter` event fires when a pointing device is moved onto an element.

continues

TABLE 7-1 *(continued)*

CATEGORY	EVENT LISTENER	DESCRIPTION
	onMouseLeave	The `mouseleave` event fires when a pointing device is moved off an element.
	onMouseMove	The `mousemove` event fires when a pointing device is moved over an element.
	onMouseOut	The `mouseout` event fires when a pointing device is moved off an element that has the `onMouseOut` event listener attached to one of its children.
	onMouseOver	The `mouseover` event fires when a pointing device is moved onto an element that has the `onMouseOver` event listener attached to one of its children.
	onMouseUp	The `mouseup` event fires when a pointing device button is released over an element.
Pointer Events	onPointerDown	The `pointerdown` event fires when a pointer device (such as a mouse, pen, or touch) becomes active, for example when a button is clicked or a touch-sensitive device is touched.
	onPointerMove	The `pointermove` event fires when a pointer changes coordinates.
	onPointerUp	The `pointerup` event fires when a pointer is no longer active.
	onPointerCancel	The `pointercancel` event fires when a browser decides there are unlikely to be more pointer events (such as when the browser window becomes inactive).
	onGotPointerCapture	The `gotpointercapture` event fires when the `setPointerCapture` method is used to capture a pointer.
	onLostPointerCapture	The `lostpointercapture` event fires when a captured pointer is released.
	onPointerEnter	The `pointerenter` event fires when a pointer moves into the boundaries of an element on a device that doesn't support hover (such as a pen or touch device with no mouse).
	onPointerLeave	The `pointerleave` event fires when a pointer moves out of the boundaries of an element.

CATEGORY	EVENT LISTENER	DESCRIPTION
	`onPointerOver`	The `pointerover` event fires when a pointing device moves into an element's boundaries.
	`onPointerOut`	The `pointerout` event fires when a pointer leaves the boundaries of an element.
Selection Events	`onSelect`	The `select` event fires when text is selected.
Touch Events	`onTouchCancel`	The `touchcancel` event fires when a touch point has been disrupted.
	`onTouchEnd`	The `touchend` event fires when a touch point is removed from a touch surface.
	`onTouchMove`	The `touchmove` event fires when a touch point is moved along a touch surface.
	`onTouchStart`	The `touchstart` event fires when a touch point is placed on a touch surface.
UI Events	`onScroll`	The `scroll` event fires when the document or an element is scrolled.
Wheel Events	`onWheel`	The `wheel` event fires when a wheel button of a pointing device is rotated.
Media Events	`onAbort`	The `abort` event fires when playback of the media is aborted.
	`onCanPlay`	The `canplay` event fires when enough data is available that the media can start playing.
	`onCanPlayThrough`	The `canplaythrough` event fires when enough of a media file is downloaded that the file can play without interruption.
	`onDurationChange`	The `durationchange` event fires when the metadata indicating the duration of the media file changes, such as when enough of it has downloaded that the duration is known.
	`onEmptied`	The `emptied` event fires when the media has become empty, such as when it's reloaded.
	`onEncrypted`	The `encrypted` event fires when the media indicates that it's encrypted.
	`onEnded`	The `ended` event fires when playback of the media ends.

continues

TABLE 7-1 *(continued)*

CATEGORY	EVENT LISTENER	DESCRIPTION
	onError	The `error` event fires when an error occurs.
	onLoadedData	The `loadeddata` event fires when the media has finished loading.
	onLoadedMetadata	The `loadedmetadata` event fires when the media's metadata is loaded.
	onLoadStart	The `loadstart` event fires when loading of the media starts.
	onPause	The `pause` event fires when playback is paused.
	onPlay	The `play` event fires when playback begins or resumes as a result of the `play` method.
	onPlaying	The `playing` event fires after the `play` event, when the media has enough data to begin playing.
	onProgress	The `progress` event fires during loading of media and contains information about the amount of data loaded.
	onRateChange	The `ratechange` event fires when playback changes speed.
	onSeeked	The `seeked` event fires when a seek operation finishes.
	onSeeking	The `seeking` event fires when a seek operation starts.
	onStalled	The `stalled` event fires when loading of media is unexpectedly not happening.
	onSuspend	The `suspend` event fires when loading of media is paused or completed.
	onTimeUpdate	The `timeupdate` event fires when the `currentTime` attribute of the element changes.
	onVolumeChange	The `volumechange` event fires when the audio volume changes.
	onWaiting	The `waiting` event fires when a requested operation is delayed.
Image Events	onLoad	The `load` event fires when an image is fully loaded.
	onError	The `error` event fires when an error occurs in loading of an image.

CATEGORY	EVENT LISTENER	DESCRIPTION
Animation Events	onAnimationStart	The animationstart event fires when an animation starts.
	onAnimationEnd	The animationend event fires when an animation stops.
	onAnimationIteration	The animationiteration event fires when one iteration of an animation ends and another starts.
Transition Events	onTransitionEnd	The transitionend event fires when a CSS transition completes.
Other Events	onToggle	The toggle event fires when the state of a details element (open or closed) is toggled.

EVENT HANDLER FUNCTIONS

Once your React component has detected an event, you can write a function that will take some action in response to the event. This function is called an *event handler function*.

Writing Inline Event Handlers

An inline event handler is an anonymous function that's written as the value of an event listener attribute. Inline event handlers are often used as wrappers for calling another function that's defined outside of the return statement. They may also be used for performing simple tasks that perhaps don't warrant the creation of a full event handler function.

Listing 7-5 shows an example of an inline event handler.

LISTING 7-5: Using an inline event handler to show an alert

```
function WarningButton(){

return (
  <button onClick={()=>{alert('Are you sure?');}}>Don't Click Here</button>
);

}

export default WarningButton;
```

It's possible to call multiple functions or execute a block of code from inside an inline event handler, but there are several reasons for not using inline event handlers for complex code:

1. Inline event handlers aren't reusable.

2. Inline event handlers can be difficult to read and they reduce the organization of your code.

3.   Inline event handlers are re-created every time the component re-renders. In function components, this is what happens to all inner functions. But, in class components, inline event handlers may affect performance, although the effect is not likely to be noticeable, and prematurely optimizing your code for this kind of problem before you have it will cause you more problems (in terms of time wasted alone) than it solves.

> **NOTE** I'll talk about how to use React Hooks to cache event handler functions in function components in Chapter 11.

Inline event handlers are often also used when the result of some user interaction should be simply to update the state in some way. In a class component, this means that setState is called, or in a function component, when the state setter function is called. Listing 7-6 shows an example of using an inline event handler to call setState.

LISTING 7-6: Using an inline event handler to call setState

```
import {Component} from 'react';

class ScreenDoor extends Component {
  constructor(props){
    super(props);
    this.state={
      isOpen:true
    }
  }
  render(){
    return(
      <button onClick={()=>this.setState({isOpen:!this.state.isOpen})}>
        {this.state.isOpen?'Close the Door':'Open the Door'}
      </button>
    )
  }
}

export default ScreenDoor;
```

Writing Event Handlers in Function Components

An event handler inside a function component is written as an inner function, using either arrow syntax or the function keyword.

If you're comfortable with the class method of writing components, you can think of function components as being the render method from a class component. The event handlers in a function component only exist for a single render, unlike in class components where they're methods of the class and persist between renders.

Function components don't have the `this` keyword, and so there's no need to bind event handlers declared inside of functions.

Writing functions inside of function components is as simple as writing a function anywhere else. Once you've written an event handler function, you can assign it to a particular event listener by passing the name of the function as the value of an event listener attribute, as shown in Listing 7-7.

LISTING 7-7: Using an event handler function in a function component

```
import {useState} from 'react';

function Search(props){

  const [term,setTerm] = useState('');
  const updateTerm = (searchTerm)=>{
    setTerm(searchTerm);
  }

  return(
    <>
      <input type="text" value={term} onChange={(e)=>{updateTerm(e.target.value)}}
/><br />
      You're searching for: {term}
    </>
  );

}

export default Search;
```

Writing Event Handlers in Class Components

Event handlers in class components are methods of the class. They're written outside of the `render` method and must be bound to the specific instance of the class.

Listing 7-8 shows one way to write and bind an event handler method in a class component.

LISTING 7-8: Writing and binding an event handler method in a class

```
import {Component} from 'react';

class CoffeeMachine extends Component {
  constructor(props){
    super(props);
    this.state={
      brewing:false
    }
    this.toggleBrewing = this.toggleBrewing.bind(this);
  }
```

continues

LISTING 7-8 *(continued)*

```
  toggleBrewing = function(){
    this.setState({brewing:!this.state.brewing});
  }

  render(){

    return(
      <>
        The Coffee Maker is {this.state.brewing?'on':'off'}.<br />
        <button onClick={this.toggleBrewing}>toggle brewing state</button>
      </>
    );
  }
}

export default CoffeeMachine;
```

JAVASCRIPT LESSON: METHOD DEFINITION SYNTAX

In JavaScript classes, functions in the class (also known as methods) can be created using *method definition syntax*, which is a shorthand way of assigning a function to a method name.

For example, you can define a method by assigning a function to a property, like this:

```
toggleBrewing = function(){
    this.setState({brewing:!this.state.brewing});
}
```

Or you can use method definition syntax, like this:

```
toggleBrewing(){
    this.setState({brewing:!this.state.brewing});
}
```

Binding Event Handler Functions

To be useful, event handler functions need to be passed as values to React's built-in components that support event listener attributes. For example, the built-in `input` element represents an input component that can receive an `onChange` event handler prop and will call an associated callback function when it receives a `change` event.

Because event handler functions are passed to child components via props, they need to be bound to the context in which they were created so that the value of `this` will refer to the parent component in which the event handler was defined.

Only class components have a this keyword, so binding only applies in class components. Plus, as you'll see, binding only applies in class components to methods defined using function or method definition syntax.

Using bind

If you're still not clear on how this and bind work in JavaScript classes, go back and review the JavaScript lesson from Chapter 4. Or, just remember this rule:

> In class components, if a function defined using method definition syntax or the function keyword will be passed as a prop, bind it.

Functions can be bound in one of two ways. The first is the method you've seen most often so far: in the constructor. In this method, you overwrite the value of the unbound function with a new function that includes the context of the class, as shown in Listing 7-9.

LISTING 7-9: Binding a function in the constructor

```
import {Component} from 'react';

class ColorWheel extends Component {

  constructor(props){
    super(props);
    this.state = {
      currentColor: '#ff0000'
    }
    this.changeColor = this.changeColor.bind(this);
  }

  changeColor(e) {
    this.setState({currentColor:e.target.value});
  }

  render(){
    const wheelStyle = {
        width: "200px",
        height: "200px",
        borderRadius: "50%",
        backgroundColor: this.state.currentColor
    }
    return(
      <>
        <div style={wheelStyle}></div>
        <input onChange={this.changeColor} value={this.state.currentColor} />
      </>
    )
  }
}

export default ColorWheel;
```

The other method of binding a function is to do it inline. In this method, you bind the function inside the value of the event listener attribute, as shown in Listing 7-10.

LISTING 7-10: Binding an event handler inline

```
import {Component} from 'react';

class ColorWheel extends Component {

  constructor(props){
    super(props);
    this.state = {
      currentColor: '#ff0000'
    }
  }

  changeColor(e) {
    this.setState({currentColor:e.target.value});
  }

  render(){
    const wheelStyle = {
        width: "200px",
        height: "200px",
        borderRadius: "50%",
        backgroundColor: this.state.currentColor
    }
    return(
      <>
        <div style={wheelStyle}></div>
        <input onChange={this.changeColor.bind(this)} value={this.state.currentColor} />
      </>
    )
  }
}

export default ColorWheel;
```

While the inline method may be more convenient in some cases, it has the drawback of living inside the `render` method, which means that it will re-run every time the component renders. Also, it may result in duplication of effort if you use the same event handler function more than once in a class.

Because the constructor only runs once, binding in the constructor has the benefit of being efficient as well as of keeping your code tidy.

Using Arrow Functions

Arrow functions use lexical `this` binding. What this means is that they are automatically bound to the scope in which they're created. As a result, if you define your event handlers using arrow functions, or write your event handlers as inline arrow functions, they don't need to be bound.

Listing 7-11 shows how to use an arrow function as an event handler.

LISTING 7-11: Using an arrow function as an event handler

```
import {Component} from 'react';

class ColorWheel extends Component {

  constructor(props){
    super(props);
    this.state = {
      currentColor: '#ff0000'
    }
  }

  changeColor = (e)=>{
    this.setState({currentColor:e.target.value});
  }

  render(){

    const wheelStyle = {
        width: "200px",
        height: "200px",
        borderRadius: "50%",
        backgroundColor: this.state.currentColor
    }

    return(
      <>
        <div style={wheelStyle}></div>
        <input onChange={this.changeColor} value={this.state.currentColor} />
      </>
    )
  }
}

export default ColorWheel;
```

Using the same syntax that you used to eliminate the binding of the event handler in the constructor, you may also be able to eliminate the constructor completely and define your component's state using a class property, as shown in Listing 7-12.

LISTING 7-12: Defining state using a class property

```
import {Component} from 'react';

class ColorWheel extends Component {

  state = {currentColor: '#ff0000'};
```

continues

LISTING 7-12 (continued)

```
  changeColor = (e)=>{
    this.setState({currentColor:e.target.value});
  }

  render(){

    const wheelStyle = {
        width: "200px",
        height: "200px",
        borderRadius: "50%",
        backgroundColor: this.state.currentColor
    }

    return(
      <>
        <div style={wheelStyle}></div>
        <input onChange={this.changeColor} value={this.state.currentColor} />
      </>
    )
  }
}

export default ColorWheel;
```

Passing Data to Event Handlers

Event handlers often need to receive data from within the render method. Most commonly, event handlers need access to the Event object so they can make use of its properties to get form field values, mouse position, and the other properties that you saw in Table 7-1.

If you specify your event handler using just the name of the event handler function, the good news is that there's nothing more to do. The Event object is passed to the event handler function automatically, as demonstrated in Listing 7-13.

LISTING 7-13: The Event object is passed automatically

```
function LogInput(){
    const logChange=(e)=>{
        console.dir(e);
    }
    return(
        <input onChange={logChange} />
    )
}

export default LogInput;
```

If you use an anonymous arrow function to call your event handler, you do need to specifically pass the Event object into the event handler, as shown in Listing 7-14.

LISTING 7-14: Passing the Event object to the event handler

```
function LogInput(){
    const logChange=(e)=>{
        console.dir(e);
    }
    return(
        <input onChange={(e)=>{logChange(e)}} />
    )
}

export default LogInput;
```

SUMMARY

Through its use of a familiar and simple interface and standard, idiomatic JavaScript, React allows programmers to enable interactivity within user interfaces while also gaining the benefits of one-way data flow.

In this chapter, you learned:

➤ What SyntheticEvents are.

➤ How to log the properties of the `SyntheticBaseEvent` object.

➤ What event listeners React can respond to.

➤ How to write event handlers in both function and class components.

➤ How to bind event handlers in class components.

➤ How to pass data into event handlers.

In the next chapter, you'll learn how to create interactive forms in React and how to listen for and respond to form events.

Forms

HTML form elements are what make it possible for web applications to gather user input. React has built-in HTML DOM components that create native HTML form elements. The built-in React components that create HTML form elements behave somewhat differently from native HTML form elements in some important ways, however. In this chapter, you'll learn:

➤ How to use form components in React with one-way data flow.

➤ The difference between controlled and uncontrolled form inputs.

➤ How and why to prevent a form's default action.

➤ How to use each of React's form elements.

➤ How to retrieve and use data from a form.

FORMS HAVE STATE

Form elements in HTML are unique in that they maintain their own internal state. When you type into a text input or check a checkbox or select something from a dropdown menu, it changes the internal state of the element.

For example, in an HTML `input` element, this state is kept in the `value` attribute and in a `checkbox` element, the state is kept in a Boolean attribute named `checked`. It's possible in HTML for the internal state of a form element to be set either by a person interacting with the form (typing into it or checking boxes, for example) or by changing the value of the attribute that determines the state.

If you've been paying close attention, you'll recognize this default behavior of HTML forms as two-way data flow, which is generally discouraged in React. Ideally, everything that changes in a React user interface should be the result of changes to the state object. However, with forms, there are times when implementing one-way data flow is unnecessary and maybe even a little ridiculous, as I'll demonstrate. Rather than forcing the programmer to always implement one-way data flow for form elements, React has two different ways to work with form inputs that you can choose between depending on the needs of a particular form. React calls these two different ways of working with inputs *controlled* and *uncontrolled*.

CONTROLLED INPUTS VS. UNCONTROLLED INPUTS

The default behavior of an `input` element is to allow the user to change its value directly. In one-way data flow, on the other hand, every interaction with the user interface results in an event which, when handled, updates the state. Changes to state then update the user interface.

React calls a form input that can be directly manipulated by the user an *uncontrolled input*, and one that can only be changed through changes to the state object a *controlled input*.

Figure 8-1 illustrates the difference between controlled and uncontrolled inputs.

Uncontrolled

`<input type="text" />`

Strawberry

Controlled

`<input type="text" value="Strawberry" />`

Strawberry

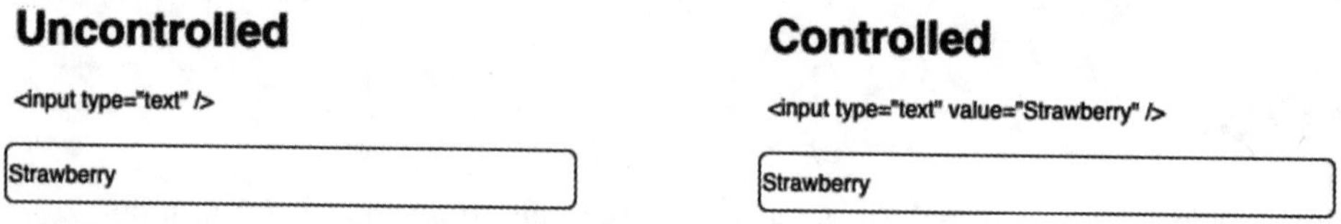

FIGURE 8-1: Controlled and uncontrolled inputs

To create an uncontrolled input, omit the `value` attribute from the JSX code for that input, as shown in Listing 8-1.

LISTING 8-1: Omiting the value attribute creates an uncontrolled input

```
function SignUp(props) {
  return(
    <form>
      <input type="text" name="emailAddress" />
      <button>Sign up for our newsletter</button>
    </form>
  )
}

export default SignUp;
```

Figure 8-2 shows the result of rendering the preceding component and typing into the input. This is exactly the behavior you'd expect with an HTML form.

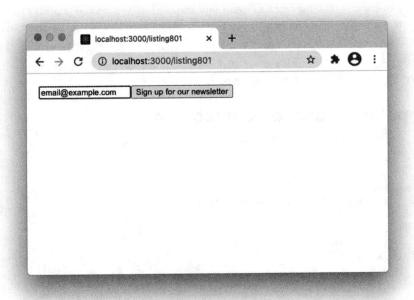

FIGURE 8-2: Rendering an uncontrolled input

To make this form be controlled, add a `value` attribute, as shown in Listing 8-2.

LISTING 8-2: Adding the value attribute creates a controlled input

```
function SignUp(props){
  return(
    <form>
      <input value="" type="text" name="emailAddress" />
      <button>Sign up for our newsletter</button>
    </form>
  )
}

export default SignUp;
```

Simply adding the `value` attribute causes React to "control" the input. Now, when you render the `SignUp` component and try to type into it, nothing will happen. It's impossible to demonstrate nothing happening in a figure, so if you'd like to see this, you can create a component similar to the one in Listing 8-2 or download the example code from this book's GitHub repository.

Updating a Controlled Input

Unless your goal is to create an input that can't be edited, a controlled input must also have an event listener attribute and an event handler function. Even though the internal state of the input element in Listing 8-2 doesn't change when you type into it, it still fires a `change` event with every keystroke.

Using the onChange event listener, you can detect this event and use the target.value property of the Event object to update the state property, which can then be assigned to the value attribute of the input.

The process for controlling a controlled input is the same in function and class components, but the JavaScript code you need to write in each differs somewhat.

Controlling an Input in a Function Component

Listing 8-3 shows a controlled text input that updates using one-way data flow in a function component.

LISTING 8-3: Updating an input element with one-way data flow

```
import {useState} from 'react';

function SignUp(props){

  const [emailAddress,setEmailAddress] = useState('');

  const handleChange = (e)=>{
    setEmailAddress(e.target.value);
  }

  return(
    <>
      <form>
        <label>Enter your email address:
          <input value={emailAddress} onChange={handleChange} type="text" />
        </label>
      </form>
      <p>Your email address: {emailAddress}</p>
    </>
  )
}

export default SignUp;
```

When you run this component in a browser, typing into the input updates the value of the emailAddress state variable, which is used as the value of the input and is also output in the paragraph below the input. The input behaves like a normal HTML input, but the component also has access to the value of the input.

Controlling an Input in a Class Component

In a class component, controlling an input works the same way, but the JavaScript is slightly different and a bit more verbose because of the need to write and bind the event handler and to correctly address the state property.

Listing 8-4 shows the same controlled input as Listing 8-3, but written as a class component.

LISTING 8-4: Controlling an input in a class component

```
import {Component} from 'react';

class SignUp extends Component{

  constructor(props){
    super(props);
    this.state = {
      emailAddress:''
    }
    this.handleChange = this.handleChange.bind(this);
  }

  handleChange(e){
    this.setState({emailAddress:e.target.value});
  }

  render(){

    return(
      <>
      <form>
        <label>Enter your email address:
        <input value={this.state.emailAddress} onChange={this.handleChange}
            type="text" />
        </label>
      </form>
      <p>Your email address: {this.state.emailAddress}</p>
      </>
    )
  }
}

export default SignUp;
```

The class component in Listing 8-4 can be written a bit more succinctly by using arrow functions, an inline event handler, and by creating `state` as a class property, as shown in Listing 8-5.

LISTING 8-5: Simplifying a controlled input in a class

```
import {Component} from 'react';

class SignUp extends Component{

  state = {emailAddress:''};

  render(){

    return(
      <>
      <form>
        <label>Enter your email address:
          <input value={this.state.emailAddress}
              onChange={ (e)=>{this.setState({emailAddress:e.target.value})}}
              type="text" />
```

continues

LISTING 8-5 *(continued)*

```
          </label>
        </form>
        <p>Your email address: {this.state.emailAddress}</p>
      </>
    )
  }
}

export default SignUp;
```

LIFTING UP INPUT STATE

Most of the time, when you have a form in a user interface, input into the form should affect some other part of the user interface. For example, words typed into a search form are used to perform a search, and then the searched-for words and the search results are presented in some sort of results component, as shown in Figure 8-3.

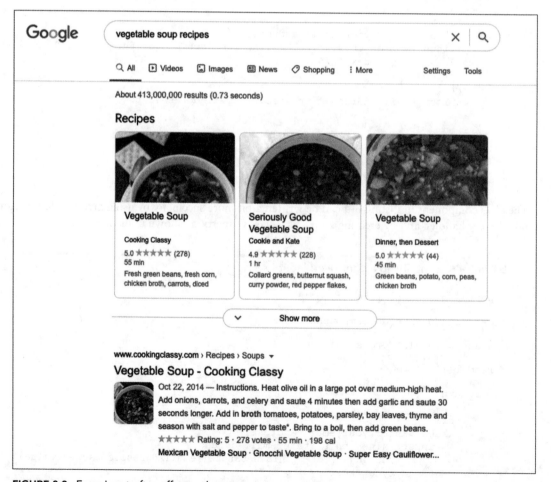

FIGURE 8-3: Form input often affects other components

Because the search term entered into the search form in Figure 8-3 needs to be used by other components, the state variable that the search form updates should be lifted up to a common ancestor of the search form and search results components.

Listings 8-6, 8-7, and 8-8 show three components that might make up a very basic version of the search interface from Figure 8-3. Notice that the setSearchTerm function is passed down to the SearchInput component and the searchTerm variable is passed down to both the SearchInput and SearchResults components.

LISTING 8-6: The SearchBox component

```
import {useState} from 'react';
import SearchInput from './SearchInput';
import SearchResults from './SearchResults';

function SearchBox(){
  const [searchTerm,setSearchTerm] = useState('');

  return(
    <>
      <SearchInput searchTerm = {searchTerm} setSearchTerm = {setSearchTerm} />
      <SearchResults searchTerm = {searchTerm}/>
    </>
  );
}
export default SearchBox;
```

LISTING 8-7: The SearchInput component

```
function SearchInput(props){

  const handleChange = (e)=>{
    props.setSearchTerm(e.target.value);
  }

  return(
    <label>Enter your search term:
      <input type="text" value={props.searchTerm} onChange={handleChange} />
    </label>
  );
}

export default SearchInput;
```

LISTING 8-8: The SearchResults component

```
function SearchResults(props){
  return(
    <p>You're searching for: {props.searchTerm}</p>
```

continues

LISTING 8-8 *(continued)*

```
    );
  }

export default SearchResults;
```

As you saw in Chapter 6, lifting state up minimizes the number of components that need to be stateful. Having a single stateful component eliminates duplication of data processing and provides the application with a single source of truth. In other words, the behavior of the subcomponents can be known and tested based on how the state changes in the stateful component.

USING UNCONTROLLED INPUTS

Using controlled inputs ensures that your user interface strictly adheres to the pattern of one-way data binding, and it enables you to easily work with the current values of your input fields. However, it also creates a lot of overhead work that may be unnecessary.

For example, a "Contact Us" form within a user interface doesn't need to store the data entered into it or do anything with the data as it's being entered. Essentially, such a form isn't really part of the larger application at all, and there's maybe no reason for React to track and run an event handler function for every keystroke that someone enters into a textarea input. Binding each input of a large form can be tedious and the additional processing that it takes to listen for and respond to a large number of form inputs can create performance issues.

In cases where you don't need to track the user's input as they're typing and you don't need to store the input in state, it may be a better choice to use uncontrolled inputs and simply attach an event listener to the form itself to run a function when the form is submitted.

Listing 8-9 shows a comment form, such as you might see on a blog, which uses an uncontrolled input. When the user submits the form, an event handler function runs that retrieves the data from the uncontrolled input and adds it to the state.

LISTING 8-9: A blog comment interface using an uncontrolled input

```
import {useState,useRef} from 'react';

function BlogComment(props){
    const [comments,setComments] = useState([]);
    const textAreaRef = useRef(null);
    const recordComment = (e)=>{
        e.preventDefault();
        setComments([...comments,textAreaRef.current.value]);
    }

    const commentList = comments.map((comment,index)=>{
        return (<p key={index}>{comment}</p>);
    })

    return(
        <>
```

```
                <form onSubmit={recordComment}>
                <p>Enter your comment:</p>
                <textarea ref={textAreaRef}></textarea><br />
                <button>Submit Comment</button>
                <p>All Comments:</p>
                {commentList}
                </form>
            </>
        );
    }

    export default BlogComment;
```

To get values from uncontrolled inputs, you can use a technique called a *ref*. The ref creates a reference to the underlying DOM node, which allows React to access its properties directly. You'll learn more about refs and how and when to use them in Chapter 9.

USING DIFFERENT FORM ELEMENTS

HTML input elements are the most commonly used types of interactive elements. By changing the `type` attribute of the `input` element, you can create inputs for a large and growing number of data types, including:

➤   button

➤   checkbox

➤   color

➤   date

➤   datetime-local

➤   email

➤   file

➤   hidden

➤   image

➤   month

➤   number

➤   password

➤   radio

➤   range

➤   reset

➤   search

➤   submit

➤   tel

➤ `text`

➤ `time`

➤ `url`

➤ `week`

The different input types may look different or have different validation that they perform on user input. For example, the `number` input type will only allow numbers to be entered, the `color` input type will display a color picker (in browsers that support it), and the `hidden` input type doesn't display anything in the browser window.

Controlling the Input Element

With the exception of the input types that create buttons, and the special case of the `file` input type, the way to get the value of a controlled input element in React is by using the `onChange` attribute.

The button inputs (`submit`, `reset`, and `button`) use the `onClick` attribute. The `button` element, which does the same thing as an input with a `type` of `button`, also uses the `onClick` attribute.

The `file` input, which allows you to choose a file from your computer to upload to the browser, is a read-only input. In React, an input with the type of `file` is always uncontrolled.

Controlling a textarea

In HTML, a `textarea` element's value is its children, as shown in Listing 8-10.

LISTING 8-10: An HTML textarea's value is its children

```
<textarea name="terms-of-use">
  Make sure to read all of these terms of use. By reading this book, you agree
to learn React and to never try to mutate a prop or forget to bind an event
handler in a class component. Furthermore, although it is not required, you
agree to consider writing a review of this book and to tell your friends how
great this book is.
</textarea>
```

In React, a `textarea` is written more like an `input` element: as an empty element (meaning it doesn't have an end tag or content) with a `value` attribute. You can use the `onChange` event listener to handle input into a `textarea` in React, as shown in Listing 8-11.

LISTING 8-11: Using a textarea in React

```
function TermsOfUse(props) {
  return(
    <textarea value={props.terms} onChange={props.updateTerms} />
  );
}

export default TermsOfUse;
```

Controlling a Select Element

A `select` element in HTML creates a dropdown list, with any number of `option` element children forming the items in the dropdown list. In HTML, each `option` element has a Boolean attribute named `selected`, which determines the current value of the `select` element, as shown in Listing 8-12.

LISTING 8-12: A select element in HTML

```
<select name="pizza-type">
  <option value="thin">Thin Crust</option>
  <option value="thick">Thick Crust</option>
  <option value="deep">Deep Dish</option>
  <option value="detroit" selected>Detroit-style</option>
  <option value="chicago">Chicago-style</option>
</select>
```

In React, the `select` element has a `value` attribute that determines which `option` is currently selected, and the `onChange` attribute on the `select` input can be used to detect and handle changes to the currently selected option, as shown in Listing 8-13.

LISTING 8-13: Using a select input in React

```
function SizeSelect(props){
  return(
    <select name="size" value={props.size} onChange={props.changeSize}>
      <option value="xs">Extra Small</option>
      <option value="sm">Small</option>
      <option vlue="md">Medium</option>
      <option value="lg">Large</option>
      <option value="xl">Extra Large</option>
    </select>
  );
}

export default SizeSelect;
```

PREVENTING DEFAULT ACTIONS

When you submit a form in a browser window, the default action that the browser will take is to reload the current page, passing the values from the form as a querystring appended to the URL. You can change the default action of the `form` element by using the `action` and `method` attributes of the `form` element. The `action` attribute changes the URL that the form will submit to, and the `method` attribute changes the HTTP method used to submit the form (either using HTTP GET or HTTP POST).

In user interfaces written using JavaScript, you don't want the `form` element to submit data to a URL at all. Instead, the form data should be handled by JavaScript. The reason for this is that default action of a form reloads the form or loads a different URL, which has the effect of reloading the underlying JavaScript library and erasing the state of the user interface.

React doesn't have its own method for preventing default actions. Instead, it just uses the `prevent-Default` method of the `Event` object. Any time you write an event handler to respond to a `submit` event, you must include a call to `preventDefault`, as shown in Listing 8-14.

LISTING 8-14: Using preventDefault

```
function SignUpForm(props){

  const handleSubmit = (e)=>{
    e.preventDefault();
    props.commitFormData();
  }

  return(
    <form onSubmit={handleSubmit}>
      <input type="email" value={props.email} onChange={props.setEmail} />
      <button>Sign Up!</button>
    </form>
  )
}

export default SignUpForm;
```

SUMMARY

Because of one-way data flow, using forms and inputs in React is somewhat different from using them in native HTML or in other frameworks and libraries. Controlled inputs give your application complete access to user input and maintain the fundamental React pattern of data flowing down and events flowing up.

However, there may be times when it's better to give up control. For this, React provides refs and the ability to have uncontrolled inputs.

In this chapter, you learned:

➤ The difference between controlled and uncontrolled inputs.

➤ How to use events to get data from a controlled input.

➤ How to use refs to get data from an uncontrolled input.

➤ How to use different types of input elements.

➤ How to prevent a form's default action.

In the next chapter, you'll learn about refs, which, when used wisely, can do much more than just getting data from uncontrolled inputs.

Refs

Refs are one of the most-often debated and controversial topics in React. Hundreds of blog posts and articles on the web will caution you to avoid refs. The official documentation for React even says (several times, in fact) that you should avoid using them, except in particular situations.

Knowing exactly when it's okay to use refs and what the problem is with using them is one of the things you'll pick up with more experience, but my aim in this chapter is to give you a head start on understanding why refs are such a hot-button issue, and some practical advice on how to use them correctly.

In this chapter, you'll learn:

➤   How to use refs in class components.

➤   How to use refs in function components.

➤   When you should use refs.

➤   When you shouldn't use refs.

➤   How to maintain the correct focus in a form.

WHAT REFS ARE

Nothing is perfect, and that includes React. There are rare, but unavoidable, times when one-way data flow and the declarative way of only modifying children via props break down. In these cases, which I'll demonstrate in more detail and with plenty of examples in this chapter, a React developer needs to be able to imperatively get into a child component or a DOM node to make changes or access some property directly. For these cases, React provides an "escape hatch" called *refs*.

A ref is reference to a child component that allows you to modify a child component or DOM node from the parent component, rather than by using the standard method of modifying children only by passing props into them.

HOW TO CREATE A REF IN A CLASS COMPONENT

In a class component, refs are created using `React.createRef`. Once you have a ref, you can assign it to a child component by passing it as the value of the `ref` attribute. Listing 9-1 shows how to create a ref to a `textarea` element from a component called `TextReader`.

LISTING 9-1: Creating a ref in a class component

```
import React,{Component} from 'react';

class TextReader extends Component {
  constructor(props) {
    super(props);
    this.textView = React.createRef();
  }
  render() {
    return (
      <textarea ref={this.textView} value={this.props.bookText} />
    );
  }
}
```

HOW TO CREATE A REF IN A FUNCTION COMPONENT

In a function component, you can use the `useRef` hook to create a ref, as shown in Listing 9-2.

LISTING 9-2: Creating a ref with useRef()

```
import {useRef} from 'react';

function TextReader(props) {

  const textView = useRef(null);

  return (
    <textarea ref={textView} value={props.bookText} />
  );

}

export default TextReader;
```

USING REFS

Once you have a ref and you've assigned it to a child element, you can access the properties of that child element by using a property of the ref called `current`. When you create a ref to a DOM element, `current` contains the properties of the DOM node (meaning what's rendered in the browser).

When you create a ref to a custom React element, `current` receives the mounted instance of the component.

Refs can only be passed to class components and DOM elements. Although they can be created inside function components, refs can't be passed to function components. The reason why you can't create a ref to a function component is that functions don't have an instance.

If you need to pass a ref to a component that's currently a function component, the easiest way to do it is by converting the function component to a class component.

> **NOTE** Remember: Function components and class components can co-exist within the same React UI. There's no need to choose one over the other. Use what you're comfortable with or what works best for a component.

With access to the properties and methods of the child, the parent component can pretty much do whatever it wants with it. You could think of creating a ref as like being able to implant a chip into your child that will allow you to remotely control them. But, no one would actually do that or want to.

Listing 9-3 shows how to call the DOM `focus` method on a `textarea` from its parent component. The reason to do this is to make sure that the `textarea` containing the text will have focus when it mounts so that the user can scroll through it using arrow keys without having to click on it first.

LISTING 9-3: Calling a DOM method on a child using a ref

```
import React,{Component} from 'react';

class TextReader extends Component {

  constructor(props) {
    super(props);
    this.textView = React.createRef();
  }

  componentDidMount(){
    this.textView.current.focus();
  }

  render(){
    return (
      <textarea style={{width:'380px',height:'400px'}}
                ref={this.textView}>{this.props.bookText}</textarea>
    );
  }

}

export default TextReader;
```

Figure 9-1 shows what the `TextReader` component looks like rendered in a browser. Notice the highlight around the text area, which indicates that it has focus.

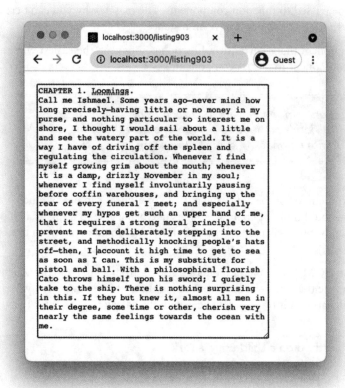

FIGURE 9-1: The TextReader component

CREATING A CALLBACK REF

A third way to create a ref is with a callback ref. A callback ref doesn't use the `createRef` function or the `useRef` hook. Instead, it's a function that you pass into the `ref` attribute, which receives the React component instance or the HTML DOM element as its argument.

Using a ref callback rather than `createRef` or `useRef` is useful when the child you're attaching the ref to is dynamic. The function you pass into the `ref` attribute will be called (with the instance or element passed into it) when the component mounts, and then it will be called again with `null` when the component unmounts.

Listing 9-4 shows an example of creating a callback ref. Notice the use of the condition in the `focusTextView` method, which allows you to avoid calling the `focus` method on the ref if the child element is unmounted.

LISTING 9-4: Creating a callback ref

```
import {Component} from 'react';

class TextReaderCallback extends Component {

  constructor(props) {
    super(props);
    this.textView = null;

    this.setTextViewRef = element => {
      this.textView = element;
    };

    this.focusTextView = () => {
      if (this.textView) this.textView.focus();
    };
  }

  componentDidMount(){
    this.focusTextView();
  }

  render(){
    return (
      <textarea style={{width:'380px',height:'400px'}}
                ref={this.setTextViewRef}
                value={this.props.bookText} />
    );
  }

}

export default TextReaderCallback;
```

Ref callbacks are often passed to child components as inline functions, as shown in Listing 9-5.

LISTING 9-5: Passing a ref callback as an inline function

```
import {Component} from 'react';

class TextReaderCallback extends Component {

  constructor(props) {
    super(props);
    this.textView = null;

    this.focusTextView = () => {
      if (this.textView) this.textView.focus();
    };
  }

  componentDidMount(){
```

continues

LISTING 9-5 *(continued)*

```
      this.focusTextView();
    }

  render(){
    return (
        <textarea style={{width:'380px',height:'400px'}}
                  ref={(e)=>this.textView = e}
                  value={this.props.bookText} />
    );
  }

}

export default TextReaderCallback;
```

One minor caveat to using the inline ref callback syntax is that it will cause the ref callback to be executed twice when the component first mounts—once with null, and then again with the element passed into it. This is not a major concern, but if you want to avoid this extra execution of the callback you can simply define the callback in the constructor.

WHEN TO USE REFS

Because they allow you to directly manipulate React components and DOM elements from parent components, refs are a powerful tool. Certain important tasks in a web application are perfect jobs for refs. These include:

➤ Managing focus

➤ Automatically selecting text within a child element

➤ Controlling media playback

➤ Setting scroll position on a child element

➤ Triggering imperative animations

➤ Integrating with third-party libraries (such as jQuery, for example)

Although you may not need to perform any of these tasks very often, when you do need them, they're impossible or nearly impossible to do simply by passing props.

WHEN NOT TO USE REFS

With great power comes great responsibility. In theory, you could use refs to bypass all the features of React and just change the contents of elements, call methods of components, change element styles, and anything else you need to do in your application in an imperative way. But, this would defeat the purpose of using React.

As a rule, if there's a way to do something by passing props to children (what we call the "React Way") that's what you should do. Breaking out of the fundamental pattern that makes React work so well will make your app more complicated, harder to debug, and likely less performant.

EXAMPLES

Finding working examples of some of the use cases for refs on the web can be difficult. So, for the rest of this chapter, I'll provide some code that you can study and try out to better understand the appropriate uses for refs.

Managing Focus

Properly managing focus, especially in a web form, is an important part of web user interface usability and accessibility.

The most basic use case for managing focus is shown in Listing 9-3. The same technique is also commonly used to automatically place the cursor into the first field in a login form when it loads.

Another common use for managing focus is to return a user to the same field they were editing before a modal window was opened or after they save their input into a form and return to it at a later time.

Automatically Selecting Text

Selecting text in a child element can be useful for making components that display text and provide a button for copying the text. This is often done in applications that generate some kind of a code or key. Listing 9-6 shows an example of a text input with a button for copying the contents.

This example also demonstrates how to display a temporary notification in a React component. After you copy the code, the component updates a state variable called message to display a success message. This state change triggers the componentDidUpdate lifecycle hook, which uses JavaScript's setTimeout method to wait three seconds and then set message back to an empty string, thus removing the success message.

LISTING 9-6: Selecting and copying text with a ref

```
import React,{Component} from 'react';

class CodeDisplay extends Component {

  constructor(props) {
    super(props);
    this.state={message:''};

    this.codeField = React.createRef();
    this.copyCode = this.copyCode.bind(this);
  }
```

continues

LISTING 9-6 *(continued)*

```
componentDidUpdate(){
  setTimeout(() => this.setState({message:''}), 3000);
}

copyCode(){
  this.codeField.current.select();
  document.execCommand('copy');
  this.setState({message:'code copied!'});
}

render(){
  return (
    <>
      <input value={this.props.yourCode}
             ref={this.codeField} /> {this.state.message}<br />
      <button onClick={this.copyCode}>Copy your Code</button>
    </>
  );
}

}

export default CodeDisplay;
```

Figure 9-2 shows the value of the text input selected and the success message that displays right after you click the button.

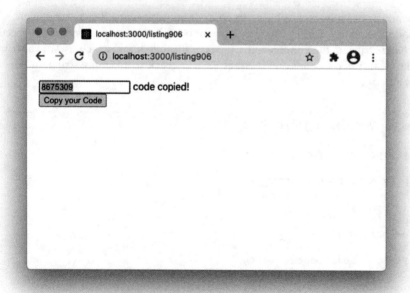

FIGURE 9-2: Selecting text and displaying a temporary message

Controlling Media Playback

HTML's `audio` and `video` elements can be controlled using several DOM methods, including `play`, `pause`, and `load`. You can attach refs to media elements to use these methods, as shown in Listing 9-7.

LISTING 9-7: A React audio player

```
import React,{Component} from 'react';

class AudioPlayer extends Component {

  constructor(props) {
    super(props);
    this.mediaFile = React.createRef();
    this.playToggle = this.playToggle.bind(this);
  }

  playToggle(){
    if (this.mediaFile.current.paused){
      this.mediaFile.current.play();
    } else {
      this.mediaFile.current.pause();
    }
  }

  render(){
    return (
      <>
        <audio ref={this.mediaFile}>
          <source src="/music/thebestsongever.mp3" type="audio/mpeg" />
        </audio><br />
        <button onClick={this.playToggle}>Play/Pause</button>
      </>
    );
  }

}

export default AudioPlayer;
```

Setting Scroll Position

The DOM `window.scrollTo` method takes coordinates in a document (specified as x and y pixel values) and scrolls the window to those coordinates. One way to use this is to find out the position of a certain element in a document (using the `offsetTop` property) and then scroll the window to that element.

This can be useful for navigating long documents, or for remembering a user's position between sessions.

Listing 9-8 demonstrates how to use a ref to get the position of an element and then scroll to that element. Previous examples have used class components, so I'll use a function component for this one.

LISTING 9-8: Scrolling to an element with a ref

```
import {useRef} from 'react';

const ScrollToElement = (ref)=>{window.scrollTo(0,ref.current.offsetTop)};

function ScrollToDemo(){

  const bookStart = useRef();

  return (
    <>
      <h1 ref={bookStart}>CHAPTER 1. Loomings.</h1>

      <div style={{width:'300px'}}><p>...</p></div>

      <button onClick={() => ScrollToElement(bookStart)}>
        Scroll to the Beginning
      </button>
    </>
  );

}

export default ScrollToDemo;
```

SUMMARY

In this chapter, you learned about React's escape hatch, refs. Refs are an important and useful part of React. Used incorrectly, however, they're antithetical to the goals and purpose of React and can have a detrimental effect on your React UI. Fortunately, the use cases for refs are relatively few, and I've covered most of them with examples in this chapter. In this chapter, you learned:

➤ What refs are and why they exist.

➤ How to create refs in both function and class components.

➤ How to use refs to access component and DOM elements from a parent.

➤ What callback refs are and how to use them.

➤ How to implement basic versions of several of ref's use cases.

In the next chapter, you'll learn about another hotly debated and sometimes controversial aspect of React, namely, how to apply style to React components.

10

Styling React

How to style React components, and React user interfaces in general, can be a polarizing topic. There are many ways to handle style in React, and you're likely to see several of them used side-by-side on most React projects.

In this chapter, you'll learn:

- ➤ How to include and use CSS files in React.
- ➤ How to write inline styles in React.
- ➤ How to use CSS Modules.
- ➤ How to use CSS-in-JS.

THE IMPORTANCE OF STYLES

Style in web applications determines how individual elements look, including typefaces, weight of text, colors, backgrounds, width, and height, for example. It also determines how elements relate to each other and to the HTML document or browser window—their borders, margins, alignment, and position. Certain CSS styles create animations. Still others affect how elements behave and how they look when they're in different states, such as hovered over, clicked, focused, and so on.

Even if you don't add any style at all to your user interface, it's still affected by the browser's default styles, which are rarely ideal. Styles also determine how your user interface will look on different sized devices, when printed, and even how it will sound when read by a text-to-speech reader.

With styles determining so much of what the end user's experience with your application will be, it's essential for a developer or a development team to give more than a little thought to how style will be managed and implemented in a user interface.

Because React is just JavaScript and because everything in your React user interface will start its life as JavaScript, you have more options for how to implement style with React than if you were developing an application using plain old HTML and CSS files.

Using ordinary CSS with React is an option, however, and it's the option that we'll talk about first.

IMPORTING CSS INTO THE HTML FILE

The most basic way to style a React user interface is by importing one or more CSS files into the HTML file that loads React. This can be done as simply as by opening up `index.html`, which lives in the `public` folder in a Create React App project, and adding an HTML `link` element between the `<head>` and `</head>` tags, as shown in Listing 10-1.

LISTING 10-1: Adding an HTML link to the HTML file

```
<!DOCTYPE html>
<html lang="en">
  <head>
    <meta charset="utf-8" />
    <link rel="icon" href="%PUBLIC_URL%/favicon.ico" />
    <meta name="viewport" content="width=device-width, initial-scale=1" />
    <meta name="theme-color" content="#000000" />
    <meta
      name="description"
      content="Web site created using create-react-app" />

    <link rel="stylesheet" href="%PUBLIC_URL%/css/style.css" />

    <link rel="apple-touch-icon" href="%PUBLIC_URL%/logo192.png" />

    <link rel="manifest" href="%PUBLIC_URL%/manifest.json" />

  </head>
  <body>
    <noscript>You need to enable JavaScript to run this app.</noscript>
    <div id="root"></div>

  </body>
</html>
```

In Create React App projects, the `index.html` file is a template, which gets compiled when you run **npm start** or **npm run build**. Variables in the template are surrounded by the `%` character. So, in the CSS link added in Listing 10-1, the `%PUBLIC_URL%` variable will be replaced with the actual URL where the application is being served.

To use this method of styling React, just put a CSS file in the right place inside the public directory or point the `link` to an external URL (such as a hosted stylesheet or a stylesheet library like Bootstrap).

This method of styling React is useful for providing an overall style to the user interface, or a theme. However, it should be used carefully, since the styles included in the HTML file will affect every component in your application, and it's easy to accidentally cause problems lower in the component tree or create unnecessary complexity by adding styles at this level.

USING PLAIN OLD CSS IN COMPONENTS

Create React App has built into it the ability to load and bundle ordinary CSS files into your user interface. If you're familiar with CSS and how to use CSS selectors to apply style to elements, classes, and IDs, you'll find using CSS in React comfortable and familiar. Listing 10-2 shows how to include a CSS file into a React component and then use the CSS classes.

LISTING 10-2: Including CSS in a component

```
import "styles.css";

function ArticleLink(props) {

return (

  <div className="article-link">
    <h1 className="title">{props.title}</h1>
    <p className="firstPara">{props.firstPararaph}</p>
    <p><a className="articleLink" href={props.link}>read more</a></p>
  </div>

);
}

export default ArticleLink;
```

Importing a stylesheet into a React component has the benefit of being a familiar way to work, and it also allows you to use existing stylesheets that you may have.

As with importing styles into the HTML file, CSS imported into the components cascades to the component's children. For example, Listing 10-3 shows a stylesheet, a parent component, and a child component rendered by the parent component. The styles are imported into the parent component, but the class and element styles defined in the stylesheet are only used in the child.

LISTING 10-3: Cascading styles in components

```
/* style.css */
p {
    font-size: 80px;
}

.red {
    color: red;
}
```

continues

LISTING 10-3 *(continued)*

```
// StyledParent.js
import StyledChild from './StyledChild';

import './style.css';

function StyledParent(props){
    return (<StyledChild />)
}

export default StyledParent;


// StyledChild.js
function StyledChild(props){
    return (<p className="red">This is testing whether styles cascade.</p>)
}

export default StyledChild;
```

The result of rendering `StyledParent` in your browser is shown in Figure 10-1.

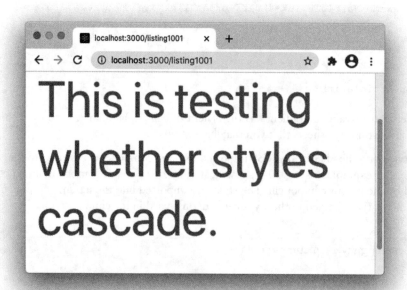

FIGURE 10-1: Cascading styles from parent to child

This trickling down of styles from parent elements to child elements and the complex series of steps that a browser goes through to determine the priority of different styles is the way that CSS was designed. It can often be useful to be able to apply styles to a tree of elements and to make use of the CSS cascade to apply styles, but more often it creates confusion and results in components that have access to far more styles than they actually use.

One way to tame CSS is to only use the class selector. This is an approach used by many CSS libraries, including Bootstrap. By only applying styles using the class selector (which is created using the ". " symbol in CSS stylesheets and matches the value of the `className` attribute in JSX) you eliminate the problem of styles that are applied to IDs overriding styles that are applied to classes, and styles applied to elements overriding classes and IDs, and styles marked as `!important` overriding everything.

But, no matter what you do, CSS is not a programming language, and it doesn't have scope as programmers understand it or many of the conveniences of programming languages. This is why many developers who use CSS directly in their components or HTML file use a CSS preprocessor, such as SASS.

> **NOTE** A discussion of CSS preprocessors is beyond the scope of this book, but if you want to learn more, visit `sass-lang.com/`.

However, React has built into it another way to style components that gives you all of the capabilities of a CSS preprocessor, without having to learn the language used by the CSS preprocessor: you can simply use JavaScript to apply style to components.

WRITING INLINE STYLES

React's built-in DOM elements have a `style` attribute that accepts a style object as its value. When you pass DOM style properties into this attribute, those properties will be applied to the resulting HTML element.

To demonstrate a basic use of the `style` attribute, Listing 10-4 shows a React component that returns a styled paragraph of text.

LISTING 10-4: Using inline styles in React

```
function WarningMessage(props) {
  return (
    <p style={{color:"red",padding:"6px",backgroundColor:"#000000"}}>
      {props.warningMessage}
    </p>
  )
}

export default WarningMessage;
```

In this example, notice that the style object, which is written as an object literal (using curly brackets) must itself be surrounded by curly brackets to indicate that it's to be treated as literal JavaScript rather than JSX, which is why there are double curly brackets around the style properties.

JavaScript Style Syntax

The properties that you can access and manipulate using JavaScript mirror the CSS properties, and you can do anything using JavaScript styles that you can do with CSS. Because of the differences between JavaScript and CSS, however, JavaScript styles are written differently.

The first difference is that a CSS rule-set does not follow the rules of JavaScript object literals, although it does resemble one. In particular, CSS style rules don't have quotes around the values, while in JavaScript style objects, quotes are required around strings.

The second difference between CSS rule-sets and JavaScript objects is that the individual rules in CSS are separated by semicolons, while in JavaScript objects, properties are separated by commas.

The third difference is that CSS property names containing more than one word have hyphens between the words. In JavaScript, this would result in an error, so JavaScript style properties use camelCase for multi-word names.

Finally, CSS has the concept of selectors, which is how styles can be selectively applied to only certain elements. A rule-set attached to a class selector (which is indicated by a . before the name of the rule-set) will apply to elements that have that class (or `className` in JSX).

In JavaScript, style objects that aren't inline styles must be assigned to a variable and that variable can be used as the value of a DOM element's `style` attribute.

Listing 10-5 shows a CSS rule-set, followed by the JavaScript style object that accomplishes the same thing.

LISTING 10-5: CSS rule-sets vs. JavaScript style objects

```
/* CSS rule-set */
.headingStyle{
  background-color: #999999;
  color: #eee;
  border: 1px solid black;
  border-radius: 4px;
  width: 50%;
}

//JavaScript style object
const headingStyle = {
  backgroundColor: '#999999',
  color: '#eee',
  border: '1px solid black',
  borderRadius: '4px',
  width: '50%'
};
```

Why to Use Inline Styles

Inline styles make it easy to see how a component will be styled. If you're only applying a couple of style properties to an element, and you're not going to reuse that particular combination of properties in another component, writing them as inline styles is easy and fast. Using inline styles also increases the portability of a component, since the styles are part of the component file and don't rely on an external module being present.

Why Not to Use Inline Styles

In a React application with many different components, using inline styles can become a maintenance nightmare. It's simply a good user interface design practice to reuse certain styles, including how headings are styled, colors and sizes of buttons, sizes and typefaces of different types of text, and so forth.

If you were to write the same style object, containing the same style properties, each time you styled a block of text, you'd soon come to the realization that writing inline style objects is a waste of effort. At that point, logically, the thing to do is to create variables to store your style objects.

Improving Inline Styles with Style Modules

Rather than writing your style objects directly in the `style` attribute of each element, you can create variables to hold the styles, as shown in Listing 10-6.

LISTING 10-6: Using variables to hold style objects

```
function WarningMessage(props){

  const warningStyle = {color:"red",padding:"6px",backgroundColor:"#000000"};

  return (
    <p style={warningStyle}>
      {props.warningMessage}
    </p>
  )
}

export default WarningMessage;
```

Variables created to hold style objects can be kept inside the component, as shown in Listing 10-6, or you can put them into separate files and export them using either named exports (if you want to create a style library containing the styles for multiple components) or a default export.

Listing 10-7 shows an example of a style object library containing styles for multiple different components.

LISTING 10-7: A style object library

```
export const warningStyle = {color:"red",padding:"6px",backgroundColor:"#000000"};
export const infoStyle = {color:"yellow",padding:"6px",backgroundColor:"#000000"};
export const successStyle = {color:"green",padding:"6px",backgroundColor:"#000000"};
```

Ignoring how ugly these styles will actually look in reality, they could be saved in a file called `messageStyles.js` and then imported individually or as a group into each component that needs to display a message.

Listing 10-8 shows how to import an entire style object library into a component that will display text in a different style, depending on the type of message passed into the component.

LISTING 10-8: Importing multiple styles

```
import {warningStyle,infoStyle,successStyle} from './messageStyles.js';

function DisplayStatus(props){
let messageStyle;
switch(props.message.type){
  case 'warning':
    messageStyle = 'warningStyle';
    break;
  case 'info':
    messageStyle = 'infoStyle';
    break;
  case 'success':
    messageStyle = "successStyle";
    break;
  default:
    messageStyle = "infoStyle";
    break;
}

  return (
    <p style={messageStyle}>{props.message.text}</p>
  );
}

export default DisplayStatus;
```

CSS MODULES

CSS Modules give you some of the benefits of using JavaScript style objects while using standard CSS stylesheets. Specifically, CSS Modules solve the problem of name conflicts and scoping in CSS.

CSS modules can be written like normal CSS files, and then imported into your components as if they were JavaScript. In fact, what happens during the compilation of your components is that CSS modules are converted into JavaScript objects. This gives CSS modules some special powers, which we'll talk about in a moment. Listing 10-9 shows a basic CSS module.

LISTING 10-9: A CSS Module

```css
/* my-component.module.css */
.bigText {
  font-size: 4em;
}

.redText {
  color: #FF0000;
}
```

To import the preceding CSS module into a component, make sure to save the file with `.module.css` at the end and use the following import statement:

```
import styles from './my-component.module.css';
```

When your component is compiled, the classes in the CSS module will be rewritten using a format called ICSS, which stands for Interoperable CSS.

You can then access the imported styles using dot notation and pass them into the `className` attribute, as shown in Listing 10-10.

LISTING 10-10: Using a CSS Module

```
import styles from './my-component.module.css';

function DisplayMessage(props) {

    return (<p className = {styles.redText}>This text is red.</p>);

}

export default DisplayMessage;
```

CSS Modules isn't specific to React. It's a separate specification, which can be used with any front-end library. However, support for it is built into Create React App, so to use it in your React applications built using Create React App, you don't need to do anything special to start using it.

Naming CSS Module Files

Although CSS module files resemble ordinary CSS files, when you use them inside of Create React App, their filenames must end with `.module.css` to indicate to the compiler that they need to be processed as CSS modules.

The standard naming convention for CSS module files is to lowercase and hyphenate the component name that the module will be used in, and then follow that with .module.css.

So, if your React component is named NavBar, the CSS module file for the NavBar component would be named nav-bar.module.css. You can import the styles contained in the CSS module file using any name you want, but it's normal to import them as an object named styles, like this:

```
import styles from './nav-bar.module.css';
```

Because each component can import its own styles object, you can write the CSS for any component without having to worry that a class name you use for one component's styles will interfere with a style having the same name in another component.

The styles inside a CSS module file should use camelCase so that when you use them inside your JSX, you can access them using dot notation.

Advanced CSS Modules Functionality

CSS module files can be just plain CSS, but they also have some additional capabilities that can make them more powerful than plain old CSS.

Global Classes

By default, the rules you create in CSS module files are scoped locally to the component you import the styles into. If you want to create a global rule, you can do so by prefixing the name of the class with :global, like this:

```
:global .header1 {
    font-size: 2rem;
    font-weight: bold;
}
```

In this example, the header1 class will be available to all of your components.

Class Composition

Class composition lets you create new classes in CSS modules by extending existing ones. For example, you might have a class named bodyText that determines how standard text in your component should display. With class composition, different types of text can extend the base bodyText class to create variations. Class composition in CSS modules uses a special property called composes, which takes as its value any number of classes that should be used as the starting point for the current class.

Listing 10-11 shows an example of using class composition to create a firstParagraph class based on bodyText.

LISTING 10-11: Using class composition

```
.bodyText {
    font-size: 12px;
    font-family: Georgia serif;
    color: #333;
```

```
    text-indent: 25px;
}

.firstParagraph {
  composes: bodyText;
  text-indent: 0px;
}
```

You can also import styles from other stylesheets to use as the base class for a new style, as shown in Listing 10-12.

LISTING 10-12: Basing a new class on an external style

```
.checkoutButton {
  composes: button from './buttons';
  background-color: #4CAF50;
  font-size: 32px;
}
```

CSS-IN-JS AND STYLED COMPONENTS

CSS-in-JS refers to a pattern of composing styles using JavaScript. Several third-party libraries exist for implementing CSS-in-JS. Perhaps the most popular and commonly used is *Styled Components*.

Because Styled Components is a separate library, which is not installed by Create React App by default, the first step in using it is to install it:

```
npm install --save styled-components
```

Once installed, you can include the `styled-components` package into any component where you want to use it.

Styled Components uses tagged template literals to let you write new components using CSS. See the "JavaScript Lesson: Tagged Template Literals" sidebar in this chapter to learn more about this relatively new feature of JavaScript.

Styled Components creates a styled component that you can wrap around the elements you want to style. The result is that your JSX code is free from style objects, class names, and style attributes, because all the styling is done with reusable styled elements. Styled Components is a declarative way of styling React components, as we say.

Listing 10-13 shows a simple example of using Styled Components to create a component called `Heading` that applies styles to its contents.

LISTING 10-13: Using Styled Components

```
import styled from 'styled-components';

const Heading = styled.h1`
```

continues

LISTING 10-13 *(continued)*

```
  width: 50%;
  margin: 0 auto;
  font-size: 2.2em;
  color: #333300;`

const ExampleComponent = ()=>{
  return(
    <Heading>Example Heading</Heading>
  );
}

export default ExampleComponent;
```

Styled Components can be defined in separate files just like other components and then imported into multiple files, they can be nested to create more complex components through composition, and because they're JavaScript, they can be scripted.

JAVASCRIPT LESSON: TAGGED TEMPLATE LITERALS

Tagged template literals are a more advanced form of template literals, so I'll start by reviewing template literals.

Template literals use the backtick character (`) to turn a JavaScript string into a template. A string surrounded by backticks can include JavaScript expressions by surrounding the expression with ${}. For example, if you want to dynamically generate a message to display after someone has placed an order on your website, you could use something like the following:

```
const thankYouMessage = `Thank you, ${customer.name}, for your
order.`;
```

Prior to template literals, the preceding code had to be written like this:

```
const thankYouMessage = "Thank you, " + customer.name + " for
your order.";
```

Tagged template literals let you parse a string with a function. The `tag` function takes a template literal as its argument, and returns a new string. For example, if you have a function that reverses the letters in a string, you could use it as a `tag` function, like this:

```
reverseString`Bet you can't read this.`;
```

Because the `tag` function only takes one argument, the parentheses around the argument are optional and are usually omitted when using tagged templates.

If you include variables in the string that you pass into a `tag` template, those variables are passed to the function as arguments. In the following example, the tag function receives a sentence with a price variable that's used to display a customized message:

```
let orderTotal = 42;

function determineShipping(strings, price) {
  let str0 = strings[0]; // "Your order "
  let str1 = strings[1]; // " for free shipping."

  let qualifyStr;
  if (price > 50){
    qualifyStr = 'qualifies';
  } else {
    qualifyStr = 'does not qualify';
  }

  return `${str0}${qualifyStr}${str1}`;
}

let output = determineShipping`Your order ${orderTotal} for
free shipping.`;

console.log(output);
// Your order does not qualify for free shipping.
```

SUMMARY

Because React doesn't give developers many rules about exactly how to structure user interfaces, you're free to mix and match solutions and patterns and find out what works best. Nowhere is this more apparent than in the multiple approaches to styling components that have been devised for React.

In this chapter, you learned:

- ➤ How to import CSS into components.
- ➤ How to use inline styles.
- ➤ How to import and use JavaScript style modules.
- ➤ How to write and use CSS Modules.
- ➤ About CSS-in-JS.

In the next chapter, you'll learn how to use hooks to give function components most of the same functionality as class components.

11

Introducing Hooks

React Hooks give function components access to much of the functionality of React that was previously only available with class components. Hooks also give developers a simpler syntax for using state, performing tasks in response to lifecycle events, and reusing code.

In this chapter, you'll learn:

- ➤ What hooks are.
- ➤ General rules and best practices for using hooks.
- ➤ How to use React's built-in hooks.
- ➤ How to write custom hooks.
- ➤ How to find and use other custom hooks.

WHAT ARE HOOKS?

Hooks are functions that are part of the React library which give you access to features of React that were previously only available by extending the `React.Component` class. These features include state and lifecycle, as well as refs and caching of function results (aka memoization). Hooks "hook into" React from functions.

WHY WERE HOOKS INTRODUCED?

Hooks were introduced to solve several problems with the React library. The first is that React didn't have a simple way to share reusable functionality between components. Prior to React Hooks, solutions such as *higher-order components* and *render props* (both of which are covered in Chapter 12) were commonly used (and still are) for sharing functionality. However, higher-order components tend to result in code and component trees that are difficult to read and overly complex. Code that renders multiple levels of components within components within components in order to provide reusable functionality to a deeply buried component is what is commonly known in the React world as "wrapper hell." Figure 11-1 shows a view of the React Developer Tools for a component tree that's suffering badly from this condition.

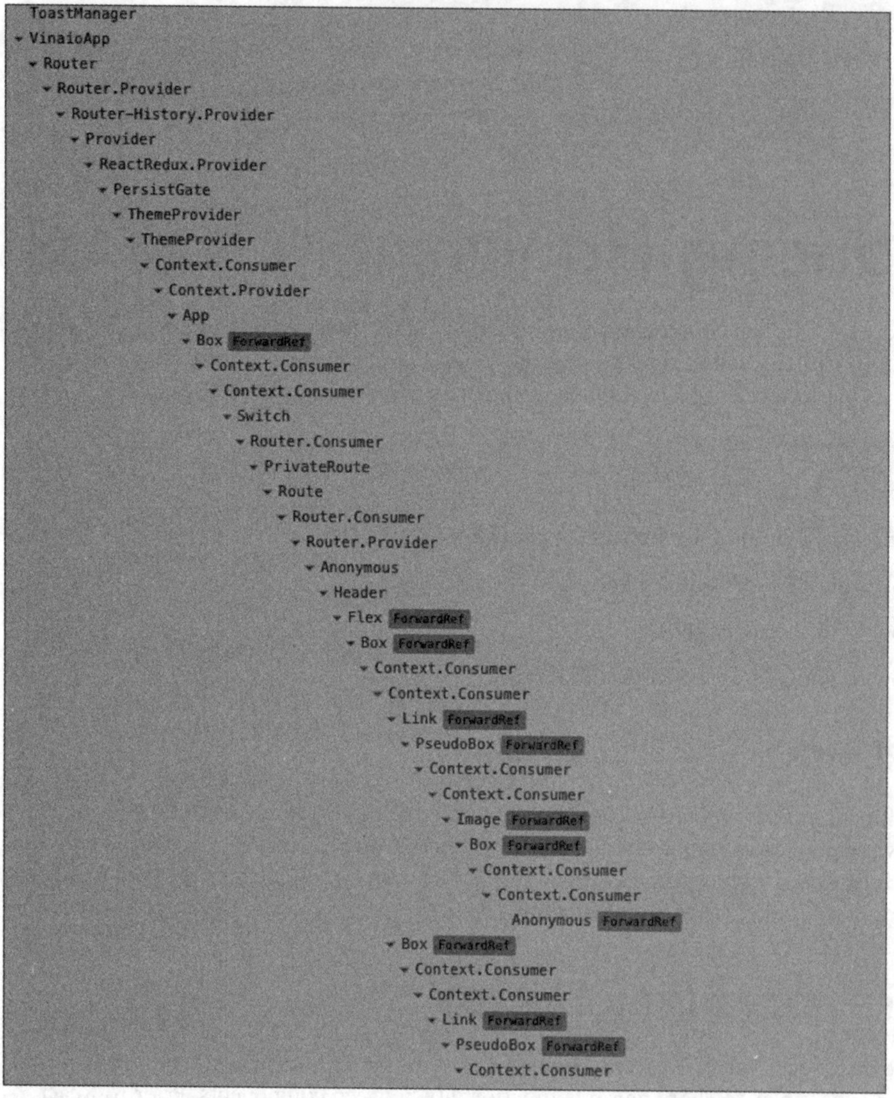

```
ToastManager
▾ VinaioApp
  ▾ Router
    ▾ Router.Provider
      ▾ Router-History.Provider
        ▾ Provider
          ▾ ReactRedux.Provider
            ▾ PersistGate
              ▾ ThemeProvider
                ▾ ThemeProvider
                  ▾ Context.Consumer
                    ▾ Context.Provider
                      ▾ App
                        ▾ Box ForwardRef
                          ▾ Context.Consumer
                            ▾ Context.Consumer
                              ▾ Switch
                                ▾ Router.Consumer
                                  ▾ PrivateRoute
                                    ▾ Route
                                      ▾ Router.Consumer
                                        ▾ Router.Provider
                                          ▾ Anonymous
                                            ▾ Header
                                              ▾ Flex ForwardRef
                                                ▾ Box ForwardRef
                                                  ▾ Context.Consumer
                                                    ▾ Context.Consumer
                                                      ▾ Link ForwardRef
                                                        ▾ PseudoBox ForwardRef
                                                          ▾ Context.Consumer
                                                            ▾ Context.Consumer
                                                              ▾ Image ForwardRef
                                                                ▾ Box ForwardRef
                                                                  ▾ Context.Consumer
                                                                    ▾ Context.Consumer
                                                                      Anonymous ForwardRef
                                              ▾ Box ForwardRef
                                                ▾ Context.Consumer
                                                  ▾ Context.Consumer
                                                    ▾ Link ForwardRef
                                                      ▾ PseudoBox ForwardRef
                                                        ▾ Context.Consumer
```

FIGURE 11-1: Wrapper hell

React's other big problem prior to hooks was that people found using classes to be unnecessarily confusing and verbose. If you've made it this far into the book, I don't need to explain this one to you again. Most of the time, what requires 50 lines of code in a class can be done with a fraction of that by using a function.

As you'll see, beyond just having the ability to accomplish the same thing with less code, hooks also give you the ability to split up your components into smaller parts by creating custom hooks.

Now that you understand the motivation for hooks, let's take a look at the specifics.

RULES OF HOOKS

Although different hooks accomplish different things, all of them have two important rules which must be followed:

1. Hooks can only be used in function components.

2. Hooks must be called at the top level of your function components—meaning inside the function, but not inside of a statement or inner function. Because hooks need to run just once every time your function component runs, they can't be called from inside of conditional statements, loops, or nested functions.

THE BUILT-IN HOOKS

React has 10 built-in hooks that you can use without needing to install anything else. These built-in hooks are:

➤ useState

➤ useEffect

➤ useContext

➤ useReducer

➤ useCallback

➤ useMemo

➤ useRef

➤ useImperativeHandle

➤ useLayoutEffect

➤ useDebugValue

The first three hooks—useState, useEffect, and useContext—are the basic hooks. They're the ones you'll use most often and that are therefore the most important ones to understand.

The other seven hooks are called "Additional Hooks" in the React documentation. These are hooks that you may only use occasionally (or never) or which are variations on the three basic hooks. There are some really useful things (and a couple that are essential, in my opinion) in this set of hooks, however, so I'm going to spend some time covering them and showing examples of how to use them as well.

Managing State with useState

On the first render of a function component containing it, the useState hook creates a stateful value from the argument passed to it, along with the function for updating it. After the first render, useState returns its most recent value after updates are applied. Like class properties (such as this .state), values created with useState persist between renders.

As with all of the hooks, the first step in using useState is to import it:

```
import {useState} from 'react';
```

IMPORTING ALL THE HOOKS

In reality, since hooks are part of the React library, you can import all of the hooks at once by importing the entire React library and then referencing them using dot notation, like this:

```
import React from 'react';
const [state,setState] = React.useState();
```

Although there's no real problem with using hooks this way, it's more common, and perhaps more efficient, to import just the hooks you need individually using named imports. If your component makes use of multiple hooks, separate them with commas inside of the curly braces, like this:

```
import {useState,useEffect,useCallback} from 'react';
```

Once you import useState into a component, you can use it as many times as you need to create stateful variables. React keeps track of stateful values in a function component based on the order in which they appear in the code, which is how it can return the latest value for each stateful variable each time the function renders. This is why hooks can't be used inside of conditional or looping code—doing so would cause the hooks in a function component to not always be called, or to not be called in the same order with each render, which would cause React to return unexpected values.

Listing 11-1 shows a simple example of using useState to keep track of the score and the current guess in a number guessing game.

LISTING 11-1: A number guessing game with useState

```
import {useState} from 'react';

function NumberGuessing(props){
  const [score,setScore] = useState(0);
  const [guess,setGuess] = useState('');

  const checkNumber =()=>{
    const randomNumber = Math.floor(Math.random() * 10)+1;
    if (Number(guess) === randomNumber){
```

```
        setScore(()=>score+1);
      }
    }

    return (
      <>
        What number (between 1 and 10) am I thinking of?
        <input value={guess}
               type="number"
               min="1"
               max="10"
               onChange={(e)=>setGuess(e.target.value)}
        />
        <button onClick={checkNumber}>Guess!</button>
        <p>Your score: {score}</p>
      </>
    )
  }

export default NumberGuessing;
```

In the preceding example, the user's guess is updated using an inline event handler in the onChange event listener when the user enters a number into the number input field.

When the button is clicked, the checkNumber function generates a random number between 1 and 10 and then compares that number with the latest value stored in the guess stateful variable.

One important thing to notice with the comparison is that I used the Number function to convert guess to a number. This is necessary because even numeric values from <input> elements are stored in the browser as strings. The random number variable is of the number data type, however, so to be able to do a strict comparison between them, one of them has to be converted.

If the two numbers match, the score variable is updated to its current value plus 1.

JAVASCRIPT LESSON: STRICT EQUALITY

JavaScript has two equality operators, == and ===. The difference between them is that == will disregard the data type when comparing, and the === operator will compare both the value and the data type of the values being compared.

If you're coming to JavaScript from another programming language, the behavior of the == operator will seem strange and mysterious. It's simply not correct that "0" is equal to 0, for example.

In fact, the existence of the == operator (and its opposite, the != operator) in JavaScript is widely regarded as a flaw in the language, because it has the potential to create mysterious behavior and errors. It is therefore best to avoid using == and to always perform strict equality comparisons.

Setting the Initial State

To set the initial state of a stateful variable created using useState, pass the initial value into useState. The useState hook accepts a single argument, which can be any of JavaScript's data types (or an expression that evaluates to a single value) or a function.

If you don't pass an argument into useState, the resulting stateful variable will be created with an initial value of undefined.

If the initial state is an expression, that expression will still run on each render, but the result will be ignored after the first render. For this reason, if your initial state is the result of an expensive calculation (for example, it requires a network request), pass a function that returns the initial value to useState, as shown here:

```
const [mailingList,setMailingList] = useState(()=>{
  const initialMailingList = loadMailingList(props);
  return initialMailingList;
});
```

The function will only be run on the first render of the component. React calls this *lazy initial state*.

Using the Setter Function

Like the setState function in a class component, the setter function returned by useState will trigger a render. If you pass a setter function down to a child component and call it from that child component, it will still operate on the original variable it was created with, as demonstrated by Listing 11-2.

LISTING 11-2: Setter functions are bound to their creator components

```
import {useState} from 'react';

function ButtonContainer(){

  const [count,setCount] = useState(0);

  return (
    <>
      <MyButton count = {count} setCount = {setCount} /><br />
      count value: {count}
    </>
  );
}

function MyButton(props){
  return (
    <button onClick = {()=>props.setCount(props.count+1)}>
      Add 1 to the Count
    </button>
  );
}

export default ButtonContainer;
```

Figure 11-2 shows the result of rendering the `ButtonContainer` component and clicking the button (which is rendered by the `MyButton` child component).

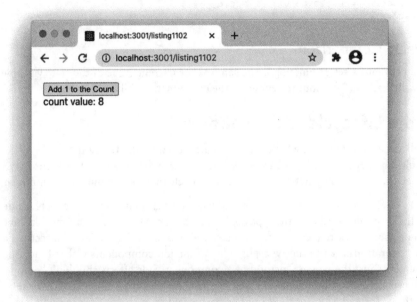

FIGURE 11-2: Passing a setter function as a prop

The setter function returned by `useState` can be used in two different ways: by passing it a function or by passing it a single value.

Passing a Value to a Setter

When you pass a single value (or an expression that evaluates to a single value) into a `useState` setter function, the stateful variable attached to that `useState` function call will be set to the new value you pass it:

```
const [guess,setGuess] = useState(''); // guess === ''
setGuess('7'); // guess === '7'
setGuess('3'); // guess === '3'
```

Unlike when you use `setState` in a class component, `useState`'s setter functions do not merge objects. If you pass an object into a `useState` setter function, the variable connected to that `useState` function will be set to exactly that object.

Passing a Function to a Setter

The other way to use `useState` setter functions is to pass them a function. This is the method that should be used when the new state of the variable is based on the previous state of the variable. Passing a function ensures that the setter function will always receive the latest value of the variable.

The function you pass to a setter function will receive the previous value of the stateful variable as an argument, and it's common to name this argument prev or the name of the variable with prev before it:

```
const [score,setScore] = useState(0); // score === 0
setScore((prevScore)=>prevScore+1); // score === 1
```

Setter Function Value Comparison

If the value that you pass into a setter function is the same as the current value of the state variable, the setter function will "bail out" without re-rendering the component's children.

Hooking into the Lifecycle with useEffect

The useEffect hook accepts a function, which it will run after each render of the function component by default. The useEffect hook can be used to simulate the componentDidMount(), componentDidUpdate(), and componentWillUnmount() lifecycle methods in function components.

The purpose of useEffect is to allow you to run imperative code that may have side effects inside a function component. These side effects are the types of things that aren't otherwise allowed in function components, such as network requests, setting timers, and manipulating the DOM directly. The reason these types of operations aren't otherwise possible in function components is that function components are essentially just the render method of a component. Side effects shouldn't be done in the render method, even in class components, because the render method is likely to overwrite the results of any side effects. Instead, side effects should be performed after the render method has run and the DOM has been updated.

This is why side effects are handled inside of lifecycle methods, such as constructor(), componentDidMount(), and componentDidUpdate() in class components.

JAVASCRIPT LESSON: SIDE EFFECTS

The term "side effects" comes up frequently in React, but it's not a React-specific term. In computer science, a side effect is a result of an impure function. If you recall, a pure function is one whose return value is always the same when given the same arguments, and that doesn't do anything that lasts past the running of the function except return a value.

Anything that a function does that has an effect outside of the function, other than producing a return value, is a side effect.

Side effects in a browser-based application can include:

➤ Modifying global variables.

➤ Making a network request.

➤ Changing the DOM.

➤ Writing to a database or a file.

➤ Modifying an argument.

Using the Default useEffect Behavior

In its most basic form, useEffect simply accepts a function and executes it after each render is complete, as shown in Listing 11-3.

LISTING 11-3: The most basic form of useEffect

```
import {useEffect,useState} from 'react';

function RenderCounter(){

  const [count,setCount] = useState(0);

  useEffect((()=>{console.log(count)});

  return(
    <>
      This component will count how many times it renders.
      <button onClick={()=>setCount((prev)=>prev+1)}>Update State</button>
    </>
  );
}

export default RenderCounter;
```

When you run the component in Listing 11-3, it will count each time the function passed to useEffect runs and log the current count to the browser's JavaScript console.

This use of useEffect is similar to if you had passed this same function into both the componentDidMount() and the componentDidUpdate() lifecycle methods in a class component. However, there is an important difference between these lifecycle methods and how useEffect works. Namely, the timing of when a class component's lifecycle methods run and when useEffect runs are different. Most of the time this isn't an issue, but in some cases it can cause problems or glitches in the layout in the browser. I'll discuss this and how to solve it when I cover the useLayoutEffect hook.

Cleaning Up After Effects

If you use useEffect to set up subscriptions, set event listeners, or create timers, you run the risk of introducing memory leaks into your React application. In class components, the componentWillUnmount() lifecycle method is used for cleaning up and avoiding memory leaks, as you saw in Chapter 4.

To clean up after effects in function components you can return a function from the function passed into useEffect. This function will run before the component is removed from the user interface. In addition, it will also run before every update of the component.

Although it may seem inefficient for the cleanup function to run before every update of a component, if you think about how function components work, you'll understand why this is necessary. Since JavaScript functions aren't persistent, effects will run every time a component renders. If you're creating a subscription to a data source, or a timer, this means that a new timer or subscription will be created each time the component renders. If it renders multiple times and there's nothing cleaning up the multiple timers or subscriptions, you'll have a memory leak.

Using a cleanup function in useEffect is optional.

Customizing useEffect

There are times when you don't want to run an effect on every render, but instead only on the initial render, or only when a specific value changes. To customize the behavior of useEffect, you can pass it an optional second argument. The second argument is an array of values that the effect depends on.

For example, Listing 11-4 shows a component that starts a timer and uses the default useEffect behavior. With the default useEffect behavior, this timer is re-created each time the component renders.

LISTING 11-4: Starting a timer with each render

```
import {useEffect} from 'react';

function TimerFun(){


    useEffect(() => {
      let time = 0;
      const interval = setInterval(() => {
        console.log(time++);
      }, 1000);
        return () => clearInterval(interval);
    });

    return (<p>Check the console to see the timer.</p>);
}

export default TimerFun;
```

Since this component doesn't use state or accept any props, there's no reason for it to re-render, so the timer will continue to increment and log a higher number each second for as long as the component is mounted in the browser window.

If this component were to re-render, however, the default behavior of useEffect would cause the cleanup function to run and a new timer to be created with each render, as shown in Listing 11-5.

LISTING 11-5: Creating a new timer with each render

```
import {useEffect,useState} from 'react';

function TimerRestartFun(props){

  const [count,setCount] = useState(0);
```

```
  useEffect(() => {
    let time = 0;
    const interval = setInterval(() => {
      console.log(time++);
    }, 1000);
    return () => clearInterval(interval);
  });

  return (
    <p>Check the console to see the timer.
      <button onClick={()=>setCount((prev)=>prev+1)}>{count}</button>
    </p>
  );
}

export default TimerRestartFun;
```

Each time you click the button in the preceding example component, the state changes and the return value changes, which causes the component to render, which causes a new timer to start, as shown in Figure 11-3.

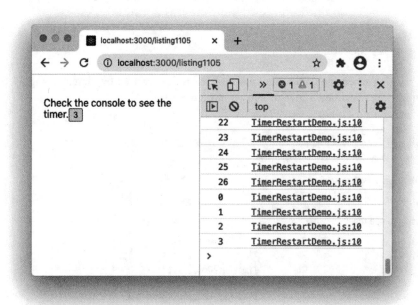

FIGURE 11-3: Starting a new timer with each render

But what if you want to create a game that runs a timer to test how quickly you can click the button? One way to do this would be to only start the timer after the component first mounts, rather than after every render. The way to do this with useEffect is to pass it an empty array as the second argument, as shown in Listing 11-6.

LISTING 11-6: Passing an empty array to only run useEffect on mount

```
import {useEffect,useState} from 'react';

function TimerOnceFun(props){

  const [count,setCount] = useState(0);

  useEffect(() => {
    let time = 0;
    const interval = setInterval(() => {
      console.log(time++);
      if(time===10){
        console.log(`time's up!`);
        clearInterval(interval);
      }
    }, 1000);
    return () => clearInterval(interval);
  },[]);

  return (<p>Check the console to see the timer.
    <button onClick={()=>setCount((prev)=>prev+1)}>{count}</button>
  </p>);
}

export default TimerOnceFun;
```

With the effect only running when the component mounts, the render caused by incrementing the count variable no longer creates a new timer, as shown in Figure 11-4.

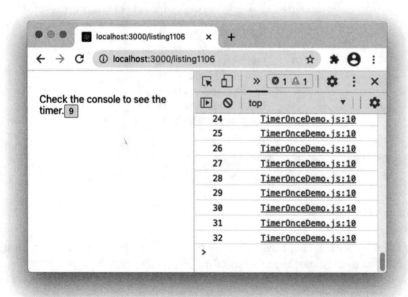

FIGURE 11-4: Running an effect only after mounting

Passing an empty array as the second argument of `useEffect` causes it to simulate the behavior of the `componentDidMount()` lifecycle method, and makes it a good place to put fetch requests for data that won't change during the life of the component, for example. The empty dependency array works because the dependency array's job is to say, "run the function when one of these values has changed." If there are no values in the dependency array, the effect only runs when it's first created.

But, what if you wanted to change the game so that the timer could be restarted when the user wants, or when the count gets up to a certain number, for example? What you need is to conditionally run `useEffect`. To do this, you can make `useEffect` depend on one or more values that will determine when it runs, as shown in Listing 11-7.

LISTING 11-7: Specifying useEffect's dependencies

```
import {useEffect,useState} from 'react';

function TimerConditionalFun(props){

  const [count,setCount] = useState(0);
  const [gameNumber,setGameNumber] = useState(0);

  useEffect(() => {
    let time = 0;
    const interval = setInterval(() => {
      console.log(time++);
      if(time===10){
        console.log(`time's up!`);
        clearInterval(interval);
      }
    }, 1000);
    return () => clearInterval(interval);
  }, [gameNumber]);

  return (
    <>
      <h1>Game Number {gameNumber}</h1>
      <p>Click as fast as you can!
        <button onClick={()=>setCount((prev)=>prev+1)}>{count}</button>
      </p>
      <p>
        <button onClick={()=>setGameNumber((prev)=>prev+1)}>New Game</button>
      </p>
    </>
  );
}

export default TimerConditionalFun;
```

When the component in Listing 11-7 mounts, the timer will start, and it will only be restarted when the value of `gameNumber` changes.

Even when the benefits and results of conditionally running an effect aren't as apparent as those in Listing 11-7, specifying the dependencies of an effect can often be a way to increase the performance of your user interface by eliminating unnecessary renders of components, as you'll see in the next section.

Running Asynchronous Code with useEffect

Because useEffect is asynchronous and runs after the component has rendered, it's the ideal place to perform asynchronous tasks such as fetching data. Listing 11-8 shows a postal code lookup component that uses an effect hook to look up the U.S. city and state whenever the ZIP code entered into an input field changes.

LISTING 11-8: Asynchronous requests with useEffect

```
import {useEffect, useState} from 'react';

function ShippingAddress(props){
  const [zipcode,setZipcode] = useState('');
  const [city,setCity] = useState('');
  const [state,setState] = useState('');

  const API_URL = 'https://api.zip-
codes.com/ZipCodesAPI.svc/1.0/QuickGetZipCodeDetails/';
  const API_KEY = 'DEMOAPIKEY';

  const updateZip = (e)=>{
    e.preventDefault();
    setZipcode(e.target.zipcode.value);
  }

  useEffect(()=>{
    if (zipcode){
      const loadAddressData = async ()=>{
        const response = await fetch(`${API_URL}${zipcode}?key=${API_KEY}`);
        const data = await response.json();
        setCity(data.City);
        setState(data.State);
      }

      loadAddressData();

    }
  },[zipcode]);

  return (
    <form onSubmit={updateZip}>
      Zipcode: <input type="text" name="zipcode" />
      <button type="submit">Lookup City/State</button><br />

      City: {city}<br />
      State: {state}<br />
```

```
        </form>
    )
}

export default ShippingAddress;
```

The result of running the component in Listing 11-8 is shown in Figure 11-5.

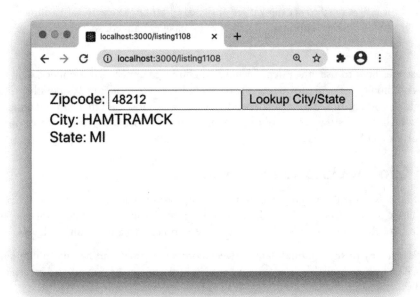

FIGURE 11-5: Performing an asynchronous request using useEffect

This example uses a number of the techniques that you've learned about in the last couple of chapters, plus a couple of new ones, so let's take a walk through the code step by step:

1. On its initial render, the `zipcode`, `city`, and `state` variables are set to empty strings. The `useEffect` hook runs, but the conditional statement that checks whether `zipcode` has a value that evaluates to a Boolean `true` prevents the inner function, `loadAddress()`, from being created or running.

2. The user can enter text into an uncontrolled input. Because the input is uncontrolled, it doesn't cause the UI to render and `useEffect` doesn't run. If this input were controlled, the effect would run on each keystroke because the value of `zipcode` would be changing.

3. When the user clicks the button, the `zipcode` state variable is set by the `updateZip()` function.

4. The change to the `zipcode` variable causes a render. Because `zipcode` is listed as a dependency for the `useEffect` hook, the effect runs.

5.   This time, `zipcode` has a value that evaluates to `true`, so the inner function is created and then runs.

6.   The `loadAddress()` function is an *async function*. Using the `async` keyword before the function definition allows the function to use the `await` statement to perform asynchronous tasks. In the case of this function, it will call the `fetch` command and then wait for a response. When a response is received, the `json()` command reads the response into an object named `data`.

7.   The data from the API is used to set the values of the `city` and `state` stateful variables. This causes another render of the component. The `zipcode` hasn't changed, so the `useEffect` hook won't run.

This component illustrates how to use effect dependencies to eliminate unnecessary renders, which are one of the most common types of performance problems in React components. It's possible that this component would still function without the dependency array, but it would make many unnecessary API requests, which would slow down your component (at the least) and possibly cost you money if the API charges you for requests.

Subscribing to Global Data with useContext

Global data is data that's used by all or many components in a program, such as a theme or user preferences. It can be a hassle to have to pass global data from parent components to child components for every component in an React app—especially when your component tree has multiple levels.

React Context provides a way to share global data between components without having to manually pass values as props. The `useContext` hook accepts a `Context` object as its argument and returns the most recent value of that object.

> **NOTE** Chapter 17 covers the React Context API in detail, along with when and exactly how to use it.

One example of global data that can be passed to child components using Context is a style theme. A theme refers to styles that are used by multiple components to give them a common look within an app.

Listing 11-9 shows an example of using the `useContext` hook in the child component to subscribe to a `Context` object.

LISTING 11-9: Using Context with the useContext hook

```
import { ThemeContext } from './theme-context'

function App() {
  const { theme } = React.useContext(ThemeContext)
```

```
    return (
      <>
        <header
          className="App-header"
          style={{ backgroundColor: theme.backgroundColor, color: theme.color }}
        >
          <h1>Welcome to my app.</h1>
        </header>
      </>
    )
}

export default App;
```

Combining Logic and State with useReducer

The useReducer hook is an alternative to useState that's useful for complex state updates or situations where the new state depends on the previous state. Whereas useState takes just an initial state as its argument, useReducer takes an initial state and a *reducer* as its arguments. A reducer is a pure function that takes the current state and an object called an *action* and returns the new state. In other words, here's the signature of a reducer function:

```
(state, action) => newState
```

The useReducer hook returns a value and a *dispatch function*. A dispatch function can be used in response to events, but instead of taking a value to set the stateful variable to, it takes an action object. An action object has a type and an optional payload.

Using reducers is quite a bit more complicated than simple state updates, but once you see some examples, they become much clearer. Listing 11-10 shows our old friend the Counter component, but rewritten to use a reducer.

LISTING 11-10: A Counter with useReducer

```
import {useReducer} from 'react';

const initialState = {count: 0};

function reducer(state, action) {
  switch (action.type) {
    case 'increment':
      return {count: state.count + 1};
    case 'decrement':
      return {count: state.count - 1};
    default:
      throw new Error();
  }
}

function Counter() {
  const [state, dispatch] = useReducer(reducer, initialState);
```

continues

LISTING 1-10 *(continued)*

```
    return (
      <>
        Count: {state.count}
        <button onClick={() => dispatch({type: 'decrement'})}>-</button>
        <button onClick={() => dispatch({type: 'increment'})}>+</button>
      </>
    );
}

export default Counter;
```

In Listing 11-10, the action only has a `type` property. But, if you wanted to have a more advanced counter, you could add a payload that could be used to indicate how much to increment or decrement the counter by, as shown in Listing 11-11.

LISTING 11-11: Passing a payload to a reducer

```
import {useReducer} from 'react';
const initialState = {count: 0};

function reducer(state, action) {
  switch (action.type) {
    case 'increment':
      return {count: state.count + action.payload};
    case 'decrement':
      return {count: state.count - action.payload};
    default:
      throw new Error();
  }
}

function Counter() {
  const [state, dispatch] = useReducer(reducer, initialState);
  return (
    <>
      Count: {state.count}
      <button onClick={() => dispatch({type: 'decrement', payload:4})}>-4</
button>
      <button onClick={() => dispatch({type: 'increment', payload:4})}>+4</
button>
    </>
  );
}

export default Counter;
```

Memoized Callbacks with useCallback

Functions that you define in components are normally re-created with each render. This is not usually a problem. However, sometimes you do need to (or should for performance reasons) return a memoized version of a function to keep it available between renderings. This is where useCallback comes in.

Listing 11-12 shows the most common use case for useCallback. In this example, the useEffect hook should call a function passed into it (which we call a callback function) when the value of the phoneNumber variable changes. The useEffect hook has two dependencies—the function and the variable.

Because callback functions are re-created on each render, the effect in this example will still call its internal function each time the component renders.

Listing 11-12 Function dependencies cause unnecessary renders

```
import {useEffect,useState,useRef} from 'react';

function CallMe(props){

    const [phoneNumber,setPhoneNumber] = useState();
    const [currentNumber,setCurrentNumber] = useState();

    const phoneInputRef = useRef();

    const handleClick = (e)=>{
        setPhoneNumber(currentNumber);
    }

    const placeCall = () => {
      if(currentNumber){
        console.log(`dialing ${currentNumber}`);
      }
    };


    useEffect(() => {
      placeCall(phoneNumber);
    }, [phoneNumber,placeCall]);

    return(
      <>
        <label>Enter the number to call:</label>
        <input type="phone" ref={phoneInputRef}
onChange={()=>{setCurrentNumber(phoneInputRef.current.value)}}/>
        <button onClick={handleClick}>
          Place Call
        </button>
```

continues

LISTING 11-12 *(continued)*

```
        <h1>{currentNumber}</h1>
      </>
    );
}

export default CallMe;
```

If you try to run the preceding component using Create React App, you'll get a warning in the console, as shown in Figure 11-6.

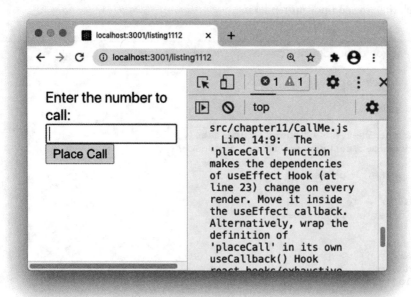

FIGURE 11-6: Unnecessary renders warning due to a function dependency

When you type into the input field, you'll see that the `placeCall()` function is called each time the component renders, which happens every time you type a character.

As the warning message tells you, there are two solutions to this problem. The first is to just define the `placeCall()` function inside of the `useEffect` hook and then remove it from the dependencies list, like this:

```
useEffect(() => {
  const placeCall = () => {
    if(phoneNumber){
      console.log(`dialing ${phoneNumber}`);
    }
  };
```

```
    placeCall(phoneNumber);

  },[phoneNumber]);
```

The other solution, which is the correct one if you're going to use the `placeCall()` function in more than one place, is to memoize the callback function using `useCallback`, like this:

```
const placeCall = useCallback(() => {
  if(phoneNumber){
    console.log(`dialing ${phoneNumber}`);
  }
},[phoneNumber]);
```

The `useCallback` hook creates a persistent version of the function that will only be re-created when the `phoneNumber` variable changes. With this change, the `useEffect` hook will behave the way you want it to—only calling the inner function when the value of `phoneNumber` changes—as shown in Listing 11-13.

LISTING 11-13: Memoized callbacks fix the unnecessary effect problem

```
import {useEffect,useState,useRef,useCallback} from 'react';

function CallMe(props){

  const [phoneNumber,setPhoneNumber] = useState();
  const [currentNumber,setCurrentNumber] = useState();

  const phoneInputRef = useRef();

  const handleClick = (e)=>{
    setPhoneNumber(currentNumber);
  }

  const placeCall = useCallback(() => {
    if(phoneNumber){
      console.log(`dialing ${phoneNumber}`);
    }
  },[phoneNumber]);


  useEffect(() => {
    placeCall(phoneNumber);
  },[phoneNumber,placeCall]);

  return(
    <>
      <label>Enter the number to call:</label>
      <input type="phone"
             ref={phoneInputRef}
             onChange={()=>{setCurrentNumber(phoneInputRef.current.value)}}
      />
      <button onClick={handleClick}>
        Place Call
```

continues

LISTING 11-13 *(continued)*

```
        </button>
        <h1>{currentNumber}</h1>
      </>
    );
}

export default CallMe;
```

Caching Computed Values with useMemo

The useMemo hook memoizes (caches) values between renderings of a function component. It works the same way as useCallback, except that it can cache any value type, not just functions.

As with useCallback, there are two reason to use useMemo:

➤   To solve problems with unnecessary renders.

➤   To solve performance problems related to computationally expensive calculations.

Solving Unnecessary Renders

I covered the first case already in the "Memoized Callbacks with useCallback" section. The issue comes up when you have an object, array, or function serve as a dependency for a function that should only be run when its dependencies change.

In JavaScript, when you create two objects (or functions, or arrays) with exactly the same properties, the two objects are not equal to each other. You can test this by opening your browser's JavaScript console and executing the following expressions:

```
{} === {}
[] === []
() => {} === () => {}
```

In each case, the result will be false, as shown in Figure 11-7.

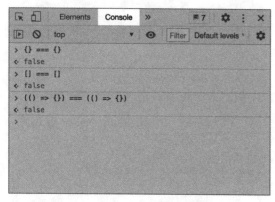

FIGURE 11-7: Testing referential equality

Because of this, using an object, array, or function in a dependency array will result in the function running on every render of the function component. Just as `useCallback` is the solution for callback functions, `useMemo` is the solution to unnecessary renders due to object or array dependencies.

Solving Performance Problems

Normally, JavaScript (and therefore calculations within React) is very fast. However, in rare cases, or when you do encounter a performance problem due to a computationally expensive operation, `useMemo` can be used to solve it.

For example, the component in Listing 11-14 generates a chart from a large set of data. By using `useMemo` to cache the chart, you can prevent it from being regenerated each time the component renders. Instead, it will only be generated when the data supplied to it changes.

LISTING 11-14: Solving performance problems with useMemo

```
import {useMemo} from 'react';
import {chartGenerator} from 'some-chart-library';

function Chart(props){

   const giantChart = useMemo(()=>{
       return chartGenerator(props.chartData);
     },[props.chartData]);

   return {giantChart};
}

export default Chart;
```

Accessing Children Imperatively with useRef

The `useRef` hook returns a `ref` object with a mutable property named `current`. One use for a `ref` object is to imperatively access the DOM. When a DOM node that a ref is attached to changes, the `ref` object's current property is updated. Changes to a ref do not cause the component to re-render.

Listing 11-15 shows a component that uses a ref to get the value of an uncontrolled `<textarea>` in order to count the number of words in it.

LISTING 11-15: Getting the value of a textarea and counting its words

```
import {useState,useRef} from 'react';

function WordCount(props){

   const textAreaRef = useRef();
   const [wordCount,setWordCount] = useState(0);
```

continues

LISTING 11-15 *(continued)*

```
const countWords = () => {
  const text = textAreaRef.current.value;
  setWordCount(text.split(" ").length);
}

return (
  <>
    <textarea ref={textAreaRef} /><br />
    <button onClick={countWords}>Count Words</button>
    <p>{wordCount} words.</p>
  </>
)
}

export default WordCount;
```

Customizing Exposed Values with useImperativeHandle

The useImperativeHandle hook lets you create a "handle" or custom name for a value exposed to a parent component using a ref. This is useful when using React.forwardRef to forward a ref attribute from one component to its child.

For example, in Listing 11-16, a component called CountingBox is created that contains a <textarea>. The ref attribute passed into the CountingBox component will be forwarded and attached to the <textarea>. The useImperativeHandle hook is then used to make a new property of the ref.current object (called count in this case) available to the parent component.

LISTING 11-16: Customizing a value exposed by a ref

```
import {useState,useRef,useImperativeHandle,forwardRef} from 'react';

const CountingBox = forwardRef((props, ref) => {

  const [text,setText] = useState('');

  useImperativeHandle(ref, () => {
    return {count: text.split(" ").length}
  }, [text]);

  return (
    <>
      <textarea value={text} onChange={(e)=>setText(e.target.value)} />
    </>);
});

function TextEdit(props){

  const countingBoxRef = useRef();
  const [wordCount,setWordCount] = useState(0);
```

```
  const handleClick = (count) => {
    setWordCount(count)
  }

  return (
     <>
       <CountingBox ref={countingBoxRef} /><br />
       <button onClick={()=>handleClick(countingBoxRef.current.count)}>
         count words
       </button><br />
         current count: {wordCount}<br />
     </>
  )
}

export default TextEdit;
```

> **NOTE** Notice that `useImperativeHandle` has a third argument, which is a dependency array (similar to that used by `useEffect`, `useCallback`, and `useMemo`). In the current version of React, `useImperativeHandle` memoizes the value of the handle, which can be a problem if you're trying to get an updated value (as in this case). Specifying a dependency that changes with each render solves the problem.

The `useImperativeHandle` hook is the least important hook to fully understand. In most cases, anything you want to do using `useImperativeHandle` can be better done by passing props from parent components to child components.

Updating the DOM Synchronously with useLayoutEffect

The `useLayoutEffect` hook is identical to `useEffect` in every way, except in when and how it executes. Whereas `useEffect` runs its functions asynchronously (that is, without blocking anything else) after the component appears in the browser, `useLayoutEffect` runs its function before the DOM is painted to the browser, and it runs synchronously.

The `useLayoutEffect` hook can be used in cases where an effect results in changes to the DOM and where the `useEffect` hook may cause flicker or inconsistent display of the results.

WRITING CUSTOM HOOKS

Custom hooks are functions that make use of the built-in hooks to encapsulate reusable functionality. Many different custom hooks have been written and are available for free on the web, either by themselves as standalone components, or as features within React libraries. You can also write your own custom hooks.

Custom hooks, like the built-in hooks, have names that start with use. This is a helpful convention rather than a requirement. To write a custom hook, write a function that uses at least one built-in hook and export a value from the function.

Listing 11-17 shows a custom hook based on the zipcode lookup component from earlier in this chapter. When imported into a component, useZipLookup will take a zipcode as its argument and return an array containing the corresponding city and state.

LISTING 11-17: useZipLookup: a custom hook to return location data based on a ZIP code

```
import {useEffect,useState} from 'react';

function useZipLookup(zipcode){
  const [city,setCity] = useState('');
  const [state,setState] = useState('');

  const API_URL = 'https://api.zip-
codes.com/ZipCodesAPI.svc/1.0/QuickGetZipCodeDetails/';
  const API_KEY = 'DEMOAPIKEY';

  useEffect(()=>{
    if (zipcode){
      const loadAddressData = async ()=>{
        const response = await fetch(`${API_URL}${zipcode}?key=${API_KEY}`);
        const data = await response.json();
        setCity(data.City);
        setState(data.State);
      }

      loadAddressData();

    }
  },[zipcode]);

  return [city,state];
}

export default useZipLookup;
```

To use the useZipLookup hook, import it into a component, pass it a ZIP code, and deconstruct the returned array into two local variables, as shown in Listing 11-18.

LISTING 11-18: Using the useZipLookup custom hook

```
import {useRef,useState} from 'react';
import useZipLookup from './useZipLookup';

function ShippingAddress2(props){
  const [zipcode,setZipcode] = useState('');
  const [city,state] = useZipLookup(zipcode);
```

```
      const setZip = (e)=>{
        e.preventDefault();
        setZipcode(e.target.zipcode.value);
      }

      return (
        <form onSubmit={setZip}>
          Zipcode: <input type="text" name="zipcode" />
          <button type="submit">Lookup City/State</button><br />

          City: {city}<br />
          State: {state}<br />

        </form>
      )
}

export default ShippingAddress2;
```

By creating the useZipLookup custom hook, we've made this functionality reusable and we simplified the component that outputs the user interface.

LABELING CUSTOM HOOKS WITH USEDEBUGVALUE

When you use a custom hook, it shows up in the React Developer Tools as a hook when you inspect a component, as shown in Figure 11-8.

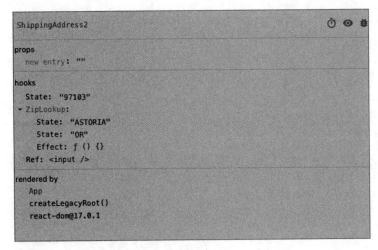

FIGURE 11-8: Inspecting a custom hook

It can be helpful for debugging in some cases to output a value from a custom hook. Normally, the time-honored practice of JavaScript developers everywhere is to use console.log to output debugging code to the console. However simple this may be, it doesn't provide any context as to what function wrote the log message, unless you add that information into the `console.log` message. Logged messages tend to build up in your code over time, unless you're careful about removing them when you no longer need them. But, when you remove them, you often end up adding them again when you're debugging something related. Logging to the console, while essential sometimes, is less than ideal.

The `useDebugValue` hook lets you export a value from a custom hook that will be visible next to the name of the hook in the React Developer Tools component inspector. This value can be anything you want. Listing 11-19 shows how to use `useDebugValue` in the `useZipLookup` component to display the value of the `zipcode` parameter passed into it.

LISTING 11-19: Using useDebugValue

```
import {useEffect,useState,useDebugValue} from 'react';

function useZipLookup(zipcode){
  const [city,setCity] = useState('');
  const [state,setState] = useState('');

  useDebugValue(zipcode);

  const API_URL = 'https://api.zip-
codes.com/ZipCodesAPI.svc/1.0/QuickGetZipCodeDetails/';
  const API_KEY = 'DEMOAPIKEY';

  useEffect(()=>{
    if (zipcode){
      const loadAddressData = async ()=>{
        const response = await fetch(`${API_URL}${zipcode}?key=${API_KEY}`);
        const data = await response.json();
        setCity(data.City);
        setState(data.State);
      }

      loadAddressData();

    }
  },[zipcode]);

  return [city,state];
}

export default useZipLookup;
```

Figure 11-9 shows how the value from `useDebugValue` displays in the component inspector.

The `useDebugValue` hook can also optionally accept a formatting function as its second parameter. This function receives the debug value and can be used for doing conversions or other formatting to the debug value. The function only runs when the hook is actually being inspected.

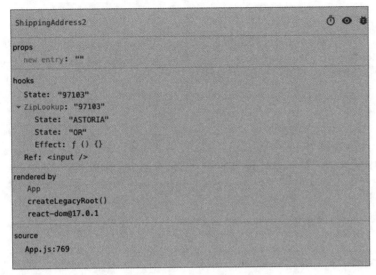

FIGURE 11-9: Viewing a Custom Hook's debug value

One example of where using the formatting function is helpful would be a case where a date is stored as a UNIX timestamp, but you want to be able to view it in the component inspector in a human-readable form. By using the formatting function, you can avoid doing the conversion except when the hook is actually being inspected. Here's what that might look like, using a function from the moment .js date library:

```
useDebugValue(timestamp, timestamp=>timestamp.format("HH/mm/ss"));
```

FINDING AND USING CUSTOM HOOKS

Custom hooks deliver on React's promise of a simple way for developers to share reusable components. Thousands of custom hooks have been created for just about any common functionality that a developer might need.

Unfortunately, finding out which custom hooks are available isn't always easy, and this is complicated by hooks that have the same purpose and name but are part of different Node.js packages and have different APIs. Here are a few of the more popular custom hooks that are currently available.

use-http

The useFetch hook that's part of the use-http package (https://use-http.com) makes isomorphic HTTP requests. What this means is that it can be used both on the server and in the browser. It features caching, TypeScript support, automatic aborting of pending requests when a component unmounts, React Native, GraphQL, and retrying.

react-fetch-hook

React Fetch Hook's `useFetch` hook (https://www.npmjs.com/package/react-fetch-hook) takes a URL and a response formatter function as parameters and returns a Boolean named `isLoading` and formatted data. In its most basic form, using this hook looks like this:

```
const {isLoading,data} = useFetch("http://example-url.com/api/users/1");
```

axios-hooks

The `useAxios` hook (https://www.npmjs.com/package/axios-hooks) executes HTTP requests using the popular Axios library. It takes a URL and an options object as parameters and returns an object containing data, the loading status, and any error message that was returned by the URL. It also returns a function that you can use to manually execute the HTTP request.

Listing 11-20 shows a simple example of using the `useAxios` hook.

LISTING 11-20: Using useAxios

```
import {useState} from 'react';
import useAxios from 'axios-hooks';
import {API_KEY} from './config';

function WeatherWidget() {
  const [city,setCity] = useState('London');
  const [{data, loading, error}, refetch] =
useAxios(`https://api.openweathermap.org/data/2.5/weather?q=${city}&appid=${API_KEY}`);
  if (loading) return <p>Loading...</p>;
  if (error) return <p>There was an error. {error.message}</p>;

  return (
  <>
    <input type="text" value={city} onChange={e=>setCity(e.target.value)} />
    <pre>{JSON.stringify(data,null,2)}</pre>
  </>
  );
}

export default WeatherWidget;
```

react-hook-form

React Hook Form's `useForm` hook makes building forms and validating data input simple. The `useForm` hook returns a function called `register()` that you can pass as a ref to uncontrolled inputs with `name` attributes. The `handleSubmit()` method returned by `useForm` will then handle all of the data from your form.

You can pass options to each `register()` function to validate fields, make them required, and specify other limits such as minimum and maximum values.

Listing 11-21 shows a basic use of `useForm`.

LISTING 11-21: Using useForm

```
import {useForm} from 'react-hook-form';

function SignUpForm() {
  const {register, handleSubmit} = useForm();
  const onSubmit = data => {
    console.log(data);
  };

  return (
    <form onSubmit = {handleSubmit(onSubmit)}>
      <label>First Name: </label>
      <input name="firstname" {...register("firstname",{required:true})} />

      <label>Last Name: </label>
      <input name="lastname" {...register("lastname",{required:true})} />

      <input type="submit" />
    </form>
  );
}

export default SignUpForm;
```

@rehooks/local-storage

The useLocalStorage hook, which is part of the Rehooks library (https://github.com/rehooks), provides functions for working with the browser's local storage. Browser local storage is useful for storing data between browser sessions. This is helpful for creating offline apps, for increasing the performance of a web app, and for remembering the user's state between sessions.

Another feature of useLocalStorage is that it can sync data between browser tabs.

use-local-storage-state

The useLocalStorageState hook (https://www.npmjs.com/package/use-local-storage-state) takes a key and an optional default value and returns an array with three values: a value, a setter function, and a Boolean named isPersistent. Here's an example:

```
const [reminders, setReminders, isPersistent] =
useLocalState('reminders',['sleep','eat food']);
```

The first two return values work the same as the values returned by useState. The third tells you whether the value is stored in memory or in local storage. By default, of course, any value you create using useLocalStorageState will be stored in localStorage. In the event that localStorage isn't available for some reason, useLocalStorageState will fall back to just keeping the value in memory.

Other Fun Hooks

Going beyond the basic tasks that are used in most modern user interfaces, other custom hooks encapsulate functionality that's more specialized or even just for fun. Here are a few custom hooks that fall into this category:

➤ The `useGeolocation` hook (`https://github.com/streamich/react-use`) tracks a user's geographic location.

➤ The `useNetworkStatus` hook (`https://github.com/rehooks/network-status`) returns information about a user's current network status.

➤ The `useKonomiCode` hook (`https://stackblitz.com/edit/use-konami-code`) is an easter egg hook for detecting when a user has entered the famous Konomi Code (↑ ↑ ↓ ↓ ← → ← → B A), which is used as a cheat code in many video games.

Lists of Hooks

Finding custom hooks for just about any purpose is becoming easier thanks to some great lists of hooks being maintained and updated by the React community. Here are a few of the lists of hooks that are currently available:

➤ Hooks.guide (`https://hooks-guide.netlify.app/`). A curated and categorized list of hooks.

➤ Collection of React Hooks (`https://nikgraf.github.io/react-hooks/`). A searchable collection of hooks that anyone can add to.

➤ Use Hooks (`https://use-hooks.org/`). Provides a tool for scaffolding React hooks and a list of hooks created using the scaffolding.

SUMMARY

Hooks aren't just a new and better way of doing something in React; they dramatically improve the entire React development experience, they make learning React easier, and they solve the problem of creating a standard and simple way to share code between components.

In this chapter, you learned:

➤ What React Hooks are.

➤ Why React Hooks were created.

➤ How to use each of the built-in hooks.

➤ How to use and create custom hooks.

➤ How to find pre-built custom hooks.

In the next chapter you'll learn how to manage complex user interfaces and applications by associating URLs with components and layouts using React Router.

12

Routing

Until now, every user interface example you've seen in this book has only had a single screen and everything the application can do is displayed at once. In the real world, apps have multiple modes, tabs, and screens. The ability to change from an app's main screen to a settings screen, for example, makes it possible for user interfaces to do more while not overwhelming the user with complexity and clutter.

In this chapter, you'll learn:

> ➤   What routing is and why you need it.

> ➤   How routing works in single page applications.

> ➤   How to install and use React Router.

> ➤   How to create basic routes.

> ➤   How to create navigation.

> ➤   How to create nested routes.

> ➤   How to use React Router's hooks.

WHAT IS ROUTING?

The most basic concept behind the web (what we call Web 1.0) is that a web browser requests a web page from a web (HTTP) server using a unique URL. The web server then responds with an HTML page that is rendered in the browser, as shown in Figure 12-1.

When a user clicks a link on a web page, it requests a new HTML page, which the browser downloads and displays instead of the current page. Browsers and servers maintain a user's state between different web pages by using browser cookies, the localStorage API, and server-side data.

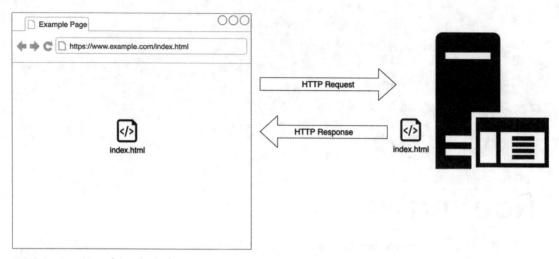

FIGURE 12-1: How the web works

The problem with loading a new web page each time a user clicks a link is that it doesn't create a smooth experience for the user, and it doesn't allow for refreshing data dynamically. The whole web page is downloaded and rendered each time a new URL is loaded.

AJAX (which stands for Asynchronous JavaScript and XML) was created to solve this problem. With AJAX, JavaScript dynamically loads data into a web page without loading a new HTML page. AJAX made dynamic web user interfaces possible, and JavaScript libraries and frameworks made building them easier. This is what was referred to as Web 2.0.

Now instead of the web browser requesting new pages from a web server, the browser only loads the first page containing the JavaScript code and the JavaScript virtual machine takes over from there and dynamically loads data and updates the browser using the DOM API.

JavaScript user interface libraries hijack the original request/response model that the web was built on. This works well, but it means that the browser is always displaying the same HTML page. This is what we call a *single page application (SPA)*. Having a website or web application that only consists of one web page makes it impossible for other sites to link to specific data within your app or site using a URL, and it makes it more difficult for search engines to index the data on your site or in your app.

The solution is to have the JavaScript that runs your web application simulate the browser's built-in ability to load web pages that correspond to unique URLs, as shown in Figure 12-2.

This mapping of URLs to things happening inside a JavaScript application is what we call *routing*.

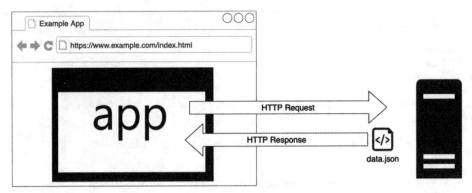

FIGURE 12-2: JavaScript routing

HOW ROUTING WORKS IN REACT

In React, routing has two purposes:

1. To change the `window.location` property of the browser (when used with a web browser).

2. To detect the current location and use it to show or hide different components or combinations of components.

The browser's `window.location.href` property is what indicates the current URL of the web page. By setting `window.location.href` without making a server request, a JavaScript routing program can simulate the native way that browsers change the rendered view. What this means is that a user or search engine can navigate to or link to a specific URL, such as `www.example.com/aboutUs`.

Once the value of `window.location.href` changes, this property can be read using JavaScript and different URLs can be associated with different components. This association is called a *route*.

Listing 12-1 shows a simple use of React Router to create two routes, such as you might do in a configuration utility, a survey, or a text-based adventure game.

LISTING 12-1: A simple routing component

```
import React from "react";
import {LessTraveledPath,MoreTraveledPath} from './PathOptions';
import {
  BrowserRouter,
  Switch,
  Route,
  Link
} from "react-router-dom";
```

continues

LISTING 12-1 *(continued)*

```
function ChooseYourAdventure() {
  return (
    <BrowserRouter>
      <div>
        <p>You come to a fork in the road. Which path will you take?</p>
        <ul>
          <li>
            <Link to="/worn">The More Well-traveled Path</Link>
          </li>
          <li>
            <Link to="/untrodden">The Less Well-traveled Path</Link>
          </li>
        </ul>


        <Switch>
          <Route path="/worn">
            <MoreTraveledPath />
          </Route>
          <Route path="/untrodden">
            <LessTraveledPath />
          </Route>
        </Switch>

      </div>
    </BrowserRouter>
  );
}

export default ChooseYourAdventure;
```

In this example, the `Link` component changes the current browser location. The `Route` components render the correct child component depending on the browser's location. When the browser's location (after the domain name) is /worn, the `MoreTraveledPath` component will be displayed, and when the location is /untrodden, the `LessTraveledPath` component will be displayed.

You can verify that the `window.location.href` property changes by opening the JavaScript console and typing **window.location.href**, as shown in Figure 12-3.

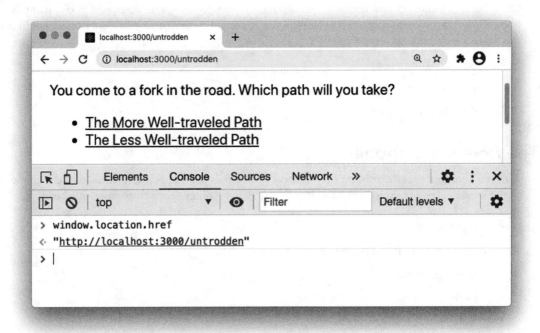

FIGURE 12-3: Changing routes and viewing the window.location.href property

USING REACT ROUTER

React Router can be used for routing in web applications or in mobile apps. Because of the fundamental differences in routing in a browser versus routing in a native mobile app, there are two different versions of React Router:

➤ `react-router-dom` is the version of React Router for the web.

➤ `react-router-native` is the version of React Router for native apps.

Since this book is primarily about creating user interfaces for the web, we'll use `react-router-dom`. However, the basic process that you'll use to create routes and links in React Router applies for either version.

Installing and Importing react-router-dom

React Router isn't installed with Create React App by default, so you'll need to install it before you can start using it. Once you have a React application built with Create React App, you can install `react-router-dom` using npm by entering the following command into the terminal:

```
npm install react-router-dom@5.3.0
```

Once `react-router-dom` is installed, you can import components, functions, and hooks from the library into any of your components that will use routing. For most uses of React Router, you'll need three parts:

➤ A router component.

➤ A linking component.

➤ A route component.

The Router Component

A router component is the top-level component that makes routing possible. It handles the changing of the `window.location` property and it provides React Router props to components below it.

Selecting a Router

React Router contains five different router components:

➤ `BrowserRouter`

➤ `HashRouter`

➤ `MemoryRouter`

➤ `StaticRouter`

➤ `NativeRouter`

No matter which router you choose, it's a convention to import the router component using the name `Router`, like this:

```
import {BrowserRouter as Router} from 'react-router-dom';
```

Importing the router as `Router` also simplifies things later if you want to change the router.

> **NOTE** The five router components listed here are the "high-level" routers. React Router also has a component named `Router`, which is the "low-level" router. The low-level `Router` component is used for synchronizing routes with state management libraries (such as Redux). Unless you have a good reason to use the low-level `Router`, you can safely ignore it.

BrowserRouter

`BrowserRouter` is the `Router` component that you'll use most, if not all, of the time. It uses the HTML5 history API to change the browser's `window.location.href` property. Using `Browser-Router` allows your React UI to simulate the familiar way of navigating the web using URL paths.

HashRouter

`HashRouter` uses the part of the URL after the hash symbol (#) to synchronize the location and the displayed components. `HashRouter` relies on the fact that anything after a # in a URL won't cause a browser to load a new page by default. For example, the following two addresses both use the same HTML page:

```
https://www.example.com/
```

```
https://www.example.com/#/aboutUs
```

The second URL passes a path after a #, which can be read using JavaScript and used to change the displayed components.

Prior to the widespread availability of the HTML5 history API in browsers, which allows JavaScript to change the address without loading new pages, hash routing was how JavaScript routing always worked. Today, `HashRouter` is mostly still around for backwards compatibility with older apps and browsers.

MemoryRouter

`MemoryRouter` doesn't update or read the browser's `window.location` property at all. Instead, it keeps the routing history in memory. `MemoryRouter` is useful for non-browser environments such as React Native, and for in-memory tests of your user interface.

StaticRouter

`StaticRouter` creates a router that never changes. It's useful for server-side rendering of React, where the web server passes a path to React on the server and React generates static code to serve to the user.

NativeRouter

`NativeRouter` is used for creating navigation in iOS and Android apps built using React Native. Keep in mind that React apps can be rendered to many different types of user interface devices (as you saw in Chapter 4). Native apps handle routing differently from web browsers, and the `NativeRouter` component translates the lower-level React Router components to routing commands that work with your target mobile operating system.

Using the Router Component

Whichever router component you choose, it needs to wrap around the other React Router components. One common way to make sure that the router is available to your entire app is by rendering it around your root component in the `ReactDOM.render` method.

This is one of the few times that you'll have a need to modify `index.js` after you initially create it. If you recall from Chapter 2, the `ReactDOM.render` method is used once in a React UI and takes a component (called the `root` component) and a DOM node where that component should be rendered as arguments.

For example, the default Create React App `ReactRouter.render` method looks like this:

```
ReactDOM.render(
  <React.StrictMode>
    <App />
  </React.StrictMode>,
  document.getElementById('root')
);
```

The `React.StrictMode` component is optional in the preceding example and may or may not be present depending on how and when you bootstrapped your app with Create React App. But, just as `React.StrictMode` wraps around the root component, `App`, you can wrap a router component around `App` to provide routing capabilities to your entire app.

After you've imported your router component, enclose the root component in a router like this:

```
import React from 'react';
import ReactDOM from 'react-dom';
import {BrowserRouter as Router} from 'react-router-dom';

ReactDOM.render(
  <React.StrictMode>
    <Router>
      <App />
    </Router>
  </React.StrictMode>,
  document.getElementById('root')
);
```

With the router in place, you can move on to creating links and routes.

Linking to Routes

React Router has three different linking components:

➤   `Link`

➤   `NavLink`

➤   `Redirect`

The first two linking components are essentially wrappers around the HTML `a` element with some additional features and capabilities added. The `Redirect` component changes the current URL without user interaction.

Internal Linking with Link

Because React Router overrides the default behavior of links in a browser, you can't simply link between routes using the `a` element as you normally would in a website. The `Link` element is the basic linking element in React Router. All it requires is a path to link to, which can be provided using the `to` attribute, and a single child node, as in the following example:

```
<Link to="/user/login">Log in</Link>
```

The value of the `to` attribute can be a string (or an expression that evaluates to a string) or an object. If the `to` property is specified as an object, the properties of the object are concatenated to create the destination location.

Linking with a String

If you pass a string to the `to` attribute, it can be any valid internal path that you would normally use as the value of the `href` attribute with the HTML a element. Any path that you pass to the `Link` component will be used to update the browser location relative to the path of the app. Because using `Link` updates the URL relative to the app, the following example won't work as you might expect:

```
<Link to="https://chrisminnick.com">Link to my website</Link>
```

Figure 12-4 shows what happens in the address bar when you click the preceding link in a React Router app.

FIGURE 12-4: React Router can't be used for external linking

If you want to link to an external site from a React app, just use the a element.

Linking with an Object

To use an object as the value of the `to` attribute, specify a combination of the allowed properties:

➤ `pathname`: A string containing the path to link to.

➤ `search`: A string containing query parameters (the question mark followed by the `name=value` pairs that form an HTML querystring).

➤ `hash`: A string containing the hash symbol (#) followed by any values you want to provide to the destination route in the hash portion of the URL.

➤ `state`: An object containing state that you want to persist in the destination location.

For example, the following `Link` component, when followed, will pass a `path` and `querystring` to the destination `Route` component:

```
<Link to={{path: '/orders, search: '?filterBy=new'}}>
    View New Orders
</Link>
```

Additional Link Props

The `Link` component can receive several optional props. These include `replace`, `component`, and pass-through props, which are discussed next.

replace

Normally, when a `Link` element is clicked, React Router adds a new location entry to the browser history stack. If you want to return to the route you were previously at, you can use the browser back button or change the browser's position in the history stack. The `replace` attribute replaces the current entry in the history stack rather than adding a new one:

```
<Link to="/somepath" replace>Go to the new location</Link>
```

component

The `component` attribute takes a custom navigation component as its value. You can use the `component` attribute to supply the name of the component you'd like to use in place of the default `Link` component. To create a custom navigation component that you want to use for the link and pass the prop from the `Link` component through to it, do this:

```
const SpecialLink = (props)=>(
  <a {...props}>***Super Special Link*** {props.children}</a>
);

<Link to="/somepath" component={SpecialLink}>Click the special link</Link>
```

pass-through props

If you want to attach additional props to the a element that results from the `Link`, you can specify them as well. Examples include `className`, `id`, and `title`.

Internal Navigation with NavLink

Navigation links are a subset of internal links within an app. They're used for changing modes, tabs, or pages within a web application. Examples of navigation links include the links in a navigation bar or mobile site navigation menu.

Navigation links function the same as any other link in a web application, but it's good user interface design to indicate which link is currently active, as shown in Figure 12-5.

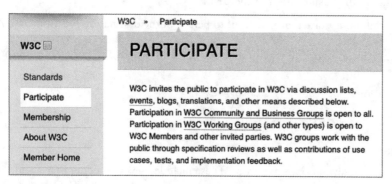

FIGURE 12-5: Navigation links indicate the current position

React Router's `NavLink` component creates navigation links. The difference between a `NavLink` and a `Link` component is that the `NavLink` has attributes that allow it to be styled when the value of its `to` attribute matches the browser's current location.

You can style a `NavLink` component using either the `activeClassName` attribute, which accepts a CSS class name, or the `activeStyle` attribute, which accepts a style object:

```
<NavLink to="/home" activeClassName="active">Home</NavLink>
```

Depending on how your app is designed, there are options to consider when deciding when a `NavLink` will display in its "active" style. For example, in the navigation menu shown in Figure 12-6, should the "Home" and "About Us" menus be highlighted when the "Meet the Team" sub-menu link is active?

Listing 12-2 shows the JSX used to build the navigation menu in Figure 12-6.

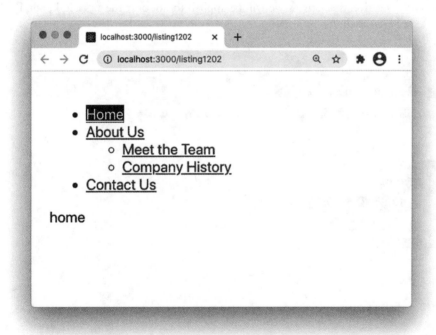

FIGURE 12-6: A navigation menu with sub-items

LISTING 12-2: A list of NavLinks with sub-items

```
<ul>
  <li><NavLink to="/" activeClassName="active">Home</NavLink></li>
  <li><NavLink to="/aboutUs" activeClassName="active">About Us</NavLink>
    <ul>
      <li>
        <NavLink to="/aboutUs/team" activeClassName="active">
```

continues

LISTING 12-2 *(continued)*

```
            Meet the Team
          </NavLink>
        </li>
        <li>
          <NavLink to="/aboutUs/history" activeClassName="active">
          Company History
          </NavLink>
        </li>
      </ul>
    </li>
    <li><NavLink to="/contactUs" activeClassName="active">Contact Us</NavLink></li>
  </ul>
```

By default, NavLink will apply the active style when part of the path matches. In the preceding example, when the Team link is active, the active style will be applied to not only the Team link, but also to the aboutUs and Home links, as shown in Figure 12-7.

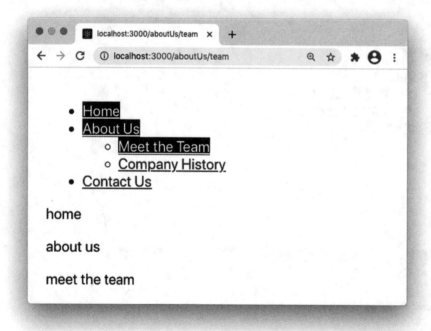

FIGURE 12-7: Partial matches activate the active style

If you only want to activate the active style when there's an exact match, you use the Boolean exact attribute, as shown in Listing 12-3.

LISTING 12-3: Using the exact attribute on NavLink components

```
<ul>
  <li><NavLink exact to="/" activeClassName="active">Home</NavLink></li>
  <li><NavLink exact to="/aboutUs" activeStyle={{color:'green'}}>About
Us</NavLink>
    <ul>
     <li><NavLink exact to="/aboutUs/team" activeClassName="active">Meet the
Team</NavLink></li>
      <li><NavLink exact to="/aboutUs/history" activeClassName="active">
Company History</NavLink></li>
    </ul>
  </li>
  <li><NavLink exact to="/contactUs" activeClassName="active">Contact
Us</NavLink></li>
</ul>
```

Figure 12-8 shows the resulting navigation bar after the exact attribute has been added to each of the NavLink components.

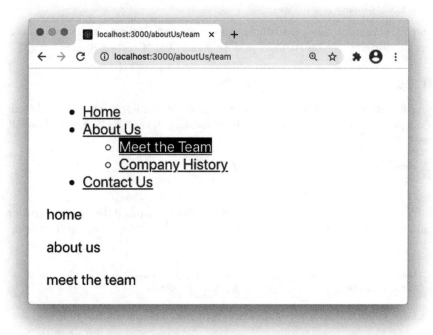

FIGURE 12-8: Using the exact attribute on NavLink components

If you need an even more strict matching of paths, the `strict` attribute can be used with `NavLink` components to also take into account the trailing slash in a URL path:

```
<li><NavLink strict to="/aboutUs" activeClassName="active">About Us</NavLink>
```

In the preceding link, the active style will be applied if the location is /aboutUs, but not if it's /aboutUs/.

Automatic Linking with Redirect

The `Redirect` component changes the current URL by replacing the current location in the history stack when it renders. Like the `Link` and `NavLink` components, `Redirect` takes an attribute named to, which can have a value of a string or object. Unlike `Link` and `NavLink`, a `Redirect` doesn't have children.

`Redirect` is often used to change the URL in response to the result of a conditional statement, as in the following example:

```
{loginSuccess?<Redirect to="/members" />:<Redirect to="/forgotPassword" />}
```

If you want to add a new location to the history stack, rather than replacing the current one, use the `push` attribute:

```
<Redirect push to="/pageNotFound" />
```

The `Redirect` component can also take an attribute called `from`, which causes it to function as a routing component. I'll discuss the `from` attribute in the next section, "Creating Routes."

Creating Routes

The `Route` component is the one that actually creates routes. In its simplest form, `Route` takes an attribute named `path`, which it compares with the current location. If there's a match, `Route` will render its children:

```
<Route path="/login">
  <LoginForm />
</Route>
```

By default, the path only needs to match part of the location. For example, if the current browser location is /login, the component in Listing 12-4 will render both the `Home` component and the `Login` component.

LISTING 12-4: Multiple routes in a component may have matches

```
import {BrowserRouter as Router, Route} from 'react-router-dom';

function HomeScreen(props) {
  return (
    <Router>
      <Route path="/">
        <Home />
      </Route>
```

```
        <Route path="/login">
          <Login />
        </Route>
      </Router>
    )
  }

  export default HomeScreen;
```

Figure 12-9 shows what the resulting page might look like when the location is /login, with the Home and Login components both displaying.

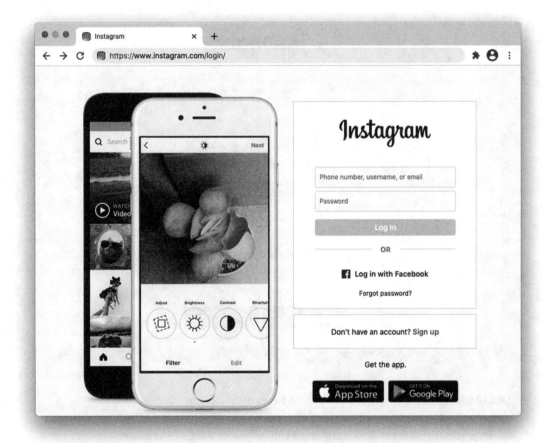

FIGURE 12-9: Multiple routes can match the URL

The ability to match and display multiple routes means that you can compose pages and create subnavigation with React Router.

Restricting Path Matching

You can use the `exact` attribute with `Route` to restrict path matching to exact matches. Figure 12-10 shows the result of adding `exact` to both of the `Routes` from the previous example and visiting the `/login` path.

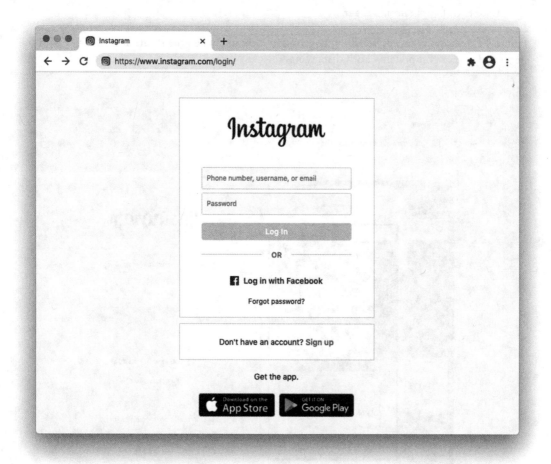

FIGURE 12-10: Add the exact attribute to Routes to restrict matching

If you want to enforce the ending slash in path matching, use the `strict` attribute:

```
<Route strict path="/user/">
  <UserProfile />
</Route>
```

Using URL Parameters

URLs frequently contain dynamic data that need to be available inside of child components. For example, in the following path, the directory name `user` is followed by a slash and then a number:

```
/user/5455
```

This type of URL usually indicates that the number represents a unique identifier for a user, rather than a component named "5455" (which isn't a valid component name).

A `Route` component to match this path would look for the `/user/` path and then indicate that the characters after the path are a parameter that should be available inside the child component, as shown in Listing 12-5.

LISTING 12-5: Using URL parameters

```
import {BrowserRouter as Router, Route} from 'react-router-dom';

function HomeScreen(props){
  return (
    <Router>
      <Route exact path="/">
        <Home />
      </Route>
      <Route exact path="/login">
        <Login />
      </Route>
      <Route path="/user/:id">
        <UserProfile />
      </Route>
    </Router>
  )
}

export default HomeScreen;
```

Inside the rendered child component, you can access URL parameters using the `useParams` hook, as shown in Listing 12-6.

LISTING 12-6: Using the useParams hook

```
function UserProfile() {

  let { id } = useParams();

  return (
    <div>
      <h3>User ID: {id}</h3>
    </div>
  );
}
```

The component Prop

Instead of specifying the component to be rendered by a matching route using children of the `Route` component, you can use the `component` attribute, as shown in Listing 12-7.

LISTING 12-7: Using the component attribute

```
import React from "react";
import {
  BrowserRouter as Router,
  Route,
  Link
} from "react-router-dom";

function ComponentProp(props) {

    const OrderDetails = (props)=>{
        return (
            <h1>Details for order # {props.match.params.orderid}</h1>
        )
    }

    return (
        <>
          <Router>
              <Link to="/orders/4">Order #4</Link>
              <Route path="/orders/:orderid" component={OrderDetails} />
          </Router>
        </>

      );
}

export default ComponentProp;
```

React Router will use the component passed to the component attribute to create and render a new React element. Using the component attribute results in the component being unmounted and rendered with every render.

Render Props

Another option for rendering components when routes match is to specify a function inside the render attribute. When the route matches, this function will be called. Using the render attribute doesn't require React Router to create an element, so it avoids the unmounting and mounting on each render that using the component attribute does.

Listing 12-8 shows an example of using the render attribute.

LISTING 12-8: Using the render attribute

```
import React from "react";
import {
  BrowserRouter as Router,
  Route,
  Link
} from "react-router-dom";
```

```
function ComponentProp(props) {

  return (
    <>
      <Router>
        <Link to="/orders/4">Order #4</Link>
        <Route path="/orders/:orderid" render={props => (
          <h1>Details for order # {props.match.params.orderid}</h1>
            )
          } />
      </Router>
    </>

  );
}

export default ComponentProp;
```

Use of Route's render attribute is an example of an advanced technique in React known as *render props*. A render prop is a function provided to a component using props that the component calls instead of using its own render method.

Render props can be used to share functionality between components and to dynamically determine what the child component will render. Inside of a component that accepts a render prop (such as Route in this case), the component will call the provided function. Listing 12-9 shows a simplified version of what happens inside the Route component when you use the render prop.

LISTING 12-9: Rendering a render prop

```
function Route(props) {

  return (
    <>
      {props.render({})}
    </>
  );
}

export default Route;
```

Switching Routes

The Switch component causes only the first matching Route to be rendered. This is useful in cases where you don't want to render multiple routes when there are multiple matches. To use Switch, wrap the routes that you want it to choose the first match from with a <Switch> element, as shown in Listing 12-10.

LISTING 12-10: Switching between multiple routes

```
<Switch>
  <Route path="/">
    <p>home</p>
  </Route>
  <Route path="/aboutUs">
    <p>about us</p>
  </Route>
  <Route path="/aboutUs/team">
    <p>meet the team</p>
  </Route>
</Switch>
```

In this example, if the current URL is /aboutUs/team, only that route will be rendered.

Rendering a Default Route

Switch can also be used to render a default route when no other routes match. The default route should be the last one, and a Route with no path can be used so that it matches any location, as shown in Listing 12-11.

LISTING 12-11: Rendering a default route

```
<Switch>
  <Route path="/">
    <p>home</p>
  </Route>
  <Route path="/aboutUs">
    <p>about us</p>
  </Route>
  <Route path="/aboutUs/team">
    <p>meet the team</p>
  </Route>
  <Route>
    <PageNotFound />
  </Route>
</Switch>
```

Routing with Redirect

The Redirect component can take a parameter named from that will be compared with the current URL and automatically redirect to a new location if it matches. Any matched parameters specified by the from attribute can be received by the to attribute by specifying them in both places. A Redirect with a from attribute can only be used inside a Switch component.

One use for a Redirect with a from attribute is in cases where more than one location should map to the same URL, or where the URL has changed. For example, in Listing 12-12, the /users route will redirect to /user/list.

LISTING 12-12: Redirecting from one location to another

```
import { BrowserRouter as Router, Redirect, Route, Switch, Link, useLocation }
from "react-router-dom";

function Header(props){
  return(<Link to="/users">View a list of users</Link>);
}

function UsersList(props){
  const location = useLocation();
  return(
    <>
      <h1>User List</h1>
      path: {location.pathname}
    </>);
}

function NoMatch(props){
  const location = useLocation();
  return(<h1>{location.pathname} is not a matching path</h1>)
}

function App(props){
  return(
    <Router>
      <Header />
        <Switch>
          <Route path="/users/list">
            <UsersList />
          </Route>

          <Redirect from="/users" to="/users/list" />

          <Route>
            <NoMatch />
          </Route>
        </Switch>
      </Router>
  );
}

export default App;
```

The App component in the previous example will render a link to /users. When that's clicked the Redirect component will change the location to /users/list and render the appropriate Route child component.

Behind the Scenes: location, history, and match

Routing depends on and uses three related objects: the history object, the location object, and the match object. By manipulating or reading values from these objects, you can gain greater control over how routing works in your app.

The history Object

The `history` object refers to the `history` package, which is separate from React Router, but which React Router depends upon. The `history` object's job is to keep a record of the locations navigated to in the current session and to make changing the location possible. The concept of session history is device-independent, but is implemented in several different ways for different environments (which correspond to the router components in React Router):

➤ Browser history.

➤ Hash history.

➤ Memory history.

You can gain access to the `history` object in your React code by using the `useHistory` hook or by using the `withRouter` higher-order function.

Listing 12-13 shows how to use `withRouter` to gain access to the `history.push` method and use it to create a link.

LISTING 12-13: Using withRouter

```
import React from "react";
import {
  withRouter
} from "react-router-dom";

function NavMenu(props) {
  function handleClick() {
    props.history.push("/home");
  }

  return (
    <button type="button" onClick={handleClick}>
      Go home
    </button>
  );
}

export default withRouter(NavMenu);
```

The `useHistory` hook is the newer, and slightly simpler, way of gaining access to the `history` object, as shown in Listing 12-14.

LISTING 12-14: Using useHistory

```
import React from "react";
import {
  useHistory
} from "react-router-dom";
```

```
function NavMenu(props) {

  const history = useHistory();

  function handleClick() {
    history.push("/home");
  }

  return (
    <button type="button" onClick={handleClick}>
      Go home
    </button>
  );
}

export default NavMenu;
```

JAVASCRIPT LESSON: HIGHER-ORDER FUNCTIONS

Higher-order functions and higher-order components are tools for abstracting and reusing code. They can be confusing at first, however, so I'll explain them with simple examples.

Higher-Order Functions

A higher-order function is a function that operates on another function. Higher-order functions aren't specific to React or to JavaScript. Rather, they're a common technique in mathematics and in computer science. Higher-order functions may take a function as a parameter and/or return a function.

For example, consider this function, which just adds one to a number and returns the result:

```
const addOne = (a)=>a+1;
```

This function is called a first-order function.

The following higher-order function takes a function as a parameter and returns the result of that function with some text appended to it:

```
const addText = f => x => f(x) + ' is the result.';
```

A new function can then be defined using the addText function with addOne supplied to it as a parameter:

```
const addWithText = addText(addOne);
```

The addWithText function can then be called, like this:

```
addWithText(8);
```

The result will be that the string "9 is the result" will be returned. You can test this out by copying each of the previous lines into your browser's JavaScript console one at a time.

continues

continued

Higher-Order Components

In React, a higher-order component is a function that takes a component and returns a new component. In the process, it enhances the original component in some way. For example, in React Router, the `withRouter` function returns a new component that has access to the `history` object.

To use a higher-order function, you can define a normal component, and then use the higher-order component to enhance that original component, as shown in this example:

```
import React from "react";
import { withRouter } from "react-router";

class ShowTheLocation extends React.Component {

  render() {
    const { match, location, history } = this.props;

    return <div>You are now at {location.pathname}</div>;
  }
}
const ShowTheLocationWithRouter = withRouter(ShowTheLocation);
export default ShowTheLocationWithRouter;
```

In the preceding example, when you render a `ShowTheLocationWithRouter` component, it will have access to the `match`, `location`, and `history` props from React Router.

Table 12-1 shows all the properties and methods of the `history` object.

TABLE 12-1: Properties and Methods of history

PROPERTIES AND METHODS	DESCRIPTION
`length`	The number of `location` items in the history stack.
`action`	The current action (such as PUSH or REPLACE).
`location`	The current `location`.
`push()`	Adds a new item to the history stack.
`replace()`	Replaces the current location on the history stack.
`go()`	Moves the pointer by the passed-in number of entries in the history stack.
`goBack()`	Go back one entry in the history stack.
`goForward()`	Go forward one entry in the history stack.
`block()`	Prevents navigation. For example, if the user clicks the Back button, `block` can be used to interrupt the navigation to display a message or confirmation dialog.

The location Object

A `location` object contains information about where the app is or has been or will be. It can contain a pathname, a querystring, a hash, state data, and a key. Location objects are stored in the history stack and can be accessed in a `Route` component or by using the `withRouter` higher-order function.

Listing 12-15 shows how to access properties of the `Location` object using `withRouter`.

LISTING 12-15: Viewing properties of the current location object

```
import React from "react";
import {
  withRouter
} from "react-router-dom";

function ViewLocation(props) {

    return (
        <>
            <h1>Current Location</h1>
            <ul>

                <li>pathname: {props.location.pathname}</li>
                <li>hash: {props.location.hash}</li>
                <li>search: {props.location.search}</li>
                <li>key: {props.location.key}</li>

            </ul>
        </>

    );
}

export default withRouter(ViewLocation);
```

With this component rendered, try changing the location by adding a `querystring` or hash in the browser's address bar, as shown in Figure 12-11.

The match Object

The `match` object contains information about how a Route's path matches the URL. Just as with the `location` and `history` objects, you can access the `match` object in several different ways:

➤ Inside a `Route` component.

➤ By using the `withRouter` higher-order component.

➤ By using a hook.

FIGURE 12-11: Modifying the current location

The `match` object contains the following properties:

➤ `params`: An object containing the key/value pairs passed from the URL, which correspond to dynamic parts of the URL. For example, if the route's path is `/user/:id`, `id` will be in the `params` property.

➤ `isExact`: A Boolean that's true if the entire URL matches, with no characters after it.

➤ `path`: The pattern that was used to make the match.

➤ `url`: The matched portion of the URL.

The `match` object is useful for dynamically constructing links and routes in nested routes, as shown in Listing 12-16.

LISTING 12-16: Dynamic links and routes in nested routes

```
import {
  BrowserRouter as Router,
  Switch,
  Route,
  Link,
  useParams,
  useRouteMatch
} from "react-router-dom";

function Reports() {
  let { path, url } = useRouteMatch();
```

```
    return (
      <div>
        <h2>Reports</h2>
        <ul>
          <li>
            <Link to={`${url}/profitloss`}>Profit and Loss</Link>
          </li>
          <li>
            <Link to={`${url}/balancesheet`}>Balance Sheet</Link>
          </li>
          <li>
            <Link to={`${url}/payroll`}>Payroll</Link>
          </li>
        </ul>

        <Switch>
          <Route exact path={path}>
            <h3>Select a report.</h3>
          </Route>
          <Route path={`${path}/:reportId`}>
            <Report />
          </Route>
        </Switch>
      </div>
    );
  }

  function Report() {

    let { reportId } = useParams();

    return (
      <div>
        <h3>{reportId}</h3>
      </div>
    );
  }

function Nav() {

  return(
    <div>
      <ul>
        <li>
          <Link to={`/reports`}>Reports</Link>
        </li>
      </ul>

      <hr />

      <Switch>
        <Route path={`/reports`}>
          <Reports />
        </Route>
      </Switch>
```

continues

LISTING 12-16 *(continued)*

```
      </div>
    )
  }
function App() {
  return (
    <Router>
      <Nav />
    </Router>
  );
}

export default App;
```

This sub-navigation menu contains `Link` elements that use the URL from the `match` object as the base for the `to` attribute. To match these new links, `Route` components use the path from the `match` object as the base for their own path attribute values.

Figure 12-12 shows the result of rendering Listing 12-16 and clicking the Reports link.

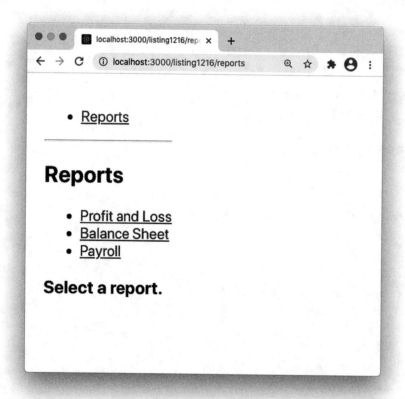

FIGURE 12-12: Dynamic link and path attributes with the match object properties

REACT ROUTER HOOKS

As you've seen in the previous examples, React Router includes several hooks that give you access to the state of the Router. These hooks are:

➤ useHistory: Gives you access to the history object.

➤ useLocation: Gives you access to the current location object.

➤ useParams: Returns an object containing the current URL parameters.

➤ useRouteMatch: Attempts to match the current URL. The useRouteMatch hook works the same way as the Route component matches URLs, but it can do so without rendering a Route.

useHistory

To use the useHistory hook, assign the return value of the useHistory hook to a new variable. The properties and methods of the history object then become available through the new object:

```
const history = useHistory();
```

useLocation

The useLocation hook works the same way as the useHistory hook. Create a new object from the returned value of useLocation to gain access to the properties of the location object:

```
const location = useLocation();
```

useParams

The useParams hook returns an object containing key/value pairs for each of the current Route's params. You can deconstruct the object to use individual params:

```
const {orderNumber,size,color} = useParams();
```

useRouteMatch

The useRouteMatch hook attempts to match the current URL in the same way that a Route component would, but without rendering anything. For example, if you have the following Route with a render prop:

```
<Route
  path="/order/:orderId"
  render={(({ match }) => {

    return <> {match.path}</>;
  }}
/>
```

you could gain access to the same match object without rendering anything like this:

```
let match = useRouteMatch("/order/:orderId");
```

The useRouteMatch hook can be used with a single argument, which is the path to match against, or it can be used without an argument, in which case it will return the match object of the current Route.

SUMMARY

Routing makes navigation and organization within React apps possible. React Router's declarative and composable API is logical and conforms to standard React best practices. With hooks, gaining access to the inner workings of routing when you need to is also easy.

In this chapter, you learned:

- ➤ What routing is.
- ➤ How JavaScript and React Router enable routing in SPAs.
- ➤ About the different routers in React Router.
- ➤ How to link between routes.
- ➤ How to create routes.
- ➤ How to use the Redirect component.
- ➤ How to use React Router's hooks.
- ➤ What higher-order functions and components are.

In the next chapter, you'll learn how to properly handle errors in React components by using error boundaries.

13

Error Boundaries

Even if it were possible to write perfect code, the nature of interactive web applications guarantees that once in a while something is going to break. Error boundaries will help you ensure that when something goes wrong, it won't result in the user seeing a crashed user interface.

In this chapter, you'll learn:

➤ What error boundaries are.

➤ What kinds of errors can be caught with error boundaries.

➤ How to log caught errors.

➤ What errors can't be caught with error boundaries.

➤ How to use JavaScript's try/catch.

THE BEST LAID PLANS

Any kind of software development involves balancing money, time, and quality. Too often, money and time are the limiting factors, especially on the web. Add to this the number of dependencies involved in a typical JavaScript application and other factors that are completely out of your control (such as network availability), and it's guaranteed that at some point or another a React user interface isn't going to function as you intended.

By default, when React encounters an error inside any of the components in a UI, it will emit an error on the next render that will fill the screen with either a big red message (in development mode) or a "white screen of death" (in production) that's not very helpful to anyone, as shown in Figure 13-1.

Crashed user interfaces and cryptic error messages are especially not helpful to end users. Usually, the only way to recover an app from a crashed UI is to restart it by refreshing the browser window, thus resetting the state of the application. In the worst-case scenario, an error message intended to be used by developers can reveal details of the internal workings of your application that could give someone with malicious intent the information they need to hack your application in some way.

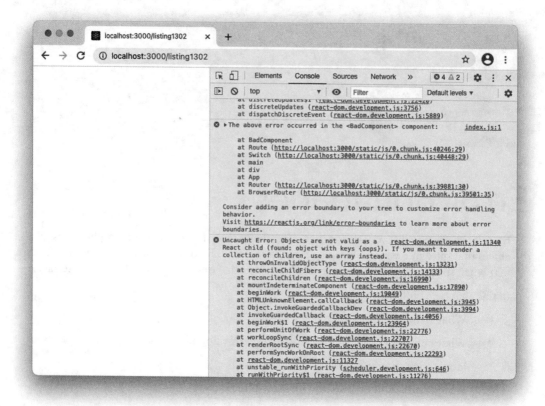

FIGURE 13-1: A crashed React app

Error boundaries catch many kinds of errors in a user interface and display a user-friendly alternative user interface. They also allow the parts of your application that were unaffected by the error to continue to function.

WHAT IS AN ERROR BOUNDARY?

An error boundary is a component that catches errors that happen in its child components. Once an error is caught, the error boundary can provide a fallback UI and log the error, as well as provide the user with a way to recover the use of the UI without refreshing the browser window. Think of it as like a firewall that keeps an explosion inside a component's child tree from blowing up your whole app.

For an example of why error boundaries are necessary, take a look at the diagram of a typical React user interface shown in Figure 13-2.

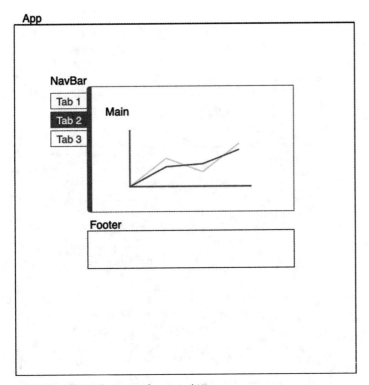

FIGURE 13-2: A diagram of a typical UI

This app consists of an `App` component that encloses several sub-components, including a navigation menu, a footer, and the main part of the user interface. It can be shown as an outline like this:

```
<App>
  <NavBar />
  <Main />
  <Footer />
</App>
```

The main part of the user interface may have many levels of components, and it may depend on outside sources of data and user input. All of these are factors that contribute to the likelihood of errors.

Starting with version 16 of React, the default behavior when an error is encountered in rendering any component in your app is to unmount the entire component tree and display a blank page, with details logged to the console. In development mode, an overlay window with an error message will also appear.

Figure 13-3 shows what happens to this user interface when something goes wrong in any of the app's components—in this case, the component was expecting a function to be passed as a prop, but it wasn't.

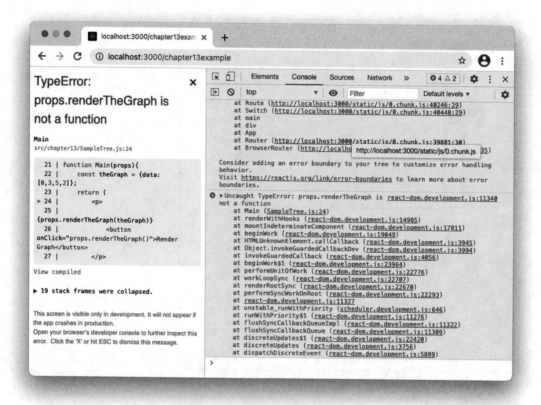

FIGURE 13-3: An uncaught error

Once the UI has been unmounted, there's no way for the user (or for the developer) to navigate elsewhere in the app. An error boundary around the `Main` component will ensure that the rest of the user interface continues to be usable even if something goes wrong inside `Main`. Here's what the new app looks like as an outline with an error boundary around `Main`:

```
<App>
  <NavBar />
  <ErrorBoundary>
    <Main />
  </ErrorBoundary>
  <Footer />
</App>
```

With this change, the `ErrorBoundary` component can now handle errors any way you want, while the rest of the UI is still functional, as shown in Figure 13-4.

If you want to, you can put an error boundary around the `NavBar` component and one around the `Footer` component as well. You could even put an `ErrorBoundary` around each of the subcomponents of `Main`, or just have one around the `App` component that handles events from all of the sub-components. More granularity (meaning more components wrapped in the ErrorBoundary) can give you more information about where the error happened as well as keep more of your app functional when something goes wrong.

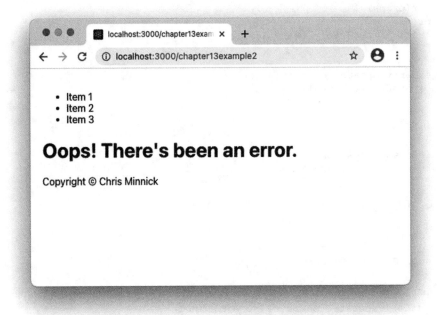

FIGURE 13-4: Handling an error with an error boundary

IMPLEMENTING AN ERROR BOUNDARY

An error boundary isn't a specific function or component in React. Instead, it's any component that you create that defines a static getDerivedStateFromError or componentDidCatch lifecycle method (or both). Because error boundaries make use of lifecycle methods, they must be class components. Once you define an ErrorBoundary component, you can reuse it as many times as you need it—or even reuse it in multiple React apps. So, if you want, an ErrorBoundary component may be the only class component you need to write.

Building Your Own ErrorBoundary Component

One way to get an ErrorBoundary component is to build your own. Listing 13-1 shows a simple example of an ErrorBoundary, which just uses static getDerivedStateFromError to show a fallback UI when an error occurs.

LISTING 13-1: An ErrorBoundary component

```
import {Component} from 'react';

class ErrorBoundary extends Component {
  constructor(props) {
    super(props);
    this.state = { hasError: false };
  }

  static getDerivedStateFromError(error) {
    return { hasError: true };
  }

  render() {

    if (this.state.hasError) {
      return <h1>Oops! There's been an error.</h1>;
    }

    return this.props.children;
  }
}

export default ErrorBoundary;
```

To understand what's happening in this ErrorBoundary component, you need to know a couple of things about the getDerivedStateFromErrors lifecycle method.

getDerivedStateFromErrors Is a Static Method

The getDerivedStateFromErrors lifecycle method is a *static method*. Static methods are commonly used to define functionality that belongs to the class as a whole, such as utilities. In React, the get-DerivedStateFromErrors and getDerivedStateFromProps lifecycle methods are defined as static to make it more difficult for them to have side effects.

In other words, because these methods are static, they belong to the component but they don't have access to the properties of an instance of a component (like this.props, this.state, and so forth). By limiting what the method has access to, React is limiting your ability to write anything but pure functions, which makes sure that this lifecycle method doesn't cause unpredictable results in the render method.

JAVASCRIPT LESSON: STATIC METHODS

Static methods are methods that are defined on a class and that can't be called on instances of the class. For example, the following class, Cashier, has a static method called makeChange. The makeChange method doesn't need to access the unique data in an instance of Cashier. It just takes a total and an amountTendered and returns the change:

```
class Cashier{
  static makeChange(total,amtTendered){
    return amtTendered - total;
  }
}
```

The makeChange method isn't available in an instance of Cashier, as shown here:

```
const bob = new Cashier();
bob.makeChange(2,10); // bob.makeChange is not a function
```

You can call makeChange on the class, however, like this:

```
Cashier.makeChange(2,10); // 8
```

getDerivedStateFromErrors Runs During the Render Phase

The render phase of a component's lifecycle is the time when it's not permitted to perform operations that have side effects. The correct time to perform side effects is before or after the render phase. If you want your ErrorBoundary to perform a side effect—such as logging the error—the place to do that is in the ComponentDidCatch lifecycle method (which we'll discuss in a moment).

getDerivedStateFromErrors Receives the Error as a Parameter

When an error happens in a descendant component of a component that uses getDerivedState-FromErrors, the method is called and the error message is passed. The error message is a string containing information about where the error happened and what the error was. As in the example in Listing 13-1, you don't actually need to do anything with the error. You can just use the fact that getDerivedStateFromErrors was called to trigger the rendering of the alternate user interface.

getDerivedStateFromErrors Should Return an Object for Updating State

The return value of getDerivedStateFromErrors will be used to update the state. In the example in Listing 13-1, getDerivedStateFromErrors returns a value for changing hasError to true. You're not limited to updating just one value, of course, and a more complex error boundary might also store the error itself in state, like this:

```
static getDerivedStateFromError(error) {
  return { hasError: true,
           error
         };
}
```

If getDerivedStateFromErrors doesn't run, ErrorBoundary will just render its children, as if it's not there at all, by returning this.props.children.

If getDerivedStateFromErrors does run, the resulting state can be used to display an alternate, or fallback, user interface. The conditional statement that checks the value of the hasError state value must go before return this.props.children so that if hasError is true, the component will return the fallback UI and not even get to the section of the `render` method that returns the children (since a function can only execute one `return` statement):

```
render() {

  if (this.state.hasError) {
    return <h1>Oops! There's been an error.</h1>;
  }

  return this.props.children;
}
```

Testing Your Boundary

Once you've created your `ErrorBoundary` component, you can test it out by wrapping it around a component that you know will produce an error that can be caught. Listing 13-2 contains a component that would normally produce an error, because it tries to return an object in the `render` method, which isn't allowed.

LISTING 13-2: A component with an error

```
function BadComponent(){
  return (
    {oops:"this is not good"}
  );
}

export default BadComponent;
```

Attempting to render this component without an error boundary will result in an error message and/or a blank screen.

To prevent this kind of error (short of fixing the actual component, of course) you can wrap the Bad-Component component in an error boundary in its parent's `render` method, or you can export it with the `ErrorBoundary` around it, as shown in Listing 13-3.

LISTING 13-3: Exporting with an ErrorBoundary

```
import ErrorBoundary from './ErrorBoundary';

function BadComponentContainer(){
  return (
    <ErrorBoundary>
      <BadComponent />
    </ErrorBoundary>
  )
}
```

```
function BadComponent(){
    return (
       {oops:"this is not good"}
    );
}

export default BadComponentContainer;
```

With the error boundary around the component with the error, the fallback UI will now render, as shown in Figure 13-5.

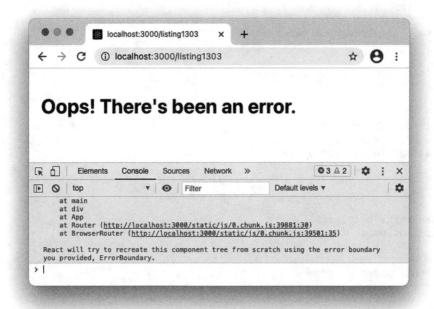

FIGURE 13-5: Rendering a fallback UI

Logging Errors with ComponentDidCatch()

Minimizing the impact on users when errors happen in your React component tree is one thing, but actually learning why and where the error occurred can help you prevent the error from happening in the future. This is where the ComponentDidCatch lifecycle method comes in.

ComponentDidCatch runs during React's *commit phase*. The commit phase happens after the render phase. In addition to ComponentDidCatch, this is also when ComponentDidMount and Component-DidUpdate run. During the commit phase, ReactDOM actually applies (or *commits*) the changes from the render phase to the browser. The commit phase is when it's safe for components to do operations that have side effects, because the commit phase only happens once per change, whereas the render phase may happen multiple times for any change to the state.

ComponentDidCatch receives two parameters: the error that was thrown, and an info object containing information about which component threw the error. Listing 13-4 adds the ComponentDid-Catch method to the ErrorBoundary we created earlier. In this version, ComponentDidCatch just logs the values of the error and info parameters to the browser console.

LISTING 13-4: Logging the error and the info object to the console

```
import {Component} from 'react';

class ErrorBoundary extends Component {
  constructor(props) {
    super(props);
    this.state = { hasError: false };
  }

  static getDerivedStateFromError(error) {
    return { hasError: true };
  }

  componentDidCatch(error,info){
    console.log(`error: ${error}`);
    console.log(`info: ${info}`);
  }

  render() {

    if (this.state.hasError) {
      return <h1>Oops! There's been an error.</h1>;
    }

    return this.props.children;
  }
}

export default ErrorBoundary;
```

With this change made to ErrorBoundary, you can now mount the BadComponent component and open the console to see the parameters passed to ComponentDidCatch, as shown in Figure 13-6.

Using a Logging Service

Logging errors to the console is fine during development, but once your app is out in the wild and being used by other people, all of those log messages that show up in the console window stay in the user's console window and don't do anyone any good.

To find out what errors are happening for real users, either they need to tell you about them (which is unlikely unless the error is very bad) or you need to implement a system that logs errors outside of the user's browser automatically.

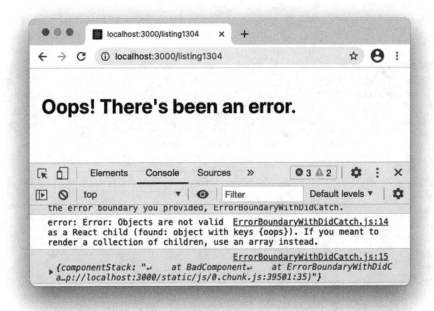

FIGURE 13-6: Viewing the error and info parameters in the console

A cloud-based logging service can capture events (such as errors) that happen in your application and provide you with reports that you can use to improve your app or to gain information about how people are using it.

One such service is Loggly (https://loggly.com). Loggly has a free trial that you can use for testing out the following example code.

After you've signed up for Loggly's trial, you'll need to install the Loggly Software Development Kit (SDK). You can do this by entering the following at the root of your app:

```
npm install loggly-jslogger
```

Once the Loggly SDK is installed, create a new component, Logger, that will provide the Loggly SDK's functionality to other components (such as your error boundary). Listing 13-5 shows what your Logger component should contain.

LISTING 13-5: The Logger component

```
import { LogglyTracker } from 'loggly-jslogger';

const logger = new LogglyTracker();

logger.push({ 'logglyKey': 'YOUR CUSTOMER TOKEN HERE' });

export default logger;
```

To get the customer token, log in to your Loggly trial account and go to the Source Browser, as shown in Figure 13-7.

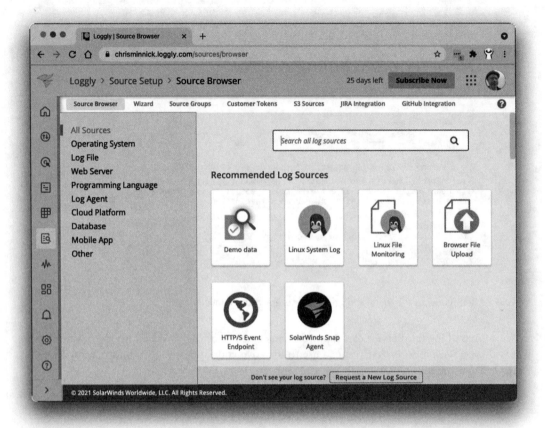

FIGURE 13-7: Add a log source

Find the Customer Tokens link (shown in Figure 13-8) and click it to view the token you'll need to enter into the Logger component.

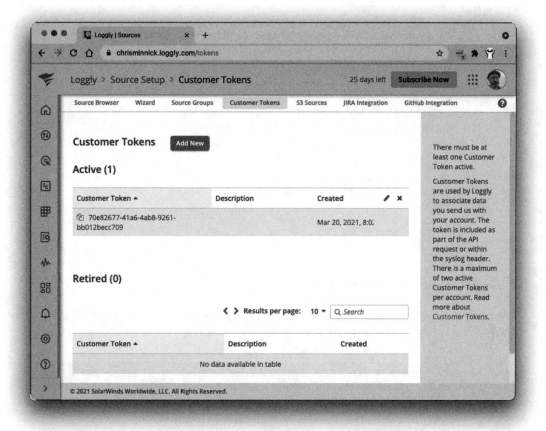

FIGURE 13-8: The Customer Token link in Loggly

The last step in installing Loggly and configuring it to log errors in your React UI is to import it into `ErrorBoundary` and pass the parameters of `ComponentDidCatch` to it, as shown in Listing 13-6.

LISTING 13-6: The updated ErrorBoundary with remote logging

```
import {Component} from 'react';
import logger from './logger';

class ErrorBoundary extends Component {
  constructor(props) {
    super(props);
    this.state = { hasError: false };
  }
```

continues

LISTING 13-6 *(continued)*

```
    static getDerivedStateFromError(error) {
      return { hasError: true };
    }

    componentDidCatch(error,info){
      logger.push({ error, info });
    }

    render() {

      if (this.state.hasError) {
        return <h1>Oops! There's been an error.</h1>;
      }

      return this.props.children;
    }
  }

  export default ErrorBoundary;
```

Now that the `ErrorBoundary` is logging caught errors to Loggly, you can go to your Loggly dashboard and see information about caught errors that happen, as shown in Figure 13-9.

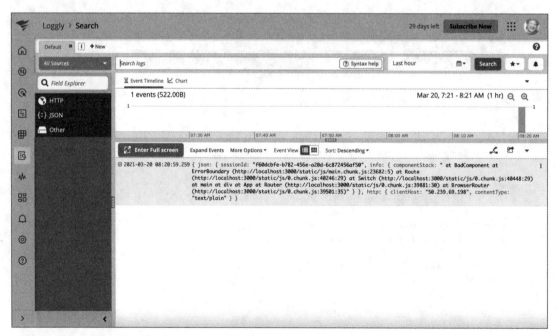

FIGURE 13-9: Viewing caught errors in Loggly

Resetting the State

If the error that triggers an error boundary is a temporary one, such as can happen when a network service is unavailable, providing a way for the user to try again can improve the user experience.

Since our `ErrorBoundary` component determines whether to render the fallback UI or its children based on the `hasError` state value, resetting the value of `hasError` will cause it to try to render the children again.

To demonstrate resetting the state, let's first make a component that doesn't always return an error. The component in Listing 13-7 will randomly result in an error when you click a button.

LISTING 13-7: A component that sometimes errors

```
import ErrorBoundary from './ErrorBoundary';
import {useState} from 'react';

function SometimesBad(){
  const [message,setMessage] = useState();

  const handleClick = () => {
    const randomNumber = Math.floor(Math.random() * 2);
    if (randomNumber === 1){
      setMessage({error:"there has been an error"});
    } else {
      setMessage("great");
    }
  }
  return (
    <div>
      <button onClick={handleClick}>Mystery Button</button>
      {message}
    </div>
  );
}

export default SometimesBad;
```

If you render this component and click the button, it may result in the value of `message` being set to an object, which will attempt to render. The result will be the unmounting of the React component tree and an error message.

If you use one of the `ErrorBoundary` components that you've seen so far in this chapter, it will prevent the user from seeing a blank screen and will leave the rest of the app intact. However, because this error isn't necessarily fatal, we can give the user an option to try their luck again. To do so, provide a way for the value of `hasError` to be reset to `false`, as shown in Listing 13-8.

LISTING 13-8: Providing a reset link in the Error Boundary

```
import {Component} from 'react';
import logger from './logger';

class ErrorBoundary extends Component {
  constructor(props) {
    super(props);
    this.state = { hasError: false };
  }

  static getDerivedStateFromError(error) {
    return { hasError: true };
  }

  componentDidCatch(error,info){
    logger.push({ error, info });
  }

  render() {

    if (this.state.hasError) {
      return (<>
                <h1>Oops! There's been an error.</h1>
                <button onClick={()=>this.setState({hasError:false})}>Try
again</button>
              <>)
    }

    return this.props.children;
  }
}

export default ErrorBoundary;
```

With this ErrorBoundary wrapped around SometimesBad, when it does result in an error, the user will be able to click the button to get back to the user interface with the button and try again, as shown in Figure 13-10.

Installing a Pre-Built ErrorBoundary Component

The other way to get an ErrorBoundary component is to install one that someone has already built, such as the one at https://www.npmjs.com/package/react-error-boundary.

To install react-error-boundary, enter the following into your terminal:

```
npm install react-error-boundary
```

The react-error-boundary package provides a configurable ErrorBoundary component that you can use instead of writing your own. To use it, import it into your component and wrap it around components that you want to catch errors in. React-error-boundary is highly customizable, but the most basic use of it simply requires a fallback component that should be displayed when an error occurs, as shown in Listing 13-9.

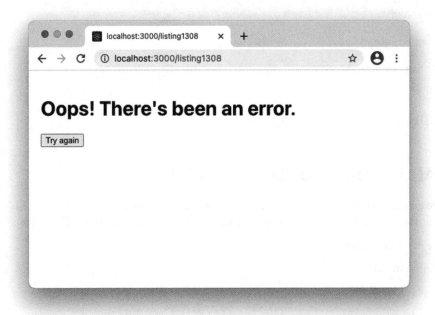

FIGURE 13-10: Providing a reset option in the error boundary

LISTING 13-9: Specifying a fallback component with react-error-boundary

```
import ErrorBoundary from 'react-error-boundary';

function ErrorFallback({error}) {
  return (
    <div role="alert">
      <p>Something went wrong:</p>
      <pre>{error.message}</pre>
    </div>
  )
}

function BadComponentContainer(){
    return (
        <ErrorBoundary
          FallbackComponent={ErrorFallback}>
            <BadComponent />
        </ErrorBoundary>
    )
}
```

continues

LISTING 13-9 *(continued)*

```
function BadComponent(){
    return (
      {oops:"this is not good"}
    );
}


export default BadComponentContainer;
```

WHAT CAN'T AN ERROR BOUNDARY CATCH?

Error boundaries are a great tool for capturing most of the errors that you're likely to encounter in your components, but there are a few types of errors that error boundaries can't handle. These are:

➤   Errors in the `ErrorBoundary`.

➤   Errors in event handlers.

➤   Errors in server-side rendering.

➤   Errors in asynchronous code.

Catching Errors in Error Boundaries with try/catch

One way to catch the errors that error boundaries can't, is to use JavaScript's built-in `try/catch` syntax.

For example, an error boundary can't catch an error in itself, only in its child components. Theoretically, you could wrap your `ErrorBoundary` in an `ErrorBoundary`, but that's a never-ending task. It's better to use `try/catch` in the `ErrorBoundary` component, as shown in Listing 13-10.

LISTING 13-10: Using try/catch to catch errors in an ErrorBoundary

```
import {Component} from 'react';
import logger from './logger';

class ErrorBoundary extends Component {
  constructor(props) {
    super(props);
    this.state = { hasError: false };
  }

  static getDerivedStateFromError(error) {
    return { hasError: true };
  }

  componentDidCatch(error,info){
    try {
      logger.push({ error, info });
    } catch(error){
```

```
      // handle the error here
    }
  }

  render() {

    if (this.state.hasError) {
      return <h1>Oops! There's been an error.</h1>;
    }

    return this.props.children;
  }
}

export default ErrorBoundary;
```

In this example, if something goes wrong with calling `logger.push`, that error can be handled by the code in the catch block.

Catching Errors in Event Handlers with react-error-boundary

Event handlers in React don't happen during the rendering, unlike the lifecycle methods and the `render` method. Because of this, errors in event handlers don't have the potential to cause the collapse of the entire UI, and so event boundaries aren't needed or supported in event handlers.

However, rather than writing separate error handling code for your event handlers and your error boundary, it would be ideal to be able to handle both the same way.

If you use the `react-error-boundary` package, it includes a hook named `useErrorHandler` that you can use to hand off errors that happen in an event handler to the nearest `ErrorBoundary` component, as shown in Listing 13-11.

LISTING 13-11: Using useErrorHandler()

```
function Greeting() {
  const [greeting, setGreeting] = React.useState(null)
  const handleError = useErrorHandler()

  function handleSubmit(event) {
    event.preventDefault()
    const name = event.target.elements.name.value
    fetchGreeting(name).then(
      newGreeting => setGreeting(newGreeting),
      error => handleError(error),
    )
  }

  return greeting ? (
    <div>{greeting}</div>
  ) : (
```

continues

LISTING 13-11 *(continued)*

```
    <form onSubmit={handleSubmit}>
      <label>Name</label>
      <input id="name" />
      <button type="submit">get a greeting</button>
    </form>
  )
}
```

In this example, when an error happens in the `handleSubmit` method, it will be handled by the `ErrorBoundary` that encloses the `Greeting` component (or one of its ancestors).

SUMMARY

The goal of error handling (also known as exception handling) in software is to minimize the impact that errors in your application have on the user experience. Once you've handled an error, logging it can help you get to the root cause and fix the problem. Both error handling and logging are enabled and simplified in React through the use of error boundaries.

In this chapter, you learned:

➤ What an error boundary is.

➤ How to write your own error boundary.

➤ How to use an error boundary to display a fallback UI.

➤ How to use an error boundary to log errors to a logging service.

➤ How to use the `react-error-boundary` package.

➤ How to catch errors using `try/catch`.

➤ How to use `react-error-boundary`'s `useErrorHandler` hook.

In the next chapter, you'll learn how to put everything you've learned so far together and actually deploy your React app to the web.

14

Deploying React

Now that you know how to build a React UI, implement routing, catch and log errors, and several methods for fixing performance problems, you're ready to move beyond the confines of your local development machine and make your app available to its audience. In software and web development, we call this step deployment.

In this chapter, you'll learn:

> ➤ The differences between the development and production versions of React.

> ➤ How to build your app for deployment.

> ➤ Different options for hosting a React UI.

> ➤ How to enable continuous integration with Git.

WHAT IS DEPLOYMENT?

Software deployment is the process of making software available for use. For web apps, this means putting an app on the web. For mobile apps, it usually means putting an app in an app store.

Deployment of a web app generally involves running the code through several steps to prepare it for the web, followed by actually transferring the processed files to a server where they'll become accessible through a non-local URL.

BUILDING AN APP

Building, or compiling, an app is the process of transforming your development, or source, files into a standalone app. In the case of a React project, this means your app must go through several steps, including the following:

> ➤ Linking to the optimized production version of the React and ReactDOM libraries.

> ➤ Bundling other linked libraries that are required for your app to run on a server (such as React Router).

➤ Transpiling your source files to a lowest-common-denominator version of JavaScript that will run in all of your target web browsers.

➤ Combining your source files into bundles for efficient transfer over the web.

➤ Minifying your source files to reduce the bandwidth required for the end user to load the app.

➤ Moving static files (such as HTML, CSS, the compiled JavaScript, and images) into a distribution directory.

Building a React app is a complex process involving several tools and scripts working together to process the hundreds of files that make up your React project. Fortunately, Create React App makes building an app simple. When you're ready to compile your React app that was bootstrapped with Create React App for deployment, you only need to know one simple command: npm run build.

Running the build Script

When you're ready to deploy your app (or any time you want to try it out, really) you can create a production version of your app by going into the terminal and typing **npm run build**.

What happens next will be that Create React App will go through a similar process to what it does when you run npm start, except that instead of opening the compiled app in a browser, it will save the compiled files in a directory named build.

Examining the build Directory

Figure 14-1 shows the files in the resulting build directory after running npm run build in the React Bookstore project from Chapter 5.

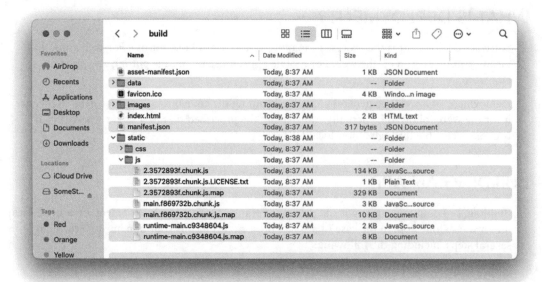

FIGURE 14-1: The build directory

If you compare the `build` directory with the rest of the project, you'll notice the following:

- The contents of the `public` directory become the root of the `build` directory. The `images` and `data` directories, along with the `favicon.ico`, `index.html`, and the `manifest.json` files, have all been copied over to `build`.
- A new `static` directory has been created. This directory contains a `css` subfolder and a `js` subfolder.
- A new `asset-manifest.json` file has been created.

The Built index.html

If you open the `index.html` from the `public` directory and the `index.html` from the `build` directory, you'll see that the one in the `build` directory is minified, comments have been removed, template code (marked by `%` characters) has been replaced, and links to scripts and CSS have been inserted. If you look hard enough, however, you'll notice your root node, where the React app will run, is still in there, as shown in Figure 14-2.

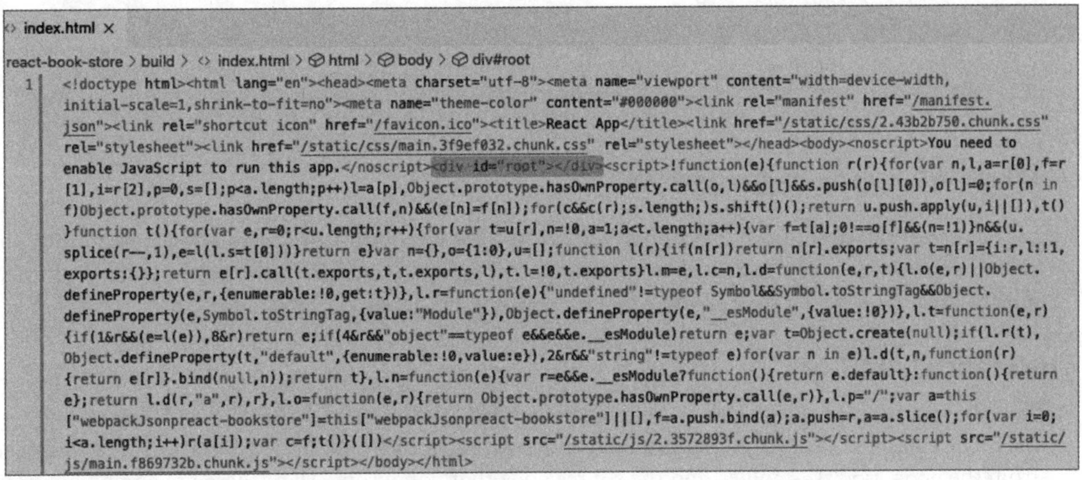


```
1 <!doctype html><html lang="en"><head><meta charset="utf-8"><meta name="viewport" content="width=device-width,
initial-scale=1,shrink-to-fit=no"><meta name="theme-color" content="#000000"><link rel="manifest" href="/manifest.
json"><link rel="shortcut icon" href="/favicon.ico"><title>React App</title><link href="/static/css/2.43b2b750.chunk.css"
rel="stylesheet"><link href="/static/css/main.3f9ef032.chunk.css" rel="stylesheet"></head><body><noscript>You need to
enable JavaScript to run this app.</noscript><div id="root"></div><script>!function(e){function r(r){for(var n,l,a=r[0],f=r
[1],i=r[2],p=0,s=[];p<a.length;p++)l=a[p],Object.prototype.hasOwnProperty.call(o,l)&&o[l]&&s.push(o[l][0]),o[l]=0;for(n in
f)Object.prototype.hasOwnProperty.call(f,n)&&(e[n]=f[n]);for(c&&c(r);s.length;)s.shift()();return u.push.apply(u,i||[]),t()
}function t(){for(var e,r=0;r<u.length;r++){for(var t=u[r],n=!0,a=1;a<t.length;a++){var f=t[a];0!==o[f]&&(n=!1)}n&&(u.
splice(r--,1),e=l(l.s=t[0]))}return e}var n={},o={1:0},u=[];function l(r){if(n[r])return n[r].exports;var t=n[r]={i:r,l:!1,
exports:{}};return e[r].call(t.exports,t,t.exports,l),t.l=!0,t.exports}l.m=e,l.c=n,l.d=function(e,r,t){l.o(e,r)||Object.
defineProperty(e,r,{enumerable:!0,get:t})},l.r=function(e){"undefined"!=typeof Symbol&&Symbol.toStringTag&&Object.
defineProperty(e,Symbol.toStringTag,{value:"Module"}),Object.defineProperty(e,"__esModule",{value:!0})},l.t=function(e,r)
{if(1&r&&(e=l(e)),8&r)return e;if(4&r&&"object"==typeof e&&e&&e.__esModule)return e;var t=Object.create(null);if(l.r(t),
Object.defineProperty(t,"default",{enumerable:!0,value:e}),2&r&&"string"!=typeof e)for(var n in e)l.d(t,n,function(r)
{return e[r]}.bind(null,n));return t},l.n=function(e){var r=e&&e.__esModule?function(){return e.default}:function(){return
e};return l.d(r,"a",r),r},l.o=function(e,r){return Object.prototype.hasOwnProperty.call(e,r)},l.p="/";var a=this
["webpackJsonpreact-bookstore"]=this["webpackJsonpreact-bookstore"]||[],f=a.push.bind(a);a.push=r,a=a.slice();for(var i=0;
i<a.length;i++)r(a[i]);var c=f;t()}([])</script><script src="/static/js/2.3572893f.chunk.js"></script><script src="/static/
js/main.f869732b.chunk.js"></script></body></html>
```

FIGURE 14-2: The minified and compiled index.html

This built `index.html` is the file that a web browser will load that will kick off the React app and display your root component (and its children) in the root node.

The `index.html` file uses absolute paths to load linked files. So, if you open `index.html` in a web browser now, you'll see error messages in the console that the JavaScript and CSS files weren't found.

If you change all of the absolute paths in `index.html` to relative ones (by putting a `.` before the path) you can actually run the built app locally on your computer without a web server, as shown in Figure 14-3.

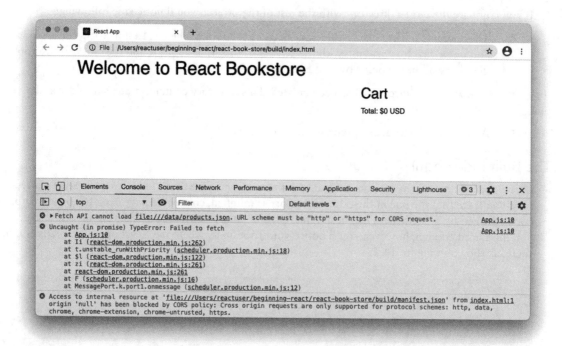

FIGURE 14-3: Running a built app from the filesystem

In the case of the React Bookstore, however, loading the app locally produces two errors in the console due to browser requirements for loading the app's data. Namely, for the `fetch` command to be able to load `data.json`, the app must be viewed using HTTP or HTTPS.

The static Directory

The `static` directory inside `build` holds the compiled JavaScript and CSS files and sourcemap files. The compiled JavaScript files are built from the React and ReactDOM libraries, other packages from the `node_modules` folder, and the source code that you wrote. All of these are combined, transpiled to be compatible with your target browsers, minified, and output as static files. The same thing happens with the CSS files.

The sourcemap files (which end in `.map`) provide mappings between the minified static files and the original formatted code. Sourcemap files can be read by web browsers to allow you to view and debug readable code in the browser developer tools.

asset-manifest.json

As part of the build process, a file named `asset-manifest.json` will be created. This file functions much like the `.map` files, but for filenames. It lists the files that were generated in the compilation of your app along with their original filenames. This file doesn't affect the rendering of your app, but rather, it can be used by tools to find out what assets your app uses without having to parse the `index.html` file.

What's in a Name?

The filenames generated by Create React App include unique strings between the original name of the file and the file extension, as you can see here:

```
/static/js/main.ee531687.chunk.js
```

This string of seeming random letters and numbers is actually a *hash string*. A hash string is a string of text calculated based on the contents of the file. As a result of the build process inserting hash strings into the filenames, whenever you change your React components and rebuild your app, the built filenames will change. This enables your application's files to be cached by servers and browsers and automatically updated when you modify the app.

Files may also be split into multiple "chunks" to optimize downloading and loading of the files. This is done automatically during the build process.

HOW IS A DEPLOYED APP DIFFERENT?

When you use Create React App's `start` command, it creates the `build` directory in memory and serves it using a development server. When you use the `build` command, it creates the `build` directory on disk so that it can be served using a static file server. Other than where it's created and served, the biggest difference between the version of your app that you've been working on and testing using `npm start` and the version that's created when you use `build` is that the version created in the `build` directory uses the production version of React.

DEVELOPMENT MODE VS. PRODUCTION

The production version of React is a minified version of the library with all the helpful warning messages and other tools for debugging your components stripped out. Minification and removal of unnecessary code makes a big difference in the file sizes of React and ReactDOM. The total file size for the React and ReactDOM libraries in the development version is currently 1045Kb, while the production version is just 132Kb.

You can tell whether a React app is running in development or production by clicking the React icon in the Chrome extensions menu. The icon will be red for an app running in development mode and blue for an app running in production mode, as shown in Figure 14-4.

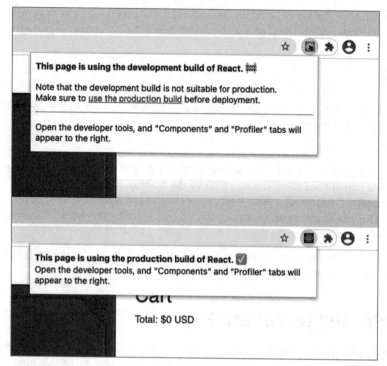

FIGURE 14-4: Development vs. production in the Developer Tools

PUTTING IT ON THE WEB

React web apps can be published to the web in a variety of different ways. Which way you choose will depend on the amount of traffic you expect the app to get, whether you want to integrate deployment with your version control system, and your budget for hosting.

Web Server Hosting

The easiest way to publish a React app on the web is to upload the contents of the `build` directory to any HTTP server, such as Apache or NGINX. Publishing a React app in this way is not much different from publishing any static website built using HTML, CSS, and JavaScript.

If you sign up with any standard web host that allows FTP upload or upload of files using a browser-based file browser, the steps for publishing your app to the web will be similar to the following:

1. Create or find out your FTP login credentials, or find out if your web host has a web-based file uploader.

2. Use FTP (or the web-based file uploader) to connect to your site and upload everything inside the `build` directory to your web directory (which should be named something like `www` or `htdocs`).

3. Test that your app works and that you uploaded it correctly by navigating to the root of your website (for example, `www.example.com`) in a web browser.

For a simple app that doesn't use routing, the preceding process will work. If your app does use routing, you'll need to do an additional configuration to redirect any requests for subdirectories of the site back to index.html so they can be properly handled by React Router.

For an Apache server, create a file named .htaccess containing the following code:

```
Options -MultiViews
RewriteEngine On
RewriteCond %{REQUEST_FILENAME} !-f
RewriteRule ^ index.html [QSA,L]
```

Add this file to your public directory, and then upload it from the build directory with the rest of your app.

Node Hosting

If your web server has Node.js installed, you can deploy your React app by installing the serve package and running it.

Run the following command to install serve globally:

```
npm install -g serve
```

To start up serve and use it to serve a particular React app, run the following command in the root of your project:

```
serve -s build
```

The server will start up and your site will become available at your web server's domain name at port 5000. If you wish to modify the port, you can do so by using -listen (or -l for short) in the serve build command, like so:

```
serve -s build -l 5050
```

Deploying with Netlify

Modern web apps are increasingly being hosted on cloud and *backend as a service (BaaS)* platforms that offer one-step deployment and continuous integration and continuous deployment (CI/CD). CI/CD means that when you commit changes to a version control system, those changes can be pushed to your live production environment automatically.

One popular target for deploying React applications is Netlify.

To get started with hosting your React app on Netlify, first go to https://netlify.com and sign up for a free account. Because Netlify publishes directly from a Git server, you should first sign up with a Git repository host such as GitHub, GitLab, or Bitbucket and push your code to one of these services, if you haven't already.

The first step in setting up hosting at Netlify is to click the **New site from Git** button on the Overview page, as shown in Figure 14-5.

The next screen will ask you to choose your Git provider. Click the one that you use, as shown in Figure 14-6.

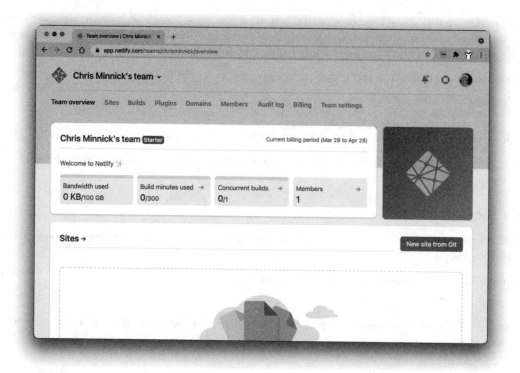

FIGURE 14-5: Click the New site from Git button

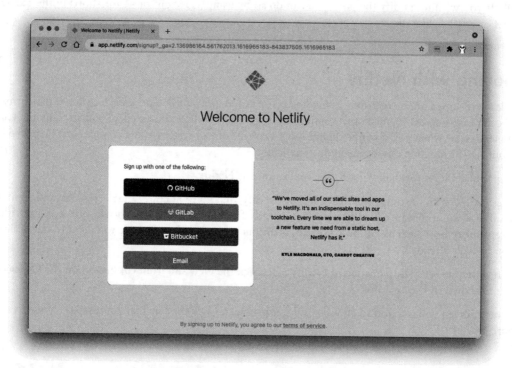

FIGURE 14-6: Choose your Git provider

Once you authorize Netlify to access your Git provider, you can select a repository to import from, as shown in Figure 14-7.

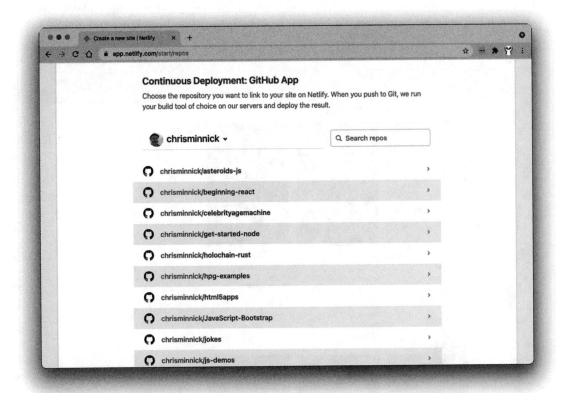

FIGURE 14-7: Choose a repository

On the next screen, you'll be asked to provide a branch of your repository that should be deployed to Netlify, and to enter the build command and publish directory. For Create React App, the build command is npm run build, and the publish directory is build.

Enabling Routing with Netlify

If your app uses routing, create a directory inside your public directory named _redirects and enter the following into it to correctly redirect any requests for files in the site to index.html:

```
/*   /index.html   200
```

After you've selected the repository that contains your app and entered the build command and the publish directory, Netlify will start the process of cloning and building your project and deploying it to a custom domain. If there are errors during the deployment, Netlify will let you know that deployment was unsuccessful and display an error log.

If your site is deployed successfully, it will become accessible using a `netlify.app` subdomain, as shown in Figure 14-8.

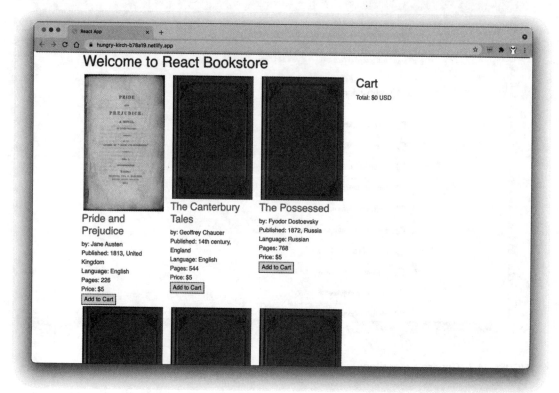

FIGURE 14-8: A deployed React app

Enabling Custom Domains and HTTPS

For most public web apps, you'll want to have a custom domain name (such as `example.com`) and to enable encrypted serving of your app using HTTPS. Both of these can be configured in Netlify's Domain management area, which is shown in Figure 14-9.

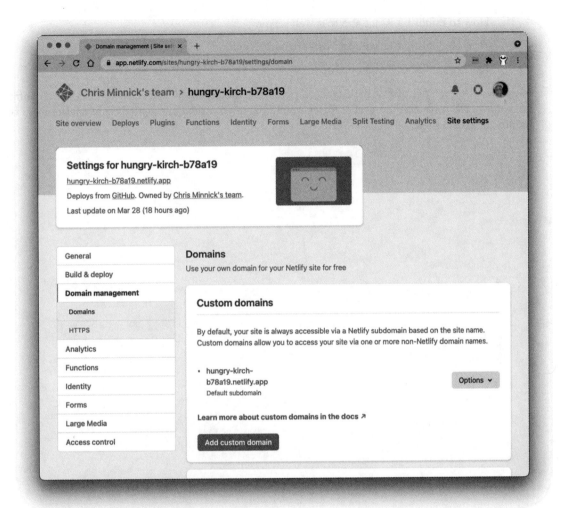

FIGURE 14-9: Domain management in Netlify

SUMMARY

Building and deployment of a React application can be done in many different ways. Tools and techniques that have become common for automating the process have made making your application available to the world reliable, repeatable, and simple.

In this chapter, you learned:

➤   How to use Create React App to build your application.

➤   How the `build` directory created by Create React App is structured.

➤   How to publish a React app to a web server.

➤   How to publish a React app to a node server.

➤   How to publish a React app to Netlify.

In the next chapter, the first of the advanced part of the book, you'll learn how to install and configure some of the tools used by Create React App to make your own automated build environment or modify an existing one.

15

Initialize a React Project from Scratch

Using a pre-built build toolchain, such as Create React App, is convenient and allows React programmers to focus on the most important job at hand—programming with React. However, there are times when you'll need to customize your toolchain or adjust settings in one of the tools that make up Create React App. Knowing what tools make up your toolchain and learning how to install and configure each of them and wire them together will give you a head start.

In this chapter, you'll learn:

➤ How to install and configure a module bundler.

➤ How to install and configure ESLint.

➤ How to use Babel.

➤ How to automate tasks with npm scripts.

➤ How to create a production build of your React app.

➤ Options for organizing a React project.

BUILDING YOUR OWN TOOLCHAIN

Create React App is an invaluable tool for automating and simplifying many of the tasks involved in starting, testing, deploying, and maintaining React apps. Under the hood of Create React App, many different Node.js packages are working together, mostly seamlessly. As a React developer, having such a powerful set of tools that is continually being maintained and improved is liberating.

Create React App is not the only build toolchain for React, however. There are alternatives to each of the components of Create React App and there are other toolchains available that have strengths and features that Create React App lacks.

Prior to the creation of Create React App, it was common for React developers to link together the individual tools needed for a toolchain themselves. Rolling your own is seldom a requirement today, and you'll actually be better off in most cases by using a toolchain built and maintained by someone else.

But just as a homeowner should have some basic skills in home repair, the experience of learning to install, configure, and link together different tools is something that every JavaScript and React developer should have.

Initializing Your Project

The build toolchain and the files that make up your React application are two separate things. Even a project that's bootstrapped using Create React App can easily be taken out of Create React App and used with another toolchain. To show you how simple it can be to start a React project without a toolchain, in this chapter we'll start with just three files and build a complete app and toolchain from scratch:

1.   Select File ⇨ New Window in VS Code.

2.   Click Open Folder from the Welcome Screen and select an empty directory on your computer where you want to put your new project.

3.   Open a new terminal window in VS Code by selecting Terminal ⇨ New Terminal from the top menu.

4.   Initialize a new Node.js package and skip over answering questions about your project by entering npm init -y into the terminal. A package.json file will be created.

5.   Open package.json in VS Code so you can watch the changes that are made to it as you install and configure required packages.

6.   Install React and ReactDOM into the new project with this command:

```
npm install react react-dom
```

The HTML Document

The first file to set up is the single HTML document that will load when a browser visits the app. This can be extremely simple:

1.   Make a new folder named src. This is where we'll keep our source files for the project.

2.   Make a new file named index.html inside the src directory.

3.   In index.html, type the ! character and then press the Tab key. This is a shortcut that will automatically enter the bones of an HTML document.

4.   Create an empty div element between <body> and </body> and give it an id attribute with a value of root:

```
<div id="root"></div>
```

Listing 15-1 shows the finished index.html.

LISTING 15-1: The finished index.html

```html
<!DOCTYPE html>
<html lang="en">
<head>
    <meta charset="UTF-8">
    <meta name="viewport" content="width=device-width, initial-scale=1.0">
    <title>My App</title>
</head>
<body>
    <div id="root"></div>
</body>
</html>
```

The Main JavaScript File

The main JavaScript file is the one that calls `ReactDOM.render` to render the root component in the browser:

1. Create a new file named `index.js` inside `src` and open it for editing.

2. Import React and ReactDOM:

```js
import React from 'react';
import ReactDOM from 'react-dom';
```

3. Import your root component (which we'll create shortly):

```js
import App from './App.js';
```

4. Call `ReactDOM.render`, passing in the root component and the target DOM node:

```js
ReactDOM.render(<App />, document.getElementById('root'));
```

Listing 15-2 shows the finished `index.js`.

LISTING 15-2: The finished index.js

```js
import React from 'react';
import ReactDOM from 'react-dom';
import App from './App';

ReactDOM.render(<App />, document.getElementById('root'));
```

The Root Component

The root component is the one that's the parent of every other component in your app:

1. Create a new file named `App.js` inside `src`.

2. Inside `App.js`, create a simple function component to use as your root. For our purposes here, this component can be anything. Listing 15-3 shows a component that will track your mouse position.

LISTING 15-3: A component to track mouse position

```
import React from 'react';

const App = () => {
    const [position,setPosition] = React.useState({x:0,y:0});

    const onMouseMove = (e) => {
        setPosition({x: e.nativeEvent.offsetX, y: e.nativeEvent.offsetY })
    }

    const { x, y } = position;

    return (
        <div style={{width:"500px",height:"500px"}}
            onMouseMove = {onMouseMove}>
            <h1>x: { x } y: { y }</h1>
        </div>
    )

}

export default App;
```

Running in the Browser

In a perfect world, it should be possible to just import index.js into your index.html document and everything would work. Let's try that out:

1. Use a script element to import index.js into index.html, as shown in Listing 15-4.

LISTING 15-4: Importing index.js into index.html

```
<!DOCTYPE html>
<html lang="en">
<head>
    <meta charset="UTF-8">
    <meta name="viewport" content="width=device-width, initial-scale=1.0">
    <title>My App</title>
</head>
<body>
    <div id="root"></div>
    <script src="index.js"></script>
</body>
</html>
```

2. Install and run a basic local web server and serve your app by entering the following into your terminal:

```
npx http-server src
```

3. Open the URL that the web server gives you when it starts. The result will be a blank screen with an error in the JavaScript console, as shown in Figure 15-1.

FIGURE 15-1: Attempting to load index.js without compiling

For our JavaScript imports and React code containing JSX to work in a browser, they need to be compiled first. We'll use the Webpack module bundler to do this.

4. Install Webpack, the Webpack Development Server, and the Webpack command-line interface:

```
npm install webpack webpack-dev-server webpack-cli --save-dev
```

Notice that with this install, we're using `--save-dev` to indicate that these tools are development dependencies that won't be deployed to production. The result of using `--save-dev` is that these packages will be listed in a separate section of `package.json` called `devDependencies`.

5. Try to compile the app now, using the following command:

```
npx webpack
```

You'll get an error saying that you need a loader, as shown in Figure 15-2. The problem is that Webpack doesn't know how to compile JSX code on its own.

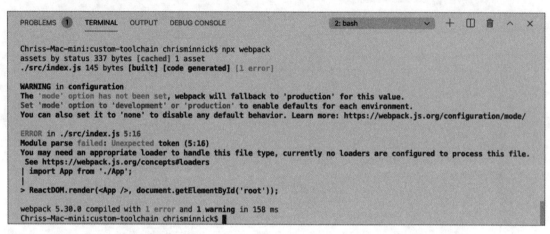

FIGURE 15-2: JSX requires a loader

6. Install Babel, the Babel loader for Webpack, and the Babel presets for modern JavaScript and for React:

```
npm install @babel/core babel-loader @babel/preset-env @babel/preset-react --save-dev
```

7. Create a new file named babel.config.json and enter the following code into it:

```
{
    "presets": ["@babel/preset-env", "@babel/preset-react"]
}
```

8. Make a Webpack config file named webpack.config.js, and link to the Babel loader:

```
module.exports = {
  mode: 'development',
  module: {
    rules: [
      {
        test: /\.js$/,
        exclude: /node_modules/,
        use: ["babel-loader"]
      }
    ]
  }
};
```

9. Run `npx webpack`. A new directory named `dist` will be created, containing the bundled `main.js` file.

10. Make a copy of `index.html` (from the `src` directory) and put it in the new `dist` directory.

11. Change the `script` element in `index.html` to import `main.js`:

```
<script src="main.js"></script>
```

12. Serve the new `dist` directory using `http-server` by entering the following into the terminal:

```
npx http-server dist
```

13. Open the localhost URL in your browser. It should work now, and as you move your mouse over the rectangle created in `App.js`, the x and y values should display the current position of your mouse, as shown in Figure 15-3.

FIGURE 15-3: The working React app

HOW WEBPACK WORKS

Webpack's primary function is to combine the modules used in modern JavaScript development into optimized output files for use in a browser. Webpack does its magic by starting with an entry point (which is `src/index.js` by default) and building a dependency graph. A dependency graph is a list of every module linked from the entry point and what the dependencies of each module are. By using the dependency graph, Webpack can bundle all of these files together.

Webpack can bundle together files that use any of several different module formats, including JavaScript's `import` statement, CommonJS, AMD Modules, `@import` statements in CSS, and HTML `<img>` elements.

Loaders

Loaders tell Webpack how to process and bundle file types that it doesn't natively support. Many loaders have been written, including CSS loaders, HTML loaders, file loaders, and more.

Loaders can be configured in `webpack.config.js` by specifying a `test` property and a `use` property. The `test` property is a regular expression that tells which files should be affected by a loader, and the `use` property tells which loader to use for the files matching the `test`. You can also use an optional property named `exclude`, which tells what files shouldn't be affected by the loader.

For example, in our project, we configured a loader with the following settings:

```
rules: [
  {
    test: /\.js$/,
    exclude: /node_modules/,
    use: ["babel-loader"]
  }
]
```

This rule says to use the `babel-loader` to transform any file that ends with `.js`, but to ignore files inside `node_modules`.

Plugins

Plugins extend the capabilities of Webpack. Examples of plugins include:

➤ `HtmlWebpackPlugin`: Creates HTML files to serve the bundle.

➤ `NpmInstallWebpackPlugin`: Automatically installs missing dependencies during bundling.

➤ `ImageminWebpackPlugin`: Minifies images in your project during bundling.

Plugins can be configured in the `plugins` array in `webpack.config.js`.

AUTOMATING YOUR BUILD PROCESS

Now that you've gone from writing React code, to compiling it, to deploying it—in a very basic way—let's automate the process and make our development and build toolchain a bit more functional.

Making an HTML Template

Copying the HTML document from `src` to `dist` and inserting the correct path to the main script isn't difficult, but it's a step that you shouldn't have to remember to do in an automated build. Here's how to use a Webpack plugin called `HtmlWebpackPlugin` to automate this process:

1. Install `HtmlWebpackPlugin`:

    ```
    npm install html-webpack-plugin --save-dev
    ```

2. Open `webpack.config.js` in VS Code and insert the following at the beginning of the file to import `HtmlWebpackPlugin`:

    ```
    const HtmlWebpackPlugin = require('html-webpack-plugin');
    ```

3. Create a new property in `webpack.config.js` named `plugins`, as shown in Listing 15-5.

LISTING 15-5: Creating the plugins object

```
module.exports = {
    mode: 'development',
    module: {
      rules: [
        {
          test: /\.js$/,
          exclude: /node_modules/,
          use: ["babel-loader"]
        }
      ],
    },
    plugins: []
};
```

The `plugins` property should contain an array of configuration objects for the plugins you want to use with Webpack.

4. Configure `HtmlWebPackPlugin`. You can read more about the features and capabilities of `HtmlWebPackPlugin` at `https://webpack.js.org/plugins/html-webpack-plugin/`. We're going to use it to copy `index.html` from the `src` directory to the `dist` and to inject the `main.js` script into it. Use the following configuration object inside the `plugins` array:

    ```
    new HtmlWebpackPlugin({
      template: __dirname + '/src/index.html',
      filename: 'index.html',
      inject: 'body'
    })
    ```

5. Open `src/index.html` and remove the `<script>` element from it.

6. Delete the `dist` directory.

7. Run `npx webpack` to test out your Webpack configuration. If you entered everything correctly, the `index.html` file should be copied from `src` to `dist`, and the compiled version in `dist` will have a script tag that imports `main.js`.

8. Start up your development server and open your app in your browser to confirm that everything still works.

Development Server and Hot Reloading

Hot reloading, in a development environment, is the ability to make changes to an app and then see those changes reflected automatically without needing to enter a compile command. To enable hot reloading with Webpack, you can use the Webpack Dev Server.

You already installed Webpack Dev Server in an earlier step. To use it, enter `npx webpack serve` into the terminal. Instead of compiling to the `dist` directory, Webpack will serve your app at `localhost:8080` (by default).

With your app being served by Webpack, try making and saving a change to `App.js`. Your changes will be reflected immediately in the browser window. When you're finished and want to stop the dev server, press Ctrl+C in the terminal window.

Testing Tools

We'll talk more about testing in Chapter 20. Although a detailed explanation of how to test React apps is beyond the scope of this chapter, automated testing is a critical part of any professional development environment. A good toolchain will include at least two testing-related components:

➤ A static code analysis tool (also known as a linter).

➤ An automated unit testing tool.

Installing and Configuring ESLint

The job of a static code analysis tool is to check the code you write for syntax errors and code style. This process is called *linting*. The tool that's currently most often used for linting JavaScript code is *ESLint*.

ESLint is highly configurable. It can be used just for checking your code for syntax errors, or it can check syntax, best practices, and code style. It can even fix some kinds of problems for you.

To get started with ESLint, install it into your project:

```
npm install eslint --save-dev
```

Once installed, ESLint includes an initialization script that will ask you questions about how you want to use it and create a configuration file based on your answers. Follow these steps to configure ESLint:

1. Type the following command to run the initialization script:

```
npx eslint --init
```

The configuration wizard will start and ask you an initial question about how you want to use ESLint, as shown in Figure 15-4.

```
Chriss-Mac-mini:custom-toolchain chrisminnick$ npx eslint —init
? How would you like to use ESLint? …
  To check syntax only
) To check syntax and find problems
  To check syntax, find problems, and enforce code style
```

FIGURE 15-4: Starting the configuration wizard

2. Use the arrow keys on your keyboard to choose any of the options. If you make a mistake or change your mind later, you can always run the configuration wizard again, or edit the configuration file manually.

3. Go through all of the questions in the configurator. When in doubt, choose the default option. At the end of the questions, the ESLint React plugin should be installed and a configuration file for ESLint will be created and named `.eslintrc.js`.

4. Open `.eslintrc.js` in VS Code to see what the configuration wizard generated.

5. Check your code in the `src` directory by running the following command:

    `npx eslint src`

    If your code doesn't have any errors or problems or style issues, as defined by the configuration file, ESLint shouldn't produce any output.

6. Introduce an error into `App.js`. For example, delete an ending tag in the `return` statement.

7. Run ESLint again to confirm that it produces an error.

ESLint Configuration

The easiest way to configure ESLint is to run the initialization script. But, ESLint has far more options than the ones that the initialization script asks you about. The primary way to configure ESLint is through rules in the configuration file.

If your configuration file has a property named `extends`, it's bringing in the rules from the configurations or plugins listed there. You can override them or add additional rules in the `rules` property.

ESLint rules determine what will produce output when you run ESLint, and the severity (called "error level") of the output. For example, if your style is to use single quotes around strings in JavaScript, you can tell ESLint to show a warning when it finds double quotes with the following rule:

```
"quotes": ["warn", "single"]
```

The error level can be one of three values:

➤ 0 or `"off"`: Disables the rule.

➤ 1 or `"warn"`: Displays a warning message.

➤ 2 or `"error"`: Displays an error and sets the exit code to 1, which will cause your automated build script to fail, as you'll see later in this chapter.

You can find a complete list of ESLint's rules at `https://eslint.org/docs/rules/`.

How to Fix Errors

When ESLint reports errors, you have at least two ways to resolve the problem. The first way is by modifying your source code to eliminate the error or fix the bug. The second way, which is quite common when you're first starting to configure ESLint, is to change ESLint's configuration so that it doesn't count the source of the error as an error.

For example, if your ESLint configuration reports use of double quotes as an error, this may cause problems and errors that you don't care about when ESLint checks configuration files, such as `webpack.config.js`.

Some of the ways you can tell ESLint not to report a certain error are:

1. Add files that you don't want checked to a file called `.eslintignore` in the root of your project.

2. Change the rule in question to a lower-level error or disable it.

3. Disable a single rule for that file by adding a block comment with an `eslint-disable` instruction to the file. For example, to disable the `no-console` rule for a file, add the following to the top of the file:

   ```
   /* eslint-disable no-console */
   ```

Depending on the error, you may also have a third way to fix errors: let ESLint do it. After it finishes running, ESLint may report that some of the errors are potentially fixable by ESLint, as shown in Figure 15-5.

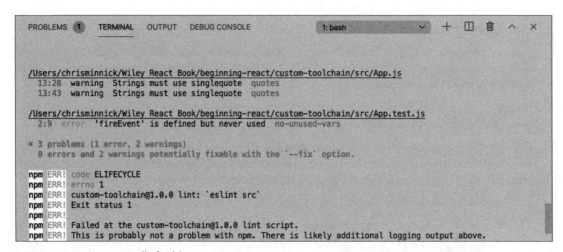

FIGURE 15-5: Automatically fixable errors or warnings

When this happens, you can have ESLint try to fix the errors by adding `--fix` to your ESLint command and running it again. If ESLint is able to fix the problems, it will just do so when it finds them.

Testing with Jest

Jest is an automated unit testing framework. Unit testing is the process of testing the components of an application in isolation. By writing tests for each component and function of your app as you write it (or before you write it, in the case of *test-driven development*), you'll detect problems in your app earlier and improve the quality of your code.

Listing 15-6 shows an example of a basic test for the mouse tracker app from earlier in this chapter.

LISTING 15-6: Testing the mouse tracker

```
import React from 'react';
import {render, screen} from '@testing-library/react';
import App from './App';

  test('initial position displays as 0,0', () => {
    render(
      <App />,
    );

    expect (screen.getByText(/x:/i).textContent).toBe('x: 0 y: 0')
});
```

Follow these steps to install and configure Jest:

1. Install the Jest package, React Testing Library, the Babel plugin for Jest, and the React Test Renderer:

    ```
    npm install jest @testing-library/react babel-jest react-test-renderer --save-dev
    ```

2. Run Jest:

    ```
    npx jest --env=jsdom
    ```

    By default, Jest will look for tests in directories named __tests__, or files that end with .spec.js, or files that end with .test.js. Because you don't currently have any files or directories that match these patterns, Jest will return a message that no tests were found, as shown in Figure 15-6.

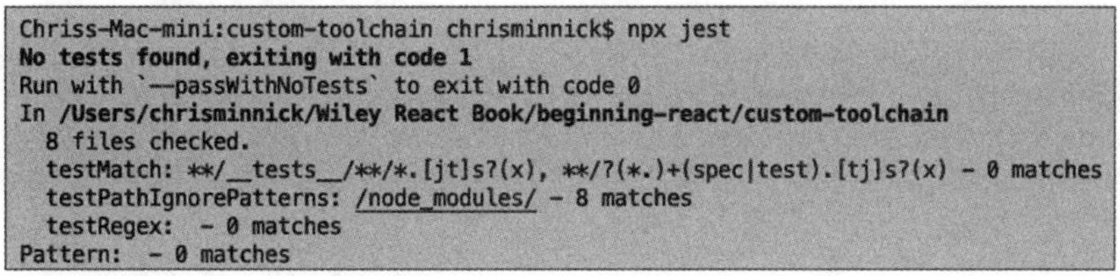

```
Chriss-Mac-mini:custom-toolchain chrisminnick$ npx jest
No tests found, exiting with code 1
Run with `—passWithNoTests` to exit with code 0
In /Users/chrisminnick/Wiley React Book/beginning-react/custom-toolchain
  8 files checked.
  testMatch: **/__tests__/**/*.[jt]s?(x), **/?(*.)+(spec|test).[tj]s?(x) - 0 matches
  testPathIgnorePatterns: /node_modules/ – 8 matches
  testRegex:  – 0 matches
Pattern:  – 0 matches
```

FIGURE 15-6: No tests found

If you save the test from Listing 15-6 into a file named `App.test.js` in the `src` directory and run Jest again, it will run the test and report that it passed, as shown in Figure 15-7.

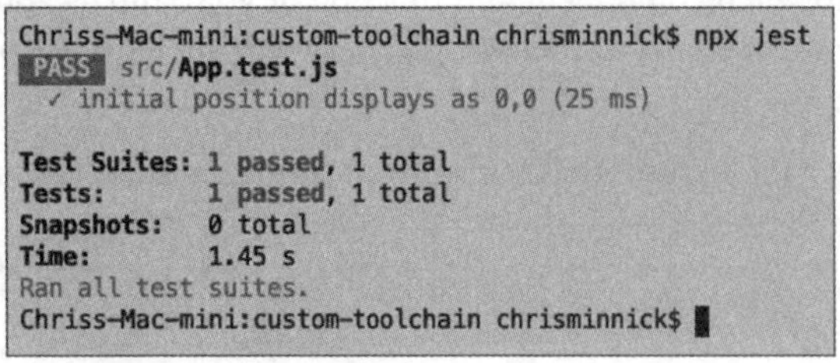

```
Chriss-Mac-mini:custom-toolchain chrisminnick$ npx jest
 PASS  src/App.test.js
  ✓ initial position displays as 0,0 (25 ms)

Test Suites: 1 passed, 1 total
Tests:       1 passed, 1 total
Snapshots:   0 total
Time:        1.45 s
Ran all test suites.
Chriss-Mac-mini:custom-toolchain chrisminnick$ ▊
```

FIGURE 15-7: Test passed

If you run ESLint now, it will likely fail. The reason is that you've added new globals to your code that ESLint doesn't know about. To fix that, add Jest as an environment in `.eslintrc.js` by modifying the `env` property, like this:

```
"env": {
  "browser": true,
  "es2021": true,
  "jest": true
},
```

Creating NPM Scripts

Now that you've installed and configured several tools for developing, testing, and deploying React apps, the next step is to link them together with npm scripts.

Npm scripts are specified in the `scripts` object in `package.json` and can be run using the `npm run` command. You can create as many npm scripts as you need, but generally any toolchain will have at least the following scripts:

➤ `npm run start`: Starts the development server.

➤ `npm run test`: Runs the automated tests.

➤ `npm run build`: Compiles the production version of the app.

> **NOTE** The first two scripts (`start` and `test`) are so commonly used in Node.js projects that the word "run" can be omitted when you want to run them.

Follow these steps to write these three npm scripts, plus a couple of others that are required in our toolchain:

1. Open `package.json` in VS Code.

2. Find the `scripts` object. By default, it will have a single script, named `test`, which will simply return a message that no tests are specified and will exit with an error.

3. Modify the test script to match the following:

    `"test": "jest --env=jsdom"`

4. Save `package.json` and enter `npm test` in the terminal. It should run Jest, just as if you had entered `npx jest --env=jsdom` into the terminal.

5. Make another property in the `scripts` object, named `lint`. The value will be `eslint src`, which will run the linter on your `src` directory:

    `"lint": "eslint src"`

6. Add another script, named `start`, which will bundle your code and start the development server:

    `"start": "webpack serve"`

7. Add a `bundle` script:

    `"bundle": "webpack"`

At this point, the `scripts` object in `package.json` should look like Listing 15-7.

LISTING 15-7: Adding npm scripts

```
"scripts": {
  "test": "jest",
  "lint": "eslint src",
  "start": "webpack serve",
  "bundle": "webpack"
},
```

The powerful thing about npm scripts is that you can link them together and run them in sequence to automate complex processes. To see this in action, create a `build` script that runs the `lint` script, followed by the `test` script, followed by the `bundle` script:

`"build": "npm run lint && npm run test && npm run bundle"`

When you run the `build` script, it will go through each of the component scripts in order. If one of them encounters an error, the `build` script will fail.

STRUCTURING YOUR SOURCE DIRECTORY

Once you have a basic toolchain in place, you can save it by itself, for example in a Git repository, and then clone it any time you need to start a new React project. Or, you can use Create React App, but with a new confidence that you know how to fix or customize your toolchain when you need to.

Either way, the toolchain is just a necessary step before you can get to the real work of writing an app. The next step in the process is to give some thought to how to efficiently organize your source files. In the end, of course, your entire project will get rolled up into bundles by Webpack and organization of your source code doesn't have a direct effect on the final `dist` or `build` directory. But, organization of your source files helps you and other developers to visualize the structure of the project without having to read through the code, and it also gives you a framework for improving and expanding your app.

React intentionally doesn't put limits on how you write code or name your functions, files, and folders. As a result, you'll see many different opinions on the "correct" way to do things. You'll also see plenty of experienced React developers who recommend taking a flexible approach to structuring your project—just get started and evolve as the need arises.

Several approaches have become common, however, and adopting parts of someone else's evolved best practice can save you the time and frustration of reinventing the wheel for yourself.

Grouping by File Type

Grouping React source files by type typically means that you start with a single directory named components, and then expand outward from there as the need arises. For small projects, the components directory may be all you need. For larger projects, however, it can be helpful to create subdirectories inside of components and to move certain kinds of files into their own directories.

Examples of directories you might create in this strategy include:

➤ css

➤ hooks

➤ utilities (often abbreviated as utils or named helpers)

➤ api

➤ routes

➤ images

Figure 15-8 shows an example of a project that was structured using groups of file types.

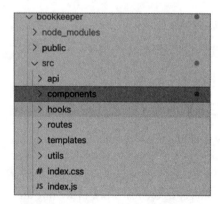

FIGURE 15-8: Grouping by file type

Grouping by Features

Grouping by features means that you create a directory structure that mirrors the main functional areas or routes in your app. For example, an app for accounting might have a route named `income` and one named `expenses`. Inside these directories, you may continue to group components and other source files by purpose, or you may decide to switch to grouping by file type inside of the functional areas.

Figure 15-9 shows an example of a project that was structured by grouping files by features.

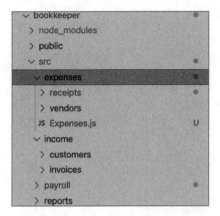

FIGURE 15-9: Grouping by features

SUMMARY

Even if you decide to use a pre-built toolchain such as Create React App (which is actually a very good idea for most people), knowing how to configure your own toolchain is an essential skill for modern JavaScript and web developers.

In this chapter, you learned:

➤ How to start a project from scratch.

➤ Why a module bundler is necessary.

➤ How Webpack works.

➤ How to automate your build.

➤ How to install ESLint and Jest.

➤ Popular ways to structure React source files.

In the next chapter, you'll learn how to reach beyond your app and fetch data from remote sources and how to store data between sessions.

16

Fetching and Caching Data

It's possible to build great user interfaces that are self-contained and don't need to interact with the outside world (such as many games, calculators, and utilities). But, most web apps have a need to receive and store data.

In this chapter, you'll learn:

- ➤ When to fetch and store data in React.
- ➤ How to use `window.fetch`.
- ➤ What promises are.
- ➤ How `async/await` works.
- ➤ How to simplify network requests with Axios.
- ➤ How to store data in `localStorage`.
- ➤ How to read data from `localStorage`.

ASYNCHRONOUS CODE: IT'S ALL ABOUT TIMING

Whenever you update state, do a side effect, or store data in the user's browser, these tasks take time. One of the trickiest, but also most important, skills that a React developer needs to have is learning how to properly handle asynchronous tasks.

With state updates, ReactDOM handles everything for you. You simply call `setState` (in a class component) or pass data to a function returned by the `useState` hook (in a function component). Most of the time, the asynchronous nature of setting React state is seamless and invisible to the developer and the user.

With network and cache requests, on the other hand, every request has the potential to adversely impact the user experience. In the worst case, a remote resource won't be available. More often, the amount of time a request takes will be wildly variable, depending on the user's internet connection, network congestion, and the remote server's current workload.

JavaScript itself is rarely the issue—JavaScript is fast and usually only gets bogged down if the developer made a mistake (such as creating an infinite loop or a memory leak). One reason why JavaScript is so fast and the reason that handling asynchronous code correctly is so important is that JavaScript doesn't wait for anything.

JAVASCRIPT NEVER SLEEPS

JavaScript doesn't have a sleep or wait command. Instead, a JavaScript engine (such as the V8 Engine built into the Chrome web browser and Node.js) starts at the beginning of your script and runs the code as fast as it can, using a single thread. Because JavaScript is single-threaded, it must complete the previous statement before moving on to the next.

The call stack in a JavaScript engine is where commands waiting to be executed sit until they can be executed in a First In Last Out (FILO) order.

You might be asking yourself at this point how it's possible to do asynchronous tasks (like network requests and caching data) in JavaScript with only one thread. The answer is that although JavaScript itself is single-threaded, the environment in which it runs (your browser or Node.js) is multithreaded.

Asynchronous tasks (like network requests) are handled by parts of the browser that are outside of the JavaScript engine, such as the Web APIs, in conjunction with two other parts of the runtime environment outside of JavaScript: the event loop and the callback queue.

Consider the following code:

```
console.log("get ready...");
setTimeout(() => {
  console.log("here it is!");
}, 1000);
console.log("end of the code.");
```

The result of running this code in a browser console is shown in Figure 16-1.

What's going on here is that when this program starts up, three function calls are added to the call stack to be executed in order. After the first statement is executed and removed from the call stack, JavaScript sees the setTimeout() function, which creates an event that is only indirectly managed by JavaScript. It hands it off to the browser to execute, and then removes it from the call stack. JavaScript can then move on to the third statement.

The Web API, in the meantime, waits for one second (because of the 1,000-millisecond timeout length you passed to it) and then adds your callback function to the browser's callback queue. The event loop (which is in charge of listening for events and registering event listeners in the JavaScript environment) picks up the function from the callback queue and adds it to JavaScript's call stack to be executed.

Figure 16-2 shows a diagram of the whole process.

Callback functions, which get executed upon completion of an asynchronous task, are how JavaScript programmers can write code that depends on the result of that asynchronous task. If you want to have multiple asynchronous tasks that happen in a particular order, you can put them inside the callback functions from other asynchronous tasks, as shown in Listing 16-1.

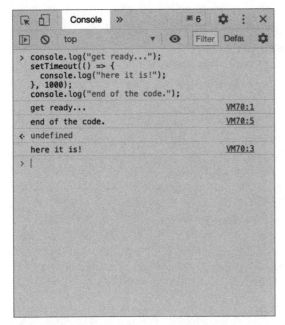

FIGURE 16-1: Executing asynchronous JavaScript

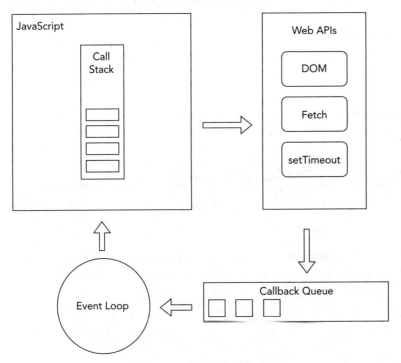

FIGURE 16-2: How asynchronous tasks are handled

LISTING 16-1: Callbacks within callbacks

```
function userCheck(username, password, callback){
  db.verifyUser(username, password, (error, userInfo) => {
    if (error) {
      callback(error)
    }else{
      db.getRoles(username, (error, roles) => {
        if (error){
          callback(error)
        }else {
          db.logAccess(username, (error) => {
            if (error){
              callback(error);
            }else{
              callback(null, userInfo, roles);
            }
          })
        }
      })
    }
  })
};
```

In the preceding example, what should happen when the `userCheck()` function is called (absent any errors) is the following:

1. Verify the user's credentials.

2. Get the user's access permissions.

3. Create a log entry.

Nested callbacks can be difficult to read, however, so more intuitive ways to perform tasks in response to asynchronous tasks have been created—namely *promises* and *async/await*.

JAVASCRIPT LESSON: PROMISES AND ASYNC/AWAIT

This JavaScript lesson examines promises, `async`, and `await`.

Promises

A promise is a placeholder for the result of an asynchronous action. It lets you write asynchronous code in a synchronous way, but instead of returning the final value, it returns a "promise" to return the final value at some point.

Promises can be in one of three states:

➤ **Pending:** This is the initial state of a promise.

➤ **Fulfilled:** The operation was completed successfully.

➤ **Rejected:** The operation failed.

When a promise becomes fulfilled, it can be chained to additional promises using the then method, as in the following example:

```
receiveHamburger
    .then(eatHamburger)
    .then(payForHamburger)
```

In order for the preceding code to work, each of the functions must return a Promise object. For example, here's what the receiveHamburger function might look like:

```
const receiveHamburger = function(){
    return new Promise((resolve,reject) => {
        getHamburger((result) => {
            resolve(result);
        })
    ))
};
```

If something goes wrong and the promise is rejected, the catch method can be used to handle the error:

```
receiveHamburger
    .then(eatHamburger)
    .then(payForHamburger)
    .catch((err)=>{ //handle the error here }
```

async/await

Promises are great, but they still require the use of callbacks. A couple of the best improvements to how asynchronous code is written are the async and await statements. With async and await, you can write code that really does look synchronous. For example, here's our hamburger example written with async and await:

```
const tradeForHamburger = async function() {
    try {
        await receiveHamburger();
        await eatHamburger();
        await payForHamburger();
    } catch(e) {
        // handle errors
    }
}
```

Although async/await is an abstraction of promises, it's easier to write and read than either callbacks or promises. Behind the scenes, an async function always returns a Promise. If the return value of an async function isn't explicitly a Promise, it will be implicitly wrapped in one.

For example, the following function:

```
async function eatHamburger(){
    return 1;
}
```

continues

> *continued*
>
> is essentially the same as this one:
>
> ```
> function eatHamburger(){
>   return Promise.resolve(1);
> }
> ```
>
> Once you make an `async` function, you can use the `await` keyword inside of it to wait for any promise inside of it without having to make any changes to other functions. Inside an `async` function, the `await` keyword will cause the function to wait until the statement following it returns before moving on to the next statement.

WHERE TO RUN ASYNC CODE IN REACT

Asynchronous code, such as data fetching, can be done at several points in the life of a component, including:

➤ When the component first mounts.

➤ In response to a user action (such as clicking a button).

➤ In response to changes in the component (such as receiving new props).

➤ In response to timers (such as apps that refresh periodically).

In a class component, initial data can be loaded using the `componentDidMount` lifecycle method, and updates to data in response to component changes can be done using the `componentDidUpdate` method, as shown in Listing 16-2.

> **NOTE** *To try out Listing 16-2 and Listing 16-3, you'll need a free API key from* https://newsapi.org/.

LISTING 16-2: Loading initial data in a class component

```
import {Component} from 'react';

class NewsFeed extends Component {
    constructor(props){
        super(props);
        this.state={
            news:[]
        }
    }
    componentDidMount(){
        fetch('https://newsapi.org/v2/top-headlines?country=us&apiKey=[YOUR KEY]')
```

```
            .then(response => response.json())
            .then(data => {
                this.setState({news:data.articles})})
            .catch(error => console.error(error))
    }
    render(){
        const todaysNews = this.state.news.map((article)=>{
            return (<p>{article.title}</p>);
        })
        return(
            <>
                <h1>Today's News</h1>
                {todaysNews}
            </>
        )
    }
}

export default NewsFeed;
```

In a function component, the useEffect hook can be used for fetching a component's initial data as well as in response to the component receiving new data, as shown in Listing 16-3.

LISTING 16-3: Loading initial data in a function component

```
import {useState,useEffect} from 'react';

const NewsFeedFunction = () => {
    const [news,setNews] = useState([]);
    useEffect(()=> {
        fetch('https://newsapi.org/v2/top-headlines?country=us&apiKey=[YOUR KEY]')
            .then(response => response.json())
            .then(data => {
              setNews(data.articles)
            })
            .catch(error => console.error(error))
    },[])

    const todaysNews = news.map((article)=>{
        return (<p>{article.title}</p>);
    })

    return(
        <>
            <h1>Today's News</h1>
            {todaysNews}
        </>
    )
}

export default NewsFeedFunction;
```

WAYS TO FETCH

Once you know how and where to run asynchronous code in React components, the rest is just a matter of knowing the properties and methods of the tool you want to use and knowing the structure of the data source.

Most single page web applications access data sources using web APIs based on the REST architecture style. Data sent and received between a user interface and a RESTful API is usually in the JSON format.

JAVASCRIPT LESSON: REST

Representational State Transfer, or REST, is an architectural style for application programming interfaces (APIs). RESTful APIs use HTTP requests to get, add, update, and delete data using unique URLs. RESTful APIs rely on the fact that HTTP has built into it different methods for accessing resources. REST maps these methods to operations that can be performed using the API:

➤ To fetch data, use the HTTP GET method.

➤ To add data, use the HTTP POST method.

➤ To update data, use the HTTP PUT method.

➤ To delete data, use the HTTP DELETE method.

For example, to get data about a user with an ID of 23 using a RESTful API, you might make an HTTP GET request to the following URL:

```
https://www.example.com/user/23/
```

To delete the user with the ID of 23, you would use the HTTP DELETE method to access that same URL.

To try out a RESTful API, open a browser window and enter the following URL into the address bar:

```
https://api.github.com/users/facebook/repos
```

This will do an HTTP GET to retrieve a list of Facebook's repositories on GitHub and display the returned JSON in the browser window.

To fetch and return the data from this same URL in a JavaScript program, you can use the Fetch API along with Promises:

```
fetch('https://api.github.com/users/facebook/repos', {
  method: 'GET',
  headers: {
    'Content-Type': 'application/json'
  }
})
  .then(response => response.json())
  .then(data => {
    console.log('Success:', data);
  })
```

GETTING DATA WITH FETCH

`window.fetch` is a method built into all modern browsers that allows you to perform HTTP requests from JavaScript without loading a separate library. Listing 16-4 shows an example of using the Fetch API to fetch data and log it to the console in a React component.

LISTING 16-4: Using Fetch in response to events

```
import {useState} from 'react';

function Restful(){
    const [repos,setRepos] = useState([]);
    const [status,setStatus] = useState();

    const getRepos = function(){
        fetch('https://api.github.com/users/facebook/repos')
            .then(response => response.json())
            .then(data => {
                setRepos(data);})
            .then(setStatus("fetched"))
            .catch(error => console.error(error))
    }

    const logRepos = function(){
        console.log(repos);
    }

    return(
        <>
          <button onClick={getRepos}>{status?"Fetched":"Fetch Repos"}</button>
          <button onClick={logRepos}>Log Repos</button>
        </>
    )
}

export default Restful;
```

GETTING DATA WITH AXIOS

Axios is a popular AJAX library that you can use instead of the browser's native Fetch API. Axios has advantages over `window.fetch` in terms of ease of use and capabilities, but using it does require you to load a separate library.

To install Axios, use the following command:

```
npm install axios
```

Axios has a method named `axios` that takes a configuration object as its parameter. The configuration object can contain many different properties, but the only ones required to perform a basic HTTP GET request are `method` and `url`:

```
axios({
    method: 'GET',
    url:'https://api.github.com/users/facebook/repos'
});
```

Like the `window.fetch` method, the `axios` method returns a `Promise`, which you can then chain to additional methods to work with the returned data.

Unlike `window.fetch`, `axios` automatically decodes the returned JSON data. What this means is that when you use Axios, you don't need to convert the response to JSON data before you can make use of it as you do with `window.fetch`.

Listing 16-5 shows an example of using Axios to perform a GET request in a component.

LISTING 16-5: Performing a GET request with Axios

```
import {useState} from 'react';
import axios from 'axios';

function Restful(){
    const [repos,setRepos] = useState([]);
    const [status,setStatus] = useState();

    const getRepos = function(){
        axios({
            method:'get',
            url:'https://api.github.com/users/facebook/repos'
            }).then(resp => {setRepos(resp.data);})
            .then(setStatus("fetched"))
            .catch(error => console.error(error))
    }

    const logRepos = function(){
        console.log(repos);
    }

    return(
        <>
          <button onClick={getRepos}>{status?"Fetched":"Fetch Repos"}</button>
          <button onClick={logRepos}>Log Repos</button>
        </>
    )
}

export default Restful;
```

In addition to the `axios` method, Axios also provides convenience functions for each HTTP method. The convenience functions are aliases to full `axios` calls that you can use without passing a configuration object. The convenience methods include:

➤ `axios.get`

➤ `axios.post`

➤ `axios.delete`

➤ `axios.put`

Using one of these methods can be as easy as passing it the URL for the request, like this:

```
axios.get('/user/1');
```

Both GET and DELETE calls are frequently made without passing any additional data, since all of the data required to perform their actions on the server are contained in the URL. The POST and PUT methods require a payload. That can be specified using the data property in the config object.

For example, to post data from a signup form using Axios, you might use the following:

```
axios.post('/user/',{
    firstName:'Frank',
    lastName:'Columbo',
    email:'f.columbo@lapdonline.org'
    });
```

USING WEB STORAGE

Web applications, by default, don't persist data between sessions. What this means for React user interfaces is that if a user leaves your application and returns later, or refreshes the browser window, the state data returns to the initial state.

One solution to persisting data between sessions is to save data on the server and associate it with the user's login info or a unique key stored in a browser cookie. When the user visits the app again, they can log in or the cookie can be read and the data can be downloaded from the server.

Downloading from the server is slow and inefficient, however, and if you can store data locally, you'll improve the performance of a user interface. The *Web Storage API*, which is supported by all modern browsers, is an easy way to store key/value pairs of string data in a user's browser.

Two Types of Web Storage

Web Storage includes two objects, `window.sessionStorage` and `window.localStorage`. Both properties work the same: they access a `Storage` object that stores data associated with the current application, as identified by its origin. A web application's origin is made up of the protocol (HTTP or HTTPS), host domain, and port. Web Storage provides at least 5MB of storage per origin.

The difference between `sessionStorage` and `localStorage` is that `sessionStorage` only lasts as long as the current browser tab is open, while `localStorage` persists between tabs and sessions. Because `localStorage` gives you all the benefits of `sessionStorage` plus persistence between sessions, it's more commonly used.

When to Use Web Storage

Web Storage can be used to remember where the user was in an application the last time they visited. For example, if your application includes a lengthy form, the user's input into that form can be saved to Web Storage so that if something happens (such as a browser crash) while they're filling it out, they can return to the form and continue where they left off. One simple and common use for Web Storage is to remember a user's login name between sessions, such as in the user interface shown in Figure 16-3.

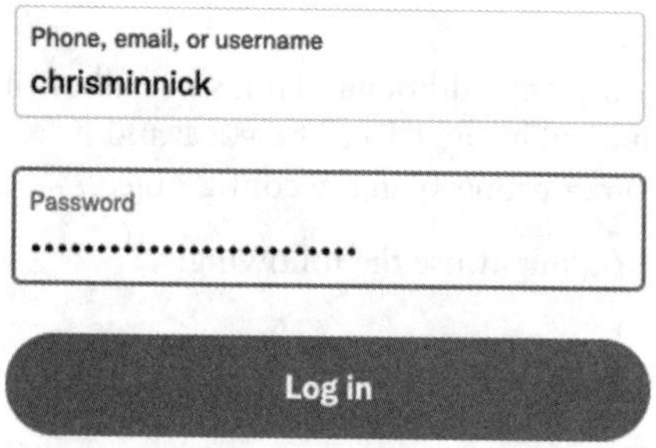

FIGURE 16-3: Remembering a user with Web Storage

When Not to Use Web Storage

Web Storage can't save data between browsers, different computers, or different origins and it will be erased if a user clears their browser's cache. For these reasons, it's not a replacement for storing data on a server that can be downloaded to any device with internet access. Instead, Web Storage should be used like a temporary cache of data entered by the user or downloaded from the server.

Web Storage should also never be used for storing sensitive data, such as credit card info or passwords. Although the same-origin policy provides some security from other sites being able to read data stored in an application's Web Storage, it's not much protection. If one of the hundreds of modules that make up a JavaScript application were to be compromised, code could be inserted into it to access and transmit stolen Web Storage data to a remote server.

Web Storage Is Synchronous

Although Web Storage is useful for improving the performance of your application, it can also cause performance problems if overused. Unlike APIs for retrieving data from servers (such as Fetch) and even other local storage APIs (such as indexedDB), Web Storage is synchronous. Each call to read or write from Web Storage blocks the execution of your app until the operation is complete.

That said, Web Storage is very fast. In most cases, using Web Storage to avoid making an HTTP request will improve the performance of your user interface. But, be careful not to overuse it.

Working with localStorage

To demonstrate how to use `localStorage`, we'll start with a simple app that doesn't use `localStorage`. Listing 16-6 shows a simple counter web application that could be used on a mobile device by someone at a retail store, for example. Every time the button is clicked, it increments a counter.

LISTING 16-6: A Clicker app

```
import {useState} from 'react';
import './style.css';

function Clicker(){
    const [count,setCount] = useState(0);

    const incrementCount = ()=>{
        setCount((prev)=>prev+1);
    }

    return(
        <div className="container">
            <h1 className="current-count">{count}</h1>
            <button className="increment-button"
                    onClick={incrementCount}>+</button>
        </div>
    )
}

export default Clicker;
```

The idea of the Clicker app is that the staff can use it to keep track of how many people visit the store during a day. But, as it's written now, the data is erased each time you leave the page and return. To fix it, we can cache its value locally.

Storing Data with localStorage

To store a key/value pair in `localStorage`, use the `setItem` method. This method takes two arguments—the key and the value:

```
localStorage.setItem('zipcode', '97103');
```

Keep in mind that Web Storage can only store string data. If you want to store another data type in Web Storage, you'll need to convert it to a string and then back again when you read it.

Because storing data in `localStorage` is a side effect, the best place to put a call to `setItem` is inside the `useEffect` hook (in a function component) or in a lifecycle method (in a class component). You can use the second parameter of `useEffect` to specify that the effect should run each time the state value you want to store changes, as shown in Listing 16-7.

LISTING 16-7: Writing to localStorage when the state changes

```
import {useState,useEffect} from 'react';
import './style.css';

function Clicker(){
    const [count,setCount] = useState(0);

    const incrementCount = ()=>{
        setCount((prev)=>prev+1);
    }

    useEffect(()=>{
        localStorage.setItem('counter',count);
    },[count]);

    return(
        <div className="container">
            <h1 className="current-count">{count}</h1>
            <button className="increment-button"
                    onClick={incrementCount}>+</button>
        </div>
    )
}

export default Clicker;
```

To verify that the value is being written to localStorage, you can open Chrome's developer console and go to the Application tab. You'll find an entry in the left pane of the Application tab for Local Storage, as shown in Figure 16-4.

Reading Data from localStorage

Now that the Clicker app is storing data in localStorage, the next thing to do is to load that data when the page loads. To get data out of localStorage, use the getItem method, which takes a key you want to get from localStorage and returns the value:

```
localStorage.getItem('zipcode');
```

The easiest place to retrieve cached data in a function component is in the initial state parameter of useState. By using a conditional operator, you can update the initial state to be set to the value from localStorage if it exists, and to a default value if it doesn't.

Listing 16-8 shows the Clicker app with the value of count being set to the cached value when it exists.

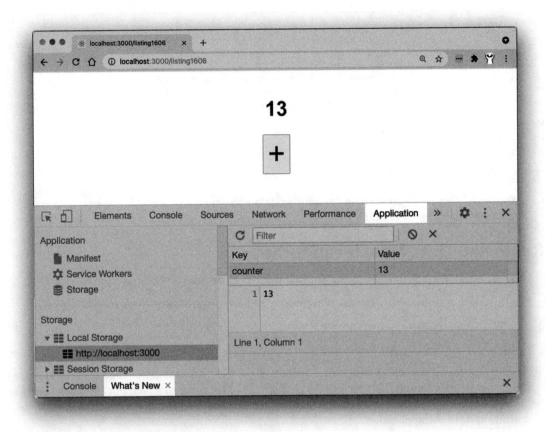

FIGURE 16-4: Viewing Local Storage in Chrome Developer Tools

LISTING 16-8: Reading localStorage data in Clicker

```
import {useState,useEffect} from 'react';
import './style.css';

function Clicker(){
    const [count,setCount] = useState(Number(localStorage.getItem('counter')) || 0);

    const incrementCount = ()=>{
        setCount((prev)=>prev+1);
    }

    useEffect(()=>{
        localStorage.setItem('counter',count);
    },[count]);
```

continues

LISTING 16-8 *(continued)*

```
    return(
        <div className="container">
            <h1 className="current-count">{count}</h1>
            <button className="increment-button"
                    onClick={incrementCount}>+</button>
        </div>
    )
}

export default Clicker;
```

Now the Clicker will increment and remember data every time it's accessed. The next step is to implement a way for the counter to be reset.

Removing Data from localStorage

To remove data from localStorage, you can use one of two methods:

➤ removeItem takes a key as its argument, and removes that key from localStorage.

➤ clear clears all of the keys for the current origin.

Since the Clicker app only has one key, we can use either method to reset localStorage. But, because we're using an effect to update localStorage when the counter changes, we could also just implement a reset button that changes the counter to 0. One thing to watch out for when resetting localStorage or removing keys is that resetting the localStorage value by itself won't change the current state of the application.

In Listing 16-9, the Clicker has been updated with a Reset button that both clears the localStorage and sets the value of the counter to 0.

LISTING 16-9: Clearing localStorage in the Clicker

```
import {useState,useEffect} from 'react';
import './style.css';

function Clicker(){
    const [count,setCount] = useState(Number(localStorage.getItem('counter')) || 0);

    const incrementCount = ()=>{
        setCount((prev)=>prev+1);
    }

    const resetCount = ()=>{
        localStorage.clear();
        setCount(0);
    }
```

```
    useEffect(()=>{
        localStorage.setItem('counter',count);
    },[count]);

    return(
        <div className="container">
            <h1 className="current-count">{count}</h1>
            <button className="increment-button"
                    onClick={incrementCount}>+</button><br />
            <button className="reset-button"
                    onClick={resetCount}>reset</button>
        </div>
    )
}

export default Clicker;
```

SUMMARY

Although React doesn't have its own AJAX and browser storage capabilities, integrating the native browser APIs or third-party APIs for these common tasks is easily done from within React components.

In this chapter, you learned:

➤   How JavaScript runs asynchronous code.

➤   How to use promises.

➤   How to use `async/await`.

➤   How to make HTTP requests using `window.fetch`.

➤   How to make HTTP requests using Axios.

➤   How to store, retrieve, and delete data using Web Storage.

In the next chapter, you'll learn how to use React's Context API to share global data in a component tree.

17

Context API

The primary way to pass data from parent components to child components in React is through props. However, in some cases props can be tedious to use and can lead to code that's more difficult to read and maintain. The Context API was created for these cases.

In this chapter, you'll learn:

➤ What prop drilling is.

➤ When the right time is to use Context.

➤ How to make a Provider.

➤ How to use Context in class components.

➤ How to use Context in function components.

➤ Best practices and conventions for Context.

WHAT IS PROP DRILLING?

React props make passing data from parent components to child components simple and intuitive. If you have a piece of data in a component and you want to make it available to subcomponents, just add an attribute to the child component's element and the value will be available in the child. If you have data in a component that you want to use in a grandchild component, you can pass the data through the child component and then into the grandchild.

This process of passing data through multiple levels of the component tree is called *prop drilling*. In a tree of components, you may have multiple levels of components that don't use a particular piece of data but just pass it along to their descendants using props, as shown in Listing 17-1.

LISTING 17-1: Using prop drilling

```
const Grandpa = (props) => {
  return (<Dad story = {props.story} />);
}

const Dad = (props) => {
  return (<Son story = {props.story} />);
}

const Son = (props) => {
  return (<Grandson story = {props.story} />);
}

const Grandson = (props) => {
  return (<p>Here's the story that was passed down to the Grandson component:
{props.story}</p>);
}

export default Grandpa;
```

HOW CONTEXT API SOLVES THE PROBLEM

Prop drilling isn't necessarily a problem. In most cases, it's exactly what you should do. However, if you have data or functions in your app that could be considered "global" (or global to a particular tree of components), Context lets you avoid prop drilling.

Here's how Context works:

1. You create a Context object, which includes the Provider and Consumer components and properties.

2. You create a Provider for the Context, which will publish a value to its descendants.

3. Any of the Provider's descendants can subscribe to the Provider.

4. Components that subscribe to a Provider will update when the Provider's data changes.

Creating a Context

To create a Context, use React.createContext:

```
const MyContext = React.createContext(defaultValue);
```

The createContext method returns a Context object. The defaultValue argument that you pass into createContext is the data that will be available to its descendants if there isn't a matching Provider. Since the default value most likely won't ever get used, many developers leave the default value as undefined or set it to some sample object.

For example, in Listing 17-2, I've created a Context for user preferences, which passes default values for the lang and timezone properties.

LISTING 17-2: A Context for user preferences

```
const PrefsContext = React.createContext({lang:'English',timezone:'Pacific
Time'});
```

You'll need to import the Context (`PrefsContext` in this case) into components where you want to use it, so it's common to put the call to `createContext` in its own module, or in a module containing a Provider.

Creating a Provider

A Context's Provider is a component that publishes changes to context data to its descendant components. The Provider component takes an attribute named `value`, which overrides the default value you set in `React.createContext`:

```
<MyContext.Provider value={/*some value here*/}>
```

The process for using a Provider is the same in function components and class components. To use a Provider, wrap it around the component or components that need access to its value. To simplify your code and make reuse of a Provider easier, it's common to create a higher-order component that renders a Provider component and its children, as shown in Listing 17-3.

LISTING 17-3: Using a Provider component

```
import React, {useState} from 'react';
import {PrefsContext} from './contexts/UserPrefs';

const UserPrefsProvider = ({ children }) => {
  const [lang, setLang] = useState("English");
  const [timezone, setTimezone] = useState("UTC");
  return (
    <PrefsContext.Provider value={{ lang, timezone }}>
      {children}
    </PrefsContext.Provider>
  );
};

function App(){
  return (
    <UserPrefsProvider>
      <Header />
      <Main />
      <Footer />
    </UserPrefsProvider>
  )
}

export default App;
```

The Provider component can be used as many times as you need, and it can be nested. Components that use a Context will access the closest Provider ancestor or will use the Context's default value if there isn't a Provider ancestor.

Consuming a Context

Once you have a Context and a Provider, descendant components can become Consumers of the Context. Context Consumers will be re-rendered when the Provider's value changes.

Using Context in a Class Component

There are two ways to consume Context in a class component:

➤ Set the contextType property on the class.

➤ Use the Context.Consumer component.

If you only need to use one Context in a class, setting the contextType class property is the easiest method. Because contextType is a class property, you can set it using public class fields syntax, as shown in Listing 17-4.

LISTING 17-4: Consuming a Context in a class component

```
import React from 'react';
import {PrefsContext} from './contexts/UserPrefs';

class TimeDisplay extends React.Component {

  static contextType = PrefsContext;

  render() {
    return (
      <>
        Your language preference is {this.context.lang}.<br />
        Your timezone is {this.context.timezone}.
      </>
    )
  }
}

export default TimeDisplay;
```

If your component needs to use multiple Context objects, you can use the Context.Consumer component. Context.Consumer requires a function as its child, and the value of the Context is passed as an argument to that function, as shown in Listing 17-5.

LISTING 17-5: Using the Context.Consumer component

```
import React from 'react';
import {PrefsContext} from './contexts/UserPrefs';
```

```
class TimeDisplay extends React.Component {

  render() {
    return (
      <PrefsContext.Consumer>
        {userPrefs => {
          <>
            Your language preference is {userPrefs.lang}.<br />
            Your timezone is {userPrefs.timezone}.
          </>
        }};
      </ PrefsContext.Consumer >
    )
  }
}

export default TimeDisplay;
```

Using Context in a Function Component

You can consume a Context in a function component by using the `Context.Consumer` component or by using the `useContext` hook.

To use `useContext`, import the Context and pass it to `useContext`, which will return the value from the Provider. Listing 17-6 shows a function component that uses `useContext` to get user preferences.

LISTING 17-6: Consuming a Context in a function component

```
import {useContext} from 'react';
import {PrefsContext} from './contexts/UserPrefs';

function TimeDisplay(props){
  const userPrefs = useContext(PrefsContext);

  return (
    <>
      Your language preference is {userPrefs.timezone}.<br />
      Your timezone is {userPrefs.timezone}.
    </>
  );
}

export default TimeDisplay;
```

COMMON USE CASES FOR CONTEXT

Context is most useful for managing global data. What fits the description of global data is a judgment call, but if some piece of data needs to be accessed by multiple components at different nesting levels, it may be a candidate for using Context.

Examples of when Context is helpful include:

➤ Theming an app (light mode or dark mode, for example).

➤ User preferences.

➤ Language preference.

➤ User authorization and roles.

WHEN NOT TO USE CONTEXT

When a component uses React Context, it becomes dependent on the global state, which makes the component less reusable.

If it's likely that a component will be reused, it's best to avoid coupling it with the global state using Context. In many cases, there are alternatives to prop drilling and Context that accomplish the same thing but maintain the standard explicit React way of passing data from parents to children. One such alternative is the *composition pattern*.

COMPOSITION AS AN ALTERNATIVE TO CONTEXT

A good alternative to Context and to prop drilling is composition. In React composition, you create a component that renders its child components and adds something to them in the process.

To understand how composition can be a better alternative to prop drilling than Context, consider the example app in Listing 17-7. This app has a login button that, when clicked, passes the username variable and the setUsername function into the Dashboard component. The username and its setter function are then passed through two levels of components that don't use them before they're used by the WelcomeMessage and Logout components.

LISTING 17-7: Getting data to a deeply nested component with prop drilling

```
import {useState} from 'react';

const App = () => {
    const [username,setUsername] = useState();
    if (username) {
        return <Dashboard setUsername={setUsername} username={username} />
    } else {
        return <button onClick={()=>setUsername('Chris')}>Login</button>
    }
}

const Dashboard = (props) => {
    return <Header setUsername={props.setUsername} username={props.username} />
}
```

```
const Header = (props) => {
    return <UserControls setUsername={props.setUsername} username={props.user-
name} />
}

const UserControls = (props) => {
    return (<>
      <WelcomeMessage username={props.username} />
      <Logout setUsername={props.setUsername} />
    </>)
}

const WelcomeMessage = (props) => {
    return <> Welcome {props.username}!</>
}

const Logout = (props) => {
    return <button onClick = {()=>{props.setUsername('')}}>Logout</button>
}

export default App;
```

Listing 17-8 shows how you might eliminate the prop drilling in this application by using React Context.

LISTING 17-8: Eliminating prop drilling with Context

```
import React,{useState,useContext} from 'react';
const UserContext = React.createContext();

const App = () => {
  const [username,setUsername] = useState();

    if (username) {
        return (
            <UserContext.Provider value={{username,setUsername}}>
              <Dashboard/>
            </UserContext.Provider>
        )
    } else {
        return <button onClick={()=>setUsername('Chris')}>Login</button>
    }
}

const Dashboard = (props) => {
    return <Header />
}

const Header = (props) => {
    return <UserControls />
}
```

continues

LISTING 17-8 *(continued)*

```
const UserControls = (props) => {
    return (<>
      <WelcomeMessage />
      <Logout />
    )</>
}

const WelcomeMessage = () => {
    const {username} = useContext(UserContext);
    return <> Welcome {username}!</>
}

const Logout = (props) => {
    const {setUsername} = useContext(UserContext);
    return <button onClick = {()=>{setUsername('')}}>Logout</button>
}

export default App;
```

Although Context has eliminated the need for prop drilling in the preceding example, it also makes the WelcomeMessage and Logout components dependent on UserContext. To illustrate why this is a bad thing, in Listing 17-9, I've attempted to reuse the Logout component outside of the Context.

LISTING 17-9: Using a component outside of a required Context

```
const App = () => {
  const [username,setUsername] = useState();
  const UserContext = React.createContext();

    if (username) {
        return (
          <>
            <UserContext.Provider value={{username,setUsername}}>
              <Dashboard/>
            </UserContext.Provider>
            <Logout />
          </>
        )
    } else {
        return <button onClick={()=>setUsername('Chris')}>Login</button>
    }
}
```

The result of this code will be an error, as shown in Figure 17-1.

Composition can be used to eliminate prop drilling while also maintaining the reusability of the WelcomeMessage and Logout components. To use composition, render the children property inside the Dashboard, Header, and UserControl components, and then compose your user interface inside the App component, as shown in Listing 17-10.

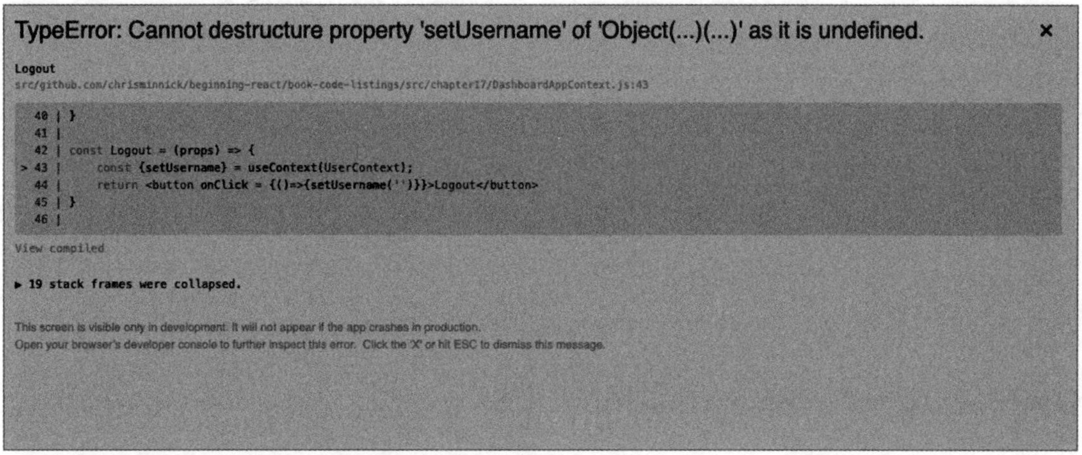

```
TypeError: Cannot destructure property 'setUsername' of 'Object(...)(...)' as it is undefined.            ✕

Logout
src/github.com/chrisminnick/beginning-react/book-code-listings/src/chapter17/DashboardAppContext.js:43

    40 | }
    41 |
    42 | const Logout = (props) => {
  > 43 |     const {setUsername} = useContext(UserContext);
    44 |     return <button onClick = {()=>{setUsername('')}}>Logout</button>
    45 | }
    46 |

View compiled

▶ 19 stack frames were collapsed.

This screen is visible only in development. It will not appear if the app crashes in production.
Open your browser's developer console to further inspect this error. Click the 'X' or hit ESC to dismiss this message.
```

FIGURE 17-1: Using a component outside of its Context

LISTING 17-10: Using composition instead of Context

```jsx
import React,{useState} from 'react';

const App = () => {
  const [username,setUsername] = useState();

    if (username) {
        return (
          <Dashboard>
            <Header>
                <UserControls>
                    <WelcomeMessage username={username} />
                    <Logout setUsername={setUsername} />
                </UserControls>
            </Header>
          </Dashboard>
        )
    } else {
        return <button onClick={()=>setUsername('Chris')}>Login</button>
    }
}

const Dashboard = (props) => {
    return (<>{props.children}</>);
}

const Header = (props) => {
    return (<>{props.children}</>);
}

const UserControls = (props) => {
    return (<>{props.children}</>);
}
```

continues

LISTING 17-10 *(continued)*

```
const WelcomeMessage = (props) => {
    return <>Welcome {props.username}!</>
}

const Logout = (props) => {
    return <button onClick = {()=>{props.setUsername('')}}>Logout</button>
}

export default App;
```

EXAMPLE APP: USER PREFERENCES

In this example app, we'll create a user interface for setting global preferences for units of temperature and units of length for an app. The larger app that this component belongs to is unimportant—it could be reused in many different types of apps.

Figure 17-2 shows the finished user interface. The user can change the dropdown menu between metric and imperial units, which changes the corresponding state changes and updates the value of the Provider.

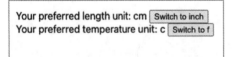

FIGURE 17-2: A user preferences component with Context

The first step in creating this user interface is to create the Context and a Provider, as shown in Listing 17-11.

LISTING 17-11: Making a Provider

```
import React, {createContext, useState} from 'react';
export const UnitsContext = createContext();

export const UnitsProvider = ({ children }) => {
    const [lengthUnit, setLengthUnit] = useState("cm");
    const [tempUnit, setTempUnit] = useState("c");
    return (
        <UnitsContext.Provider value={{ lengthUnit, setLengthUnit, tempUnit,
setTempUnit }}>
            {children}
        </UnitsContext.Provider>
    );
};
```

In a smaller app, it's common to put the call to `createContext` and the Provider higher-order component (if you create one) in the same file as the top-level component in the tree that uses the Context. If your app makes use of multiple Contexts or uses the same Context or Provider more than once, it's common to put them in a separate file, often in a directory named `context`.

The next step is to wrap the tree of components that will consume the Context with the Provider component, as shown in Listing 17-12.

LISTING 17-12: Providing a Context to a tree

```
import { UnitsProvider } from './contexts/UnitsContext';
import Header from './Header';

const App = (props) => {
    return (
        <UnitsProvider>
            <Header />
        </UnitsProvider>
    )
}

export default App;
```

With the Provider in place, you can consume the Context from anywhere inside the `Header` component and its descendants. Listing 17-13 shows a component that's a descendant of `Header` that uses the Context to display the current values of `lengthUnit` and `tempUnit` and allows the user to change them.

LISTING 17-13: Consuming a Context

```
import {useContext} from 'react';
import {UnitsContext} from './contexts/UnitsContext';

const UserPrefs = (props) => {

    const unitPrefs = useContext(UnitsContext);

    const changeLengthUnit = () => {
        unitPrefs.setLengthUnit((unitPrefs.lengthUnit === 'cm')?"inch":"cm");
    }

    const changeTempUnit = () => {
        unitPrefs.setTempUnit((unitPrefs.tempUnit === 'c')?"f":"c");
    }

    return (
        <>
            Your preferred length unit: {unitPrefs.lengthUnit} 
            <button onClick={changeLengthUnit}>Switch to {(unitPrefs.lengthUnit
=== 'cm')?"inch":"cm"}</button><br />
```

continues

LISTING 17-13 *(continued)*

```
        Your preferred temperature unit: {unitPrefs.tempUnit} 
        <button onClick={changeTempUnit}>Switch to {(unitPrefs.tempUnit ===
'c')?"f":"c"}</button><br />
<br />
        </>
    )
}

export default UserPrefs;
```

SUMMARY

The ability to consume Context from function components with the useContext Hook makes React Context easy and convenient. But, React Context is a tool that should be used sparingly or not at all in most apps. When you need it, however, it's invaluable as a way to manage small pieces of global data.

In this chapter, you learned:

➤   What prop drilling is and how React Context can eliminate it.

➤   When to use React Context.

➤   When not to use React Context.

➤   How to use composition as an alternative to Context.

In the next chapter, you'll learn about using React Portals to break out of the confines of a React app's root DOM node.

18

React Portals

ReactDOM.render renders a React application in a single DOM node in a web page. But it may be a big document outside that node, and there are times when your application may need access to that larger world. React Portals provide you with a way to access and control DOM nodes beyond the root in which it's rendered.

In this chapter, you'll learn:

➤ How to create a Portal.

➤ Common use cases for Portals.

➤ How to make a modal dialog with Portals.

➤ How to listen for and handle events within Portals.

➤ How to properly handle keyboard focus with Portals.

WHAT IS A PORTAL?

A Portal is a way to render child components into different DOM nodes than the root of your React application. For example, if you have a modal dialog box that appears when the user clicks a help link, a Portal lets you render that dialog box in a separate element in the HTML that's styled to appear on top of the React application, as shown in Figure 18-1.

How to Make a Portal

Because Portals interact with the DOM, they're a part of the ReactDOM library. To create a Portal, use the ReactDOM.createPortal method within a React component. ReactDOM.createPortal works the same way as ReactDOM.render, except that it works inside a React component's render method. Like ReactDOM.render, it takes two arguments: the component to render and the DOM node in which to render it.

FIGURE 18-1: Portals enable modal dialogs

Making a React Portal starts with knowing the structure of the HTML document in which your app is rendered. Unlike every example you've seen so far, Portals depend on having more than just a root node inside the HTML body element. Listing 18-1 shows an HTML document with two elements inside the body.

LISTING 18-1: An HTML document with multiple nodes in the body

```
<!DOCTYPE html>
<html lang="en">
<head>
    <meta charset="UTF-8">
    <meta name="viewport" content="width=device-width, initial-scale=1.0">
    <title>Portal Demo</title>
</head>
<body>
    <div style="display:flex;">
      <div id="root" style="width:50%"></div>
      <div id="sidebar" style="width:50%"></div>
    </div>
</body>
</html>
```

The `div` element with the `id` of `root` is where we want to render the React app with `ReactDOM` `.render`. The `div` element with the `id` of `sidebar` is where we want to render a Portal.

Any component in your React app can call `ReactDOM.createPortal`. In Listing 18-2, a component named `SidebarHelp` renders a paragraph of text as a Portal.

LISTING 18-2: Creating a Portal

```
import {createPortal} from 'react-dom';

function SidebarHelp(props){
  return createPortal(
    <p>{props.helpText}</p>,
    document.getElementById('sidebar')
  );
}

export default SidebarHelp;
```

Listing 18-3 shows an example of a component that renders the `SidebarHelp` component. Notice that from the perspective of this component, rendering a component containing a Portal is no different from rendering any other component.

LISTING 18-3: Using the SidebarHelp component

```
import Chart from './Chart';
import SidebarHelp from './SidebarHelp';

function SalesChart(props){
  return (
    <>
      <Chart type="sales" />
      <SidebarHelp helpText="This chart shows your sales over time." />
    </>
  )
}

export default SalesChart;
```

Figure 18-2 shows the result of rendering the `SalesChart` component.

If you inspect the resulting HTML in the Chrome Developer Tools, you'll see the HTML generated by the `SidebarHelp` component rendered outside of the root component, as shown in Figure 18-3.

If you inspect the app using the React Developer Tools, you'll see the `SidebarHelp` component rendered as a normal child component, as shown in Figure 18-4.

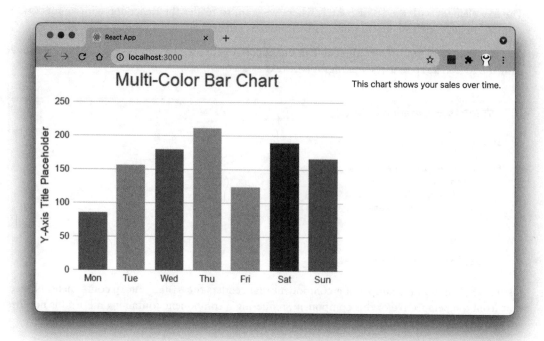

FIGURE 18-2: Rendering the SalesChart component

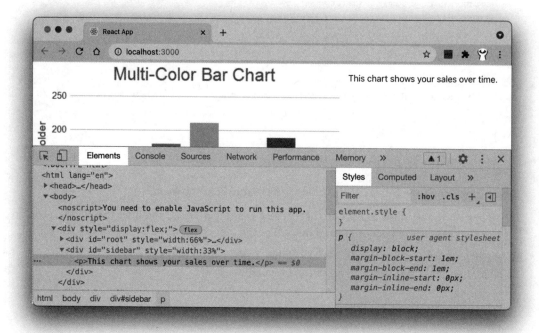

FIGURE 18-3: Inspecting an app with a Portal in Chrome Developer Tools

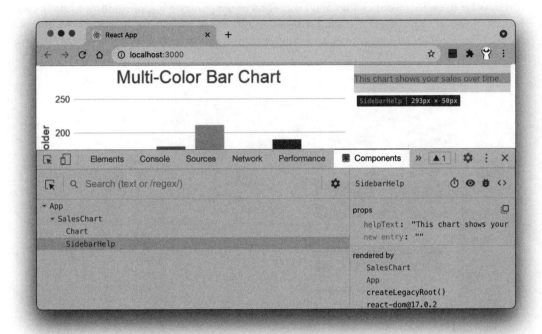

FIGURE 18-4: Inspecting an app with a Portal in React Developer Tools

Why Not Just Render Multiple Component Trees?

Another way to render React components into multiple DOM nodes is to use multiple calls to `ReactDOM.render`. If the components in the two DOM nodes don't need to interact and they use separate data, this works fine.

The benefit of using React Portals is that a Portal behaves like any other child in a React application. This means that Portals are both inside and outside of the React user interface. They mount and unmount outside of the root DOM node, but they behave the same as they would if they were normal React children—they accept props, can listen for and handle events, and so forth.

COMMON USE CASES

Portals are useful for any situation in which you need to display and interact with DOM nodes outside of the root node of your application. Common uses for Portals include:

➤ Rendering child elements elsewhere in the browser window.

➤ Modal dialogs.

➤ Tooltips.

➤ Hovercards.

It is possible to create modal dialogs and other sorts of temporary pop-up windows without using Portals. However, any element rendered without using a Portal inherits the height and width from its parent element. This can lead to problems in which a dialog box is cropped by its parent element, as shown in Figure 18-5.

FIGURE 18-5: Rendering a modal without using React Portals can have unexpected results

Rendering and Interacting with a Modal Dialog

Depending on how and why they open and close, temporary windows that overlay the main content of an HTML document go by different names, including modal dialogs, popup windows, tooltips, and hovercards. Most of the time, their opening and closing is triggered by an event happening within the application, such as a click on a help link or the mouse hovering over a line on a chart.

Follow these steps to create a modal dialog with Portals:

1. Create a node for the modal in the DOM tree. This can be any element outside of the root node. It should have an `id` attribute to make it easy to select:

```
<!DOCTYPE html>
<html lang="en">
<head>
    <meta charset="UTF-8">
    <meta name="viewport" content="width=device-width, initial-scale=1.0">
    <title>Modal Dialog with React</title>
</head>
```

```
<body>
    <div id="main"></div>
    <div id="modal"></div>
</body>
</html>
```

2. Create a modal component. Our example component will display a header and the `children` prop. By rendering the `children` prop, we make the modal dialog a flexible container that can be reused throughout the user interface:

```
import "./styles.css";

function Modal(props){
  return (
    <div className="modalOverlay">
      <div className="modalContainer">
        <h1 className="modalTitle">{props.title}</h1>
        <div className="modalContent">
          {props.children}
        </div>
      </div>
    </div>

  )
}

export default Modal;
```

3. Create a CSS document, which we'll call `styles.css`, that will position and style the modal. You can style your modal any way you like. My sample styles are shown in Listing 18-4.

LISTING 18-4: One way to style a modal

```
.modalOverlay {
  position: absolute;
  top: 0;
  left: 0;
  height: 100%;
  width: 100%;
  padding-top: 60px;
  background-color: rgba(50,50,50,0.6);
}
.modalContainer {
    border:1px solid black;
    background: white;
    width: 50%;
    margin: 0 auto;
    padding: 25px;
}
.modalTitle {
  text-align:center;
  background-color: black;
  color: white;
```

continues

LISTING 18-4 *(continued)*

```
}
.modalContent {
  background: white;
  text-align: center;
}
```

4. Create an App component that renders the modal:

    ```
    import Modal from './Modal';
    import './styles.css';

    function App() {
      return (
        <div>
          <Modal title="Warning" isOpen={isModalOpen}>
            <p>This Modal is awesome.</p>
          </Modal>
        </div>
      );
    }

    export default App;
    ```

5. Add a stateful variable to App to set whether the modal is open, and create a function, buttons, and event listener to toggle the open state. Notice that passing an event listener to a Portal and handling the events that happen in a Portal works the same as if the Portal were any other child element. Everything you learned in Chapter 7 about event listeners and event handlers applies to Portals.

    ```
    import {useState} from 'react';
    import Modal from './Modal';
    import './styles.css';

    function App() {

      const [isModalOpen, setModalOpen] = useState(false);
      const toggleModal = () => setModalOpen(!isModalOpen);

      return (
        <div>
          <button onClick={toggleModal}>Open the Modal</button>

          <Modal title="Warning" isOpen={isModalOpen}>
            <p>This Modal is awesome.</p>
            <button onClick={toggleModal}>close modal</button>
          </Modal>
        </div>
      );
    }

    export default App;
    ```

The current `App` component is shown in Listing 18-5. At this point, we're just passing a Boolean prop named `isOpen` to the `Modal` component. In the next steps, we'll use this value to determine whether to display the Portal.

LISTING 18-5: The App component

```
import {useState} from 'react';
import Modal from './Modal';
import './styles.css';

function App() {

  const [isModalOpen,setModalOpen] = useState(false);
  const toggleModal = () => setModalOpen(!isModalOpen);

  return (
    <div>
      <button onClick={toggleModal}>Open the Modal</button>

      <Modal title="Warning" isOpen={isModalOpen}>
        <p>This Modal is awesome.</p>
        <button onClick={toggleModal}>close modal</button>
      </Modal>
    </div>
  );
}

export default App;
```

6. Import `ReactDOM` and wrap the child element in the `Modal` component with `ReactDOM` `.createPortal` and pass a pointer to the DOM node where it should be rendered:

```
import ReactDOM from 'react-dom';
import "./styles.css";

function Modal(props){
  return (
  ReactDOM.createPortal((
    <div className="modalOverlay">
      <div className="modalContainer">
        <h1 className="modalTitle">{props.title}</h1>
        <div className="modalContent">
          {props.children}
        </div>
      </div>
    </div>)
  ,document.getElementById('modal'))
  )
}

export default Modal;
```

7. Use the Boolean prop passed from the `App` component to conditionally render the Portal:

```
import ReactDOM from 'react-dom';
import "./styles.css";

function Modal(props){

  return (
    <>
      {props.isOpen &&
        ReactDOM.createPortal((
          <div className="modalOverlay">
            <div className="modalContainer">
              <h1 className="modalTitle">{props.title}</h1>
              <div className="modalContent">
                {props.children}
              </div>
            </div>
          </div>)
        ,document.getElementById('modal'))}
    </>
  )
}

export default Modal;
```

The finished `Modal` component is shown in Listing 18-6.

Listing 18-6: The finished Modal component

```
import ReactDOM from 'react-dom';
import "./styles.css";

function Modal(props){

  return (
    <>
      {props.isOpen &&
        ReactDOM.createPortal((
          <div className="modalOverlay">
            <div className="modalContainer">
              <h1 className="modalTitle">{props.title}</h1>
              <div className="modalContent">
                {props.children}
              </div>
            </div>
          </div>)
        ,document.getElementById('modal'))}
    </>
  )
}
export default Modal;
```

Figure 18-6 shows the UI with the `isOpen` variable set to `true`.

FIGURE 18-6: The opened modal

Managing Keyboard Focus with Modals

Modal dialogs, such as tooltips, help dialogs, and modal forms, can make a user interface more usable. They also have the potential to confuse users if they aren't implemented correctly. One particularly important consideration with modal dialogs is to properly manage keyboard focus when closing a modal.

For example, a long signup or application form may make use of modal windows for entering detailed information and viewing help content, as shown in Figure 18-7.

When a user clicks a link to open a modal and interacts with the content of that modal (even just to click a "close" button), focus leaves the main content of the form. When the modal closes, the user will be forced to click in or tab to the next form field again to fill it out. At the least, this is inconvenient. At worst, it's an accessibility issue for users who rely on screen readers.

To properly set focus when returning from a modal, use the useEffect hook along with a ref to check whether the value of isModalOpen has changed to false and set the focus, as shown in Listing 18-7.

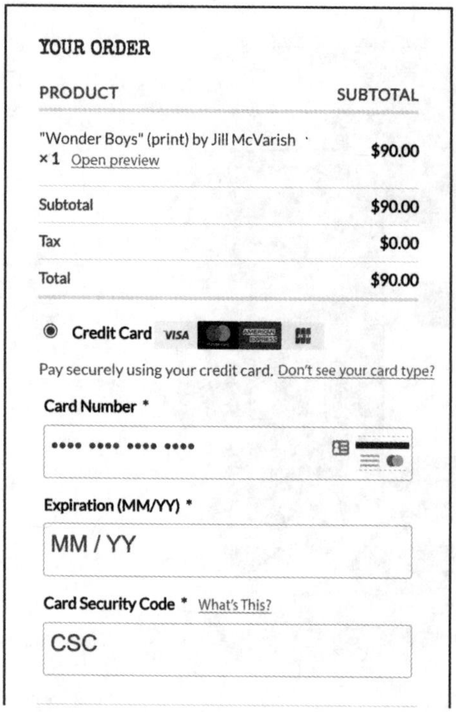

YOUR ORDER

PRODUCT	SUBTOTAL
"Wonder Boys" (print) by Jill McVarish · ×1 Open preview	$90.00
Subtotal	$90.00
Tax	$0.00
Total	$90.00

◉ **Credit Card** VISA

Pay securely using your credit card. Don't see your card type?

Card Number *

•••• •••• •••• ••••

Expiration (MM/YY) *

MM / YY

Card Security Code * What's This?

CSC

FIGURE 18-7: A checkout form with help links

Listing 18-7: Using a ref to set keyboard focus

```
import {useState,useRef,useEffect} from 'react';
import Modal from './Modal';
import './styles.css';

function App() {
  const CSCRef = useRef()
  const [isModalOpen,setModalOpen] = useState(false);

  const toggleModal = () => {
    setModalOpen(()=>!isModalOpen);
  }

  useEffect(() => {
    setTimeout(()=>{!isModalOpen && CSCRef.current.focus()},1000)
  }, [isModalOpen]);

  return (
    <>
    <div style={{padding:"60px"}}>
      <label>Card Security Code:<input ref={CSCRef} /></label>
      <button onClick={toggleModal}>What's This?</button>
```

```
            <Modal title="What is the CSC Code?" isOpen={isModalOpen}>
              <p>A credit card security code is the 3-4 digit number that
                is printed, not embossed, on all credit cards. The length
                and location of a credit card's security code depend on
                what network the card is on. </p>
              <button onClick={toggleModal}>close modal</button>
            </Modal>
          </div>
        </>
      );
    }

    export default App;
```

In Listing 18-7, I used a `setTimeout` function to make the setting of the focus take 1,000 milli-seconds (1 second) so that it will be obvious when you test it out. In an actual application you can eliminate the `setTimeout` function so that the focus gets set as quickly as possible when the modal dialog is closed.

SUMMARY

Occasionally, it's helpful to be able to break out of the root node and render React components in a different DOM node. React Portals, which is enabled by `ReactDOM.createPortal`, is the way to do this.

In this chapter, you learned:

➤   What a React Portal is.

➤   When Portals are useful.

➤   How to create a Portal.

➤   How to interact with a Portal.

➤   How to manage keyboard focus when closing a Portal.

In the next chapter, you'll learn about accessibility concerns when programming React user interfaces.

19

Accessibility in React

Accessibility (also known as *a11y*, because all those letters between the a and the y are too hard to type) means that websites and web applications are designed and built in such a way so that people with disabilities can use them. The qualities that make a user interface built with React accessible are no different from those that make any web user interface accessible, but the way in which accessibility is implemented differs in some instances.

In this chapter, you'll learn:

➤ What makes a web application accessible.

➤ Special considerations for making single page applications accessible.

➤ What ARIA is.

➤ How and why to use semantic HTML.

➤ The importance of proper labeling of form elements.

➤ How to use media queries in React components.

WHY IS ACCESSIBILITY IMPORTANT?

According to the World Health Organization, about 15 percent of the global population has some form of disability. Accessibility studies have found that between 6 and 10 percent of people over 15 years old have a sight or hearing impairment. For people over 65, that number is over 20 percent. Eight percent of people over 65 have difficulty grasping objects—including a computer mouse.

With the average age increasing worldwide, the number of people who require some sort of alternative device or assistive technology to use the web is in the tens of millions, even by conservative estimates.

Implementing web accessibility is not just the right thing to do or good for business, it's increasingly required by law. Public sector websites in many countries (including the U.S., Canada, and the E.U.) have been required to meet certain accessibility standards for years, and private-sector websites in many countries will be required by law to meet accessibility standards in the coming years.

ACCESSIBILITY BASICS

Most of the techniques you'll use for making web applications accessible are just good practices in general, and they make your application better and easier to use for all users, not just those with disabilities.

A short list of the considerations to keep in mind when designing your app for accessibility includes:

➤ Use valid HTML.

➤ Make sure all images have `alt` attributes.

➤ Add alternative content for all audio and video content.

➤ Your app should be navigable without a mouse.

➤ Form elements should be properly labeled.

➤ The application should be usable by people with color blindness.

Web Content Accessibility Guidelines (WCAG)

The World Wide Web Consortium (W3C) has developed and maintains a collection of documents that explain how to make websites accessible, which are collectively known as the Web Content Accessibility Guidelines, or WCAG. WCAG is the standard used by governments for laws that require accessibility.

The WCAG has four main principles:

➤ **Perceivable.** All user interface elements must be presentable to users in a way that they can receive it. For example, images must have text alternatives that can be read by screen readers for the blind. Perceivability also encompasses techniques such as responsive design, which ensures that content can be presented in different ways without losing information or structure. For example, a user interface should respond to changes in orientation of a mobile device (from portrait to landscape) and to different sized screens.

➤ **Operable.** Users should be able to operate the user interface. For example, it should be possible for all content and navigation and components to be used with a keyboard instead of a mouse.

➤ **Understandable.** How the user interface works must be understandable. This principle includes making sure the language of the content is specified in the code, providing proper labels to user interface controls, and providing help to the user.

➤ **Robust.** Content must be usable by a wide variety of devices and user agents, including assistive technologies. The most important factor in determining whether web content is robust is whether it complies with the HTML standard. For example, while a visual web browser may be able to render something that works just fine from faulty markup, it's much more difficult, or impossible, for an assistive device such as a screen reader to parse HTML that has duplicate attributes or missing end tags.

A complete guide to implementing WCAG is beyond the scope of this book, but you can find the complete document, as well as a quick reference guide to the latest version of the standard, at `https://www.w3.org/WAI/`.

Web Accessibility Initiative - Accessible Rich Internet Applications (WAI-ARIA)

The Web Accessibility Initiative - Accessible Rich Internet Applications (WAI-ARIA) document, published by the W3C, defines techniques for making web applications accessible to people who use assistive technologies, including people who use screen readers and people who cannot use a mouse.

ARIA provides standard HTML attributes that can be used to identify user interaction features and specify how they relate to each other as well as their current state:

➤ ARIA's `role` attribute can be added to elements to point out landmarks such as nav, search, tab, and so forth to screen readers.

➤ The `aria-live` attribute can be used to tell screen readers that particular content is updated. This is particularly important in dynamic single page applications.

➤ The `tabindex` attribute allows you to make the order of tabbing between user interface elements explicit. This is useful when the position of the elements in the document and the order in which you want them to be accessed are different.

➤ Attributes such as `aria-label` and `aria-required` can be used to give more information about form controls to screen readers.

To find out more about ARIA, visit the WAI-ARIA overview at `https://www.w3.org/WAI/standards-guidelines/aria/`.

IMPLEMENTING ACCESSIBILITY IN REACT COMPONENTS

Because the result of compiling a React application is a standard HTML, CSS, and JavaScript web page, implementing accessibility in user interfaces built with React is largely done using the same standards and techniques that you use with a static HTML document.

However, because you write the output of React components using JavaScript and JSX rather than HTML, there are some differences that you should be aware of.

The main things to consider when implementing accessibility with React are:

➤ ARIA attributes.

➤ Semantic HTML.

➤ Form accessibility.

➤ Managing focus.

➤ How to use media queries.

ARIA Attributes in React

JSX supports all the ARIA attributes. Unlike most other attributes that you write in JSX, ARIA attributes with multiple words, such as `aria-label`, are written the same as in HTML, using a hyphen between words rather than camelCase.

For example, the following JSX code tells a screen reader that an input is required and specifies the control's label:

```
<input
  type="text"
  aria-label={labelText}
  aria-required="true"
  onChange={onchangeHandler}
  value={inputValue}
  name="name"
/>
```

Semantic HTML

Semantic HTML refers to using HTML elements that indicate the purpose, or role, of an element in the document. For example, a page's navigation should be written using the nav element, and the address element should be used to mark up contact information.

When you use semantic HTML elements, the ARIA role of the element is implied, meaning there's no need to explicitly define the ARIA `role` attribute. Writing semantic and valid HTML is the most important thing you can do to make a page or application usable by assistive technologies.

Because each React component must return a single element, there's a tendency when writing React to wrap the return value of a component in an unnecessary div element, such as in the component shown in Listing 19-1.

LISTING 19-1: Using unnecessary elements to group elements

```
function ListItem({ item }) {
  return (
    <div>
      <dt>{item.term}</dt>
      <dd>{item.description}</dd>
    </div>
  );
}
```

These unnecessary elements can confuse screen readers, especially when they're used inside lists. For example, the component shown in Listing 19-2 makes use of the ListItem component to generate a definition list.

LISTING 19-2: Using unnecessary grouping elements can result in invalid HTML

```
function Glossary(props) {
  return (
    <dl>
      {props.items.map(item => (
        <ListItem item={item} key={item.id} />
      ))}
    </dl>
  );
}
```

The returned HTML from Listing 19-2 will have a `div` element around each group of terms and descriptions. The result is a definition list that doesn't comply with the HTML standard way to make definition lists.

The solution to this problem is to use `React.Fragment` (or its shorthand element) to group elements in cases where there shouldn't be a resulting HTML element from the necessary JSX grouping, as shown in Listing 19-3.

LISTING 19-3: Using React.Fragment to eliminate unnecessary HTML elements

```
function ListItem({ item }) {
  return (
    <>
      <dt>{item.term}</dt>
      <dd>{item.description}</dd>
    </>
  );
}
```

Form Accessibility

Form inputs need to have labels that are readable by screen readers and that are specifically associated with the inputs. It's not enough, for example, to have a label that visually appears above or next to an input, like this:

```
<form>
  first name: <input type="text" />
</form>
```

An accessible form is one that uses a `label` element and/or an `aria-label` attribute to label each input field. The `label` element in JSX works the same as the HTML `label` element, except that the `for` attribute in the HTML `label` element becomes the `htmlFor` attribute in JSX.

The value of `htmlFor` should be the value of the `id` attribute in the associated form control. Listing 19-4 shows an accessible form written in JSX.

LISTING 19-4: An accessible form, written using JSX

```
<form onSubmit={handleSubmit}>
  <label htmlFor="firstName">First Name</label>
  <input id="firstName" type="text" />

  <label htmlFor="lastName">Last Name</label>
  <input id="lastName" type="text" />

  <label htmlfor="emailAddress">Email Address</label>
  <input id="emailAddress" type="email" />

  <button type="submit">Submit</button>
</form>
```

Focus Control in React

Your web application should be fully accessible and usable with only the keyboard. One important aspect of making an application usable with only the keyboard is to properly manage focus.

Skip Links

Users who navigate using the keyboard or voice commands typically must move from one interactive element on the page to the next using the Tab key. For applications with a large number of navigation elements at the top of the page, this can mean that the user must tab through each element to get to the main body of the page. To help keyboard or screen reader users to navigate to the part of the page they want to use, you can implement a "Skip Navigation" link.

Skip Navigation links are links at the top of a page that may be visible, or that are only visible for keyboard and screen reader users. The Skip Navigation link uses an HTML anchor to move the focus past the navigation and directly to the main content of the page. You can implement Skip Navigation links easily yourself with a link and some styling, or you can use a pre-built component that makes it easier. Listing 19-5 shows a React component that implements a Skip Navigation link using the react-skip-nav component, which is available at npmjs.com/package/react-skip-nav or by running npm install react-skip-nav.

LISTING 19-5: Implementing Skip Navigation links with react-skip-nav

```
import React from 'react';
import SkipNav from 'react-skip-nav';

import "react-skip-nav/lib/style.css";

const MyComponent = (props) => {
  return (
    <>
      <SkipNav
        id='main-content'
        text='skip to main content'
```

```
        targetDomId='main-content'
    />
      <Header/>
      <div id="main-content">
        <MainContent />
      </div>
    </>
  )
}

export default MyComponent;
```

Managing Focus Programmatically

When the browser's focus is taken away from the normal flow of a page and then returned to it (such as what happens when a modal dialog is opened and closed), even users with a mouse must manually return the focus to the form field or interactive element they were using prior to the opening of the modal dialog. Without proper focus management, users of keyboard navigation or screen readers must start again at the top of the page and move through each element until they get to the spot where they were when focus moved to the modal.

You can use a ref and the `window.focus` method to return focus to the correct place when a modal dialog is closed. Listing 19-6 shows how to open a modal and return the focus to the appropriate element when the modal is closed.

LISTING 19-6: Managing focus upon closing a modal

```
import ReactDOM from 'react-dom';
import {useState,useRef,useEffect} from 'react';
import './styles.css';

function Modal(props){

  return (
  <>
  {props.isOpen &&
  ReactDOM.createPortal((
    <div className="modalOverlay">
      <div className="modalContainer">
        <div className="modalContent">
          {props.children}
        </div>
      </div>
    </div>)
  ,document.getElementById('modal'))}
  </>
  )
}

function App() {
  const PasswordRef = useRef()
```

continues

LISTING 19-6 *(continued)*

```
const [isModalOpen, setModalOpen] = useState(false);

const toggleModal = () => {
  setModalOpen((()=>!isModalOpen);
}

useEffect(() => {
  !isModalOpen && PasswordRef.current.focus()
}, [isModalOpen]);

return (
  <>
  <div style={{padding:"60px"}}>
    <label>Choose a Password:<input ref={PasswordRef} /></label>
    <button onClick={toggleModal}>?</button>

    <Modal title="Password Requirements" isOpen={isModalOpen}>
      <p>Your password must contain at least 8 characters, an uppercase letter,
         the name of your pet, your birthday, your child's birthday, the word
         "password" and several sequential numbers.</p>
      <button onClick={toggleModal}>close modal</button>
    </Modal>
  </div>
  </>
  );
}

export default App;
```

Media Queries in React

Media queries provide different CSS to a page or application based on the properties of the browser. The most common use for media queries is for implementing responsive design.

Responsive design is the technique used to make web pages and web applications adapt to different-sized devices. Besides making your application more usable for visual web browsers, responsive design also makes it possible for users with low vision to resize the user interface without needing to scroll horizontally. Media queries can also be used to detect non-visual browsers and customize the CSS for these devices.

Because inline styles in React components are actually JavaScript, rather than CSS, it's not easily possible to write media queries as style modules or using inline styles. Two common ways to use media queries in React components are by including a CSS stylesheet into the component or by using a custom hook.

Media Queries in Included CSS

If your React toolchain is configured to allow the importing of CSS files (as is the case if you use Create React App), you can use media queries in React the same way that you'd use them in any web application.

Listing 19-7 shows how to use media queries in CSS to format a web application differently at different viewport widths. Each width at which the styles change in responsive design is called a "breakpoint."

HOW MANY BREAKPOINTS SHOULD YOU HAVE?

At the very least, a responsive web application should have a separate design for mobile devices and desktop devices. While a mobile layout may work fine on a desktop device, mobile-specific user interface controls (especially those involving touch events) may not work correctly on desktop computers.

The breakpoints specified in the sample CSS shown in Listing 19-7 are much more granular, and you can even refine your breakpoints further to customize the CSS for devices that may fall in between these standard ones.

Many websites and organizations have created sample media queries that you can copy and paste into your applications. The ones in Listing 19-7 come from `https://responsivedesign.is`.

LISTING 19-7: Responsive media queries in a CSS file

```
/* Smartphones (portrait and landscape) ----------- */
@media only screen and (min-device-width : 320px) and (max-device-width : 480px) {
/* Styles */
}

/* iPads (portrait and landscape) ----------- */
@media only screen and (min-device-width : 768px) and (max-device-width : 1024px) {
/* Styles */
}
/* Desktops and laptops ----------- */
@media only screen  and (min-width : 1224px) {
/* Styles */
}

/* Large screens ----------- */
@media only screen  and (min-width : 1824px) {
/* Styles */
}
```

Using useMediaQuery

The useMediaQuery hook is part of the react-responsive library. To use it, you first need to install it using **npm install react-responsive** and then import it into your component. Once you've imported it, you can use either the MediaQuery component or the useMediaQuery hook.

To use the useMediaQuery hook, pass a query to it as a parameter. The result will be a Boolean value that you can use to conditionally render JSX. Listing 19-8 shows an example of using useMediaQuery to conditionally render one of four different components based on the size of the viewport.

LISTING 19-8: Conditionally rendering children based on a media query

```
import { useMediaQuery } from 'react-responsive'

const Desktop = ({ children }) => {
  const isDesktop = useMediaQuery({ minWidth: 992 })
  return isDesktop ? children : null
}
const Tablet = ({ children }) => {
  const isTablet = useMediaQuery({ minWidth: 768, maxWidth: 991 })
  return isTablet ? children : null
}
const Mobile = ({ children }) => {
  const isMobile = useMediaQuery({ maxWidth: 767 })
  return isMobile ? children : null
}
const Default = ({ children }) => {
  const isNotMobile = useMediaQuery({ minWidth: 768 })
  return isNotMobile ? children : null
}

const Example = () => (
  <div>
    <Desktop>Desktop or laptop</Desktop>
    <Tablet>Tablet</Tablet>
    <Mobile>Mobile</Mobile>
    <Default>Not mobile (desktop or laptop or tablet)</Default>
  </div>
)

export default Example;
```

SUMMARY

Accessibility is an essential element in the design and implementation of any user interface. It helps to ensure that the largest possible number of users will be able to access and make use of your application. The techniques for implementing accessibility with React are largely the same as with any web UI, but with some important technical differences.

In this chapter, you learned:

➤ Why accessibility is important.

➤ What the main accessibility standards are.

➤ How ARIA attributes help to identify user interface components.

➤ The importance of semantic and valid HTML.

➤ How to make forms accessible.

➤ How to control focus in a React component.

➤ How to implement media queries in React.

In the next chapter, you'll be introduced to some additional tools and resources that will help you to continue to become a better React programmer long beyond the limits of this book.

20

Going Further

I've covered a lot of material in this book, but your React learning journey is just beginning. The React ecosystem is giant, active, and growing. What this means is that developers are constantly creating new tools to use with React and improving existing ones.

With all the activity, having a guide to the next steps can be invaluable. In this chapter, I'll give you a head start on where to go from here by discussing or expanding on some of the topics that I didn't have room for earlier in the book.

In this chapter, you'll learn:

- ➤ About testing and popular testing libraries.
- ➤ What server-side rendering is.
- ➤ How GraphQL works.
- ➤ How to use GraphQL with Apollo.
- ➤ What Flux and Redux are.
- ➤ What Next.js and Gatsby are and how they're used.
- ➤ What organizations and people to follow to keep up to date on React.

TESTING

The process of testing React components and user interfaces is similar to the process for testing any JavaScript application, and there are many automated testing tools to choose from. If you're using Create React App, the most straightforward choice is simple—Create React App installs and configures Facebook's Jest testing framework for you.

Although Jest is popular and quite good, other tools and libraries may offer features or a way of working that you prefer. You might choose to use some of these tools together with Jest or in place of similar functionality that's provided by Jest. Here are a few of the most popular testing tools for React besides Jest.

Mocha

Mocha, like Jest, is an automated testing framework. Mocha is more configurable than Jest, and as a result, it may require more initial configuration. Mocha tests run sequentially, unlike Jest, which runs tests in parallel. Also unlike Jest, Mocha doesn't include its own assertion library. Instead, it's commonly used along with the Chai assertion library, which you'll learn about in the next section.

Test suites created with Mocha look very similar to those created with Jest. They use a function named `describe()` to create a test suite, and a function named `it` to define assertions (aka tests). Listing 20-1 shows a simple test suite created with Mocha and the Assert assertion library.

LISTING 20-1: A test suite created with Mocha

```
const assert = require('assert');
describe('Array', function() {
  describe('#indexOf()', function() {
    it('should return -1 when the value is not present', function() {
      assert.equal([1, 2, 3].indexOf(4), -1);
    });
  });
});
```

Enzyme

Enzyme is a testing utility for React that was developed by AirBnB. It can be used in place of React's built-in testing library (which you saw in Chapter 15). Enzyme's interface for selecting and working with nodes in the output of components is similar to how jQuery works with the DOM. With Enzyme, you can use familiar CSS-style selectors to locate nodes that you want to test. Enzyme makes it easier to traverse and inspect the elements output from your application's React components, which is an essential part of unit testing a React application.

To use Enzyme, you first render a component using one of its three render methods:

➤ `shallow`: Renders a single component. The `shallow` method is most often used for unit testing, in which it's important to be sure that you're not indirectly testing the behavior of child components.

➤ `mount`: Renders a component and mounts it in the DOM. The `mount` method is typically used with a browser simulator such as jsdom. Jsdom is a "headless" browser that runs completely in JavaScript. Use `mount` for testing higher-order components and components that interact with the DOM.

➤ `render`: Renders static HTML from your component. You can use the `render` method to test the structure of the HTML returned by a component.

Among the functions included with Enzyme is the `find` method, which is a simple way to locate and select elements in a component. The `find` method takes the place of several functions that are included with ReactDOM's testing utilities, including `findRenderedDOMComponentWithClass`, `findRenderedDOMComponentWithTag`, and `findRenderedComponentWithType`.

Listing 20-2 shows how to use the `shallow` method to render a component and the `find` method to locate a node within it. Once you've rendered the component and made a selection with `find`, you can test the selected node using an assertion library (such as Chai, in this example).

LISTING 20-2: Rendering and finding a node with Enzyme

```
import React from 'react';
import { expect } from 'chai';
import { shallow } from 'enzyme';

import MyComponent from './MyComponent';
import Foo from './Foo';

describe('<MyComponent />', () => {
  it('renders three <Foo/> components', () => {
    const wrapper = shallow(<MyComponent />);
    expect(wrapper.find(Foo)).to.have.lengthOf(3);
  });
});
```

Chai

Chai is an assertion library. Assertion libraries are used with testing frameworks and testing libraries to provide functions for declaring what result you expect in a test. Chai is often used along with Mocha and Enzyme, but it can also be used with Jest.

Chai has three different ways that you can write assertions:

➤ Assert

➤ Expect

➤ Should

Assert

The assert style is similar to the assert function that comes with Node.js. It uses the `assert` function, followed by a matcher function, as shown in Listing 20-3.

LISTING 20-3: Using Chai's assert method

```
const assert = require('chai').assert;
let foo = 'bar';
const beverages = { tea: [ 'chai', 'matcha', 'oolong' ] };

assert.typeOf(foo, 'string'); // without optional message
assert.typeOf(foo, 'string', 'foo is a string'); // with optional message
assert.equal(foo, 'bar', 'foo equal `bar`');
assert.lengthOf(foo, 3, 'foo`s value has a length of 3');
assert.lengthOf(beverages.tea, 3, 'beverages has 3 types of tea');
```

Expect

Expect is commonly used for Behavior Driven Development (BDD). It uses a chain of functions to produce an assertion that resembles how you would describe a test in English. An example of using expect is shown in Listing 20-4.

LISTING 20-4: Using Chai's expect method

```
const assert = require('chai').assert;
let foo = 'bar';
const beverages = { tea: [ 'chai', 'matcha', 'oolong' ] };

expect(foo).to.be.a('string');
expect(foo).to.equal('bar');
expect(foo).to.have.lengthOf(3);
expect(beverages).to.have.property('tea').with.lengthOf(3);
```

Should

The should method extends each object with a should property that starts a chain similar to the chains used by expect. Listing 20-5 shows examples of assertions written with should.

LISTING 20-5: Using Chai's should method

```
const should = require('chai').should(); //actually call the function
let foo = 'bar';
const beverages = { tea: [ 'chai', 'matcha', 'oolong' ] };

foo.should.be.a('string');
foo.should.equal('bar');
foo.should.have.lengthOf(3);
beverages.should.have.property('tea').with.lengthOf(3);
```

Karma

Jest and Mocha both run in Node.js and can test your code using a simulated web browser. Even the best simulated web browser isn't the same as a real one, however, and there's a possibility that your React code may not run exactly the same in Firefox as it does in Chrome running on an Android device.

Karma is a tool for testing JavaScript code in real browsers. It works by launching an HTTP server and then loading your tests (written with whichever tools you prefer) into each of a list of browsers that you specify. Karma then reports the result of running each test in each browser.

Nightwatch.js

Nightwatch is an end-to-end testing tool. The idea of end-to-end testing is to test scenarios as if from the eyes of the user. Nightwatch controls web browsers to simulate user actions.

Listing 20-6 shows an example test suite (from the `nightwatchjs.org` website) that opens the Ecosia search engine, searches for "nightwatch," and checks that the first result is the `nightwatchjs.org` website.

LISTING 20-6: A Nightwatch test suite

```
module.exports = {
  'Demo test ecosia.org' : function(browser) {
    browser
      .url('https://www.ecosia.org/')
      .waitForElementVisible('body')
      .assert.titleContains('Ecosia')
      .assert.visible('input[type=search]')
      .setValue('input[type=search]', 'nightwatch')
      .assert.visible('button[type=submit]')
      .click('button[type=submit]')
      .assert.containsText('.mainline-results', 'Nightwatch.js')
      .end();
  }
};
```

SERVER-SIDE RENDERING

Most of the time, React runs in a web browser and manages rendering and updating of components by manipulating the DOM. However, because React components are just JavaScript functions, they can also run inside of any other JavaScript engine. Server-side React runs React components to generate static files that can be sent to a web browser when a React user interface is first requested. The result is that the initial rendering of the page is faster, because it doesn't have to happen in the user's browser.

Server-side rendering works by having an instance of the ReactDOMServer library on the server (typically in a Node.js server) and using one of its render methods to generate static HTML. ReactDOM-Server has four render methods you can choose from, depending on your needs:

➤ `renderToString`: Renders the app to a static HTML string. Inside the browser, this HTML string can be turned into a functioning React user interface using the `ReactDOM.hydrate` method.

➤ `renderToStaticMarkup`: Renders the app to static HTML, without the attributes that React normally adds to HTML. The result is a smaller file, but one that can't be made interactive using `ReactDOM.hydrate`. You can use `renderToStaticMarkup` to create a static file server.

➤ `renderToNodeStream`: Returns the same HTML as `renderToString` but encoded as a Node Stream rather than as a string.

➤ `renderToStaticNodeStream`: Returns the same HTML as `renderToStaticMarkup`, but formatted as a Node Stream.

Flux

Flux is a pattern for how to manage data within an application. With the Flux pattern, data is kept in stores that can be subscribed to by user interface components. When a store that a component is subscribed to changes, the user interface component (also known as the view) fetches the new data and uses it to update.

Changing the data in a store is done using actions, which are dispatched in response to events in the view. All data in a Flux application flows in a single direction. Figure 20-1 shows the basic Flux pattern.

FIGURE 20-1: The Flux pattern

Redux

As your user interface gets larger, it can be helpful to centralize some or all of the data used in it, rather than having stateful variables spread throughout your components.

Redux is a library for managing state in a React application that implements the Flux pattern. Redux centralizes the state data in an application into a single state tree. This state tree is modified from within components by dispatching "actions." These actions, in turn, trigger pure functions called reducers, which update the Redux state tree. Figure 20-2 shows how data flows in a Redux application.

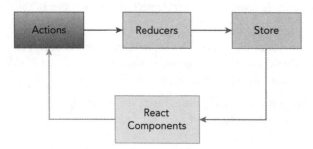

FIGURE 20-2: Data flow in a Redux application

A React application that uses Redux has a single object that contains all of its data. This object is called the Redux *store*. A store is created using the `createStore` method. The `createStore` method takes a function parameter, called a *reducer*, as its argument. The reducer contains all the methods that can be used to work with the data in the store.

The following is an example of a reducer function for a simple counter application:

```
const counterReducer = (state = 0, action) => {
  switch (action.type) {
```

```
      case 'INCREMENT':
        return state + 1
      case 'DECREMENT':
        return state - 1
      default:
        return state
    }
  }
```

To create a store, pass the reducer function into Redux's `createStore` function, like this:

```
import { createStore } from 'redux';

const store = createStore(counterReducer)
```

Each possible case in the reducer's `switch` statement corresponds to an action that can be dispatched in response to an event in the user interface.

An *action* in Redux is a JavaScript object that has a type and an optional payload. For example, in a Redux counter app, clicking an "Increment" button doesn't call a `setState` function. Rather, it triggers the Redux dispatcher (which is a method of the store object) and passes it an action object:

```
<button onClick={() => store.dispatch({ type: 'INCREMENT' })}>
  +
</button>
<button onClick={() => store.dispatch({ type: 'DECREMENT' })}>
  -
</button>
```

The store's reducer function receives the action and uses its `type` property to decide how to change the store. Changing the store causes the application to re-render.

Putting it all together, Listing 20-7 shows a complete Redux counter example.

LISTING 20-7: A Redux counter

```
import React from 'react'
import ReactDOM from 'react-dom'
import { createStore } from 'redux'

const counterReducer = (state = 0, action) => {
  switch (action.type) {
    case 'INCREMENT':
      return state + 1
    case 'DECREMENT':
      return state - 1
    default:
      return state
  }
}

const store = createStore(counterReducer)
const rootEl = document.getElementById('root')
```

continues

LISTING 20-7 *(continued)*

```
const Counter = (props)=>{

  return (
      <p>
        Clicked: {props.value} times
        <button onClick={props.onIncrement}>
          +
        </button>
        <button onClick={props.onDecrement}>
          -
        </button>
      </p>
    )
  }

const render = () => ReactDOM.render(
  <Counter
    value={store.getState()}
    onIncrement={() => store.dispatch({ type: 'INCREMENT' })}
    onDecrement={() => store.dispatch({ type: 'DECREMENT' })}
  />,
  rootEl
)

render()
store.subscribe(render)
```

If this example looks complicated to you, that's because it is. Redux is not meant to be used for such simple applications. However, even for larger applications, Redux often involves more complexity than is necessary.

GraphQL

GraphQL is a query language for APIs. GraphQL services are created by defining types and fields on those types. For example, you might have a type named User that might look like this:

```
type User {
  id: ID
  fname: String
  lname: String
}
```

A GraphQL server accepts requests and returns JSON data to the client application. Here's an example of a GraphQL query:

```
{
  user(id:"1") {
    fname
    lname
  }
}
```

The response from the preceding query might look something like the following:

```
{
  "data": {
    "user": {
      "fname": "Chris",
      "lname": "Minnick"
    }
  }
}
```

Because a GraphQL query has the same shape as the returned data, GraphQL is a more declarative way to fetch remote data than using REST.

Apollo

Like Redux, Apollo is a state management library. Unlike Redux, Apollo lets you manage both your local and remote data. Apollo has a client component that interacts with a remote GraphQL server to fetch data, and a provider component that makes the data available to components in your React app.

The first step in using Apollo is to have a GraphQL server to connect to. This is the most involved part of the process of using GraphQL and Apollo. You can create your own GraphQL server by following the instructions from the "How to Create a GraphQL Server" tutorial on Apollo's website at `https://www.apollographql.com/blog/tutorial-building-a-graphql-server-cddaa023c035/`.

Once you have a GraphQL server, you can connect to it with the Apollo client. Listing 20-8 shows how to create an Apollo client.

LISTING 20-8: Creating an Apollo client

```
import { ApolloClient, InMemoryCache } from '@apollo/client';

const client = new ApolloClient({
  uri: 'https://my.graphql.server',
  cache: new InMemoryCache()
});
```

To connect an Apollo client to your React app, you can use the `ApolloProvider` component, as shown in Listing 20-9.

LISTING 20-9: Using an Apollo provider

```
import React from 'react';
import { render } from 'react-dom';
import { ApolloClient, InMemoryCache } from '@apollo/client';
import { ApolloProvider } from '@apollo/client/react';
```

continues

LISTING 20-9 *(continued)*

```
const client = new ApolloClient({
  uri: 'https://my.graphql.server',
  cache: new InMemoryCache()
});

function App() {
  return (
    <div>
      <h2>My first Apollo app</h2>
    </div>
  );
}

render(
  <ApolloProvider client={client}>
    <App/>
  </ApolloProvider>,
  document.getElementById('root'),
);
```

React Native

React Native is a framework for creating native mobile apps using React. React Native works the same way as React: components are JavaScript functions or classes that return JSX. The difference between React and React Native is that React Native doesn't manipulate the HTML DOM. Instead, React Native components return JSX elements that map to mobile user interface building blocks such as Text, View, and Image. React Native was explored further in Chapter 4.

Next.js

Next.js is a React development web framework, similar to Create React App. Like Create React App, Next.js helps you to get started with your React app quickly and provides tools that you'll use throughout the development and building of your application.

In terms of features, the two main differences between Next.js and Create React App are:

➤ Next.js is more configurable than Create React App.

➤ Next.js supports server-side rendering. Create React App can be configured to support server-side rendering, but it doesn't support it by default.

Gatsby

Gatsby is a static site generator. It pre-renders React user interfaces and pre-fetches data on the server, which makes rendering of the site happen faster on the client. Besides speed, another benefit to serving static pages to browsers is that static pages may be more easily accessible by search engines, which can mean that static sites will receive higher search engine placement. Since static sites don't interact with the server or a database from the browser, they are also often more secure and provide less opportunity for a malicious script or user to access or modify data they're not authorized to access.

PEOPLE TO FOLLOW

Given how active the React developer community is and how popular React is, it's important to stay on top of the latest developments. A great place to find out about the latest React news and trends in the React community is on Twitter. The following is a list of React and JavaScript developers and organizations you may want to follow:

➤ **React News (@ReactExpo):** ReactJS and React Native news, templates, and jobs.

➤ **Rectiflux (@reactiflux):** A chat community of over 147,000 React and React Native developers.

➤ **Andrew Clark (@acdlite):** ReactJS developer at Facebook. Co-creator of Redux.

➤ **ReactJS News (@ReactJSNews):** The latest ReactJS news and articles.

➤ **React (@reactjs):** The official ReactJS Twitter account.

➤ **React Newsletter (@reactnewsletter):** The free, weekly newsletter of the latest React news, tutorials, resources, and more.

➤ **Becca Bailey (@beccaliz):** Engineering manager at Formidable labs.

➤ **MadeWithReactJS (@madewith_react):** A collection of projects made with ReactJS.

➤ **Jessica Carter (@jesss_codes):** Freelance software engineer who frequently tweets about React.

➤ **Dan Abramov (@dan_abramov):** Software engineer at Facebook. Co-creator of Redux and Create React App.

➤ **Mark Dalgleish (@markdalgleish):** React developer and co-creator of CSS Modules.

➤ **John-David Dalton (@jdalton):** JavaScript developer and creator of the Lodash library.

➤ **Sean Larkin (@TheLarkinn):** Webpack developer.

USEFUL LINKS AND RESOURCES

When you need help or have questions about how to do something in React, chances are good that someone else has had a similar problem and the solution can be found with a quick search. If you run into a new problem, finding help is usually not a problem and your question may help others who are having the same issue. The open source community thrives because of users helping each other out, and as you gain more experience, you may be able to solve others' problems as well. Here are some of the best places to give and find help with React programming:

➤ **Stack Overflow:** Stack Overflow is the first place to check, and the place where you're most likely to find an answer. You can find questions tagged with `reactjs` at `https://stack-overflow.com/questions/tagged/reactjs`.

➤ **Reddit's React community:** Although you're less likely to find answers to specific questions on Reddit, you can often find interesting discussions or projects posted at `https://www.reddit.com/r/reactjs/`.

➤ **Dev.to:** The `react` tag on Dev.to is an active place to find links to articles and tutorials about React and React-related topics. `https://dev.to/t/react`

➤ **React Community on Facebook:** React was created by Facebook, and so it's logical that there would be an active React Facebook community. In reality, this isn't really the case, but following the React Facebook community is a good way to stay on top of announcements from Facebook related to React.

➤ **Reactiflux:** The Reactiflux website and the online chat at `https://discord.gg/reactiflux` are both great resources for learning about React and for getting and giving help.

➤ **Hashnode:** Hashnode is another site with an active React community. Check it out at `https://hashnode.com/n/reactjs`.

SUMMARY

You've come to the end of this book, and hopefully you've gained a good understanding of the foundations of ReactJS. There's always more to learn, and the brief summaries in this chapter should give you some good jumping off points.

In this chapter, you learned:

➤ Several popular testing libraries and frameworks.

➤ What server-side rendering is.

➤ What GraphQL and Apollo are.

➤ About Next.js and how it compares to Create React App.

➤ About using Gatsby for static site generation.

➤ Who to follow on Twitter.

➤ Resources to use for getting help with React.

Every React developer benefits from the amazing React community. Now that you have a solid foundation of React knowledge, one of the best ways to continue to learn and to ensure that React will continue to thrive is by giving back. Ways to give back include answering React questions on Stack Overflow and elsewhere, contributing to an open source project, or teaching React to someone else or writing a book. Best wishes!

INDEX

A

Abramov, Dan (React developer community), 435
accessibility
  also known as a 1 1 y, 413
  basics of, 414–415
  form accessibility, 417–418
  implementing of in React components, 415–422
  why is it important, 413–414
addEventListener, 200
AJAX (Asynchronous JavaScript and XML), 290
AMD (Asynchronous Module Definition), 25
Angular (angular.io), 18
animation events, 211
Apollo, 433–434
App component
  adding methods and binding them to, 191–192
  converted App component, 193–195
  copying and modifying of JSX in, 191
  initializing state in, 190
  listing for, 407
  rendering NavBar inside of, 87
  static version of, 163
apply function, 67
apps
  building of, 339–343
  Clicker app, 381, 383, 384
  example of, 396–398
  inspecting of with Portal in Chrome Developer Tools, 402
  inspecting of with Portal in React Developer Tool, 403
  putting it on the web, 344–349
  running built app from filesystem, 342
  what's in a name, 343
  working React app, 357
ARIA attributes, 416
array
  changing of with spread, 158
  copying of with spread, 158–159
  passing an empty array to only run useEffect on mount, 268
array.map function, 53
arrow functions, 39, 216–217
assertions, writing of with Chai, 427–428
asset-manifest-json, 342–343
async, 372
asynchronous code
  described, 369–370
  where to run in React, 374–377
Asynchronous JavaScript and XML (AJAX), 290
Asynchronous Module Definition (AMD), 25
asynchronous tasks, 371
attributes
  ARIA attributes, 416
  component attribute, 305–306
  custom attributes, 56
  exact attribute, 301–303, 304
  non-standard attributes, 56
  vs. props, 52–56
  React as supporting many HTML attributes, 55
  renaming of, 54
  render attribute, 306–307
  some as behaving differently, 55
  standard HTML attributes, 54–56
  as using camelCase, 54
  using event listener attributes, 202
await, 372
Axios, getting data with, 377–379
axios-hooks, 286

B

Babel, 31–32
backend as a service (BaaS), 345
back-end environment, 20
Bailey, Becca (React developer community), 435
bidirectional data flow, 125
bind function, 67, 215–216
breakpoints, 421
browser incompatibilities, elimination of, 33
BrowseRouter, 294
build directory, examining of, 340
build script, running of, 340
build toolchain, React without, 1–7
built app, running of from filesystem, 342
built-in components, 47–56
built-in hooks
  accessing children imperatively with useRef, 279–280
  caching computer values with useMemo, 278–279
  combining logic and state with useReducer, 273–274
  customizing exposed values with useImperativeHandle, 280–281
  hooking into lifecycle with useEffect, 264–272
  list of, 259
  managing state with useState, 260–264
  memoized callbacks with useCallback, 275–278
  subscribing to global data with useContext, 272–273
  updating DOM synchronously with useLayoutEffect, 281
bytecode, 31

C

call function, 67
callback function, 67
callback refs, creating of, 236–238
callbacks
  within callbacks, 372
  memoized callbacks with useCallback, 275
camelCase, 33, 54, 201, 248, 252, 416
caption, rendering of, 74
Carter, Jessica (React developer community), 435
cascading styles, in components, 245–246

CDN links, 3
Chai, testing with, 427–428
Change Detection, 19
checkout form, with help links, 410
children
  accessing of imperatively with useRef, 279–280
  cloning of in NavBar.js, 88
  conditionally rendering children based on media query, 422
  creating new CartItem children, 110
  defined, 84, 104
  an HTML textarea's value as, 230
  making us of props in, 88–89
  manipulating, 86–88
  rendering of using props.children, 87–88
CJS (CommonJS), 26–27
Clark, Andrew (React developer community), 435
class, basing new class on external style, 253
class body, and constructor method, 62–63
class components
  consuming a Context in, 390
  controlling of inputs in, 224–225
  converting to, 190–197
  creating ref in, 234
  defined, 103
  differences between function and class components, 84
  initializing state in, 146–147
  introduction to, 57–68
  loading initial data in, 374–375
  managing state in, 71–72
  updating state with setState, 150
  using Context in, 390
  using state and setState in, 72
  writing event handlers in, 213–214
class composition, use of, 252–253
class declarations, 60–61
class expression, 61–62
class property, initializing state in, 147
Clicker app, 381, 383, 384
clipboard events, 206
cloneElement, 87
command-line interface (CLI), 101–102
commit phase, of component lifecycle, 89, 327
commits, 327

CommonJS (CJS), 26–27

component attribute, use of, 305–306

component data, editing of in React DevTools, 114–117

component tree, 108–110, 113

componentDidCatch(), 92, 327–328

componentDidMount method, 90

componentDidUpdate, 92

components

  as able to be imported into other components, 45

  App component. *See* App component

  attributes vs. props, 52–56

  built-in components, 47–56

  cascading styles in, 245–246

  changing state data in, 4–5

  class components, 57–68, 103, 213–214, 224–225, 234, 374–375, 390

  as compared to elements, 44–47

  Context.Consumer component, 390–391

  Counter component, 94

  creating component using a class, 58

  creating component with React .createClass, 57

  creating configurable ones, 15

  custom components, 30, 56

  defined, 15, 43

  as defining elements, 44–45

  dumb components, 79

  elements as invoking, 45

  with errors, 326

  FigureList component, 74–76

  filtering of, 112–114

  function components, 76–84, 103, 212–213, 224, 375, 391

  higher-order components, 114, 311–312

  HTML element components, 47–51

  improving performance and avoiding errors, 92–98

  including CSS in, 245

  inspecting, 107–114

  lifecycle of, 89–98

  lifecyle of, 104

  linking component, 294

  Logger component, 329

  made up of three child components, 85

  Modal component, 408

passing children into, 85–86

presentational components, 79

Provider component, 389–390

pure component, 96, 103

putting everything in one, 46–47

React component, 23–24

React.Component, 68–76

rendering of, 98–103

root component, 43, 103, 353–354

route component, 294

router component, 294

SalesChart component, 401, 402

SearchBox component, 227

searching for, 110–112

SearchInput component, 227

SearchResults component, 227–228

selecting, 114–117

setting an event listener in, 201

shell components, 163–164

SidebarHelp component, 401

simple routing component, 291–292

stateful component, 103

stateless component, 103, 147

stateless functional components, 79

terminology of, 103–104

TextReader component, 236

types of, 56–84

use of to reduce complexity, 45–46

user-defined components, 30, 56

without default props, 142

Components window, 108–109, 114, 115

componentWillUnmount, 92

composing, defined, 15

composition

  as alternative to Context, 392–396

  defined, 15

  vs. inheritance, 15–16

  use of instead of Context, 395–396

  using, 16

composition events, 206

conditional rendering

  with && operator, 37–38

  with conditional operator, 38

  defined, 36

  with if/else and element variables, 36–37

const keyword, 82, 156

constant, defined, 82
constructor
    binding function in, 215–216
    class body and constructor method, 62–63
    in mounting stage, 90
Context
    common use cases for, 391–392
    composition as alternative to, 392–396
    consuming a Context in a function component,
        391
    consuming of, 390–391, 397–398
    creating Provider, 389
    eliminating prop drilling with, 393–394
    use of composition instead of, 395–396
    use of with useContext hook, 272
    for user preferences, 389
    user preferences component with, 396
    using a component outside of a required Context,
        394–395
    using in function component, 391
    when not to use, 392
Context API, as solving the problem, 388–391
Context object, creating of, 388–389
Context.Consumer component, use of, 390–391
controlled inputs
    adding value attribute as creating, 223
    simplifying of in a class, 225–226
    vs. uncontrolled inputs, 221–226
    updating of with function components, 223–224
Counter, with useReducer, 273–274
Counter component, toggling render of, 94
CounterClass button, result of clicking, 153
Create React App
    Babel as integrated into, 31
    interactive "Hello, World" with, 7–8
    use of to build boilerplate user interface, 1–7
CSS
    advanced CSS Modules functionality, 252–253
    CSS rule-sets vs. JavaScript style objects, 248
    importing of into HTML file, 243–245
    media queries in included CSS, 421
    modules of, 250–253
    naming CSS Module files, 251–252
    responsive media queries in CSS file, 421

    using plain old CSS in components, 245–247
CSS-in-JS, and styled components, 253–254
curly braces
    putting comments in, 35–36
    use of double curly braces with objects, 35
    use of to include literal JavaScript, 35
custom attributes
    prefacing of in DOM elements with data-, 34
    written using only lower-case letters, 56
custom components, 30, 56
custom domains, enabling of and HTTPS, 348
custom hooks
    finding and using, 286–288
    inspecting of, 283
    labeling of with useDebugValue, 283–285
    other fun hooks, 288
    viewing debug value of, 285
    writing of, 281–283

D

Dalgleish, Mark (React developer community), 435
Dalton, John-David (React developer community),
    435
data
    fetching and caching of, 369–385
    getting data to a deeply nested component with
        prop drilling, 392–393
    getting of with Axios, 377–379
    getting of with fetch, 377
    reading of from localStorage, 382–385
    removing of from localStorage, 383–384
data flow
    bidirectional data flow, 125
    one-way data flow, 123–126, 224
    two-way data flow, 125
    unidirectional data flow, 123–126
data type, validation of, 133–134
declarative programming, 16–17
default actions, preventing of, 231–232
default exports, 28–29
default values, adding of to InputForm, 174–175
defaultProps object, 143, 178
defaults

destructuring props and setting of, 143

setting `defaultProps` as static property, 143–144

setting `defaultProps` for function component, 145

setting `defaultProps` outside of component body, 144–145

setting of with OR operator, 142

deployment

  defined, 339

  a deployed React app, 348

  how is a deployed app different? 343

  with `Netlify`, 345–349

destructuring assignment syntax, 81, 83

Developer Tools, 344. *See also* React DevTools

development environment, 20, 21

development mode, vs. production, 343–344

development server, and hot reloading, 360

Dev.to, 436

Document Object Model (DOM)

  defined, 13

  role of, 13

DOM method

  calling of on child using a ref, 235

  updating of synchronously with `useLayoutEffect`, 281

dumb components, 79

E

ECMAScript Modules (ESM), 27

effects

  cleaning up after, 265–266

  running of only after mounting, 268

element tree

  after user clicks a link, 100

  initial element tree, 100

`element` validator, 137

elements

  components as defining, 44–45

  as invoking components, 45

  using unnecessary elements to group elements, 416

  using unnecessary grouping elements can result in invalid HTML, 417

`elementType` validator, 137

Enzyme, testing with, 426–427

error boundaries

  best laid plans, 319–320

  building your own `ErrorBoundary` component, 323–334

  crashed React app, 320

  defined, 320–323

  `ErrorBoundary` component, 324

  `getDerivedStateFromErrors` as static method, 324

  handling an error with, 323

  implementing of, 323–338

  providing reset option in, 335

  testing of, 326–327

  what it can't catch, 336–337

error handling, as stage of component's life, 89, 92

error message

  cannot read property, 173

  cannot read property 'map' of undefined, 175

  not-renderable error message, 135

`ErrorBoundary` component

  building your own, 323–334

  exporting with, 326

  installing a pre-built one, 334–336

  listing for, 324

  providing reset link in, 334

  updated of with remote logging, 331–332

errors

  automatically fixable errors or warnings, 362

  catching ones in error boundaries with `try/catch`, 336–337

  catching ones in event handlers with `react-error-boundary`, 337–338

  component that sometimes errors, 333

  component with, 326

  how to fix, 362

  logging of and the `info` object to console, 328

  logging of with `ComponentDidCatch()`, 327–328

  uncaught error, 322

  viewing caught ones in Loggly, 332

  viewing of and info parameters in console, 329

ES205 module rules, 28–29
ESLint
  configuration of, 361
  how to fix errors, 362
  installing and configuring of, 360–361
ESM (ECMAScript Modules), 27
Event API documentation, 205
event bubbling, 202
event handler
  binding event handler functions, 214–216
  binding of, 70–71
  binding of inline, 216
  catching errors in with `react-error-boundary`, 337–338
  defining state using class property, 217–218
  `FilterSelect` with, 187–188
  functions of, 211–219
  `InputForm` component with event handlers and event listeners, 181–182
  passing data to, 218–219
  passing `Event` object to, 219
  use of arrow function as, 39, 216–217
  using inline event handler to call `setState`, 212
  using inline event handler to show an alert, 211
  writing and binding an event handler method in a class, 213–214
  writing inline event handlers, 211–212
  writing of in function components, 212–213
event handler function, 211–219
event listeners
  `FilterSelect` with, 187–188
  `InputForm` component with event handlers and event listeners, 181–182
  setting of in React component, 201
  using event listener attributes, 202
Event object
  adding properties to, 205
  base `Event` properties, 203
  passing of automatically, 218
  passing of to event handler, 219
  viewing properties of, 203
`Event.cancelable`, 203
`Event.preventDefault`, 203

events
  animation events, 211
  clipboard events, 206
  composition events, 206
  event bubbling, 202
  `Event` object, 203–204
  focus events, 206
  form events, 206–207
  generic events, 207
  how they work in React, 199–201
  image events, 210
  keyboard events, 206
  media events, 209–210
  mouse events, 207–208
  other events, 211
  pointer events, 208–209
  selection events, 209
  setting an event listener in a React component, 201
  supported events, 204–211
  `SyntheticEvent`, 201–202
  touch events, 209
  transition events, 211
  UI events, 209
  using `addEventListener`, 200
  using an event attribute in HTML, 200
  using event listener attributes, 202
  wheel events, 209
  writing of in class components, 213–214
`Event.target`, 203
`Event.type`, 203
exact attribute
  adding of to Routes to restrict matching, 304
  use of on `NavLink` components, 301–303
export statement, 27–29
exporting, with `ErrorBoundary`, 326–327
expressions, 38–39

F

Facebook
  React as created by, 11
  React Community on, 436
fecthing, ways to, 376

fetch, getting data with, 377
figure, rendering of, 74
FigureList component, 74–76
filteredReminders, creating new one, 184–185
filtering
   of components, 112–114
   reminders, 183–190
   reminders list, 185
filterList function, implementing of, 186–187
FilterSelect
   with an event handler and event listener, 187–188
   filtering reminders, 183–190
   pure FilterSelect, 172
   round two of, 166
   shell component for, 163
   validating and setting defaults for, 177–178
fixed counter class, 155
Flamegraph chart, 119
Flux, use of, 430
focus
   managing of, 239
   managing of programmatically, 419
focus control (in React), 418–420
focus events, 206
form events, 206–207
forms
   controlled inputs vs. uncontrolled inputs,
      221–226
   as having state, 221–222
   lifting up input state, 226–228
   preventing default actions, 231–232
   using different form elements, 229–231
   using uncontrolled inputs, 228–229
front-end environment, 20
function binding, 67
function components
   consuming a Context in, 391
   controlling of input in, 224
   creating ref in, 234
   defined, 79, 103
   how to write them, 79–80
   initializing state in, 147–149
   loading initial data in, 375
   managing state in, 83–85

optimizations and shortcuts with, 80
   setting defaultProps for, 145
   as simpler than class components, 76–79
   updating state with, 154–155
   use of PropTypes with, 133
   writing event handlers in, 212–213
function constructors, 58
function declarations, 61
function dependencies
   as causing unnecessary renders, 275–277
   unnecessary renders warning due to, 276
function hoisting, 61
function scope, 81
functional programming, 64
functions
   apply function, 67
   array.map function, 53
   arrow functions, 39, 216–217
   binding of in the constructor, 215–216
   call function, 67
   callback function, 67
   higher-order functions, 311–312
   immediately invoking of in JSX, 39
   passing of to a setter, 263
   setter function, 262–264

G

Gatsby, use of, 434
generic events, 207
getDerivedStateFromErrors
   receives error as parameter, 325
   as running during render phase, 325
   should return an object for updating state,
      325–326
   as static method, 324
getDerivedStateFromProps, 90, 91, 92
getElementById function, 13
getSnapshotBeforeUpdate, 91–92
Git button, clicking New site from, 346
Git provider, choosing of, 346
global data
   defined, 272
   subscribing to with useContext, 272

global scope, 82
Google, Angular (`angular.io`), 18
GraphQL, use of, 432–433

H

hash string, defined, 343
Hashnode, 436
`HashRouter`, 294, 295
Hello, World
  interactive Hello, World component, 7
  running in browser, 5
Hello React Learner, 8
higher-order components, 114, 257, 311–312
higher-order functions, 114, 311–312
`history` object, 309, 310, 312
hoisting, 61, 81
hooks
  built-in hooks, 259–281
  custom hooks, 281–288
  defined, 257
  importing of, 260
  React Router hooks, 317–318
  resources on, 288
  role of, 79, 147
  rules of, 259
  and state, 116
  why they were introduced, 257–259
hot reloading, 8, 360
HTML
  adding HTML link to HTML file, 244
  adding React to page, 1–7
  custom attributes in, 34
  element components, 47–51
  file for using React without toolchain, 4
  HTML document, 352–353
  HTML document with multiple nodes in the body, 400
  importing CSS into, 243–245
  input elements, 229–230
  making HTML template, 359–360
  React as supporting many HTML attributes, 55
  `select` element in, 231
  semantic HTML, 416

standard HTML attributes, 54–56
using an event attribute in, 200
using unnecessary grouping elements can result in invalid HTML, 417
HTTPS, enabling custom domains and, 348

I

image events, 210
immutabilty, 156
imperative programming, 16
implicit globals, 82
`import` statement, 27–29
`index.html`
  the built `index.html`, 341
  creating React App's, 99
  finished one, 352–353
  importing `index.js` into, 354
`index.js`
  attempt to load without compiling, 355
  finished `index.js`, 353
  importing of into `index.html`, 354
initial element tree, 100
initializing `state`, 146–149
inline event handlers, 211–212
inline styles
  importing multiple styles, 250
  improvement of with style modules, 249
  using of in React, 247–248
  using variables to hold style objects, 249
  why not to use, 249
  why to use, 249
`innerHTML` function, 13
input elements
  controlling of, 230
  list of, 229–230
`InputForm`
  adding PropTypes and default values to, 174–175
  converted `InputForm` component, 196–197
  with event handlers and event listeners, 181–182
  pure `InputForm`, 172
  round two of, 165–166
  shell component for, 163

inputs. *See also* controlled inputs; uncontrolled inputs
  controlling of in class component, 224–225
  controlling of in function component, 224
  lifting up input state, 226–228
  updating input element with one-way data flow, 224
isComplete, implementing isComplete changing functionality, 188–190
Isomorphic React, 103
isRequired validator, 134
isValidElement, 87

J

JavaScript
  array.map function, 53
  class body and constructor method, 62–63
  class declarations, 60–61
  class expression, 61–62
  class validation, 138
  classes in, 58–68
  CSS rule-sets vs. JavaScript style objects, 248
  equality operators, 261
  executing asynchronous JavaScript, 371
  function (or method) invocation in, 64–66
  as functional programming language, 64
  history of modules in, 25–29
  main JavaScript file, 353
  method definition syntax, 214
  method syntax, 65
  as never sleeping, 370–374
  promises and async/await, 372–374
  REST (Representational State Transfer), 376
  routing, 291
  shallow copies and spread operator, 157–160
  side effects, 264
  static methods, 324–325
  in strict mode, 65
  style syntax, 248
  subclasses with extends keyword, 63–64
  tagged template literals, 254–255
  variables in, 81–83
  when to use it in JSX, 36

Jest, testing with, 363, 425
JSX
  accessible form, writing using, 418
  Babel, 31–32
  Boolean attributes, 34–35
  conditionals in, 36
  copying and modifying of in App, 191
  defined, 30
  expressions in, 38–39
  how it works, 30–31
  JSX Transform, 31, 32
  as not HTML, 23, 33
  as requiring loader, 356
  as supporting all ARIA attributes, 416
  syntax basics of, 33–41
  transpilation, 31–33
  use of curly braces to include literal JavaScript, 35
  as using camelCase, 33
  using children in, 40
  when to use JavaScript in, 36
  as XML, 33

K

Karma, testing with, 428
key prop, 177–183
keyboard events, 206
keyboard focus, use of ref to set, 410–411

L

Larkin, Sean (React developer community), 435
let keyword, 82
lexical variable scoping, 82
lifting state up, 170–176
Link, internal linking with, 296–297
linking
  automatic linking with Redirect, 302
  with object, 297
  to routes, 296–302
  with string, 297
linking component, 294
linting, defined, 360
list virtualization, 120

literal JavaScript, using of inside JSX, 35
loader
  JSX as requiring, 356
  role of, 358
localStorage
  clearing of in the Clicker, 384–385
  reading data from, 382
  reading of in Clicker, 383–384
  removing of data from, 383–384
  storing data with, 381–382
  viewing of in Chrome Developer Tools, 383
  working with, 381
  writing to when state changes, 382
location object, 309, 313, 314
log source, adding of, 330
Logger component, 329
logging service, use of, 328–329
Loggly, 329–330, 331, 332

M

MadeWithReactJS, 435
Martin, Robert C. ("Uncle Bob"), 15
match object, 309, 313–314, 316
media events, 209–210
media playback, controlling of, 241
media queries (in React)
  overview, 420
  conditionally rendering children based on, 422
  in included CSS, 421
  responsive media queries in CSS file, 421
  using useMediaQuery, 422
memoization, 121
memory leaks
  avoiding, 93–98
  fixing, 96
  React component with potential one, 93
MemoryRouter, 294, 295
method definition syntax, 214
methods
  as properties too, 60
  this keyword in, 65–66
Microsoft, TypeScript, 19
Mocha, testing with, 426

modal
  managing keyboard focus with, 409–410
  one way to style, 405–406
  opened modal, 409
Modal component, finished Modal component, 408
modal dialog, rendering and interacting with, 404–409
model, managing focus upon closing of, 419–420
Model-View-Controller (MVC) pattern, 12
modularization, 24–29
mounting, as stage of component's life, 89, 90
mouse events, 207–208
mouse position, component to track, 354
mouse tracker, testing of, 363
multiple component trees, why not just render? 403

N

NativeEvent, 204, 205
NativeRouter, 294, 295
NavBar, 87
NavBar.js, cloning children in, 88
navigation menu with sub-items, 299
NavLink
  internal navigation with, 298–302
  list of NavLinks with sub-items, 299–300
  using exact attribute on NavLink components, 301
Netlify
  deployment with, 345–349
  domain management in, 349
  enabling routing with, 347–348
new operator, 59
Next.js, use of, 434
Nightwatch.js, testing with, 428–429
node hosting, 345
nodes, validation of, 134–137
npm scripts, creating of, 364–365

O

object, copying of with spread, 159–160
object-oriented programming (OOP), 15
oneOfType validator, 139

one-way data flow
  defined, 123
  reason for, 125
  understanding, 124–125
  updating input element with, 224
operators, equality operators, 261
optimization, 120–121

P

parameters
  using URL parameters, 304–305
  using useParams hook, 305
parent
  defined, 84, 104
  passing onClick into, 88
path matching, restricting of, 304
payload, passing of to reducer, 274
performance, solving performance problems, 279
plugins, role of, 358
plugins object, creating of, 359
pointer events, 208–209
Portals
  common use cases for, 403–411
  creating of, 401
  defined, 399
  as enabling modal dialogs, 400
  how to make, 399–403
  inspecting an app with Portal in Chrome
    Developer Tools, 402
  inspecting an app with Portal in React Developer
    Tools, 403
pre-commit phase, of component lifecycle, 89
presentational components, 79
preventDefault, use of, 232
production, development mode vs., 343–344
Profiler tab, 119
project
  automating build process, 358–365
  HTML document, 352–353
  initializing a React project from scratch, 351–367
  initializing yours, 352
  main JavaScript file, 353
  root component, 353–354

running in the browser, 354–357
structuring your source directory, 365–367
prop drilling
  defined, 387–388
  elimination of with Context, 393–394
  getting data to a deeply nested component with,
    392–393
  use of, 388
props (properties)
  accessing props, 52–54
  additional Link props, 296–297
  attributes vs., 52–56
  as being any data type, 126–127
  component Prop, 305–306
  component that uses string prop, 130
  components as receiving, 126
  creating, 126
  creating and using, 74–76
  default props, 141–145, 175–176
  defined, 103, 126
  difference between state and, 149
  key prop, 177–183
  limiting of to certain values or types, 139
  local variable and props confusion, 129
  methods as, 60
  passing props, 52
  passing setter function as, 263
  passing the wrong prop type, 131
  as read-only, 127
  render props, 257, 306–307
  rendering render prop, 307
  as storing data, 69
  string prop, 130
  validating incoming ones with PropTypes,
    129–130
  validating that a prop is a string, 130–131
  validation of required props, 134
props.children, 87
PropTypes
  adding of and default values to InputForm,
    174–175
  appending the isRequired validator, 134
  creating custom ones, 140–141
  defined, 130

PropTypes *(continued)*
  displaying a warning, 132
  failing `PropTypes.element` validation, 138
  getting started with, 131–133
  inside component's body, 132
  putting propTypes outside the class body, 133
  `Reminder` with and `defaultProps`, 178
  as telling which attribute caused the error, 136
  trying to render non-node value, 135
  use of with function component, 133
  using `PropTypes.node`, 136
  using `PropTypes.oneOf`, 139
  validating incoming props with, 129–131
  validation with, 133
`PropTypes.arrayOf`, 139
`PropTypes.exact`, 140
`PropTypes.objectOf`, 139
`PropTypes.shape`, 140
prototypal inheritance, 58–60
prototypes
  JavaScript as having, 58
  modifying and using of, 59
Provider component
  making of, 396
  use of, 389–390
public field, 147
public instance field, 147
pure component, 96, 103
pure function, 96

R

Ranked chart, 120, 121
React
  as compared to Angular (`angular.io`), 18–19
  as compared to Vue.js (`vujs.org`), 19
  as compared to what you already know, 18–19
  as declarative, 16–17
  developer community, 435
  events supported by, 206
  foundation of, 11–22
  as front-end library, 19
  as idiomatic, 17
  origins of, 11

  philosophy of, 14–21
  and ReactDOM, 12
  reason for name, 11–13
  reason to learn, 17
  Twitter account, 435
  useful links and resources, 435–436
  what it is not, 19–21
React audio player, 241
React Bookstore, 105–107, 108
React component tree, 43, 44
React DevTools
  additional functionality of, 118–119
  editing component data in, 114–117
  Flamegraph chart, 119
  getting started with, 105–107
  for inspecting components, 107–114
  installation of, 105–107
  logging component data to console, 118
  profiling, 119–121
  Ranked chart after optimizing, 121
  role of, 107
  Select tool, 115
  View Settings, 113
  viewing Ranked chart, 120
React element type, validation of, 137
React elements, validation of, 137
React Konsul, 103
React Native
  React Native CLI, 101–102
  as rendering engine, 101
  use of, 434
  your first React Native component, 101
React News, 435
React Newsletter, 435
React UI
  as having many components nested within other
    components, 84
  rendering of, 100
`React.Children`, 86
`React.Component`
  class header, 69
  constructor function, 69
  defined, 68
  importing of, 68–69

initializing local state, 69

managing state in, 71

React.createClass, 57

React.createElement(), 32

React.createElement method, 31

react.development.js, 2

ReactDOM, 12–14, 101

react-dom.development.js, 2

ReactDOM.render(), 6, 13, 98–99

ReactDOMServer, 102–103

react-error-boundary, specifying fallback component with, 335–336

react-fetch-hook, 286

React.Fragment
 use of short syntax of, 40–41
 use of to eliminate unnecessary HTML elements, 417

react-hook-form, 286

Reactiflux, 435, 436

reactive programming, defined, 12

ReactJS News, 435

React.memo(), 97–98

react.pdf, 103

React.PureComponent, 96, 97

React.render(), 6

react-router-dom
 installing and importing of, 293–294
 as one version of React Router, 293

react-router-native, as one version of React Router, 293

react-skip-nav, implementing Skip Navigation links with, 418–419

React.StrictMode, 98

reconciliation, 14, 100

Reddit's React community, 435

Redirect
 automatic linking with, 302
 routing with, 308–309

reducer, 274, 430

Redux, use of, 430–432

reference values, 157

referential equality, testing of, 278

refs
 calling a DOM method on a child using, 235

creating callback ref, 236–237

creating of in class component, 234

creating of in function component, 234

customizing value exposed by, 280–281

defined, 233

examples of, 239–242

passing ref callback as inline functions, 237–238

use of, 234–236

use of to set keyboard focus, 410–411

when not to use, 238–239

when to use, 238

regular expressions
 defined, 110
 use of, 110–112

@rehooks/local-storage, 287

Reminder
 with PropTypes and defaultProps, 178
 round two of, 167
 shell component for, 164

reminders
 adding of to list, 183
 filtering of, 183–190
 filtering of reminders list, 185

Reminders App
 building, 161–168
 initial render of, 179
 static version of, 167–168

RemindersList
 with default props and PropTypes, 175–176
 pure RemindersList, 172–173
 with Reminder imported, 164
 round two of, 166
 shell component for, 164

render(), 6

render attribute, 306–307

render function, 73–74

render method, 90, 91

render phase, of component lifecycle, 89

render props, 257, 306–307

rendering
 of caption, 74
 of children using props.children, 87–88
 of components, 98–103

rendering *(continued)*

  conditional rendering, 36–38

  conditionally rendering children based on media query, 422

  default route, 308

  a fallback UI, 327

  of figure, 74

  and finding node with Enzyme, 427

  and interacting with a modal dialog, 404–409

  modal without React Portals can have unexpected results, 404

  of `NavBar` inside of App, 87

  other rendering engines, 101

  of React UI, 100

  ReactDOM as most commonly used rendering engine, 101

  of render props, 307

  of `SalesChart` component, 402

  server-side rendering, 429–434

  of uncontrolled input, 223

renders

  function dependencies as causing unnecessary ones, 275–276

  solving unnecessary ones, 278–279

  unnecessary renders warning due to function dependence, 276

repository, choosing of, 347

RequireJS, 25–26

reserved words, cautions with, 33

rest parameters, 160

`return` statement, 40

root component, 43, 103, 353–354

route component, 294

router

  components of, 294, 295–296

  installing and importing `react-router-dom`, 293–294

  linking component, 294

  route component, 294

  router component, 294

  selecting of, 294–295

  using React router, 293–316

router component, 294, 295–296

routes

  creating of, 302–309

  dynamic links and routes in nested routes, 314–316

  linking to, 296–302

  multiple ones in component may have matches, 302–303

  multiple routes can match the URL, 303

  rendering default route, 308

  switching of, 307–308

routing

  behind the scenes, 309–316

  changing routes and viewing the `window.location.href` property, 293

  defined, 289–290

  enabling routing with `Netlify`, 347–348

  how it works in React, 291–293

  linking to routes, 296–302

  purposes of, 291

  React Router hooks, 317–318

  with `Redirect`, 308–309

  redirecting from one location to another, 309

  simple routing component, 291–292

  using React router, 293–316

S

`SalesChart` component, 401, 402

scroll position

  scrolling to element with a ref, 242

  setting of, 241–242

Search input box, 110

`SearchBox` component, 227

`SearchInput` component, 227

`SearchResults` component, 227–228

`select` elements, controlling of, 231

`select` inputs, use of in React, 231

selection events, 209

`setState` function

  as asynchronous, 72–73

  calls to as asynchronous, 152–153

  managing of in class components, 71

  merging object into state with, 151–152

  as not `setState`, 149

passing a function info, 153–154
using updater function with, 154
setState method, 150–151
setter
  passing function to, 263–264
  passing value to, 263
setter function
  as bound to their creator components, 262
  passing one as a prop, 263
  use of, 262
  value comparison, 264
shallow copy, 157, 158
shallowCompare function, 96, 97
shell components, 163–164
shouldComponentUpdate, 91, 96, 97
side effects, 264
SidebarHelp component, use of, 401
single page application (SPA), 290
single responsibility principle, 15
Skip Navigation links, 418–419
source directory
  grouping by features, 367
  grouping by file type, 366
  structuring yours, 365–367
spread operator, 157–160
Stack Overflow, 435
state
  App with lifted state, 171–172
  defined, 103
  defining of using class property, 217–218
  difference between props and, 149
  hooks and, 116
  initializing state in App, 190
  lifting it up, 170–176
  lifting up input state, 226–228
  resetting of, 333
  setter function as replacing, 156
  updating, 149–150
  updating of with function components, 154–155
  what not to put in, 168
  what to put in state, 161
  where to put it, 168–170
state object, 69–70, 71, 145–149
stateful component, 103
stateless component, 103, 147

stateless functional components, 79
static directory, 342
static method, getDerivedStateFromErrors
    as, 324
StaticRouter, 294, 295
store (in Redux), 430
string
  hash string, 343
  linking with, 297
  validating that a prop is one, 130–131
string prop, 130
style objects
  importing multiple styles, 250
  style object library, 250
  using variables to hold, 249
styled components, use of, 253–254
styles
  CSS Modules, 250–253
  CSS-in-JS and styled components, 253–254
  importance of, 243–244
  importing CSS into HTML file, 243–245
  using plain old CSS in components, 245–247
  writing inline styles, 247–250
subclasses with extends keyword, 63–64
syntactic sugar, use of term, 58
SyntheticBaseEvent object, 203–204
SyntheticEvent, 201–202, 204

T

tagged template literals, 254–255
templates, making HTML template,
    359–360
test-driven development, 363
testing tools, 360–364, 425
text
  automatic selection of, 239
  selecting and copying of with ref, 239–240
  selecting of and displaying temporary message,
    240
textarea
  controlling of, 230
  getting value of and counting its words, 279–280
  an HTML textarea's value as, 230
  use of in React, 230

TextReader component, 236
ThingsLike, 86
ThingsThatAreFunny, 85
this keyword, 64–66
this.props.children, 85
timer
  creating new timer with each render, 266–267
  starting of with each render, 266
toolchain, building your own, 351–357
touch events, 209
transition events, 211
transpilation, 31–33
try/catch, catching errors in error boundaries
    with, 336–337
two-way data flow, 125
TypeScript (Microsoft), 19

U

UI
  diagram of typical one, 321
  rendering a fallback UI, 327
UI events, 209
UI layer, 12
UMD (Universal Module Definition), 3
uncontrolled inputs
  blog comment interface using, 228–229
  vs. controlled inputs, 221–226
  omitting value attribute as creating, 222
  rendering of, 223
  use of, 228–229
unidirectional data flow, 123, 124–125
Universal React, 103
unmounting, as stage of component's life, 89, 92
updater function, 153–154
updating, as state of component's life, 89, 90–92
URL parameters, use of, 304–305
useAxios, use of, 286
useCallback
  function dependences cause unnecessary renders,
    275–277
  memoized callbacks fix the unnecessary effect
    problem, 277–278
  memoized callbacks with, 275–278

useContext
  subscribing to global data with, 272–273
  using Context with, 272–273
useDebugValue
  labeling of custom hooks with, 283–285
  use of, 284
useEffect
  asynchronous requests with, 270–271
  cleaning up after effects, 265–266
  creating new timer with each render, 266–267
  customizing of, 266–270
  hooking into lifecycle with, 264–272
  most basic form of, 265
  passing an empty array to only run useEffect
    on mount, 268
  running asynchronous code with, 270–272
  specifying useEffect's dependencies, 269
  starting timer with each render, 266
  using default useEffect behavior, 265
useErrorHandler(), use of, 337–338
useForm, use of, 287
useGeolocation, 288
useHistory, 310–311, 317
use-http, 285
useImperativeHandle, customizing exposed
    values with, 280–281
useKonomiCode, 288
useLayoutEffect, updating DOM synchronously
    with, 281
use-local-storage-state, 287
useLocation, 317
useMediaQuery, use of, 422
useMemo
  caching computed values with, 278–279
  solving performance problems with, 279
  solving unnecessary renders with, 278–279
useNetworkStatus, 288
useParams, 317
user preferences (app), 396–398
user-defined components
  custom components as also known as, 30
  as having any attributes, 34
  possibilities for, 56
useReducer

combining logic and state with, 273–274

`Counter` with, 273–274

passing payload to reducer, 274

`useRef`, accessing children imperatively with, 279–280

`useRouteMatch`, 317–318

`useState`

calling of hook as returning an array, 155–156

managing state with, 260–264

number guessing game with, 260–261

setting initial state, 262

setting initial state with, 156

use of to create and update a counter, 84–85

why use `const` with, 156

`useState` function, 147, 149

`useZipLookup`

defined, 282

use of, 282–283

V

validation

of data type, 133–134

failing `PropTypes.element` validation, 138

of incoming props, 129–131

JavaScript class validation, 138

of nodes, 134–137

with PropTypes, 133

of React element type, 137

of React elements, 137

of required props, 134

and setting defaults for `FilterSelect`, 177–178

that prop is a string, 130–131

that prop is an instance of a class, 138

validators

custom validators, 140–141

`element` validator, 137

`elementType` validator, 137

`isRequired` validator, 134

values

customizing exposure values with `useImperiatveHandle`, 280–281

customizing value exposed by ref, 280–281

debug value, 283–285

getting value of `textarea` and counting its words, 279–280

passing of to a setter, 263

`var` keyword, 81–82

variables

block scope variables with `let`, 82

changing local variables doesn't update the view, 127–128

goodbye to `var`, 81–82

in JavaScript, 81–83

local variable and props confusion, 129

use of to hold style objects, 249

using `const`, 82

Virtual DOM, 13–14, 100–101

Vue.js (`vujs.org`), 19

W

web

how it works, 290

putting app on, 344–349

Web Accessibility Initiative - Accessible Rich Internet Applications (WAI-ARIA), 415

Web Content Accessibility Guidelines (WCAG), 414–415

web server hosting, 344–345

Web Storage

remembering user with, 380

as synchronous, 380

types of, 379

use of, 379–385

when not to use, 380

when to use, 380

Webpack, how it works, 357–358

Webpack Dev Server, 360

wheel events, 209

windowing, 120

`withRouter`, use of, 310

wrapper hell, 258